*"Adventures are to the Adventurous."*

BEACONSFIELD.

*THE
ADVENTURE
SERIES.*

*POPULAR  RE-ISSUE.*

# THE ADVENTURE SERIES.

Illustrated.    Large Crown 8vo, in Decorative
Cover, price 3s. 6d.

---

### 1.

**Adventures of a Younger Son.** By E. J.
TRELAWNY.  *With an Introduction by Edward
Garnett.*  Second Edition.

### 2.

**Robert Drury's Journal in Madagascar.**
*Edited, with an Introduction and Notes, by
Captain S. P. Oliver.*

### 3.

**Memoirs of the Extraordinary Military**
Career of John Shipp.  *With an Introduction
by H. Manners Chichester.*

### 4.

**The Buccaneers and Marooners of America.**
Being an Account of the Famous Adventures
and Daring Deeds of certain Notorious Free-
booters of the Spanish Main.  *Edited by Howard
Pyle.*

### 5.

**The Log of a Jack Tar ; or, The Life of James**
Choyce, Master Mariner.   With O'Brien's Captivity in France.  *Edited, with an Introduction
and Notes, by V. Lovett Cameron, R.N.*

### 6.

**The Voyages and Adventures of Ferdinand**
Mendez Pinto.  *With an Introduction by
Arminius Vambéry.*

# THE VOYAGES AND ADVENTURES OF FERDINAND MENDEZ PINTO, THE PORTUGUESE

*(DONE INTO ENGLISH BY HENRY COGAN)*

WITH AN INTRODUCTION BY ARMINIUS VAMBÉRY

POPULAR EDITION

LONDON: T. FISHER UNWIN
PATERNOSTER SQUARE. MDCCCXCVII

# THE
# VOYAGES
## AND
# ADVENTURES,
### OF
## Ferdinand Mendez Pinto,
### A *Portugal* : During his
# TRAVELS

for the space of one and twenty years in

The Kingdoms of Ethiopia, China, Tartaria, Cauchin-
china, Calaminham, Siam, Pegu, Japan, and a
great part of the East-Indies.

With a *Relation* and *Description* of most of the Places
thereof ; their Religion, Laws, Riches, Customs, and
Government in the time of Peace and War.

Where he five times suffered Shipwrack, was sixteen times sold,
and thirteen times made a Slave.

Written Originally by himself in the Portugal Tongue,
and Dedicated to the
*Majesty* of Philip *King* of Spain.

---

Done into English by H. C. Gent.

---

*L O N D O N,*
Printed by *J. Macock,* and are to be sold by *Henry Herringman,* at the Sign
of the *Blew-Anchor* in the lower-walk of the *New-Exchange,* 1663.

# LIST OF ILLUSTRATIONS.

[*The illustrations are taken from the second Dutch edition of "The Voyage of John Huyghen Van Linschoten to the East Indies" in 1586–92. Linschoten, who was a generation after Pinto's time, made his own drawings, from which the plates were engraved.*]

# CONTENTS.

### CHAPTER I.

### CHAPTER II.

### CHAPTER III.

### CHAPTER IV.

### CHAPTER V.

## PUBLISHER'S NOTE.

THE Publisher of the present edition, in abridging Cogan's translation of 1663, has aimed at preserving (a) the most adventurous, and (b) the most curious passages of Mendez Pinto's narrative. By abridging somewhat the lengthy speeches of the Orientals, by omitting the least interesting of the adventures, and by passing over some of the descriptions of public ceremonies, it has been found practicable to reprint a work which otherwise from its length could not have come within the scope of "The Adventure Series."

# NOTE ON MENDEZ PINTO AND ON THE EDITIONS OF HIS TRAVELS.

(*Extracted from Michaud's " Biographie Universelle."*)

MENDEZ PINTO is no ordinary adventurer. The account of his voyages is written by himself, and the work is still regarded as a classic by the Portuguese. It has been translated irto almost every language ; some have read it enthusiastically, others have looked upon it as a tissue of lies. His partisans have had little difficulty in justifying their opinions, for there is a great fascination in his narrative ; the work has throughout an air of sincerity which prejudices one in the author's favour, and it seems to reflect as a faithful mirror the character and behaviour of the first conquerors of India. These men of well-tried metal display a certain ferocity which mingled with their religious ideas made them capable of great cruelties and heroic actions. So long as Pinto was the only traveller who told the tale of the particular countries he visited, his opponents could deny the truth of his account without the possibility of refutation, but now these countries are better known, one cannot fail to recognize the substantial truth of his story. Certain details are undoubtedly embellished, but one may conclude from what has been recounted in regard to many points that these rest on real facts. His travels were no doubt written chiefly from memory, and it is obvious, that instead of putting things down exactly as they really happened, he has given us rather the impressions left on his ardent imagination. Nowhere, however, is he guilty of wilful exaggeration for the sake of self-glorification.

1 *a*

Everything relating to himself is told with the utmost
simplicity.   He said that he only wrote his travels to tell his
children of the great dangers he had passed through in life,
and one might be tempted to believe it.

"The date of his death is not known.   His book was
first printed many years afterwards by the care of Francis
Andrada, at Lisbon, in folio.   This edition is rare : others were
issued from the same town in 1678 and in 1725.   In the latter
edition is also included the Itinerario of Antonio Tenego,
who in 1529, travelled overland from India to Portugal, and
the account of the conquest of the kingdom of Pegu in 1601.
These works are also to be found in the Lisbon edition of
1762, folio; but there is also a more recent one of the
same town, viz., 1833, 2 vols. 8vo.   It was translated
into Spanish six years after the first appearance by Francis
Herreva of Afalderado, who added to it a dissertation to
establish its authenticity (Madrid, 1620 folio).   This translation was well received, and was reprinted in 1627, 1645, and
1664.   The French translation by Bernard Figuier (Paris,
1628, in 4to) is still sought after.   A new edition of the translation has also appeared (Paris, 1830, 3 vols. 8vo) which was
one of a series of reprints that the Government caused to be
executed to provide employment for the compositors who were
out of work after the Revolution of July."—DE ROSSEL.

[The extreme caution with which English critics have
treated Pinto's narrative has forced the publisher to turn
for a criticism of him to a foreign source.   M. de Rossel's
remarks are perhaps as judicious as any yet published, and
are therefore translated for the English reader.]

* The English editions are limited to three.   The second edition of 1692
is, like the present, a reprint of Cogan's translation of 1663.

# INTRODUCTION.

CCOUNTS of eventful and dangerous travels have always awakened more doubts than admiration in the majority of mankind. True, the every-day man, treading the well-worn path of his prosaic life, accustomed to the occurrences and usages of his small native horizon, listens with eager delight to the exciting and fascinating accounts of travelling experiences in distant lands. He shudders at hearing of dangers avoided, he is lost in admiration at the sight of strange habits and customs, and at the mysterious doings of his fellow-men in far-away regions. He is like the child, the intelligent child, who breathlessly follows the thread of the fairy tale, but who at the end, drawing a deep breath, asks himself—"Is this possible ? Can this really be true ? "

Happily the Europe of to-day is, and for a considerable time has been, past this childish

age, but in the Middle Ages it was sticking fast
in it; and, indeed, it is scarcely a hundred years
since this incredulity and scepticism, born of
ignorance, has completely disappeared. The
modestly glittering lamp which some travellers
and men of letters have lit, could spread but
little light in the pitch dark ignorance prevailing
in the Middle Ages regarding matters geographical
and ethnological, and learning could raise but
slightly the level of general culture. But as people
and societies prefer to doubt the veracity of others
to confessing their own ignorance and stupidity,
so it is natural that the mediæval travellers and
explorers who, after traversing strange countries
at the risk of their lives and at the cost of great
privations, returned home with an account of
their wonderful experiences, were stigmatized as
liars, derided, and mostly misunderstood. That
there were some travellers who, relying on the
general ignorance, let the bridle of their imagination loose in order to heighten the interest of
the public by extravagant and grotesque descriptions, can scarcely be denied; but, on the whole,
the insinuations were unjust, and certainly the
narrow-mindedness of the respective epochs was
greater than the lying disposition of the dis-
coverers of new paths in the Asiatic world.

We find ample traces of this regretable and
malicious conception in several stereotype sayings

of those days. The mediæval Church to which, for the rest, we owe some important geographical and ethnographical discoveries, originated the saying—"Qui multum peregrinatur, raro sanctificatur," viz., "He who travelled much is seldom canonized." Similarly in England, whose inhabitants were always known for their travelling propensities, we find the expression, " a travellers' tale," applied to any not very credible story. Analogous proverbs are met with in other European languages, the Turks being the only people who are of a different way of thinking. They say—"Not he who has lived long, but who has travelled much, possesses a right understanding." Taken all in all, however, the lot of the early traveller was not an enviable one. The minorite monk, Odoric of Pordenone, who, in the beginning of the fourteenth century, travelled through a great part of Asia, owes his canonization not to his geographical discoveries, but to his having baptised, as he alleged, 60,000 Saracens; whilst Marco Polo, the Prince of Asiatic travellers, who was not renowned for apostolic zeal, was rewarded only with sneers and mockery for his great and fruitful work, and for centuries Italy designated a liar and a boaster with the expression *Marco Millioni*. A like fate befel the famous Portuguese, Fernao Mendez Pinto, who, between the years 1537–1558, journeyed through the most different parts of Asia, and during his twenty-one years' wanderings, as he himself says, was sold sixteen times, was a slave thirteen times, and was shipwrecked five times.

This extraordinary man, whose account of his journeys was published in 1614 under the title "Peregrinacao" (a book which in the course of the same century was translated into English, French, and Spanish), had an exceedingly large amount of most curious experiences and adventures. He had opportunities of getting acquainted on the spot with people and land in India, China, Japan, Tartary, and communicated so much that was extraordinary and wonderful, and even that looked incredible, that his contemporaries simply rejected all he said and stamped him as a liar. The first edition of his book had to appear with an apologetic introduction, and Congreve, wishing to characterize a liar, said—

"Mendez Pinto was but a type of thee, thou liar of the first magnitude!"

A cruel irony of fate, a sorry reward for all that the audacious Portuguese, led on by his thirst after knowledge, had to suffer during his wanderings, for having faced death in a thousand forms, for all the miseries endured, all with the sole object of satisfying a curiosity which has proved so useful to posterity.

What is the reason, what are the chief motives, of the incredulity of contemporaries and the scepticism of later generations? is a question which suggests itself to the modern man. The general indifference and ignorance of the public already alluded to must naturally be taken into account; but there were also other reasons which we cannot pass over. We find, namely, that the mediæval travellers and adventurers undertook their self-imposed task with little or no preparation, and that in spite of their lengthened sojourn amid the different peoples, they were but imperfectly familiar with the languages, customs, and religions of the same—a circumstance which caused their narratives to be incomplete, and led them sometimes into serious errors. Marco Polo himself so disfigures the Turkish, Persian, and Mongolian proper names as to be unrecognizable, and posterity had to exert all its ingenuity to find out the proper spelling and meaning of such names. The application and penetration of a Henry Yule or a Pauthier succeeded partly in remedying this great defect, but the setting right of the text so misconstructed by copyists is even yet far from complete. Besides the mysteriousness of the nomenclature, there is a great drawback in the childish tone, in the fairy-tale-like description of things seen and heard, in the style which, though in keeping with the taste of the age, yet by its tawdriness brought the contents themselves into disrepute. When Marco Polo speaks of ants as big as dogs, and Mendez Pinto relates of men with round feet and with arms entirely covered with hair; such exaggeration certainly seems to have somewhat contributed to the general distrust, although it would not justify us in denying the existence, in a reduced measure, of the said facts, as was amply proved by the researches of commentators. On the other hand, the narratives contain much that the traveller did not see himself, but related only after hearsay. Thus, for instance, Pinto speaks of the thousands of carts of the king of Tartary (*rectius* Mandshury) drawn by rhinoceroses—in which case Pinto can excuse himself by saying "*relata refero*," or else the name of the animals is erroneously given.

It is, however, entirely superfluous, if not unjust, to measure the reports of the early Asiatic travellers by a very elevated standard, as the tales and fables *bonâ fide* accepted and related by them can be recognized at a glance, and were never believed by any one but those who read for the sake of amusement and not of instruction. Whether the zealous missionaries of the twelfth and thirteenth centuries, or the wise Venetian brothers, or the Bavarian Schiltberger who was taken prisoner at Varna, or, in fine, the most remarkable among them, on account of his adventures, Mendez Pinto, they have each and all contributed their share to make Europe take an interest in the fate of Asia, and to place posterity in possession of a picture, however incomplete and defective, of the power and authority of Asia, then still unbroken. In this picture, so full of instructive details, we perceive more than one thing fully worthy of the attention of the latter-day reader. Above all, we see the fact that the traveller from the West, although obliged to endure unspeakable hardships, privation, pain, and danger, at least had not to suffer on account of his nationality and religion, as has been the case in recent times since the all-puissance of Europe has thrown its threatening shadow on the interior of Asia, and the appearance of the European is considered the foreboding of material decay and national downfall. How utterly different it was to travel in mediæval Asia from what it is at present is clearly seen from the fact that in those days missionaries, merchants, and political agents from Europe could, even in time of war, traverse any distances in Asiatic lands without molestation in their personal liberty or property just as any Asiatic traveller of Moslem or Buddhist persuasion. Only thus can it be understood, how Italian merchants had large warehouses in the thirteenth and fourteenth century in Tana and other places in immediate vicinity of Tartar hordes, and how they, during the troubles succeeding the fall of the Timurides and the accession of the Sefevides, moved about in the adjacent countries partly with their goods, partly as political agents. As far as Interior Asia in particular is concerned, it was the news of the victorious advance of the English, and of the gradual downfall of the Mogul power that awakened first the mistrust against European travellers. What Jenkinson could accomplish in 1558, namely, under the reign of Abdullah Khan, the greatest Central-Asiatic ruler of the modern era, that Sir Alexander Burnes could carry out only with difficulty under Nasrullah's rule, for it was not so much the religious fanaticism of the Moslem as rather the fear from the all-absorbing power of the Christian West that made the Asiatics suspect in every Frenghi a spy and a disguised would-be conqueror. In Persia, which owing to its inland position, thought itself less exposed to attacks, this was not the case, hence it is easy to understand how Abbas the Great could show his full favours to the Englishman Shirley, and how Chardin obtained opportunities of thoroughly studying the country and its inhabitants. It was the same in the interior of Asia Minor where Niebuhr, unlike Palgrave, who was forced to assume an incognito, could explore the Arabian peninsula.

The danger that threatened the traveller in mediæval Asia lay in the elements, in the state of temporary anarchy, and especially in the raw manners of some Asiatic tribes, who abhorred all communication from without and had absolutely no sense for contact with foreign people. The religious duty of pilgrimage has made the Moslem a good traveller, but the Buddhists and Brahmanists considered this a sacrilegious proceeding, and whoever decided to undertake a journey among them must have possessed an extraordinary amount of adventuresome spirit or an uncontrollable desire for knowledge of distant lands. This adventuresome spirit naturally received a fresh impulse from the fortunate enterprises of the Portuguese in East Asiatic waters. In this small country in westernmost Europe, we see rulers like John the Great and John the Perfect, and princes like Henry the Sailor and the Duke of Coimbra, &c., giving us proofs of how even with small means great things can be accomplished if the free development of the spirit is under fostering care; for men like Alfons de Albuquerque, Francisco de Almeida, Nuno de Cunha, Joao de Castro, Antonio de Silveira, or audacious adventurers like Duante Coelho and Mendez Pinto have not only startled the Orientals with proofs of the activity and intrepidity of the Europeans, but they also opened to us the way into the interior of several countries of the rising sun and facilitated the work of their successors, the Britons, of spreading European civilization.

Turning now to the work of the adventurous traveller so often sneered at and so severely criticised, I think it needful to give a few remarks explanatory of the origin of adventure in general, as well as the state of mind, the inner struggle and the secret motive power of the traveller so unjustly called an adventurer. I feel myself all the more called upon to do this as my own wanderings in Interior Asia were not free from the savour of adventure, and I can still distinctly recall the state of mind I was in during my peregrinations as a disguised Efendi and Dervish. And, first of all, I would remind the reader that never did a man start on travel with the intention of becoming an adventurer. No one thinks of exciting one day the curiosity and nerves of his future readers by the tale of his experiences and sufferings, and no one takes up his walking staff in the hope of being one day fêted as the hero of awe-inspiring stories and blood-thrilling episodes. The traveller, and notably the explorer, is to a certain extent aware of the dangers attending his undertaking; indeed it is this danger that attracts and allures him; but that a man should undertake a long journey solely with a view to expose himself to the dangers of thirst, hunger, prison, and a martyr's death, and after a lucky escape to be shone upon by the rays of glory, is a thing that I could never credit or understand. One becomes an adventurer, the hero of blood-stirring experiences only in the natural course of later events, through occurrences that surprise the traveller himself, that excite him in the highest degree, and try to the utmost his presence of mind and ingenuity. No serious or reasoning explorer ever set out on a journey with the firm intention of seeking adventures on his proposed route and testing his strength on the same. He is sometimes conscious of the dangers awaiting him, he suspects that everything will not run smooth; but he never, even in the moments of the greatest excitement, and in the wildest state of mind, neglects to take such measures as could be of service to him in his critical position.

When, in order to explore some parts of Central Asia never before visited by Europeans, I decided in Teheran to accompany the ragged and most horrible looking Tartars returning home from the pilgrimage to Mekka, all my friends and acquaintances in the Persian capital thought it would be my desperate looking travelling companions who would put an end to my being. I had myself some misgivings on this score. It was not their violence I feared, but rather that they would either from treachery or necessity hand me over to Central Asiatic authorities, and in order to guard myself against the agonies of a martyr's death, I asked and obtained from Dr. B——, the physician to the Turkish Mission, two strychnine pills with which to shorten, in case of need, the tortures of a possible martyr's death. These two pills which I hid away in the wadding of my rags, formed my only consolation and anchor-sheet, and when in moments of imminent peril I touched with my finger-tips these little prominences among the wadding, I felt a pleasing sensation running through me, inasmuch as by their help I thought myself safe against long death agonies. Man is more resigned to his fate where death seems an inevitable consequence of the combination of elementary forces and where defence is unavailing; but even there there is a feeble ray of hope lightening through the dark horizon and spreading a little light. On the fatiguing road from the Persian frontier to Khiva, which Conolly had to abandon after a fruitless attempt, and where ten years later Colonel Markusoff lost several thousand brave warriors, we were for five days without water and nearly dying from thirst. Two of our fellow travellers fell victims to their terrible sufferings. The ominous white spots began to appear on my palate, my tongue was heavy, I lay prostrate with high fever, and I saw the forerunners of my approaching end, but only for a short while, as presently there arose the faint hope of salvation which soon afterwards became a reality. In this continuous change of threatening peril, desperate struggle for self-preservation and never-relaxing hopes, the nerves grow so hardened that one can live for months, nay years, in mortal danger without thinking of death and the possible sudden termination of this most wonderful earthly existence. What I went through during some months—for really great danger surrounded me only in Central Asia—others before me experienced for years, and I do not doubt for a moment but they felt all the better for it, the same as I did ; for one day of such adventurous travel is worth many years spent in monotonous every-day life.

In a word, the adventurer becomes such through the combination of circumstances. In the nature of man there is only the first impulse to travel, but his desire for adventure increases at the same rate as he has learnt by experience to cope with difficulties. One victory achieved is incitement to fresh fights, and in this pleasing giddiness of the senses, adventurous travellers have sometimes accomplished extraordinary results. Concerning the acts of Mendez Pinto in particular, we have to point out that he was the first to make known the natural riches of Japan and originated the first settlement near Yokohama in 1548. His accounts of Burmah, Siam, Cochin China, and several cities of the flowery country in the interior, stand in no way behind the writings of De la Cruz, of Boterus, Paulus Jovius, Mendoza, and other contemporary men of letters and travellers ; and indeed as regards the details of the war and conquest of China by Murhachu, the Prince of the Mandshus, whom Pinto calls Tartars, are distinctly valuable. One whose fate brought him in such intimate contact with the life and doings of a strange people, and who had opportunities to study so deeply their customs and manners as Mendez Pinto had, certainly deserves to be heard. The new edition, slightly abridged, of his " Peregrinacão " or " Wanderings " is a faithful mirror of Asia three hundred years ago. We may derive from it much that is instructive and interesting.

ARMINIUS VAMBÉRY.

BUDAPEST UNIVERSITY,
*April*, 1891.

MAP OF FURTHER INDIA

AND ARCHIPELAGO.

# TRAVELS, VOYAGES, AND ADVENTURES

OF

# FERDINAND MENDEZ PINTO.

## CHAPTER I.

*After what manner I past my Youth in the Kingdom of Portugal, untill my going to the Indies.*

O often as I represent unto myself the great and continual travels that have accompanied me from my birth, and amidst the which I have spent my first years, I find that I have a great deal of reason to complain of Fortune, for that she seemeth to have taken a particular care to persecute me, and to make me feel that which is most insupportable in her, as if her glory had no other foundation then her cruelty. For not content to have made me be born, and to live miserably in my country during my youth, she conducted me, notwithstanding the fear I had of the dangers that menaced me, to the *East Indies*, where in stead of the relief which I went thither to seek, she made me find an

2

increase of my pains, according to the increase of my age. Since then it hath pleased God to deliver me from so many dangers, and to protect me from the fury of that adverse Fortune, for to bring me into a port of safety and assurance; I see that I have not so much cause to complain of my travels past, as I have to render Him thanks for the benefits which untill now I have received of Him; seeing that by His Divine bounty He hath preserved my life, to the end I might have means to leave this rude and unpolished discourse unto my children for a memorial and an inheritance. For my intention is no other, but to write it for them, that they may behold what strange fortunes I have run for the space of one and twenty years, during the which I was thirteen times a captive, and seventeen times sold in the *Indies*, in *Æthiopia*, in *Arabia*, in *China*, in *Tartaria*, in *Madagascar*, in *Sumatra*, and in divers other kingdoms and provinces of that Oriental Archipelage upon the confines of *Asia*, which the *Chineses*, *Siames*, *Gueos*, and *Lecquios* name, and that with reason, in their geography, the ey-lids of the world, whereof I hope to entreat more particularly, and largely, hereafter. Whereby men, for the time to come, may take example, and a resolution not to be discouraged for any crosses that may arrive unto them in the course of their lives. For no disgrace of Fortune ought to essoign us never so little from the duty which we are bound to render unto God; because there is no adversity, how great soever, but the nature of man may well undergo it, being favoured with the assistance of heaven. Now, that others may help me to praise the Lord Almighty for the infinite mercy He hath shewed me, without any regard to my sins, which I confess were the cause and original of all my misfortunes, and that from the same Divine Power I received strength and courage to resist them, escaping out of so many dangers, with my life saved, I take from the beginning of my voyage the time which I spent in this kingdom of *Portugal*, and say, that after I had lived there till I was about eleven or twelve years old, in the misery and poverty of my fathers house within the town of *Monte-mor Ovelho*, an uncle of mine, desirous to advance me to a better fortune then that whereunto I was reduced at that time, and to take me from the caresses and cockerings of my mother, brought me to this city of *Lisbon*, where he put me into the service of a very honourable lady : the which he was carried out of the hope he had, that by the favour of her self and her friends he might attain to his desire for my advancement ; and this was in the same year that the funeral pomp of the deceased King *Emanuel* of happy memory was celebrated at *Lisbon*, namely St. *Lucies* day, the 13. of *December*, 1521, which is the furthest thing I can remember. In the mean time my uncles design had a success clean contrary to that which he hath promised to himself in favour of me: for having been servant of this lady; about a year and a half, an accident befel me, that cast me into manifest peril of life, so that to save my self I was constrained to abandon her house with all the speed that possibly I could. Flying away then in very great fear, I arrived before I was aware at the Ford of *Pedra*, which is a small port so called ; there I found a carvel of *Alfama*, that was laden with the horses and stuff of a lord, who was going to *Setuval*, where at that instant King *Joana* the Third kept his court, by reason of a great plague that reigned in divers parts of the kingdom.

Perceiving then that this carvel was ready to put to sea, I imbarqued my self in her, and departed the next day. But alas ! a little after we had set sail, having gotten to a place named *Cezmibra*, we were set upon by a *French* pirate, who having boarded us, caused fifteen or sixteen of his men to leap into our vessel, who finding no resistance made themselves masters of her : now after they had pillaged every one of us, they emptied all the merchandise wherewithal ours was laden, which amounted to above six thousand duckats, into their ship, and then sunk her ; so that of seventeen of us that remained alive, not so much as one could escape slavery, for they clap'd us up all bound hand and foot under hatches, with an intent to go and sell us at *La Rache* in *Barbary*, whither also, as we found by being amongst them, they carried arms to the *Mahometans* in way of trade ; for this purpose they kept us thirteen dayes together, continually whipping us ; but at the end thereof it fortuned that about sun set they discovered a ship, unto which they gave chase all the night, following her close, like old pirates long used to such thieveries ; having fetcht her up by break of day, they gave her a volley of three pieces of ordnance, and presently invested her with a great deal of courage ; now though at first they found some resistance, yet they quickly rendred themselves masters of her, killing six *Portugals*, and ten or eleven slaves. This was a goodly vessel, and belonged to a *Portugal* merchant of the town of *Conde*, named *Silvestrè Godinho*, which divers other merchants of *Lisbon* had laden at Saint *Tome* with great store of sugar and slaves; in such sort that those poor people seeing themselves thus taken and robbed fell to lament their loss, which they estimated to be forty thousand duckats. Whereupon these pirates, having gotten so rich a booty, changed their design for going to *la Rache*, and bent their course for the coast of *France*, carrying with them such of ours for slaves, as they judged fit for the service of their navigation. The remainder of us they left at night in the road, at a place called *Melides*, where we were landed miserably naked, our bodies covered with nothing but with the stripes of the lashes which so cruelly we had received the dayes before. In this pitiful case we arrived the next morning at St. *Jago de Caten*, where we were relieved by the inhabitants of the place, especially by a lady that was there at that time, named *Donna Beatrix*, daughter to the Earl of *Villanova*, and wife to *Alonzo Perez Pantoia*, commander and grand provost of the town. Now after the sick and wounded were recovered, each of us departed, and got him where he hoped to find the best assistance; for my self, poor wretch, I went with 6. or 7. that accompanied me in my misery to *Setuval*: thither I was no sooner come, but my good fortune placed me in the service of *Francisco de Faria*, a gentleman belonging to the great commander of S. *Jago*, who in recompense of four years service that I did him, put me to the said commander to wait on him in his chamber, which I performed for an year and an half after. But in regard the entertainment which was given at that time in noble-mens houses was so small that I was not able to live on it, necessity constrained me to quit my master, with a design to imbarque my self by his favour to go to the *Indies* ; for that I thought was the best way I could take to free me of my poverty. So albeit I were but meanly accommodated, I imbarqued my self, notwithstanding, submitting my self to whatsoever fortune should arrive unto me in those far countries, either good or bad.

---

## CHAPTER II.

My departure from Portugal for the Indies, and my imbarquing there for the Streight of Mecqua.

IT was in the year 1537, and the 11th of *March*, that I parted from this kingdom in a fleet of five ships, whereof there was no General; for each of those vessels was commanded by a particular captain: for example, in the ship named the Queen, commanded *Don Pedro de Silva*, surnamed the Cock, son to the Admiral *Don Vasco de Gama*. In the ship called S. Rock, commanded *Don Fernando de Lima*, son to *Diego Lopez de Lima*, grand Provost of the town of *Guimaranes*, who died valiantly in defence of the fortress of *Ormuz*, whereof he was captain the year following, 1538. In the S. *Barba*, commanded *Don Fernando de Lima*, who was the governour of the town of *Chaul*; of that, which was called the *Flower of the Sea*, *Lope Vaz Vagado* was captain; and in the fifth and last ship, named *Galega*, commanded *Martin de Freitas*, born in the Isle of *Madera*, who the same year was slain at *Damao*, together with five and thirty men that followed him. These vessels sailing different wayes, arrived at length at a great port called *Mozambique;* there we met with the Saint *Michael*, that wintered there, and was commanded by *Duart Tristao*, who parted thence richly laden for to return into *Portugal ;* howbeit I believe she was taken, or suffered shipwrack, as it happens but too often in this voyage to the *Indies*, for he was never heard of since. After our five vessels were equipped with all that was necessary for them, and ready to set sail from *Mozambique*, the lieutenant of the fortress, called *Vincent Pegado*, shewed the captains of the said five ships a mandate from the Governour, named *Nunho de Cunha*, whereby he expressly commanded that all *Portugal* ships, which did arrive in that port this year should go to *Diu*, and leave their

men there for the guard of the fortress, because of the fear
they were in of the *Turkish* army, which was every hour
expected in the *Indies*, by reason of the death of *Sultan Bandur*
King of *Cambaya*, whom the said Governour had put to death
the summer before. In regard this affair was of great importance, it was the cause that all the captains assembled
together to deliberate thereupon : at length, to meet with the
present necessity they concluded, that three of those five ships,
appertaining to the King, should go to *Diu*, conformable to the
contents of the said mandate, and that the other two, which
belonged to particular merchants, should pursue their course
to *Goa* : the King's three ships sailing to *Diu*, and the other
two merchants towards *Goa*, it pleased God to conduct them
safe thither. Now as soon as the King's three ships came to
the mouth of the river of the port of *Diu*, which fell on the
5th of *September* the same year, 1538. *Antonio de Silvera*, the
brother of *Lowys Silvera*, Earl of *Sortelha*, who was captain
there at that time, gave them all the testimony that possibly
he could of the joy he took at this their arrival ; for proof
whereof he bestowed liberally on every one, keeping a set
table for above 7 hundred persons which they brought along
with them, besides his secret rewards, and extraordinary gifts,
whereby he supplied the necessities they had suffered during
their voyage. Whereupon the souldiers considering how this
captain entreated them very royally, that he payed them
before-hand, distributed their pay and munition unto them
with his own hands, caused the sick to be carefully tended,
and shewed himself most ready to assist every one, it so
wrought upon them, that of their own accord they offered to
stay there for to serve him, being no way constrained thereunto,
as they use to be (in those countries) in all the fortresses which
expect a siege. This done, as soon as the three ships had sold
the merchandise they had brought, they set sail for *Goa*, carrying none with them but the officers of the vessels, and some
sea-men to conduct them ; where they abode till such time as
the Governour had given them dispatches for to go to *Cochin*,
where being arrived they took in their lading, and returned all
five safe into *Portugal*.

Seventeen dayes after we were arrived at the fortress of *Diu*,

where at that time two foists were ready prepared to go to the
Streight of *Mecqua*, for to discover, and find out the design of
the *Turkish* army, whose coming was greatly feared in the
*Indies*, because one of those foists was commanded by a
captain that was a great friend of mine, who gave me good
hope of the voyage he was bound for, I imbarqued my self
with him; relying then on the promises which the captain
made me, that by his favor and means I should quickly be
rich, the only thing in the world that I most desired, and
suffered my self to be deceived by my hopes, I imagined that
I was already master of great wealth, never considering how
vain and uncertain the promises of men are, and that I could
not reap much benefit by the voyage I was going to undertake,
by reason it was dangerous, and unseasonable for navigation
in that country. Now being departed from *Diu*, we sailed in
a time full of storms, because it was about the end of winter,
which seemed to begin anew, so impetuous were the winds,
and so great was the rain: nevertheless, how violent soever
the tempest was, and dark the weather, we letted not to
discover the Isle of *Curia, Muria*, and *Avedalcuria*, at the
sight whereof we thought our selves quite lost, and without
hope of life. Whereupon, to decline the danger, we turned
the prow of our vessel to the south-east, knowing no other
mean then that to avoid shipwrack: but by good fortune for
us, it pleased God that we let fall an anchor at the point of
the Island of *Socotora*; there we presently anchored, a league
below the place, where *Don Francisco d' Almeyda* caused a
fortress to be built in the year 1507. when he came from
*Portugal*, as the first Vice-roy that ever was in the *Indies*. In
the said place we took in fresh water, and some provision of
victuals, that we bought of the Christians of the country,
which are the descendants of those whom the Apostle S.
*Thomas* converted in those parts. Being refreshed thus, we
parted from thence with a purpose to enter the *Streights*;
so that after we had sailed nine dayes with a favourable wind,
we found our selves right against *Mazua*; there about sun-set
we descried a sail at sea, whereunto we gave so hard chace,
that before the first watch of the night we came up close to
her; and then to satisfie the desire we had for to learn som-

thing of the captain by gentleness touching the *Turkish* army, we demanded of him whether it was parted from *Sues*, or whether he had not met with it in any place; and that we might be the better informed, we spake aloud to all those that were in the ship. But in stead of answer, without speaking a word, and in contempt of us, they gave us 12. pieces of ordnance, whereof five were small, and the other seven field pieces, together with good store of musquet shot; and withall, in a kind of jollity, and as it were believing that we were already theirs, they made all the ayr about resound again with their confused cries. After this, to brave and terrifie us the more, they flourished a many flags and streamers up and down, and from the top of their poop they brandished a number of naked scymitars, commanding us with great threatning to come aboard and yield our selves unto them. At the first view of so many rhodomontados and bravings we were in some doubt and amaze, which caused the captains of our foists to call the souldiers to councel, for to know what they should do; and the conclusion was, to continue shooting at them till the next morning, that so by day-light they might be the better fought withal and invested, it being agreed upon of all sides that they were not to be let go unpunished for their presumption; which accordingly was performed, and all the rest of the night we gave them chase, plying them with our ordnance. So morning come, their ship being shot thorow and thorow in many places, and cruelly battered all over, they render themselves into our hands. In the encounter there were 64. of their men killed, and of 80. that remained, the most part, seeing themselves reduced to extremity, cast themselves into the sea, choosing rather there to be drowned, then to be burnt in their ship with the artificial fires that we had hurled into her; so that of all the fourscore there escaped but five, very sore hurt, whereof one was the captain. This same, by force of torture, whereunto he was exposed by the command of our two captains, confessed that he came from *Judea*, and that the *Turkish* army was already departed from *Sues*, with a design to take in *Adem*, and then to build a fortress there before they attempted any thing in the *Indies*, according to an express charge sent by the great *Turk* from *Constantinople* to the *Bassa* of *grand Cairo*, who was going to be general of the army: besides this, he confessed many other things conformable to our desire; amongst the which he said, that he was a renegado Christian, a *Maliorquin* by nation, born at *Cerdenha*, and son to one named *Paul Andrez*, a merchant of that island, and that about four years before growing enamoured of a very fair *Greekish Mahumetân*, that was then his wife, for the love of her he had abjured Christianity, and embraced the law of *Mahomet*. Our captains much amazed hereat, gently perswaded him to acquit this abominable belief, and become a Christian again; whereunto the wicked caytiff made answer with a brutish obstinacy, that at no hand he would yield to forsake his law, shewing himself so hardened in the resolution to continue therein, as if he had been born in it, and never had profest any other. By these speeches of his, the captains, perceiving there was no hope of recalling him from his damnable error, caused him to be bound hand and foot, and so with a great stone tyed about his neck to be cast alive into the sea, sending him to participate with the torments of this *Mahomet*, and to be his companion in the other world, as he had been his confident in this. This infidel being executed in this sort, we put the other prisoners into one of our foists, and then sunk their vessel, with all the goods that were in her, which consisted most in packs of stained cloths, whereof we had no use, and a few pieces of chamlet that the soldiers got to make them apparel.

---

## CHAPTER III.

Our travelling from Mazua by land to the mother of Prester John; as also our reimbarquing at the Port of Arquico, and that which befel us by the encounter of three Turkish vessels.

WE departed from this place with an intent to go to *Arquico*, the territory of *Prester John*, Emperour of *Æthiopia*; for we had a letter to deliver, which *Antonio de Sylvera* sent to a factor of his, named *Aurique Barbosa*, who

had been three years resident in that country, by the
commandment of the Governour *Nuno de Cunha*. When we
were arrived at *Gottor*, a league lower then the port of *Mazua*,
we were all received there very courteously, as well by the
inhabitants, as by a *Portugal* called *Vasco Martin de Seixas*,
born in the town of *Obidos*, who was come thither by *Henrico
Barbosa's* order, and had been there a moneth attending the
arrival of some *Portugal* ships. The cause of that abode was
to deliver a letter from the said *Henrico*, as accordingly he did
to the captains of our foists; by this letter he certified the
estate of the *Turkish* army, and besought them at any hand
to send him some *Portugals*; to induce them whereunto, he
remonstrated unto them how it much imported the service
both of God and the King, and that for his own part he could
not come unto them, because he was employed with forty other
*Portugals*, in the fort of *Gileytor*, for the guard of the person
of the Princess of *Tigremahon*, mother to *Prester John*. The
two captains having perused this letter, communicated it to
the chiefest of the souldiers, and sat in councel upon it, where
it was determined that four of them should go along with
*Vasco Martins* to *Barbosa*, and that they should carry the
letter which *Antonio de Sylvera* had sent him. This was no
sooner resolved then executed; for the next day three other
*Portugals*, and my self, departed accordingly, and we went
by land mounted upon good mules, which the *Ciquaxy*,
captain of the town, sent us by the command of the
Princess, the Emperours mother, together with six *Abissins* to
accompany us. The first night we lay at a very fair
monastery, called *Satilgaon*; the next day before the sun rose
we travelled along by a river, and by that time we had rode
five leagues we arrived at a place named *Bitonte*, where we
spent that night in a convent of religious persons, dedicated
to S. *Michael*; there we were very well entertained both by
the Prior, and the Friers. A little after our arrival, the son of
*Bernagais*, Governour of that empire of *Æthiopia*, a very proper
and courteous gentleman, about seventeen years old, came to
see us, accompanied with thirty men, all mounted upon mules,
and himself on a horse furnished after the *Portugal* manner;
the furniture was of purple velvet trimmed with gold fringe,

which two years before the Governour *Nuno de Cunha* sent him
from the *Indies*, by one *Lopez Chanoco*, who was afterwards
made a slave at *Grand Cairo*; whereof this young prince
being advertised, he presently dispatched away a *Jewish*
merchant of *Azabiba* to redeem him; but as ill fortune would,
he died before the Jew could get thither, which so grieved this
prince when he understood of it, as the said *Vasco Martins*
assured us that in the said monastery of S. *Michael*, he caused
the most honourable funerals to be celebrated for him that
ever he saw, wherein assisted above four thousand priests,
besides a greater number of novices, which in their language
are called *Santilcos*: nor was this all, for this prince hearing
that the deceased had been married at *Goa*, and likewise
that he had left three daughters there behind him, which were
very young and poor, he bestowed on them three hundred
*Oqueas* of gold, that are worth twelve *Crusadoes* of our money
apiece; a liberality truly royal, and which I relate here, as
well to amplifie the nobleness of this prince, as that it may
serve for an example to others, and render them more
charitable upon like occasions.

The next morning we continued our journey, making all the
haste that possibly we could : to which end we got upon good
horses, that were given us by this prince; and withal he
appointed four of his servants to accompany us, who during
our voyage entertained us every where very sumptuously.
That day our lodging was at a goodly place, called *Betenigus*,
which signifies a royal house; and in truth it was not without
reason so named, for on whatsoever part one cast an eye, it
was invironed with great high trees for three leagues about;
nor is it to be credited how pleasing this wood was, for that
it was composed all of cedars, cypress, palm, date-trees, and
cocos, like to those in the *Indies*; here we past the night with
all kind of contentment. In the morning we proceeded on our
journey, and travelling after five leagues a day, we past over
a great plain, all full of goodly corn; then we arrived at a
mountain, named, *Vangaleu*, inhabited by Jews, which was
very white and handsome; two days and an half after we
came to a good town, called *Fumbau*, not above twelve leagues
distant from the fort of *Gyleytor*, there we found *Barbosa*, and

the forty *Portugals* aforesaid, who received us with great
demonstration of joy, but not without shedding of some tears,
for though they lived there at their ease, and were absolute
masters of all the country, as they said, yet the consideration
how they were as men banished from their country into this
place, did very much trouble them.

Now because it was night when we arrived, and that we had
all need of rest; *Barbosa* was of the opinion that we should
not see the Emperours mother till the next morning, which
was on Sunday, the 4th of *October*; that come, and we well
refreshed, we went accompanied with *Barbosa*, and his forty
*Portugals*, to the Princess palace, where we found her at Mass
in her chappel. A while after, being advertised of our arrival,
she caused us to be admitted into her presence; whereupon
we fell on our knees before her, and with all kind of humility
kissed the Ventilow that she held in her hand; to these
submissions we adjoyned many other ceremonies according to
their fashion, conformable to the instructions we had taken
from the *Portugals* that conducted us thither. She received
us with a smiling countenance; and to testifie how much she
was pleased with our coming; *Verily*, said she, *you cannot
imagine how glad I am to see you, that are right Christians;
for it hath been a thing which I have alwayes as much desired,
as a fair garden enammelled with flowers doth the morning
dew; wherefore you are most welcome; come, and may your
entrance into my house be as propitious as that of the Vertuous
Queen* Helena's *was into blessed Jerusalem.* Herewith she
made us to sit down upon mats, not above five or six paces
distant from her; then shewing her self exceedingly contented,
she questioned us about certain matters, of which she assured
us, that she very much longed to be satisfied: First, she asked
us the name of our Holy Father the Pope, also how many kings
there were in Christendome, and whether any of us had ever
been in the Holy Land; whereupon she much condemned the
Christian princes for their neglect and want of care in seeking
to ruine the power of the *Turk*, who, she said, was the
common enemy of them all. Likewise she would know of
us, whether the King of *Portugal* was great in the *Indies*,
what forts he had there, in what places they were seated, and

how defended. She made us many other like demands, to the which we answered the best we could for to content her; whereupon she dismissed us, and we returning to our lodging, continued there nine dayes, which we spent in waiting on this Princess, with whom we had much discourse on several subjects: that term expired, we went to take our leaves of her; and in kissing of her hands she seemed to be somwhat troubled at our departure. *Truly*, said she, *it grieves me that you will be gone so soon; but since there is no remedy, I wish your voyage may be so prosperous, that at your arrival in the Indies, you may be as well received by yours, as the Queen of* Sheba *was heretofore by King* Solomon *in the admirable palace of his greatness.* Now before we departed she bestowed on us twenty four *Oqueas* of gold, which make two hundred forty duckats of our money; she caused us also to be conducted by a *Naique*, and twenty *Abissins*, as well to serve us for guides, and guard us from robbers, whereof that countrey was full, as to furnish us with victuals and horses, until such time as we got to *Arquico*, where our foists attended for us. This Princess also sent a rich present of divers jewels of gold and stones by *Vasco Martins de Seixas* unto the Governour of the *Indies*, which by ill fortune was lost in this voyage, as shall be declared hereafter.

After we were returned to the port of *Arquico*, where we found our companions caulking of our foists, and furnishing them with all that was necessary for our voyage, we fell to work with them for the space of nine dayes. At length, all things being ready, we set sail, and parted from thence on Tuesday, the 6th of *November*, 1538. We carried with us both *Vasco Martins de Seixas*, that had the present, and a letter from the Princess to the Governour of the *Indies*, as also an *Abissin* bishop, who was bound for *Portugal*, with an intent to go from thence to *Galicia*, *Rome* and *Venice*, and afterwards to travel to *Jerusalem*, which especially he desired to see in regard of the holiness of the place. An hour before day we left the port, and sailed along the coast before the wind, until such time as about noon we reached the point of the Cape of *Cocam*; and before we arrived at the Island of Rocks, we discerned three vessels on the other side, that seemed

to us to be *Gelvas* or *Terrades*, which are the names of the
vessels of that country ; whereupon we gave them chase, and
with the strength of our oars, because the wind was then
somwhat down, we pursued them in such sort, that in less
then two hours, having gotten up to them, we might easily
perceieve them to be *Turkish* gallies, whereof we were no sooner
assured, but that we presently betook ourselves to flight, and
made towards the land with all the haste that might be, so (if
it were possible) to escape the danger that inevitably threatned
us : but whether the *Turks* suspected our design, or knew it,
in less than a quarter of an hour they hoisted up all their sails,
and having the wind favourable they followed us very hard,
so as in a little while getting within a small faulcon shot of us,
they discharged all their ordnance upon us, wherewith they
not only killed nine of our men, and hurt six and twenty, but
so battered our foists, that we were fain to cast a great part
of our goods into the sea ; mean while the *Turks* lost no time,
but joyned us so close, that from their poop they hurt us easily
with their pikes. Now there were four and fourty good souldiers
remaining yet unhurt in our foists, who knowing that upon
their valour and the force of their arms depended the lives both
of themselves, and all the rest, they determined to fight it out.
With this resolution they set couragiously upon the admiral of
three gallies, wherein was *Solyman Dragut*, General of the
Fleet; their onset was so furious, as they invested her from
poop to prow, and killed seven and twenty *Janizaries* ; nevertheless she being instantly succoured with fresh men by the
other two gallies, which had stayed a little behind, we were so
wearied and oppressed with numbers, that we were not able to
make any further resistance; for of four and fifty that we were
at first, there was but eleven left alive, whereof two also died the
next day, whom the *Turks* caused to be cut in quarters, which
they hung at the end of their mainyard for a sign of their
victory, and in that manner carried them to the town of
*Mocaa*, whereof the father-in-law of the said *Solyman Dragus*,
that had taken us, was Governor; who with all the inhabitants
waited the coming of his son-in-law at the entry into the port,
to receive and welcome him for his victory. In his company
he had a certain *Cacis*, who was *Moulana*, the chiefest sacer-

dotal dignity; and because he had been a little before in pilgrimage at the temple of their prophet *Mahomet* in *Mecca*, he was held by all the people for a very holy man: this imposter rode up and down the town in a triumphant charret, covered all over with silk tapistry, and with a deal of ceremony blessed the people as he went along, exhorting them to tender all possible thanks unto their Prophet for the victory which *Solyman Dragut* had obtained over us. As soon as they arrived at this place, we nine that remained alive were set on shore, tied altogether with a great chain, and amongst us was the *Abissin* bishop, so pitifully wounded, that he died the next day, and in his end shewed the repentance of a true Christian, which very much encouraged and comforted us. In the mean time all the inhabitants that were assembled about us, hearing that we were the Christians which were taken captives, being exceedingly transported with choler, fell to beating of us in that cruel manner, as for my own part I never thought to have escaped alive out of their hands, whereunto they were especially incited by the wicked *Cacis*, who made them believe they should obtain the more favour and mercy from their *Mahomet*, the worse they entreated us. Thus chained all together, and persecuted by every one, we were led in triumph over all the town, where nothing was heard but acclamations and shouts, intermingled with a world of musick, as well of instruments, as voyces. Moreover, there was not a woman, were she never so retired, that came not forth then to see us, and to do us some outrage; for from the very least children to the oldest men, all that beheld us pass by cast out of the windows and balcons upon us pots of piss, and other filth, in contempt and derision of the name of Christian, wherein every one strived to be most forward, in regard their cursed priest continued still preaching unto them, that they should gain remission of their sins by abusing us. Having been tormented in this sort until the evening, they went and laid us (bound as we were) in a dark dungeon, where we remained 17 dayes, exposed to all kind of misery, having no other victual all that time, but a little oatmeal, which was distributed to us every morning to serve us all the day: somtimes they gave us the same measure in dry peason a little soaked in water, and this was all the meat we had.

## CHAPTER IV.

A Mutiny happening in the town of Mocaa, the occasion thereof, that which
befel thereupon, and by what means I was carried to Ormuz; as also my
sailing from thence to Goa, and what success I had in that voyage.

THE next day, in regard that we had been so miserably
moiled, and our hurts that were great but ill looked
unto, of us nine there died two; whereof one was named
*Nuno Delgado*, and the other *Andre Borges*, both of them men
of courage, and of good families.  The jaylor, which in their
language is called *Mocadan*, repairing in the morning to us,
and finding our two companions dead, goes away in all haste
therewith to acquaint the *Gauzil*, which is as the judge with
us, who came in person to the prison, attended by a great
many of officers and other people; where having caused their
irons to be stricken off, and their feet to be tyed together with
a rope, he commanded them so to be dragged from thence
clean through the town, where the whole multitude, to the
very children, pursued and pelted them with staves and stones,
untill such time as being wearied with hurrying those poor
bodies in such fashion, they cast them all battered to pieces
into the sea.  At last we seven, that were left alive, were
chained altogether, and brought forth into the publique place
of the town, to be sold to them that would give most: there
all the people being met together, I was the first that was put
to sale; whereupon just as the cryer was offering to deliver
me unto whomsoever would buy me, in comes the very *Cacis
Moulana*, whom they held for a saint, with ten or eleven other
*Cacis*, his inferiours, all priests, like himself, of their wicked
sect, and addressing his speech to *Heredrin Sofo*, the Governour
of the town, who sate as president of the portsale, he required
him to send us, as an alms, unto the Temple of *Mecqua* saying,
that he was upon returning thither, and having resolved to
make that pilgrimage in the name of all the people, it were
not fit to go thither without carrying some offering to the
Prophet *Noby*, (so they termed their *Mahomet*), a thing, said
he, that would utterly displease *Razaadat Moulana*, the chief
priest of *Medina Talnab*, who without that would grant no

kind of grace or pardon to the inhabitants of this town, which by reason of their great offences stood in extream need of the favour of God and His Prophet.

The Governour having heard the *Cacis* speak thus, declared unto him that, for his particular, he had no power to dispose of any part of the booty, and that therefore he should apply himself to *Solyman Dragus* his son-in-law, who had made us slaves; so that in right it appertained only unto him to do with us as he pleased; and I do not think, added he, that he will contradict so holy an intention as this is. Thou hast reason for it, answered the *Cacis*, but with all thou must know, that the things of God, and the alms that are done in His name, lose their value and force, when they are sifted through so many hands, and turmoiled with such humane opinions; for which very cause seldom doth any divine resolution follow thereupon, especially in a subject such as this, which thou mayst absolutely dispose of, as thou art sovereign commander of this people. Moreover, as there is no body can be displeased therewith, so I do not see how it can bring thee any discontent. For besides that this demand is very just; it is also most agreeable to our Prophet *Noby*, who is the absolute lord of this prize, in regard the victory came solely from his holy hand, though with as much falsehood as malice thou goest about to attribute the glory of it to the valor of thy son-in-law, and the courage of his soldiers. At this instant a *Janizary* was present, captain of one of the three gallies that took us, a man that for his exceeding valour was in great esteem amongst them, called *Copa Geynal*, who nettled with that which he heard the *Cacis* speak, so much in contempt of both of himself and the rest of the souldiers, that had carried themselves very valiantly in the fight with us, returned him this answer. Certainly you might do better, for the salvation of your soul, to distribute some part of the excessive riches you possess among these poor souldiers, then seek with feign'd speeches, full of hypocrisie and deceit, to rob them of these slaves, which have cost the lives of so many brave men, their fellows in arms, and have been dearly bought by us that survive, even with our dearest blood, as the wounds we have upon us can but too well witness; so can it not be said of your Cabayage (a sacerdotal robe after their fashion), which for all it fits so trim and neat upon you, covers a pernicious habit you have of purloyning other mens estates from them : wherefore I would wish you to desist from the damnable plot you have laid against the absolute masters of this prize, whereof you shall not have so much as a token, and seek out some other present for the *Cacis* of *Mecqua*, to the end he may conceal your theevries, and impiety, provided it be not done with the expence of our lives and blood, but rather with the goods you have so lewdly gotten by your wicked and cunning devices.

This *Cacis Moulana* having received so bold an answer from this captain, found it very rude, and hard of digestion, which made him in bitter terms, and void of all respects, exceedingly to blame the captain, and the souldiers that were there present, who, as well *Turks* as *Saracens*, being much offended with his ill language, combined together and mutined against him, and the rest of the people, in whose favour he had spoken so insolently ; nor could this mutiny be appeased by any kind of means, though the Governor of the town, father-in-law to the said *Solyman Dragut*, together with the officers of justice, did all that possibly they could.  In a word, that I may not stand longer upon the particulars of this affair, I say, that from this small mutiny did arise so cruel and enraged a contention, as it ended not but with the death of 600 persons, of the one, and the other side : but at length the souldiers party prevailing, they pillaged the most part of the town, especially the said *Cacis Moulana's* house, killing 7 wives and 9 children that he had, whose bodies together with his own were dismembred, and cast into the sea with a great deal of cruelty. In the same manner they entreated all that belonged unto him, not so much as giving life to one that was known to be his.  As for us 7 *Portugals*, which were exposed to sale in the publique place, we could find out no better expedient to save our lives, then to return into the same hole, from whence we came, and that too without any officer of justice to carry us thither ; neither did we take it for a small favour that the jaylour would receive us into prison.  Now this mutiny had not ceased but by the authority of *Solyman Dragut*, General of the gallies aforesaid ; for this man with very gentle words

gave an end to the sedition of the people, and pacified the
mutiners, which shews of what power courtesie is, even with
such as are altogether ignorant of it. In the mean time
*Heredrin Sopho*, Governour of the town, came off but ill from
this hurly burly, by reason that in the very first encounter he
had one of his arms almost cut off. Three days after this disorder was quieted, we were led all 7 again to the market place,
there to be sold with the rest of the booty, which consisted of
our stuff, and ordnance, that they had taken in our foists, and
were sold at a very easie rate: for my self, miserable that
I was, and the most wretched of them all; fortune, my sworn
enemy, made me fall into the hands of a Greek renegado,
whom I shall detest as long as I have a day to live, because
that in the space of 3 moneths I was with him; he used me so
cruelly, that becoming even desperate, for that I was not able
to endure the evil he did me, I was seven or eight times upon
the point to have poysoned my self, which questionless I had
done, if God of His infinite mercy and goodness had not
delivered me from it, whereunto I was the rather induced to
make him lose the money he paid for me, because he was the
most covetous man in the world, and the most inhumane, and
cruellest enemy to the name of a Christian. But at the end
of three moneths it pleased the Almighty to deliver me out of
the hands of this tyrant, who for fear of losing the mony I cost
him; if I should chance to make my self away, as one of his
neighbours perswaded him I would, telling him that he had
discovered so much by my countenance, and manner of
behaviour, wherefore in pity of me he counselled him to sell
me away, as he did not long after unto a Jew, named *Abraham
Muca*, native of a town called in those quarters *Toro*, not
above a league and an half distant from Mount *Sinay*. This
man gave for me the value of 300 reals in dates, which was the
merchandize that this Jew did ordinarily trade in with my
late master; and so I parted with him in the company of
divers merchants for to go from *Babylon* to *Cayxem*, whence
he carried me to *Ormuz*, and there presented me to *Don
Fernand de Lima*, who was at that time captain of the fort,
and to *Don Pedro Fernandez*, Commissary General of the
*Indies*, that was then residing at *Ormuz*, for the service of the

King by order from the Governour *Nunho de Cunha.* These
two, namely *Fernandez* and *de Lima*, gave the Jew in recompence for me 200 *Pardaos*, which are worth three shillings
and nine pence a piece of our coyn, whereof part was their
own mony, and the rest was raised of the alms which they
caused to be gathered for me in the town, so we both remained contented, the Jew for the satisfaction he had received
from them, and I to find my self at full liberty as before.

Seeing my self by Gods mercy delivered from the miseries
I had endured; after I had been seventeen days at *Ormuz*,
I imbarqued my self for the *Indies* in a ship that belonged to
one *Jorge Fernandez Taborda*, who was to carry horses to *Goa.*
In the course that we held we sailed with so prosperous a
gale, that in 17 dayes we arrived in the view of the Fort of
*Diu*; there, by the advice of the captains, coasting along by
the land for to learn some news, we descried a great number
of fires all that night, also at times we heard divers pieces of
ordnance discharged, which very much troubled us, by reason
we could not imagine what those fires, or that shooting in the
night should mean; in so much that we were divided into
several opinions.   During this incertainty our best advice was,
to sail the rest of the night with as little cloth as might be,
until that on the next morning by favour of day light we
perceived a great many sails, which invironed the fort on all
sides.   Some affirmed that it was the Governour newly come
from *Goa*, to make peace for the death of *Sultan Bandur*, King
of *Cambaya*, that was slain a little before.   Others said that it
was the Infant, brother to the King *Dom Jovan*, lately arrived
there from *Portugal*, because he was every day expected in the
*Indies.*   Some thought that it was the *Patemarca*, with the
King of *Calicuts* hundred foists of *Camorin.*   And the last
assured us, how they could justifie with good and sufficient
reasons that they were the *Turks.*   As we were in this
diversity of minds, and terrified with that which we discerned
before our eyes, five very great gallies came forth of the midst
of this fleet, with a many of banners, flags and streamers,
which we saw on the tops of their masts, and the ends of their
sail-yards, whereof some were so long, that they touched even
the very water.   These gallies being come forth in this sort,

turned their prows towards us in such a couragious and
confident manner, that by their sailing we presently judged
them to be *Turks*; which we no sooner knew to be so indeed,
but we clapt on all our cloth for to avoid them, and to get into
the main sea, not without exceeding fear, lest for our sins we
should fall into the like estate from whence I was so lately
escaped. These five gallies having observed our flight, took
a resolution to pursue us, and chased us till night, at which
time it pleased God that they tacked about, and returned to
the army from whence they came. Seeing our selves freed
from so great a danger we went joyfully on, and two dayes
after arrived at the town of *Chaul*, where our captain and the
merchants, only landed for to visit the captain of the fort,
named *Simon Guedez*, unto whom they reported that which
had befallen them. Assuredly, said he, you are very much
bound to give God thanks for delivering you from one of the
greatest perils that ever you were in, for without His assistance
it had been impossible for you ever to have declined it, or to
tell me of it with such joy as now you do: thereupon he
declared unto them, that the army they had encountred was
the very same, which had held *Antonio de Silveyra* twenty
dayes together besieged, being composed of a great number of
*Turks*, whereof *Solyman* the *Bassa*, Vice-roy of *Caire*, was
General, and that those sails they had seen, were 58. gallies
great and small, each of which carried five pieces of ordnance
in her prow, and some of them were pieces of battery, besides
eight other great vessels full of *Turks*, that were kept in
reserve to succour the army, and supply the places of such as
should be killed: moreover, he added, that they had great
abundance of victuals, amongst the which there was 12.
Basilisks. This news having much amazed us, we rendred
infinite praise to the Lord for shewing us such grace, as to
deliver us from so imminent a danger.

We staid at *Chaul* but one day, and then we set sail for
*Goa*; being advanced as far to the river of *Carapatan*, we
met with *Fernand de Morais*, captain of three foists, who by
the command of the Vice-roy, *Dom Garcia de Noronha*, was
going to *Dabul*, to the end he might see whether he could take
or burn a *Turkish* vessel which was in the port laden with

victuals by order from the *Bassar*. This *Fernand de Morais* had no sooner gotten acquaintance of our ship, but he desired our captain to lend him 15 men, of twenty that he had, for to supply the great necessity he was in that way, by reason of the Vice-royes hastning him away upon the sudden; which, said he, would much advance the service both of God, and his highness. After many contestations of either part upon this occasion, and which, to make short, I will pass under silence; at length they were agreed, that our captain should let *Fernand de Morais* have 12 of 15 men that he requested, wherewithal he was very well satisfied: of this number I was one, as being alwayes of the least respected.    The ship departing for *Goa;* *Fernand de Morais*, with his three foists, continued his voyage towards the port of *Dabul*, where we arrived the next day about nine of the clock in the morning, and presently took a patach of *Malabar*, which laden with cotton wool and pepper, rode at anchor in the midst of the port.   Having taken it we put the captain and pilot to torture, who instantly confessed that a few dayes before the ship came into the port expresly from the *Bassa* to lade victuals, and that there was in her an embassadour, who had brought *Hidalcan* a very rich *Cabaya*, that is, a garment worn by the gentlemen of that countrey, which he would not accept of, for that thereby he would not acknowledge himself subject to the *Turk*, it being a custom among the *Mahumetans*, for the lord to do that honour to his vassal; and further, that this refusal had so much vexed the Embassador, as he returned without taking any kind of provision of victuals, and that *Hidalcan* had answered, he made much more esteem of the K. of *Portugals* amity, then of his, which was nothing but deceit, as having usurped the town of *Goa* upon him, after he had offered to aid him with his favour and forces to regain it.   Moreover, they said, that it was not above two dayes since the ship they spoke of parted from the port, and that the captain of her, named *Cide Ale*, had denounced war against *Hidalcan*, vowing that as soon as the fort of *Diu* was taken, which could not hold out above eight dayes, according to the estate wherein he had left it, *Hidalcan* should lose his kingdom, or life, and that then he should (to his cost) know how that the *Portugals*, in whom he put his confidence, could not avail him. With these news Captain *Morais* turned towards *Goa*, where he arrived two dayes after, and gave account to the Vice-roy of that which had past. There we found *Goncallo vaz Coutinho*, who was going with five foists to *Onor*, to demand of the Queen thereof one of the gallies of *Solymans* army, which by a contrary wind had been driven into her ports. Now one of the captains of those foists, my special friend, seeing me poor and necessitous, perswaded me to accompany him in this voyage, and to that end got me five ducates pay, which I very gladly accepted of, out of the hope I had, that God would thereby open me a way to a better fortune. Being imbarqued then, the captain and souldiers, pitying the case I was in, bestowed such spare clothes as they had upon me, by which means being reasonably well pieced up again, we parted the next morning from the Road of *Bardees*, and the Monday following we cast anchor in the port of *Onor*; where, that the inhabitants of the place might know how little account we made of that mighty army, we gave them a great peal of ordnance, putting forth all our fifes, beating our drums, and sounding our trumpets, to the end that by these exterior demonstrations they might conclude we regarded not the *Turks* awhit.

---

## CHAPTER V.

Goncallo vaz Coutinho's Treaty with the Queen of Onor; his assaulting of a Turkish galley, and that which hapned unto us as we were upon our return to Goa.

OUR fleet making a stand upon the discharging of our peal of ordnance, the General *Goncallo vaz Coutinho* sent *Bento Castanho*, a very discreet and eloquent man, to the Queen of *Onor*, to present her with a letter from the Vice-roy, and to tell her that he was come to complain of her, for that she had sworn a peace and amity with our King of *Portugal*, and yet suffered the *Turks*, mortal enemies to the *Portugals*, to abide in her ports. Hereunto she returned this answer: *That both himself and his company were very welcome, and that she desired to maintain the peace as long as she lived. For that which he said of the* Turks, *she took her God to witness, how much against her will she had received and suffered them in her ports; but that finding her self too weak for to resist such powerful* enemies, *she was constrained to dissemble, which she would never have done had she been furnished with sufficient forces. Furthermore, to clear her self the better unto them, she offered both her power and people for to repel them out of her ports.* To this speech she added, that *she should be as well pleased if God would give him the victory over them, as if the King of* Narsingua, *whose slave she was, should set her at the table with his wife, Goncallo vaz Coutinho* having received this embassage, and other complements from the Queen, though he had little hope of any performance on her part, yet did he wisely dissemble it. Afterwards being fully informed by the people of the country of the *Turks* intention, of the place where they were, and what they did at that instant, he called a councel thereupon, and having througly debated and considered all things, it was unanimously concluded, that both for the King of *Portugal* their masters honour, and his own, it was expedient to set upon this galley, either for to take, or fire it, wherein it was hoped that God, for whose glory we fought, would be assisting to us against those enemies of the holy faith. This resolution being made, and signed by us all, he entred some two faulcons shot within the river, where he had scarce anchored, when as a little boat, which they call an *Almadia*, came aboard us, with a *Brachman* that spake very good *Portuguez*. This man delivered a message from the Queen unto our captain, whereby she earnestly desired him, that for Vice-royes sake he would desist from the enterprise he had undertaken, and not to assault the *Turks* any manner of way, which, said she, could not be done without great disadvantage, for that she had been advertised by her spies, that they had fortified themselves with a good trench, which they had cast up near the place where they had moored their galley; in regard whereof it seemed to her almost impossible for him with no more forces then he had to be able to prevail in so great an attempt : wherefore she took her God to witness how much she was troubled with the fear she was in, lest some

mis-fortune should betide him. Hereunto our captain returned
an answer full of wisdom and courtesie, saying that he kissed
her Highness hands for the extraordinary favour she did him,
in giving him so good advice : but for his combat with the
*Turks,* he could not follow her counsel, and therefore would
proceed in his determination, it being always the custom of
the *Portugals,* not to inquire whether their enemies were few,
or many since the more they were, the more should be their
loss, and the greater his profit and honour. Thus was the
*Brachman* dismissed, our captain bestowing on him a piece
of green chamlet, and an hat lined with red sattin, wherewith
he returned very well contented.

The *Brachman* dismist, *Goncallo vaz Coutinho* resolved to
fight with the *Turks,* but before he proceeded any further, he
was advertised by spies what stratagems the enemy would use
against us, and that the precedent night, by the favour of the
Queen, they had moored up the galley, and by it raised up a
platform, whereupon they had flanked 25. pieces of ordnance ;
but all that stayed him not from advancing towards the enemy ;
seeing himself then within a cannon shot of them, he went out
of his foist, and with 80. men onely landed, the rest which he
had brought with him from *Goa* for this enterprize, being but
an hundred more, he left for the guard of the foists. So after
he had set his men in battel array, he marched couragiously
against his adversaries, who perceiving us making towards
them valiantly resolved to defend themselves, to which end
they sallied some five and twenty or thirty paces out of their
trenches, where the fight began on either side with such fury,
that in less then a quarter of an hour, five and forty lay dead
in the place, amongst the which, there was not above 8. of ours :
Hereupon our General not contented with the first charge,
gave them a second, by means whereof it pleased God to make
them turn their backs, in such sort that they retired pell-mel,
as men routed, and in fear of death. Mean while we pursued
them to their very trenches, where they turned upon us, and
made head anew, in the heat thereof we were so far engaged
and intangled together, that we knocked one another with the
pummels of our swords. Mean while our foists arrived, which
were come along by the shore to succour us, and accordingly

they discharged all their ordnance upon our enemies, to such good purpose, as they killed 11. or 12. of the valiantest *Janizaries*, which wore green turbants, as a mark of their nobility. The death of these so terrified the rest, that they presently forsook the field, by means whereof we had leasure to set the galley on fire upon the express command of our General *Goncallo*, so that having cast into her five pots of powder, the fire took hold on her with such violence, as it was apparant it could not be long before she were utterly consumed; for the mast and sail-yards were all of a flame, had not the *Turks*, knowing the danger she was in, most couragiously quenched the fire, but we laboured all that possibly we could to hinder them from it, and to make good that we had so bravely begun, which the enemies perceiving, as their last refuge they gave fire to a great piece of ordnance, which charged with stones, and other shot, killed six of ours, whereof the principal was *Diego vas Coutinho*, the Generals son, besides a dozen others were hurt, that put us quite in disorder; whereupon the enemies finding how they had spoyled us, fell to shouting in sign of victory, and to rendring of thanks to their *Mahomet*: at the naming of this their false Prophet, whom they invoked, our General, the better to encourage his souldiers, *Fellows in arms*, said he, *seeing these dogs call upon the Devil to aid them, let us pray unto our Saviour Jesus Christ to assist us.* This said, we once more assaulted the trench, which the enemies no sooner perceived, but they craftily turned their backs, and took their flight towards the galley, but they were instantly followed by some of ours, who within a while made themselves masters of all their trenches; in the mean time the infidels gave fire to a secret myne, which they had made a little within their trenches, and blew up six of our *Portugals*, and eight slaves, maiming many others besides; now the smoak was such and so thick, as we could hardly discern one another, in regard whereof our general, fearing lest some greater loss then the former should befal him, retreated to the water side, carrying along with him both the dead bodies, and all the hurt men, and so went where his foists lay, into the which every one being imbarqued, we returned with strength of rowing to the place from whence we came, where with extream sorrow he caused the slain to be interred, and all that were hurt to be drest, which were a very great number.

The same day that was so fatal to us, a list being taken of all the surviving souldiers, that so it might be known how many had been lost in the last fight upon assaulting of the trench, we found that of fourscore which we were, there was fifteen slain, fifty four hurt, and nine quite maimed for ever: the rest of the day, and the night following, we kept very good watch to avoid all surprizes of the enemy. As soon as the next morning appeared, there came an embassadour from the Queen of *Onor* to the General *Goncallo*, with a present of hens, chickens, and new layd eggs, for the relief of our sick men; now though we had great need of those things, yet in stead of receiving our General utterly refused them; and shewing himself very much displeased with the Queen, he could not forbear lashing out some words that were a little more harsher then was requisite; saying, that the Vice-roy should ere long be advertised of the bad offices she had rendred the King of *Portugal*, and how much he was obliged to pay her that debt, when occasion should serve: further, he bid him tell her, that for an assurance of that which he said, he had left his son dead and buried in her land, together with the other *Portugals*, who had been miserably slaughtered through her practices, by assisting the *Turks* against them: and in a word, that he would thank her more fully another time for the present she had sent, the better to dissemble what she had executed against him, for which he would one day return her a recompence according to her merit.

The embassadour, very much terrified with this speech, departed; and being come to the Queen his mistress, he so thoroughly represented *Goncallo's* answer unto her, as she greatly doubted that this galley would be an occasion of the loss of her kingdom; wherefore to decline so great a mischief, she thought it necessary to seek by all means possible to maintain the league with our General, to which end she assembled her Councel, by whose advice she dispatched another embassadour unto him, who was a *Brachman*, a grave and reverend personage, and her nearest kinsman. At his arrival where our foists lay, our General gave him very good

entertainment; and after the ordinary ceremonies and complements, the *Brachman*, having demanded permission to
deliver his embassage, declared that *the Queen faithfully
promiseth, within four days to burn the galley, that hath put
you to so much pain, and turn the* Turks *out of the limits of her
kingdome, which is all that she can do, and which you may be
most confident she will not fail to execute accordingly.*

Our General knowing of what importance this affair was,
presently accepted of the *Brachmans* offer, and told him that
he was contented that the league should be renewed betwixt
them, according whereunto it was instantly published on
either part with all the ceremonies accustomed in such cases;
therupon the *Brachman* returned to the Queen, who afterwards laboured all she could to make good her word; but
because *Goncallo* could not stay the four days which he had
demanded, in regard of the extream danger he should thereby
have exposed our hurt men unto, he resolved to be gone, and
so the same day after dinner we departed; howbeit he first
left one, named *Georgio Neogueyra*, there, with express order
exactly to observe all that was done concerning that affair,
and thereof to give certain intelligence to the Vice-roy, as the
Queen her self had requested.

----

## CHAPTER VI.

What passed till such time as Pedro de Faria, arrived at Malaca; his
receiving an embassadour from the King of Batas; with his sending
me to that King, and that which arrived to me in that Voyage.

THE next day our General *Goncallo vaz Coutinho* arrived
at *Goa*, with so many of us as remained alive: there
he was exceedingly welcomed by the Vice-roy, unto whom he
rendred an account of his voyage, as also of that which he
had concluded with the Queen of *Onor*, who had promised
to burn the galley within four dayes, and to chase the *Turks*
out of all the confines of her kingdom, wherewith the Vice-
roy was very well satisfied. In the mean time, after I had
remained three and twenty dayes in the said town of *Goa*,

where I was cured of two hurts which I had received in fight
at the *Turks* trenches, the necessity whereunto I saw my
self reduced, and the counsel of a frier, my friend, perswaded
me to offer my service unto a gentleman, named *Pedro de
Faria*, that was then newly preferred to the charge of captain
of *Malaca*, who upon the first motion was very willing to
entertain me for a souldier, and promised me withal to give me
something over and above the rest of his company during the
voyage which he was going to make with the Vice-roy. For
it was at that very time when as the Vice-roy *Dom Garcia
de Noronha* was preparing to go to the succour of the fortress
of *Diu*, which he certainly knew was besieged, and in great
danger to-be taken, by reason of the great forces wherewithal
it was invested by the *Turk*; and to relieve it the Vice-roy
had assembled a mighty fleet at *Goa*, consisting of about
225. vessels, whereof fourscore and three were great ones;
namely, ships, galleons, carvels, and the rest brigantines,
foists, and galleys, wherein it was said there were ten
thousand land-men, and thirty thousand mariners, besides a
great number of slaves. The time of setting sail being come,
and the foists provided of all things necessary, the Vice-roy
imbarqued himself on *Saturday* the 14. of *November*, 1538.
Howbeit five dayes past away before he put out of the haven,
in regard he stayed for his men, that were not all ready to
imbarque; the meanwhile a catur arrived from the town of
*Diu*, with a letter from *Antonio de Silveyra*, captain of the
fortress, whereby he advertised the Vice-roy, that the *Turks*
had raised the siege, and were retired. Now though these
were good news, yet was the whole fleet grieved thereat, for
the great desire every one had to fight with the enemies of
our faith. Hereupon the Vice-roy abode there five dayes
longer, during the which he took order for all things necessary
to the conservation of his government of the *Indies*, and then
commanding to hoist sail, he departed from *Goa* on a
Thursday morning, the 16. of *December*: the fourteenth of
his navigation he went and cast anchor at *Chaul*, where he
remained three dayes, during the which he entered into
conference with *Inezamuluco*, a *Mahometan* prince, and took
order for certain affairs very much importing the surety of the

fortress : after that he caused some of the vessels of the fleet
to be rigged, which he furnished with souldiers and victuals,
and then departed for to go to *Diu* ; but it was his ill fortune,
as he was crossing the gulph, to be suddenly overtaken by
such a furious tempest, that it not only separated his fleet,
but was the loss of many vessels, chiefly of the bastard galley
which was cast away at the mouth of the river *Dabul*, whereof
*Dom Alvaro de Noronha*, the Vice-royes son, and General of
the Sea-forces, was captain ; in the same gulph also perished
the galley named *Espinhero*, commanded by *Jovan de Sousa* ;
howbeit the most part of their men were saved by *Christophilo
de Gama*, who came most opportunely to their succour. During
this tempest there were seven other ships likewise cast away,
the names of which I have forgotten, in so much that it was
a moneth before the Vice-roy could recover himself of the loss
he had sustain'd, and re-assemble his fleet again, which this
storm had scattered in divers places : at length the 16. of
*January*, 1539. he arrived at the town of *Diu*, where he caused
the fortress, to be re-built, the greater part whereof had been
demolished by the *Turks*, so as it seemed that it had been
defended by the besieged, rather by miracle : then force :
now to effect it the better, he made proclamation, that all the
captains with their souldiers should each of them take in
charge to re-build that quarter which should be allotted them ;
and because never a commander there had more then *Pedro
de Faria*, he thought fit to appoint him the bulwark, which
looked to the sea, for his quarter, together with the out-wall
that was on the lands side ; wherein he bestowed such care
and diligence, that in six and twenty days space, both the one
and the other were restored to a better state then before, by
the means of 300 souldiers that were employed about it. This
done, for that it was the 14 of *March*, and a fit time for
navigation to *Malaca*, *Pedro de Faria* set sail for *Goa*, where
by vertue of a patent granted him by the Vice-roy, he furnished himself with all things necessary for his voyage ;
departing then from *Goa* on the 13 of *April*, with a fleet of
eight ships, four foists, and one galley, wherein there were
five hundred men, he had so favourable a wind, that he arrived
at *Malaca*, the 5th day of *June*, in the same year, 1539.

*Pedro de Faria* succeeding *Dom Estevano de Gama* in the charge of the captain of *Malaca*, arrived there safely with his fleet, nothing hapning in his voyage worthy of writing. Now because at his arrival, *Estevan de Gama* had not yet ended the time of his commission, he was not put into the possession of that government until the day that he was to enter upon his charge. Howbeit, in regard *Pedro de Faria*, was ere long to be governour of the fortress, the neighbouring kings sent their embassadours to congratulate with him, and to make a tender of their amity, and of a mutual conservation of peace with the King of *Portugal*. Amongst these embassadours there was one from the King of *Batas*, who raigned in the Isle of *Samatra*, where it is held for a surety that the Island of Gold is, which the King of *Portugal*, *Dom. Joana* the Third, had resolved should have been discovered, by the advice of certain captains of the country. This embassadour, that was brother-in-law to the King of *Batas*, named *Aquarem Dabolay*, brought him a rich present of wood of *Aloes, Calambaa*, and five quintals of benjamon in flowers, with a letter written on the bark of a palm-tree, [*demanding the aid of the Portuguese against the Tyrant of Achem*].

This embassadour received from *Pedro de Faria* all the honour that he could do him after their manner, and as soon as he had delivered him the letter, it was translated into the *Portugal* out of the *Malayan* tongue, wherein it was written. Whereupon the embassadour by his interpreter declared the occasion of the discord which was between the Tyrant of *Achem* and the King of *Batas*, proceeding from this, that the Tyrant had not long before propounded unto this King of *Batas*, who was a Gentile, the imbracing of *Mahomets* law, conditionally that he would wed him to a sister of his, for which purpose he should quit his wife, that was also a Gentile, and married to him six and twenty years; now because the King of *Batas* would by no means condescend thereunto, the Tyrant, incited by a *Cacis* of his, immediately denounced war against him: so each of them having raised a mighty army, they fought a most bloody battel, that continued three houres and better, during the which the Tyrant perceiving the advantage the *Bataes* had of him, after he had lost a great number of his people, he made his retreat into a mountain, called *Cagerrendan*, where the *Bataes* held him besieged by the space of three and twenty dayes; but because that time many of the Kings men fell sick, and that also the Tyrants camp began to want victuals; they concluded a peace, upon condition that the Tyrant should give the King five bars of gold (which are in value two hundred thousand crowns of our mony) for to pay his souldiers, and that the King should marry his eldest son to that sister of the Tyrant, who had been the cause of making that war. This accordingly being signed by either part, the King returned into his country, where he was no sooner arrived, but relying on this treaty of peace, he dismist his army, and discharged all his forces. The tranquillity of this peace lasted not above two moneths and an half, in which time there came to the Tyrant 300 *Turks*, whom had long expected from the Streight of *Mecqua*, and for them had sent four vessels laden with pepper, wherein also were brought a great many cases of muskets and hargebuses, together with divers pieces both of brass and iron ordnance; whereupon the first thing the Tyrant did, was to joyn 300. *Turks* to some forces he had still afoot; then making as though he would go to *Pacem*, for to take in a captain that was revolted against him, he cunningly fell upon two places, named *Jacur* and *Lingua*, that appertained to the King of *Batas*, which he suddenly surprized when they within them least thought of it, for the peace newly made between them took away all the mistrust of such an attempt, so as by that means it was easie for the Tyrant to render himself master of those fortresses. Having taken them, he put three of the Kings sons to death, and 700 *Ouroballones*, so are the noblest and the valiantest of the kingdom called. This while the King of *Batas*, much resenting, and that with good cause so great a treachery, sware by the head of his god *Quia Hocombinor*, the principal idol of the Gentiles sect, who hold him for their god of justice, never to eat either fruit, salt, or any other thing that might bring the least gust to his palate, before he had revenged the death of his children, and drawn reason from the Tyrant for this loss; protesting further, that he was resolved to dye in the maintenance of so just a war. To which end, and the better to bring it to pass, the King of *Batas* straight way assembled an army of 1500 men, as well natives, as strangers; wherewithal he was assisted by some princes his friends: and to the same effect he implored the forces of us Christians, which was the reason why he sought to contract a new amity with *Pedro de Faria*, who was very well contented with it, in regard he knew that it greatly imported, both the service of the King of *Portugal*, and the conservation of the fortress, besides that by this means he hoped very much to augment the revenue of the customes, together with his own particular, and all the rest of the *Portugals* profit, in regard of the great trade they had in those countries of the *South*.

After that the King of *Batas* embassadour had been seventeen dayes with us, *Pedro de Faria* dismissed him, having first granted whatsoever the King his master had demanded, and somthing over and above, as fire-pots, darts, and murdering pieces wherewith the embassadour departed from the fortress so contented, that he shed tears for joy; and presently imbarqued himself in the same *Lanchara*, wherein he came thither, being accompanied with eleven or twelve *Balons*, which are small barques, and so went to the Isle of *Vpa*, distant not above half a league from the port. There the *Bandara* of *Malaca* (who is as it were Chief Justicer amongst the *Mahometans*) was present in person, by the express commandment of *Pedro de Faria*, for to entertain him; and accordingly he made him a great feast, which was celebrated with hoboys, drums, trumpets, and cymbals, together with an excellent consort of voices framed to the tune of harps, lutes, and viols after the *Portugal* manner. Whereat this embassador did so wonder, that he would often put his finger on his mouth, an usual action with those of that country when they marvel at any thing. About twenty dayes after the departure of this embassador, *Pedro de Faria*, being informed that if he would send some commodities from the *Indies* to the kingdom of *Batas*, he might make great profit thereof, and much more of those which should be returned from thence, he to that effect set forth a *Jurupango*, of the bignesse of a small carvel, wherein he ventured a matter of some ten thousand ducates; in this vessel he sent, as his factor, a certain *Mahometan*, born at *Malaca*, and was desirous to have me

4

to accompany him, telling me, that thereby I should not only much oblige him, but that also under pretext of being sent as embassador thither, I might both see the King of *Batas*, and going along with him in his journey against the Tyrant of *Achem*, which some way or other would questionless redound to my benefit.  Now to the end that upon my return out of those countries I might make him a true relation of all that I had seen, he prayed me carefully to observe whatsoever should pass there, and especially to learn whether the Isle of Gold, so much talked of, was in those parts ; for that he was minded, if any discovery of it should be made, to write unto the King of *Portugal* about it.  To speak the truth, I would fain have excused my self from this voyage, by reason those countries were unknown to me, and for that the inhabitants were by every one accounted faithless and treacherous, having small hope besides to make any gain by it, in regard that all my stock amounted not to above an hundred ducates ; but because I durst not oppose the captains desire I imbarqued myself, though very unwillingly, with that Infidel who had the charge of the merchandize.  Our pilot steered his course from *Malaca* to the port of *Sorotilau*, which is in the kingdom of *Aru*, always coasting the Isle of *Samatra* towards the *Mediterranean* Sea, till at length we arrived at a certain river, called *Hicandure ;* after we had continued five dayes sailing in this manner we came to an harbour, named *Minhatoley*, distant some ten leagues from the kingdom of *Peedir*.  In the end finding our selves on the other side of the ocean we sailed on four days together, & then cast anchor in a little river, called *Gaateamgim*, that was not above seven fathom deep, up the which we past some 7 or 8 leagues.  Now all the while we sailed in this river with a fair wind, we saw athwart a wood, which grew on the bank of it, such a many adders, & other crawling creatures, no less prodigious for their length then for the strangeness of their forms, that I shall not marvel if they that read this history will not beleeve my report of them ; especially such as have not travelled ; for they that have seen little beleeve not much, whereas they that have seen much beleeve the more.  All along this river, that was not very broad, there were a number of lizards, which might more properly be called serpents,

because some of them were as big as an *Almadia*, with scales
upon their backs, and mouths two foot wide. Those of the
country assured us, that these creatures are so hardy, as there
be of them that sometimes will set upon an *Almadia*, chiefly
when they perceive there is not above four or five persons in
her, and overturn it with their tailes, swallowing up the men
whole, without dismembring of them. In this place also we
saw strange kind of creatures, which they call *Caquesseitan*;
they are of the bignesse of a great goose, very blacke and scaly
on their backs, with a row of sharp pricks on their chins, as
long as a writing pen: moreover, they have wings like unto
those of bats, long necks, and a little bone growing on their
heads resembling a cocks spur, with a very long tail spotted
black and green, like unto the lizards of that country; these
creatures hop and fly together, like grashopers; and in that
manner they hunt apes, and such other beasts whom they
pursue even to the tops of the highest trees. Also we saw
adders, that were copped on the crowns of their heads, as big
as a mans thigh, and so venomous, as the *Negroes* of the country
informed us, that if any living thing came within the reach of
their breath, it dyed presently, there being no remedy nor
antidote against it. We likewise saw others, that were not
copped on their crowns, not so venomous as the former, but
far greater and longer, with an head as big as a calves. We
were told that they hunt their prey in this manner: they get
up into a tree, and winding their tails about some branch of
it, let their bodies hang down to the foot of the tree, and then
laying one of their ears close to the ground, they hearken
whether they can hear anything stir during the stillness of the
night, so that if an ox, a boar, or any other beast doth chance
to pass by, they presently seize on it, and so carries it up into
the tree, where he devours it. In like sort we descryed a
number of baboons, both grey and black, as big as a great
mastiff, of whom the *Negroes* of the country are more afraid,
then of all the other beasts, because they will set upon them
with that hardiness, as they have much ado to resist them.

## CHAPTER VII.

What hapned to me at Penaiu, with the King of Batas expedition against
the Tyrant of Achem; and what he did after his victory over him.

BY that time we had sailed seven or eight leagues up the
river, at the end we arrived at a little town, named
*Botterendan*, not above a quarter of a mile distant from *Panaiu*,
where the King of *Batas* was at that time making preparation
for the war he had undertaken against the Tyrant of *Achem*.
This King understanding that I had brought him a letter and
a present from the Captain of *Malaca*, caused me to be entertained by the *Xabandar*, who is he that with absolute power
governs all the affairs of the army: this general, accompanied
with five *Lanchares*, and twelve *Ballons*, came to me to the
port where I rode at anchor; then with a great noise of drums,
bells, and popular acclamations, he brought me to a certain
key of the town, called *Campalator*; there the *Bandara*,
governour of the kingdom, stayed for me in great solemnity,
attended by many *Ourobalons* and *Amborraias*, which are the
noblest persons of his Court, the most part of whom, for all
that, were but poor and base, both in their habit, and manner
of living, whereby I knew that the country was not so rich as
it was thought to be in *Malaca*. When I was come to the
Kings palace, and had past through the first court, at the
entrance of the second I found an old woman, accompanied
with other persons far nobler, and better apparelled then those
that marched before me, who beckening me with her hand, as
if she had commanded me to enter:

*Man of Malaca*, said she unto me, *Thy arrival in the King
my masters land is as agreeable unto him, as a showre of rain is
to a crop of rice in dry and hot weather; wherefore enter boldly,
and be afraid of nothing, for the people, which by the goodness
of God thou seest here, are no other than those of thine own
country, since the hope which we have in the same God makes
us believe that he will maintain us all together unto the end of
the world.* Having said so, she carried me where the King
was, unto whom I did obeysance according to the manner of
the country; then I delivered him the letter and the present I

had brought him, which he graciously accepted of, and asked me what occasion drew me thither. Whereunto I answered, as I had in commission, that I was come to serve his Highness in the wars, where I hoped to have the honour to attend on him, & not to leave him till such time as we returned conqueror of his enemies; hereunto I likewise added, that I desired to see the city of *Achem*, as also the scituation and fortifications of it, and what depth the river was of, whereby I might know whether it would bear great vessels and gallions, because the captain of *Malaca* had a design to come and succor his Highnesse, as soon as his men were returned from the *Indies*, and to deliver his mortal enemy, the Tyrant of *Achem*, into his hands. This poor king presently believed all that I said to be true, and so much the rather, for that it was conformable to his desire, in such sort, that rising out of his throne where he was set, I saw him go and fall on his knees before the carcass of a cows head, set up against the wall, whose horns were gilt, and crowned with flowers; then lifting up his hands and eyes, *O thou*, said he, *that not constrained by any material love, wherunto Nature hath obliged thee, dost continually make glad all those that desire thy milk, as the own mother doth him whom she hath brought into the world, without participating either of the miseries, or paines, which ordinarily she suffers from whom we take our being, be favorable unto the prayer which now with all my heart I offer up unto thee: and it is no other but this, that in the meadows of the sun, where with the payment and recompence which thou receivest, thou art contented with the good that thou dost here below, thou wilt be pleased to conserve me in the new amity of this good captain, to the end he may put in execution all that this man here hath told me.* At these words all the courtiers, which were likewise on their knees, said three times, as it were in answer, *How happy were he that could see that, and then dye incontinently?* Wherupon the King arose, & wiping his eyes, which were all beblubbered with the tears that proceeded from the zeal of the prayer he had made, he questioned me about many particular things of the *Indies*, and *Malaca*. Having spent some time therein, he very courteously dismissed me, with a promise to cause the merchandise which the *Mahometan* had brought in

the captain of *Malaca's* name, to be well and profitably put
off, which indeed was the thing I most desired. Now for as
much as the King at my arrival was making his preparations
for to march against the Tyrant of *Achem*, and had taken
order for all things necessary for that voyage, after I had
remained nine days in *Panaiu*, the capital city of the kingdom
of *Batas*, he departed with some troops towards a place named
*Turban*, some five leagues off, where he arrived an hour before
sun-set, without any manner of reception, or shew of joy, in
regard of the grief he was in for the death of his children,
which was such as he never appeared in publique, but with
great demonstration of sorrow.

The next morning the King of *Batas* marched from *Turban*
towards the kingdome of *Achem*, being 18 leagues thither. He
carried with him fifteen thousand men of war, whereof eight
thousand were *Bataes*, and the rest *Menancabes*, *Lusons*,
*Andraguires*, *Jambes*, and *Bournees*, whom the Princes his
neighbours had assisted him with, as also fourty elephants, and
twelve carts with small ordnance, namely, faulcons, bases, and
other field pieces, amongst the which there were three that
had the arms of *France*, and were taken in the year 1526. at
such time as *Lopo Vaz de Sampayo* governed the State of
the *Indies*. Now the King of *Batas*, marching five leagues a
day came to a river, called *Quilem*; there by some of the Tyrants
spies, which he had taken, he learnt that his enemy waited for
him at *Tondacur*, two leagues from *Achem*, with a purpose to
fight with him, and that he had great store of strangers in his
army, namely *Turks*, *Cambayans*, and *Malabars*: whereupon
the King of *Batas*, assembling his councel of war, and falling
into consultation of this affair, it was concluded, as most
expedient, to set upon the enemy before he grew more strong.
With this resolution having quit the river, he marched somewhat
faster then ordinary, and arrived about ten of the clock in the
night at the foot of a mountain, half a league from the enemies
camp, where after he had reposed himself a matter of 3 hours,
he marched on in very good order; for which effect having
divided his army into four squadrons, and passing along by a
little hill, when he came to the end thereof, he discovered a
great plain sowed with rice, where the enemy stood ranged in

two battalions. As soon as the two armies descried one another, and that at the sound of their trumpets, drums, and bells, the souldiers had set up a terrible cry, they encountred very valiantly together; and after the discharge of their shot on both sides, they came to fight hand to hand with such courage, that I trembled for fear to behold their fury. The battel continued in this manner above an hour, and yet could it not possibly be discerned which party had the better. At last the Tyrant foreseeing, that if he persisted in the fight, he should lose the day, because he perceived his men to grow faint and weary, he retreated to a rising ground, that lay south to the *Bataes*, and about a faulcons shot distant from them. There his intention was to fortifie himself in certain trenches which before he had caused to be cast up against a rock in form of a garden, or tilth of rice; but a brother of the K. of *Andraguire* interrupted his design, for stepping before him with 2000 men, he cut off his way, and stopt him from passing further, in so much that the medly grew to be the same it was before, and the fight was renewed between them with such fury, as cruelly wounding one another, they testified sufficiently how they came but little short of other nations in courage. By this means the Tyrant, before he could recover his trenches, lost 1500 of his men, of which number were 300 and 60 *Turks*, that a little before were come to him from the Streight of *Mecqua*, with two hundred *Saracens*, *Malabars*, and some *Abissins*, which were the best men he had. Now because it was about mid-day, and therefore very hot; the King of *Batas* retired towards the mountain, where he spent the rest of the day in causing those that were wounded to be looked unto, and the dead to be buried. Hereupon not being well resolved what to do, in regard he was altogether ignorant of the enemies design, he took care to have good watch kept all that night in every part. The next morning no sooner began the sun to appear, but he perceived the valley, wherein the *Achems* had been the day before, to be quite abandoned, and not one of them to be seen there, which made him think the enemy was defeated in this opinion, the better to pursue the first point of his victory, he dismissed all the hurt men, as being unfit for service, and followed the Tyrant to the city, where arriving

two hours before sun-set, to shew that he had strength and
courage enough to combat his enemies, he resolved to give
them proof of it by some remarkable action before he would
encamp himself; to which effect he fired two of the suburbs
of the town, as also four ships, and two galleons, which were
drawn on land, and were those that had brought the *Turks*
from the Streight of *Mecqua*. And indeed the fire took with
such violence on those six vessels, as they were quite consumed in a little time, the enemy not daring to issue forth for
to quench it. After this, the King of *Batas*, seeing himself
favoured by fortune, to lose no opportunity began to assault a
fort, called *Penacao*, which with twelve pieces of ordnance
defended the entry of the river; to the scalado of this he went
in person, his whole army looking on, and having caused some
70 or 80 ladders to be planted, he behaved himself so well,
that with the loss only of 37 men he entred the place, and
put all to the sword that he found in it, to the number of 700
persons, without sparing so much as one of them. Thus he
did on the day of his arrival perform three memorable things,
whereby his souldiers were so heartned, as they would fain
have assaulted the city the very same night, if he would have
permitted them; but in regard it was very dark, and his men
weary, he gave thanks to God, and contented himself with
that which he had done.

The King of *Batas* held the city besieged by the space of 23
dayes, during the which two sallies were made, wherein
nothing past of any reckoning, for there were but ten men
slain on either part. Now as victories and good success in
war do ordinarily encourage the victorious; so often it happens
that the weak become strong, and cowards so hardy, as laying
aside all fear, they dare undertake most difficile and dangerous
things, whence also it as often falls out, that the one prospers,
and the other is ruined; which appeared but too evidently in
that which I observed of these two princes; for the King of
*Batas*, seeing that the Tyrant had shut himself up in his city,
thereby as it were confessing that he was vanquished, grew to
such an height of confidence, that both he and his people
believing it was impossible for them to be resisted, and trusting in this vain opinion that blinded them, were twice in

hazard to be lost by the rash inconsiderate actions which they entred into. In the third sally, made by the inhabitants, the King of *Batas* people encountred them very lustily in two places, which those of *Achem* perceiving, they made as though they were the weaker, and so retreated to the same fort that was taken from them by the *Bataes* the first day of their arrival, being closely followed by one of the Kings Captains, who taking hold of the opportunity, entred pell-mell with the *Achems*, being perswaded that the victory was sure his own; but when they were altogether in the trenches, the *Achems* turned about, and making head afresh defended themselves very couragiously. At length in the heat of their medley, the one side indeavouring to go on, and the other to withstand them, those of *Achem* gave fire to a myne, they had made, which wrought so effectually, as it blew up the captain of the *Bataes*, and above 300 of his souldiers, with so great a noise, and so thick a smoak, as the place seemed to be the very portrayture of hell. In the mean time the enemies giving a great shout, the Tyrant sallied forth in person, accompanied with 5000 resolute men, and charged the *Bataes* very furiously; Now for that neither of them could see one another by reason of the smoak proceeding from the myne, there was a most confused and cruel conflict between them; but to speak the truth, I am not able to deliver the manner of it; it sufficeth, that in a quarter of an hours space, the time this fight endured 4000 were slain in the place on both sides, whereof the King of *Batas* lost the better part, which made him retire with the remainder of his army, to a rock, called *Minacalen*, where causing his hurt men to be drest, he found them to be two thousand in number, besides those that were killed; which because they could not be so suddenly buried were thrown into the current of the river. Hereupon the two kings continued quiet for four dayes after, at the end whereof one morning, when nothing was less thought of, there appeared in the midst of the river, on *Penaticans* side, a fleet of fourscore and six sails, with a great noise of musick, and acclammations of joy. At first this object much amazed the *Bataes*, because they knew not what it was, howbeit the night before their scouts had taken five fisher-men, who put to torture confessed, that this was the army which the Tyrant had sent some two months before to *Tevassery*, in regard he had war with the *Sornau*, King of *Siam*; and it was said that this army was composed of 5000 *Lussons* and *Sornes*, all choice men, having to general a *Turk*, named *Hametecam*, nephew to the *Bassa* of *Cairo*. Whereupon the King of *Batas* making use of these fisher-mens confession, resolved to retire himself in any sort whatsoever, well considering that the time would not permit him to make an hours stay, as well because his enemies forces were far greater than his, as for that every minute they expected succours from *Pedir* and *Pazen*, whence it was reported, for certain, there were twelve ships full of strangers coming. No sooner was the King fortified in this resolution, but the night ensuing he departed very sad, and ill contented for the bad success of his enterprize, wherein he had lost above three thousand and five hundred men, not comprizing the wounded, which were more in number, nor those that were burnt with the fire of the myne. Five dayes after his departure he arrived at *Panaiu*, where he dismissed all his forces, both his own subjects and strangers; that done, he imbarqued himself in a small *lanchara*, and went up the river without any other company then two or three of his favorites. With this small retinue he be took himself to a place, called *Pachissaru*, where he shut himself up for fourteen dayes, by way of penance, in a pagode of an idol, named *Ginnassereo*, which signifies *the God of Sadness*. At his return to *Panaiu*, he sent for me, and the *Mahometan* that brought *Pedro de Faria's* merchandise; the first thing that he did, was to enquire particularly of him whether he made a good sale of it, adding withal, that if any thing were still owing to him he would command it to be presently satisfied; hereunto the *Mahometan* and I answered, that through his Highness favour all our business had received a very good dispatch, and that we were paid for that we had sold, in regard whereof the captain of *Malaca* would not fail to acknowledge that courtesie, by sending him succour for to be revenged on his enemy the Tyrant of *Achem*, whom he would inforce to restore all the places, which he had unjustly usurped upon him. The King hearing me speak in this manner stood a while musing with himself, and then in answer to my speech; *Ah* Portugal, said he, *since thou constrainest me to tell thee freely what I think ; believe me not hereafter to be so ignorant as that thou mayst be able to perswade me, or that I can be capable to imagine, that he which in thirty years space could not revenge himself, is of power to succour me at this present in so short a time ; or if yet thou thinkest I deceive my self, tell me, I pray thee now, whence comes it that thy King and his Governours could not hinder this cruel King of* Achem *from gaining from you the Fort of* Pazem, *and the galley which went to the* Molucquaes, *as also three ships in* Queda, *and the galleon of* Malaca, *at such time as* Garcia *was captain there, besides the four foists that were taken since at* Salengor, *with the two ships that came from* Bengala, *or* Lopo Chanoca's *junk and ship, as likewise many other vessels, which I cannot now remember, in the which, as I have been assured, this inhumane hath put to death above a thousand* Portugals, *and gotten an extream rich booty. Wherefore if this Tyrant should happen to come once more against me, how canst thou have me rely upon their word which have been so often overcome ? I must of necessity then continue as I am with three of my children murdered, and the greatest part of my kingdom destroyed, seeing you your selves are not much more assured in your fortress of* Malaca. I must needs confess that this answer, made with so much resentment, rendred me so ashamed, knowing he spake nothing but truth, that I durst not talk to him afterwards of any succour, nor for our honour reiterate the promises which I had formerly made him.

## CHAPTER VIII.

What past between the King of Batas and me, until such time as I imbarqued for Malaca.

THE *Mahometan* and I returning to our lodging, departed in four dayes after, imploying that time in shipping an hundred bars of tin, and thirty of benjamin, which were still on land. Then being fully satisfied by our merchants, and ready to go, I went to wait upon the King at his *Passeiran.*

which was a great place before the palace, where those of the
country kept their most solemn fairs; there I gave him to
understand, that now we had nothing more to do but depart
if it would please his Majesty to permit us: the entertainment that he gave me then was very gracious; and for answer
he said to me, I am very glad for that *Hermon Xabandar*, (who
was chief general of the wars) assured me yesterday that your
captains commodities were well sold; but it may be that that
which he told me was not so, and that he delivered not the
truth for to please me, and to accommodate himself to the
desire he knew I had to have it so; wherefore, continued he,
I pray thee declare unto me freely whether he dealt truly with
me, and whether the *Mahometan* that brought them be fully
satisfied; for I would not that, to my dishonour, those of
*Malaca* should have cause to complain of the merchants of
*Panaiu*, saying, that they are not men of their word, and that
there is not a king there who can constrain them to pay their
debts; and I swear to thee by the faith of a Pagan, that this
affront would be no less insupportable to my condition, then if
I should chance to make peace with that Tyrant, and perjured
enemy of mine, the King of *Achem*. Whereunto having
replyed, that we had dispatched all our affairs, and that there
was nothing due to us in his country: Verily, said he, I am
very well pleased to hear that it is so; wherefore since thou
hast nothing else to do here, I hold it requisite, that without
any further delay thou shouldst go, for the time is now fit to
set sail, and to avoid the great heats that ordinarily are
endured in passing the gulph, which is the cause that ships are
many times cast upon *Pazem* by foul weather at sea, from
which I pray God deliver thee; for I assure thee that if thy
ill fortune should carry thee thither, the men of *Achem* would
eat thee alive, and the Tyrant himself would have the first bite
at thee, there being nothing in the world these inhumanes so
much vaunt of, as to carry on the crest of their arms the device
of *Drinkers of the troubled blood of miserable Caffers*, who
(they say) are come from the end of the world, calling them
*tyrannical men, and usurpers in a supreme degree of other mens
kingdoms in the Indies, and Isles of the Sea*. This is the title
wherein they glory most, and which they attribute particularly

to themselves, as being sent them from *Mecqua* in recompence of the golden lamps which they offered to the Alcoran of their *Mahomet*, as they use to do every year. Furthermore, although heretofore I have often advised thy captain of *Malaca*, to take careful heed of this Tyrant of *Achem*, yet do not thou omit to advertise him of it once more from me ; for know that he never had, nor shall have other thoughts, then to labour by all means to expel him out of the *Indies*, and make the *Turk* master of them, who to that end promiseth to send him great succours ; but I hope that God will so order it, as all the malice and cunning of this disloyal wretch shall have a contrary success to his intentions. After he had used this language to me he gave me a letter in answer to my embassage, together with a present, which he desired me to deliver from him to Captain *de Faria* ; this was six small javelins headed with gold, 12 *cates* of *Calambuca* wood, every one of them weighing 20 ounces, and a box of exceeding value, made of a tortoise shell, beautified with gold, and full of great seed pearl, amongst the which there were 16 fair pearls of rich account. For my self, he gave me two *cates* of gold, and a little courtelace garnished with the same. Then he dismissed me with as much demonstration of honour as he had alwayes used to me before, protesting to me in particular, that the amity which he had contracted with our nation should ever continue inviolable on his part. Thus I imbarqued my self with *Aquarius Dabolay*, his brother-in-law, who was the same he had sent embassadour to *Malaca*, as I have related before. Being departed from the port of *Panaiu*, we arrived about two hours in the night at a little island, called *Apofingua*, distant some league and an half from the mouth of the river, and inhabited by poor people, who lived by fishing of shads.

The next morning, leaving that island of *Apofingua*, we ran along by the coast of the Ocean Sea for the space of 25 leagues, until such time as at length we entred into the Streight of *Minhagaruu*, by which we came; then passing by the contrary coast of this other *Mediterranean Sea*, we continued our course along by it, and at last arrived near to *Pullo Bugay*. There we crost over to the firm land, and passing by the port of *Junculan*, we sailed two dayes and an half with a favourable wind, by

means whereof we got to the river of *Parles* in the kingdom of
*Queda.*

[*Here follows an adventure that befell Pinto in the Kingdom
of Queda,* omitted.]

Being departed from the river of *Parles*, on a Saturday about
sun-set, I made all the speed that possibly I could, and continued my course until the Tuesday following; when it pleased
God that I reached to the isles of *Pullo Sambalin*, the first
land on the coast of *Mallayo*. There by good fortune I met
with 3 *Portugal* ships (whereof 2 came from *Bengala*, and the
other from *Pegu*) commanded by *Tristen de Gaa*, who had
somtimes been governour of the person of *Don Lorenzo*, son
to the Vice-roy, *Don Francesco d' Almeda*, that was afterward
put to death by *Miroocem* in *Chaul* Roade, as is at large
delivered in the history of the discovery of the *Indies*. This
same *Tristan* furnished me with many things that I had great
need of, as tackle, and mariners, together with two souldiers,
and a pilot; moreover, both himself and the other two ships
had alwayes a care of me until our arrival at *Malaca*; where
dis-imbarquing my self, the first thing I did was to go to
the fortress for to salute the captain, and to render him
an account of the whole success of my voyage, where I
discoursed unto him at large what rivers, ports, and havens,
I had newly discovered in the isle of *Samatra*, as well on
the *Mediterranean*, as on the Ocean Seas side, as also what
commerce the inhabitants of the country used; then I declared
unto him the manner of all that coast, of all those ports
and of all those rivers; whereunto I added the scituations, the
heights, the degrees, the names, and the depths of the ports,
according to the direction he had given me at my departure.
Therewithall I made him a description of the roade wherein
*Rosado*, the captain of a *French* ship, was lost, and another,
named *Matelote de Brigas*, as also the commander of another
ship, who by a storm at sea was cast into the port of *Diu*, in
the year 1529, during the reign of *Sultan Bandur*, King of
*Cambaya*. This prince having taken them all, made fourscore
and two of them abjure their faith, who served him in his wars
against the great *Mogor*, and where every one of them miserably
slain in that expedition. Moreover I brought him the des-

cription of a place fit for anchorage in *Pullo Botum* Roade,
where the *Bisquayn* ship suffered shipwrack, which was said to
be the very same, wherein *Magellan* compassed the world, and
was called the *Vittoria*, which traversing the Isle of *Jooa* was
cast away at the mouth of the river of *Sonda*. I made him a
recital likewise of many different nations, which inhabit all
along this ocean, and the river of *Lampon*, from whence the
gold of *Menancabo* is transported to the kingdom of *Campar*,
upon the waters of *Jambes* and *Broteo*. For the inhabitants
affirm, out of their chronicles, how in this very town of *Lampon*
there was anciently a factory of merchants, established by the
Queen of *Sheba*, whereof one, named *Nausem*, sent her a
great quantity of gold, which she carried to the Temple of
*Jerusalem*, at such time as she went to visit the wise King
*Solomon* ; from whence, some say, she returned with child of
a son, that afterwards succeeded to the Empire of *Æthiopia*,
whom now we call *Prester-John*, of whose race the *Abissins*
vaunt they are descended. Further, I told him what course
was usually held for the fishing of seed pearl betwixt *Pullo
Tiquos* and *Pullo Quenim*, which in times past were carried by
the *Bataes* to *Pazem* and *Pedir*, and exchanged with the *Turks*
of the Streight of *Mecqua*, and the ships of *Judæa*, for such
merchandise as they brought from *Grand Cairo*, and the ports
of *Arabia Fœlix*. Divers other things I recounted unto him,
having learnt them of the King of *Batas*, and of the merchants
of *Panaiu*. And for conclusion, I gave him an information in
writing, as he had formerly desired me, concerning the Island
of Gold : I told him, how this island is beyond the river
*Calandor* five degrees to the southward, invironed with many
shelfs of sand, and currents of water, as also that it was distant
some hundred and threescore leagues from the point of the
Isle of *Samatra*. With all which reports *Pedro de Faria*
remained so well satisfied, that he made present relation
thereof to the King *Dom Jovan* the Third of happy memory,
who the year after ordained *Francesco d' Almeida* for captain
to discover the Isle of Gold, a gentleman of merit, and very
capable of that charge, who indeed had long before petitioned
the king for it in recompence of the services by him performed
in the islands of *Banda*, of the *Molucques*, of *Ternate*, and

*Geilolo :* but by ill-fortune this *Francesco d' Almeida*, being
gone from the *Indies* to discover that place, dyed of a feaver in
the Isles of *Nicubar* ; whereof the King of *Portugal* being
advertised, he honored one *Diego Cabral*, born at the *Maderaes*,
with that command ; but the court of justice deprived him of
it by express order from *Martinez Alphonso de Sousa*, who was
at that time Governor, which partly proceeded, according to
report, for that he had murmured against him ; whereupon he
gave it to *Jeronymo Figuereydo*, a gentleman belonging to the
Duke of *Braganca*, who in the year 1542. departed from *Goa*
with two foists, and one carvel, wherein there were fourscore
men, as well souldiers, as mariners ; but it is said, that his
voyage was without effect, for that, according to the apparances
that he gave of it afterward, it seemed that he desired to
enrich himself too suddenly : to which end he passed to the
coast of *Tanassery*, where he took certain ships that came
from *Mecqua, Adem, Alcosser, Judæa*, and other places upon
the coast of *Persia*.   And verily this booty was the occasion of
his undoing, for upon an unequal partition thereof falling at
difference with his souldiers, they mutined in such sort against
him, as after many affronts done him they bound him hand
and foot, and so carried him to the Isle of *Ceilan*, where they
set him on land ; and the carvel, with the two foists, they
returned to the Governor *Don Joana de Castra*, who in regard
of the necessity of the time pardoned them the fault, and took
them along with him in the army, which he led to *Diu* for the
succour of *Don Joana Mascarenhas*, that was then straitly
besieged by the King of *Cambaya's* forces.   Since that time
there hath been no talk of the discovery of this island of gold,
although it seemes very much to import the common good of
our kingdom of *Portugal*, if it would please God it might be
brought to passe.

## CHAPTER IX.

The Arrival of an Embassador at Malaca from the King of Aaru to the Captain thereof; his sending me to the said King, my coming to Aaru, and that which happen'd to me after my departing from thence.

FIVE and twenty dayes after my coming to *Malaca, Dom Stephano de Gama*, being still captain of the fortress, an embassador arrived there from the King of *Aaru*, for to demand succor of men from him, and some munitions of war, as powder, and bullets, for to defend himself from a great fleet that the King of *Achem* was setting forth against him, with an intention to deprive him of his kingdom, and to be a nearer neighbour unto us, to the end that having gained that passage, he might afterwards send his forces the more easily against our fortress of *Malaca*; whereof *Pedro de Faria* was no sooner advertised, but representing unto himself how important this affair was for the service of the King, and preservation of the fortress, he acquainted *Dom Stephano de Gama* with it, in regard his command of the place was to continue yet six weeks longer; howbeit he excused himself from giving the succor which was required, saying, that the time of his government was now expiring, and that his being shortly to come in, the duty of his charge did oblige him to take care of this businesse, and to think of the danger that menaced him. Hereunto *Pedro de Faria* made answer, that if he would relinquish his government for the time he had yet to come in it, or give him full power to dispose of the publique magazins, he would provide for the succor that he thought was necessary. In a word, and not to stand long on that which past betwixt them, it shall suffice to say, that this Embassador was utterly denied his demand by these two Captains; whereof the one alleged for excuse, that he was not yet entred upon his charge; and the other, that he was upon the finishing of his : whereupon he returned very ill satisfied with this refusal, and so far resented the injustice which he thought was done unto his King, as the very morning wherein he imbarqued himself, having met by chance with the two Captains at the gate of the fortress, he said aloud before them publiquely, with the tears in his eyes

*In the name of the Prince of Portugal, I beseech you, once, twice,
nay a hundred times, that you will perform that appertaines unto
your duty to do; for this which I thus publickely demand of you
is of so great importance, that therein consists, not so much the
preservation of the Kingdom of* Aaru, *as the safety of this your
fortress of* Malaca, *which that Tyrant of* Achem, *our enemy, so
extreamly desires to possesse.*

Having finished this speech, which availed him nothing, he
stooped down to the ground, from whence taking up two stones,
he knocked with them upon a piece of Ordnance, and then the
tears standing in his eyes, he said, *The Lord, who hath created
us, will defend us if he please;* and so imbarquing himself he
departed greatly discontented for the bad answer he carried
back. Five days after his departure *Pedro de Faria* was told
how all the town murmured at the small respect that both he
and *Don Stephano* had carried to that poor King, who had ever
been a friend both to them, and the whole *Portugal* nation, and
continually done very good offices to the fort, for which cause
his Kingdom was now like to be taken from him. This advice
causing him to see his fault, and to be ashamed of his proceeding, he labored to have palliated it with certain excuses,
but at last he sent this King by way of succor fifteen quintals
of powder, an hundred pots of wild-fire, an hundred and fifty
bullets for great ordnance, twelve harquebuzes, forty sacks of
stones, threescore head-pieces, and a coat of gilt mail, lined
with crimson sattin, for his own person, together with many
other garments of divers sorts, as also twenty pieces of *Caracas*,
which are stained linnen, or cotton tapestry, that come from
the *Indies*, and cloth of *Malaya*, wherewith they usually
apparel themselves in that country, as well for his wife, as his
daughters. All these things being laden aboard a *Lanchara*
with oars, he desired me conduct and present them from him
to the King of *Aaru*, adding withall, that this business greatly
concerned the King of *Portugals* service, and that at my return,
besides the recompence I should receive from him he would
give me an extraordinary pay, and upon all occasions employ
me in such voyages, as might redound to my profit; whereupon
I undertook it, in an ill hour as I may say, and for a punishment of my sins, in regard of what arrived unto me thereupon,

as shall be seen hereafter. So then I imbarqued my self on Tuesday morning, the 5th of *October*, 1539. and used such speed, that on Sunday following I arrived at the river of *Panetican*, upon which the city of *Aaru* is scituated.

I no sooner got to the river of *Panetican*, but presently landing I went directly to a trench, which the King in person was causing to be made at the mouth of the river for to impeach the enemies' dis-imbarquing; presenting my self unto him, he received me with great demonstration of joy, whereupon I delivered him *Pedro de Faria's* letter, which gave him some hope of his coming in person to succor him, if need required, with many other complements, that cost little the saying, wherewith the King was wonderfully contented, because he already imagined that the effect thereof would infallibly ensue. But after he saw the present I brought him, consisting of powder and ammunitions, he was so glad, that taking me in his arms, My good friend, said he unto me, I assure thee that the last night I dreamt how all these things, which I behold here before me, came unto me from the King of *Portugal*, my masters fortress, by means whereof, with God's assistance, I hope to defend my kingdom, and to serve him, in the manner I have always hitherto done, that is, most faithfully, as all the captains can very well testifie, which have heretofore commanded in *Malaca*. Hereupon questioning me about certain matters, that he desired to know, as well concerning the *Indies*, as the Kingdom of *Portugal*, he recommended the finishing of the trench to his people, who wrought very earnestly and chearfully in it; and taking me by the hand, on foot as he was, attended only by five or six gentlemen, he led me directly to the city, that was about some quarter of a league from the trench, where in his palace he entertained me most magnificently, yea and made me to salute his wife, a matter very rarely practised in that country, & held for a special honor, which when I had done, with abundance of tears he said unto me, *Portugal*, here is the cause that makes me so much to redoubt the coming of my enemies; for were I not withheld by my wife, I swear unto thee by the law of a good and true Moore, that I would prevent them in their designs, without any other aid then of my own subjects; for it is not now that I begin to know what manner of man the perfidious *Achem* is, or how far his power extends; Alas! it is the great store of gold, which he possesseth, that covers his weaknesse, and by means whereof he wageth such forces of strangers, wherewith he is continually served. But now that thou maist on the other side understand how vile and odious poverty is, and how hurtful to a poor King, such as I may be, come thee along with me, and by that little which I will presently let thee see thou shalt perceive, whether it be not too true, that fortune hath been so exceeding niggardly to me of her goods. Saying so, he carried me to his Arsenal, which was covered with thatch, and shewed me all that he had within it, whereof he might say with reason, that it was nothing in com- parison of what he needed for to withstand the attempts of two hundred & thirty vessels, replenished with such warlike people, as the *Achems* and *Malabar Turks* were ; moreover, with a sad countenance, and as one that desired to discharge his mind of the grief he was in for the danger was threatned him, he recounted unto me, that he had in all but six thousand men *Aaruns*, without any forraign succor, forty pieces of small ordnance, as falconets, and bases, and one cast piece, which he had formerly bought of a *Portugal*, named *Antonio de Garcia*, sometimes a receiver of the toll and customs of the ports of the fortress of *Pacem*, whom *Georgio de Albuquerque* cause since to be hanged and quartered at *Malaca*, for that he treated by letters with the King of *Bintham* about a plot of treason, which they had contrived together. He told me besides, that he had also forty muskets, six and twenty elephants, fifty horsemen for the guard of the place, eleven or twelve thousand staves hardened in the fire, called *Salignes*, whose points were poysoned, and for the defence of the trench fifty lances, good store of targets, a thousand pots of unslack'd lime made into powder, and to be used instead of pots of wild-fire, & three or four barques full laden with great flints; in a word, by the view of these, and such other of his miseries, I easily perceived he was so unprovided of things necessary for his defence, that I presently concluded the enemy would have no great a do to seize on this kingdom. Nevertheless he having demanded of me what I thought of all this ammunition in his magazin, and

whether there were not enough to receive the guests he
expected, I answered him, that it would serve to entertain
them; but he understanding my meaning stood musing a pretty
while, and then shaking his head, Verily, said he unto me, if
your King of *Portugal* did but know what a loss it would be to
him, that the Tyrant of *Achem* should take my kingdom from
me, doubtless he would chastise the little care of his captains,
who, blinded as they are, and wallowing in their avarice, have
suffered my enemy to grow so strong, that I am much afraid
they shall not be able to restrain him when they would, or if
they could, that then it must be an infinite expence. I labored
to answer this which he had said unto me with much resentment; but he confuted all my reasons with so much truth, as
I had not the heart to make any farther reply; withal he
represented divers foul and enormous actions unto me, wherewithall he charged some in particular amongst us, which I am
contented to pass in silence, both in regard they are nothing
pertinent to my discourse, and that I desire not to discover
other mens faults. For a conclusion of his speech, he related
unto me the little punishment which was ordained for such as
were culpable of these matters, and the great rewards that he
had seen conferred on those which had not deserved them;
whereupon he added, that if the King desired throughly to
perform the duty of his charge, and by arms to conquer people
so far distant from his kingdom, and to preserve them, it was
as necessary for him to punish the wicked, as to recompence
the good. This said, he sent me to lodge in a merchants
house, who for 5 days together, that I remained there,
entertained me bravely; though to speak truth I had rather
have been at that time in some other place with any poor
victuals, for here I was always in fear, by reason of the
enemies continual alarms, and the certain news that came to
the King the next day after my arrival, how the *Achems* were
already marching towards *Aaru*, and would be there within
eight dayes at the farthest, which made him in all haste to
give directions for such things as he had not taken order for
before, and to send the women, and all that were unfit for war,
out of the city five or six leagues into the wood, amongst the
which the Queen her self made one, mounted on an elephant.

Five dayes after my arrival, the King sent for me, and asked me when I would be gone, whereunto I replied, at such time as it would please his Greatnesse to command me, though I should be glad it might be with the soonest, for that I was to be employed by my captain with his merchandise to *China*. Thou hast reason, answered he ; then taking two bracelets of massy gold off from his wrists, worth some thirty crowns, I pri'thee now, said he, giving them to me, do not impute it to miserableness that I bestow so little on thee, for thou mayst be assured, that it hath been always my desire for to have much for to give much ; withall I must desire thee to present this letter, and this diamond from me to thy captain, to whom thou shalt say, that whatsoever I am further engaged to him for the pleasure he hath done me by succouring me with those ammunitions he hath sent me by thee, I will bring it to him my self hereafter, when I shall be at more liberty then now I am.

Having taken leave of the King of *Aaru*, I presently imbarqued my self, and departed about sun-set, rowing down the river to an hamlet, that is at the entrance thereof, composed of ten or eleven houses covered with straw. This place is inhabited with very poor people, that get their living by killing of *lizards*, of whose liver they make poyson, wherewith they anoint the heads of their arrows ; for the poyson of this place, chiefly that which is called *Pocausilim*, is held by them the best of those countries, because there is no remedy for him that is hurt with it. The next day, having left this small village, we sailed along the coast with a land wind until evening, that we doubled the islands of *Anchepisan* ; then the day and part of the night following we put forth somewhat farther to sea. But about the first watch the wind changed to the north-east, for such winds are ordinary about the Isle of *Samatra*, and grew to be so tempestuous, that it blew our mast over board, tore our sails in pieces, and so shattered our vessel, that the water came in that abundance into her at two several places, as she sunk incontinently to the bottom, so that of eight and twenty persons, which were in her, three and twenty were drowned in less then a quarter of an hour. For us five (that escaped by the mercy of God) we passed the rest of the night upon a rock, where the waves of the sea had cast us. There all that we could do was with tears to lament our sad fortune, not knowing what counsel or course to take, by reason the country was so moorish, & invironed with so thick a wood, that a bird, were she never so little, could hardly make way through the branches of it, for that the trees grew so close together. We sat crouching for the space of three whole days upon this rock, where for all our sustenance we had nothing but snails, and such filth, as the foam of the sea produceth there. After this time, which we spent in great misery and pain, we walked a whole day along by the Isle of *Samatra*, in the owze up to the girdle-stead, and about sun-set we came to a mouth of a little river, some crossbow-shot broad, which we durst not undertake to swim over, for that it was deep, and we very weak and weary ; so that we were forced to pass all that night, standing up to the chin in water. To this misery was there adjoyned the great affliction which the flies and gnats brought us, that coming out of the neighbouring woods, bit and stung us in such sort, as not one of us but was gore blood. The next morning as soon as we perceived day, which we much desired to see, though we had little hope of life, I demanded of my four companions, all mariners, whether they knew the country, or whether there was any habitation thereabout, whereupon the eldest of them, who had a wife at *Malaca*, not able to contain his tears, Alas ! answered he, the place that now is most proper for you, and me, is the house of death, where ere it belong we must give an account of our sins ; it therefore behoves to prepare our selves for it without any further delay, and patiently to attend that which is sent us from the hand of God : for my part, let me intreat thee to be of a good courage whatsoever thou seest, and not to be terrified with the fear of dying, since, every thing well considered, it matters not whether it be to day, or to morrow. This spoken, he embraced me, and with tears in his eyes desired me to make him a Christian, because he beleeved, as he said, that to be so was sufficient to save his soul, which could not otherwise be done in the cursed sect of *Mahomet*, wherein he had lived till then, and for which he craved pardon of God. Having finished these last words, he remained dead in my arms, for he

was so weak, as he was not able to subsist any longer, as well
for that he had not eaten ought in three or four days before,
as in regard of a great wound the wrack of the *Lanchara* had
given him in his head, through which one might see his brains
all putrefied and corrupted, occasioned both for want of looking
unto, as by salt water and flies that were gotten into it.
Verily this accident grieved me very much, but for my self I
was in little better case, for I was likewise so weak, that every
step I made in the water I was ready to swoon, by reason of
certain hurts on my head and body, out of which I had lost a
great deal of blood. Having buried him in the owze the best
we could, the other three mariners and my self resolved to cross
the river, for to go and sleep on certain great trees, that we
saw on the other side, for fear of the tygers and crocodiles,
whereof that country is full, besides many other venemous
creatures, as an infinite of those copped adders I have spoken
of before in the sixth chapter, and divers sorts of serpents with
black and green scales, whose venom is so contagious, as they
kill men with their very breath. This resolution being thus
taken by us, I desired two of them to swim over first, and the
other to stay with me for to hold me up in the water, for that
in regard of my great weakness I could hardly stand upon my
legs : whereupon they two cast themselves presently into the
water, exhorting us to follow them, and not be afraid ; but
alas ! they were scarce in the midst of this river, when as we
saw them caught by two great *lizards*, that were before our
faces, and in an instant tearing them in pieces, dragged them
to the bottom, leaving the water all bloody, which was so
dreadful a spectacle to us, as we had not the power to cry out;
and for my self, I knew not who drew me out of the water, nor
how I escaped thence ; for I was gone before into the river as
deep as my waste, with that other mariner which held me by
the hand.

-------

## CHAPTER X.

By what means I was carried to the town of Ciaca, and that which befell me there; my going to Malaca with a Mahometan merchant; and the Tyrant of Achem's army marching against the King of Aaru.

FINDING my self reduced to that extremity I have spoken of, I was above three hours so besides my self, as I could neither speak, nor weep. At length the other mariner and I went into the sea again, where we continued the rest of that day. The next morning having discovered a barque, that was seeking the mouth of the river, as soon as it was near we got out of the water, and falling on our knees with our hands lift up we desired them to come and take us up; whereupon they gave over rowing, and considering the miserable state we were in they judged immediately that we had suffered shipwrack, so that coming somewhat nearer they asked us what we desired of them; we answered, that we were Christians, dwelling at *Malaca*, and that in our return from *Aaru* we were cast away by a storm about nine days before, & therefore praied them for Gods sake to take us away with them whithersoever they pleased. Thereupon one amongst them, whom we guessed to be the chiefest of them, spake to us thus, By that which I see you are not in case to do us any service, and gain your meat, if we should receive you into our barque, wherefore if you have any mony hidden, you shall do well to give it us aforehand, and then we will use towards you that charity you require of us, for otherwise it is in vain for you to hope for any help from us: saying so, they made shew as though they would be gone; whereupon we besought them again weeping, that they would take us for slaves, and go sell us where they pleased; hereunto I added, how they might have any ransom for me they would require, as having the honor to appertain very nearly unto the Captain of *Malaca*. Well, answered he then, we are contented to accept of thy offer, upon condition, that if that which thou saiest be not true, we will cast thee, bound hand and foot, alive into the sea. Having replied, that they might do so if they found it otherwise, four of them got presently to us, and carried us into their barque, for we were so weak at that time, as we were not able to stir of our selves. When they had us aboard, imagining that by whipping they might make us confess where we had hid our mony, for still they were perswaded that we had some, they tyed us both to the foot of the mast, and then with two double cords they whipped us till we were nothing but blood all over.   Now because that with this beating I was almost dead, they gave not to me, as they did to my companion, a certain drink, made of a kind of lime, steeped in urine, which he having taken it, made him fall into such a furious vomiting, as he cast up both his lungs and his liver, so as he dyed within an hour after. And for that they found no gold come up in his vomit, as they hoped, it pleased God that that was the cause why they dealt not so with me, but only they washed the stripes they had given me with the said liquor, to keep them from festering, which notwithstanding put me to such pain, as I was even at the point of death.   Being departed from this river, which was called *Arissumhea*, we went the next day after dinner ashore, at a place where the houses were covered with straw, named *Ciaca*, in the kingdom of *Jambes*, there they kept me seven and twenty days, in which time by the assistance of heaven I got my self throughly cured of all my hurts.   Then they that had a share in my person, who were seven in number, seeing me unfit for their trade, which was fishing, exposed me to sale three several times, and yet could meet with no body that would buy me; whereupon being out of hope of selling me, they turned me out of doores, because they would not be at the charge of feeding me.   I had been six and thirty days thus abandoned by these inhumanes, and put a grasing like a cast horse, having no other means to live but what I got by begging from door to door, which God knows was very little, in regard those of the country were extream poor, when as one day, as I was lying in the sun upon the sand by the sea side, and lamenting my ill fortune with my self, it pleased God that a *Mahometan*, born in the Isle of *Palimban*, came accidentally by.   This man, having been sometimes at *Malaca* in the company of *Portugals*, beholding me lie naked on the ground, asked me if I were not a *Portugal*, and willed me to tell him the truth; whereupon I answered, that indeed I was one, and descended of very rich parents, who would give him for my ransom whatsoever he would demand, if he would carry me to *Malaca*, where I was nephew to the captain of the fortress, as being the son of his sister. The *Mahometan* hearing me say thus, If it be true, replyed he, that thou art such as thou deliverest thy self to be, what so great sin hast thou committed that could reduce thee to this miserable estate wherein I now see thee? Then I recounted to him from point to point how I was cast away, and by what sort the fishermen had first brought me thither in their barque, and afterwards had turned me out of the wide world, because they could not find any body that would buy me. Hereat he seemed to be much astonished, so that musing a pretty while by himself; Know stranger, said he unto me, that I am but a poor merchant, all whose wealth amounts not to above an hundred *Pardains* (which are worth two shillings a piece of our mony) with which I trade for the rows of shads, thereby hoping to get my living. Now I am assured that I might gain something at *Malaca*, if so be the captain, and the officers of the Custom-house there, would not do me the wrong which I have heard say they do to many merchants that come thither to traffique; wherefore if thou thinkst that for thy sake I should be well used there, I could be contented to redeem thee from the fishermen, and go thither with thee. Thereunto I answered him, with tears in mine eyes, that considering the state I was in at the present, it was not likly he could give credit to any thing I said, because it was probable that to free my self out of my miserable captivity I would prize my person at a far higher value then it would be esteemed for at *Malaca*; howbeit if he would lend any belief to my oaths, since I had no other assurance to give him, I would swear to him, and also set it under my hand, that if he would carry me to *Malaca*, the captain should do him a great deal of honor for my sake, and besides the exempting of his merchandise from paying of custome, he should receive ten times as much as he should disburse for me. Well, replied the *Mahometan*, I am contented to redeem, and reconduct thee to *Malaca*, but thou must take heed that thou speakest not a word of what we have concluded on, for fear thy masters hold thee at so dear a rate, as I shall not be able to draw thee out of their hands though I would never so fain; whereupon I gave him my faith to do nothing but what he would have me to do, especially in that particular, which I held to be most necessary for the better effecting of our desire.

Four dayes after this agreement, the *Mahometan* merchant, that he might the more easily redeem me, used the interposure of a man born in the country, who under hand went to the fishermen, and carried the business so cunningly with them, as they quickly consented to my redemption, for they were already very weary of me, as well in regard that I was sickly, as for that I could no way stand them in any stead, and therefore, as I delivered before, they had turned me out of doores, where I had continued a month and better; so by the means of this third person, whom the *Mahometan* had emploied, the fishermen sold me to the merchant for the sum of seven *mazes* of gold, which amounts in our mony to seventeen shillings and six pence. The *Mahometan* as soon as he had redeemed me, brought me to his house, where I was five dayes out of the tyranny of these fishermen, and in a far better captivity then the former; at the end whereof my new master went five leagues off to a place, named *Sorobaya*, where he got his merchandise aboard, which, as I said before, was nothing but the rows of shads; for there is such great abundance of them in that river, as the inhabitants do therewith every year lade above two thousand vessels, which carry at least a hundred and fifty, or two hundred barrels, whereof each one contains a thousand rows, the rest of the fish not yielding them a penny. After that the *Mahometan* had laden a *Lanchara* with this commodity, he presently set sail for *Malaca*, where within a while he safely arrived, and carrying me to the fortress presented me to the captain, relating unto him what agreement we had made together. *Pedro de Faria* was so amazed to see me in such a lamentable plight, as the tears stood in his eyes, whereupon he bade me speak out aloud, that he might know whether it was I that he beheld, for that I did not seem to be my self, in regard of the strange deformity of my face. Now because that in three months space there had been no news of me, and that every one thought me to be dead, there came so many folks to see me, as the fortress could scarce hold them.

Here being demanded the occasion of my mis-fortune, and who
had brought me into that miserable case, I recounted the
adventures of my voyage, just in the same manner as I have
already delivered them, whereat the whole company were so
astonished, that I saw some go away without speaking a word,
and others shrink up their shoulders, and bless themselves in
admiration of that which they had heard from me ; but in conclusion their compassion towards me was such, that with the
very alms they bestowed on me I became far richer then I was
before I undertook that unlucky voyage. As for *Pedro de
Feria*, he caused threescore ducates to be given to the *Mahometan* merchant that brought me, besides two pieces of good
*China* damask ; moreover he freed me of all the duties he was
to pay for the custom of his merchandise, which amounted to
very near a like sum, so as he remained exceeding well satisfied of the bargain he had made with me. After this, to the
end I might be the better used and looked unto, the captain
commanded me to be lodged in the registers house of the
Kings Customs, where for that he was married there he
thought I might be better accommodated then in any other
place, as indeed I was very well entreated by him and his
wife ; so that having kept my bed about the space of a month,
it pleased God to restore me unto my perfect health.

When I had recovered my health, *Pedro de Faria* sent for
me to the fortress, where he questioned me about that which
had past betwixt me and the King of *Aaru*, as also how and
in what place I was cast away, whereupon I made him an
ample relation thereof. But before I proceed any further, it is
requisite I should here report what was the success of the war
between the Kings of *Aaru* and *Achem*, to the end, that the
desolation, which I have so often foretold, of our fortress of
*Malaca*, may the more evidently appear, it being a matter of
too much importance for to be so neglected as it is by those
who ought to have more care of it. For this is certain, that
either the power of the King of *Achem* is utterly to be ruined,
or by it we shall be miserably expelled out of the countries
we have conquered all along the southern coast, as *Malaca*,
*Bauda*, *Maluco*, *Sunda*, *Borneo*, and *Timor*, and northwards
*China*, *Japan*, and the *Lequios,* as also many other parts and

ports, where the *Portugals* are very much interessed by reason
of the traffique which they daily use there, and where they
reap more profit then in any other place that is yet discovered,
beyond the Cape of Good Hope, the extent thereof being so
great, that it contains along the coast above three thousand
leagues, as may easily be seen by the cards and globes of the
world, if so be their graduation be true.   Besides, if this loss
should happen, which God of his infinite mercy forbid, though
we have but too much deserved it for our carelessness and
sins, we are in danger in like manner to lose the customes of
*Mandorim* of the city of *Goa*, which is the best thing the King
of *Portugal* hath in the *Indies*, for they are ports and islands,
mentioned heretofore, whereon depends the greatest part of his
revenue, not comprehending the spices, namely, the nutmegs,
cloves, and maces, which are brought into this kingdom from
those countries.   Now to return to my discourse, I say, that
the Tyrant of *Achem* was advised by his councel how there was
no way in the world to take *Malaca*, if he should assail it by
sea, as he had divers times before, when as *Dom Stephano de
Gama* and his predecessors were captains of the fortress, but
first to make himself master of the kingdom of *Aaru*, to the
end he might afterwards fortifie himself on the river of *Panetican*, where his forces might more commodiously and neatly
maintain the war he intended to make : for then he might
have means with less charge to shut up the Streights of *Cinca-
pura*, and *Sabaon*, and so stop our ships from passing to the
Seas of *China*, *Sunda*, *Banda*, and the *Molucques*, whereby he
might have the profit of all the drugs which came from that
great Archipelage ; and verily this counsel was so approved by
the Tyrant, that he prepared a navy of an hundred and threescore sails, whereof the most part were *Lanchares* with oars,
galiots, *Calabuzes* of *Jaoa*, and fifteen ships high built, furnished with munition and victual.   In these vessels he
imbarqued twenty thousand men, namely twelve thousand
soldiers, the rest sailers and pioners.   Amongst these were
four thousand strangers, *Turks*, *Abissins*, *Malabares*, *Gusurates*,
and *Lusons* of the Isle of *Borneo*.   Their general was one
named *Heredin Mahomet*, brother-in-law to the Tyrant, by
marriage with a sister of his, and governour of the kingdom of

*Baarros.* This fleet arrived safely at the river of *Panetican,* where the King of *Aaru* attended them with six thousand of his own natural subjects, and not a forraigner amongst them, both in regard he wanted mony for to entertain souldiers, and that also he had a company unprovided of victual to feed them. At their arrival the enemies found them fortifying of the trench whereof I spake heretofore; whereupon without any further delay they began to play with their ordnance, and to batter the town on the sea side with great fury, which lasted six whole dayes together. In the mean time the besieged defended themselves very valiantly, so as there was much blood spilt on either side. The general of the *Achems,* perceiving he advanced but little, caused his forces to land, and mounting twelve great pieces he renewed the battery three several times with such impetuosity, that it demolished one of the two forts that commanded the river; by means whereof, and under the shelter of certain packs of cotton, which the *Achems* carried before them, they one morning assaulted the principal fortress: in this assault an *Abissin* commanded, called *Mamedecan,* who a moneth (or thereabout) before was come from *Juda,* to confirm the new league made by the Bassa of *Caire,* on the behalf of the grand *Signior,* with the Tyrant of *Achem,* whereby he granted him a custom house in the port of *Pazem.* This *Abissin* rendred himself master of the bulwark, with sixty *Turks,* forty *Janizaries,* and some *Malabar* Moors, who instantly planted five ensigns on the walls. In the meantime the King of *Aaru* encouraging his people with promises, and such words as the time required, wrought so effectually, that with a valourous resolution they set upon the enemy, and recovered the bulwark which they had so lately lost; so as the *Abissin* captain was slain on the place, and all those that were there with him. The King, following his good fortune, at the same instant caused the gates of the trench to be opened, and sallying out with a good part of his forces, he combated his enemies so valiantly, as he quite routed them. In like manner he took 8 of their 12 pieces of ordnance, and so retreating in safety he fortified himself the best he could, for to sustain his enemies future assaults.

## CHAPTER XI.

The death of the King of Aaru, and the cruel justice that was executed on
him by his enemies; the going of his Queen to Malaca, and her reception
there.

THE General of *Achem*, seeing the bad success which he
received in this encounter, was more grieved for the
death of the *Abissin* captain, and the loss of those eight pieces
of ordnance, then for all them that were slain besides; whereupon he assembled his councel of war, who were all of opinion
that the commenced siege was to be continued, and the trench
assailed on every side, which was so speedily put in execution,
that in 17 dayes it was assaulted nine several times; in so
much as by divers sorts of fire-works, continually invented by
a *Turkish* engineer that was in their camp, they demolished
the greater part of the trench; moreover, they overthrew two
of the principal forts on the south-side, together with a great
platform, which in the manner of a fals-bray defended the
entry of the river, notwithstanding all the resistance the King
of *Aaru* could make with his people, though they behaved
themselves so valiantly, as the *Achems* lost above two thousand
and five hundred men, besides those that were hurt, which
were far more then the slain, whereof the most part died
shortly after for want of looking to. As for the King of *Aaru*,
he lost not above 400 men; howbeit for that his people were
but few, and his enemies many, as also better ordered, and
better armed, in the last assault, that was given on the 13 day
of the moon, the business ended unfortunately by the utter
defeat of the King of *Aaru's* forces; for it was his ill hap, that
having made a salley forth by the advice of a *Cacis* of his,
whom he greatly trusted, it fell out that this traytour suffered
himself to be corrupted with a bar of gold, weighing about
forty thousand ducates, which the *Achem* gave him, whereof
the King of *Aaru* being ignorant, set couragiously on his
enemies, and fought a bloody battel with them, wherein the
advantage remained on his side in all mens judgement; but
that dog, the perfidious *Cacis*, whom he had left commander
of the trench, sallied forth with 500 men, under colour of

seconding the King in his pursuit of so prosperous a beginning and left the trench without any manner of defence, which perceived by one of the enemies captains, a *Mahometan Malabar,* named *Cutiale Marcaa,* hé presently with six hundred *Gusarates* and *Malabars,* whom he had led thither for that purpose, made himself master of the trench which the trayterous *Cacis,* for the bar of gold he had received had left unguarded, and forthwith put all the sick and hurt men that he found there to the sword, amounting to the number of about fifteen hundred, whereof he would not spare so much as one. In the mean time the unhappy King of *Aaru,* who thought of nothing less than the treachery of his *Cacis,* seeing his trench taken, ran to the succouring of it, being a matter that most imported him : but finding himself the weaker, he was constrained to quit the place, so that as he was making his retreat to the town ditch, it was his ill fortune to be killed by a shot of an harquebuse from a *Turk* his enemy. Upon this death of his ensued the loss of all the rest, by reason of the great disorder it brought amongst them. Whereat the enemies exceedingly rejoycing, took up the corpse of that wretched king, which they found amongst the other dead bodies, and having imbowelled and salted him they put him up in a case, and so sent him as a present to the Tyrant, who after many ceremonies of justice, caused him to be publiquely sawed into sundry pieces, and then boiled in a cauldron full of oyl and pitch, with a dreadful publication, the tenour whereof was this :

*See here the justice which* Sultan Laradin, *King of the Land of the two Seas, hath caused to be executed, whose will and pleasure it is, that as the body of this miserable Mahometan hath been sawed in sunder, and boyled here on earth, so his soul shall suffer worse torments in hell, and that most worthily, for his transgressing of the Law of* Mahomet, *and of the perfect belief of the* Musselmans *of the house of* Mecqua ; *for this execution is very just, and conformable to the holy doctrine of the Book of Flowers, in regard this miscreant hath shewed himself in all his workes to be so far without the fear of God, as he hath incessantly from time to time betrayed the most secret and important affairs of this kingdom to those accursed dogs of the other end of the world, who for our sins, and through our*

*negligence, have with notorious tyranny made themselves lord*
*of* Malaca. This publication ended, a fearful noise arose
amongst the people, who cryed out, *This punishment is bu*
*too little for so execrable a crime.* Behold truly the manner
of this passage, and how the loss of the kingdome of *Aaru*
was joyned with the death of that poor king, who lived
in such good correspondence with us, and that in my opinion
might have been succoured by us with very small charge
and pains, if at the beginning of the war he had been
assisted with that little he demanded by his embassadour
Now who was in the fault hereof, I will leave to the judgement
of them which most it concerns to know it.

After that this infortunate King of *Aaru* had miserably
ended his dayes, as I have before related, and that this whole
army was utterly defeated, both the town, and the rest of the
kingdome were easily and quickly taken in. Thereupon the
General of the *Achems* repaired the trenches, and fortified them
in such manner as he thought requisite for the conservation
and security of all that he had gained : which done, he left
there a garison of 800 of the most couragious men of his army
who were commanded by a *Lusan Mahometan*, named *Sapetu*
*de Raia*, and incontinently after departed with the rest of his
forces. The common report was that he went to the Tyrant o
*Achem*, who received him with very much honour for the
good success of this enterprize ; for, as I have already
delivered, being before but Governour and *Mandara* of the
kingdom of *Baarros*, he gave him the title of King, so tha
ever after he was called *Sultan* of *Baarros*, which is the proper
denomination of such as are kings amongst the *Mahometans*
Now whilest things passed in this sort, the desolate Queer
remained some seven leagues from *Aaru*, where being ad
vertised and assured of the death of the King her husband
and of the lamentable issue of the war, she presently resolved
to cast her self into the fire; for she had promised her husband
in his life time, confirming it with many and great oaths. But
her friends and servants, to divert her from putting so
desperate a design into execution, used many reasons unto
her, so that at length, overcome by their perswasions, *Verily*
said she unto them, *Although I yield to your request, yet .*

*would have you know, that neither the considerations you have propounded, nor the zeal you seem to shew of good and faithful subjects, were of power to turn me from so generous a determination, as that is which I promised to my King, my Husband, and my Master, if God had not inspired me with this thought, that living I may better revenge his death, as by his dear blood I vow unto you to labour as long as I live to do, and to that end I will undergo any extremity whatsoever; nay, if need be, turn Christian a thousand times over, if by that means I may be able to compass this my desire.* Saying so, she immediately got upon an elephant, and accompanied with a matter of seven hundred men, she marched towards the town with a purpose to set it on fire, where incountring some four hundred *Achems*, that were busie about pillaging of such goods as were yet remaining, she so encouraged her people with her words and tears, that they cut them all presently in pieces. This execution done, knowing her self too weak for to hold the town, she returned into the wood, where she sojourned twenty days, during which time she made war upon the townsmen, surprising and pillaging them as often as they issued forth to get water, wood, or other necessaries, so as they durst not stir out of the town to provide themselves such things as they needed, in which regard if she could possibly have continued this war other twenty days longer, she had so famished them, as they would have been constrain'd to render the town; but because at that time it rain'd continually by reason of the climate, and that the place was boggy and full of bushes, as also the fruits, wherewithal they nourished themselves in the wood were all rotten, so that the most part of our people fell sick, and no means there to relieve them, the *Queen* was constrained to depart to a river, named *Minhacumbaa*, some 5 leagues from thence, where she imbarqued her self in 16 vessels, such as she could get, which were fishermens *Paroos*, and in them she went to *Malaca*, with a belief that at her arrival there she should not be denied any thing she would ask.

*Pedro de Faria*, being advertised of the *Queens* coming, sent *Alvaro de Faria*, his son, and General of the Sea-forces, to receive her with a galley, five foists, two cátures, 20 balons,

and 300 men, besides divers persons of the country.  So she
was brought to the fortress, where she was saluted with an
honourable peal of ordnance, which lasted the space of a good
hour.  Being landed, and having seen certain things which *Pedro
de Faria* desired to shew her, as the Custom-house, the river,
the army, the manufactures, stores of powder, and other particulars prepared before for that purpose ; she was lodged in a
fair house, and her people, to the number of six hundred, in a
field, called *Ilher*, in tents and cabbins, where they were accommodated the best that might be.  During all the time of
her abode, which was about a matter of five moneths, she continued solliciting for succour, and means to revenge the death of
her husband.  But at length perceiving the small assistance she
was like to have from us, and that all we did was but a meer
entertainment of good words, she determined to speak freely
unto *Pedro de Faria*, that so she might know how far she
might trust to his promises ; to which end, attending him one
Sunday at the gate of the fortress, at such time as the place
was full of people, and that he was going forth to hear mass ;
she went to him, and after many complements between them,
she said unto him ; *Noble and valiant Captain, I beseech you by
the generosity of your race, to give me the hearing in a few things
I have to represent unto you.  Consider, I pray you, that albeit I
am a Mahometan, and that for the greatness of my sins I am altogether ignorant in the knowledge of your holy Law, yet in regard
I am a woman, and have been a Queen, you ought to carry some
respect to me, and to behold my misery with the eyes of a Christian.*
Hereunto at first *Pedro de Faria* knew not what to answer; in
the end putting off his cap, he made her a low reverence, and
after they had both continued a good while without speaking
the Queen bowed to the church gate, that was just before
them, and then spake again to *Pedro de Faria*.  *Truly,* said
she, *the desire I have alwayes had to revenge the death of my
husband, hath been, and still is so great, that I have resolved
to seek out all the means that possibly I may to effect it, since by
reason of the weakness of my sex fortune will not permit me to
bear arms.  Being perswaded then that this here, which is the
first I have tryed, was the most assured, and that I more relyed
upon then any other, as trusting in the ancient amity which hath*

*alwayes been betwixt us and you Portugals, and the obligation wherein this fortress is engaged to us, passing by many other considerations well known to you; I am now to desire you with tears in mine eyes, that for the honour of the high and mighty King of Portugal, my sovereign lord, and unto whom my husband was ever a loyal subject and vassal, you will ayd and succour me in this my great adversitie, which in the presence of many noble personages you have promised me to do. Howbeit now I see that in stead of performing the promises which you have so often made me, you alledge for an excuse that you have written unto the Vice-roy, about it, whereas I have no need of such great forces as you speak of, for that with an hundred men only, and such of my own people as are flying up and down in hope and expectation of my return; I should be able enough, though I be but a woman, in a short space to recover my country, and revenge the death of my husband, through the help of Almighty God, in whose Name I beseech and require you, that for the service of the King of Portugal, my master, and the only refuge of my widow-hood; you will, since you can, assist me speedily, because expedition is that which in this affair imports the most; and so doing you shall prevent the plot which the wicked enemy hath upon this fortress, as too well you may perceive by the means he hath used to effect it. If you will be pleased to give me the succour I demand of you, say so; if not, deal clearly with me, for that you will prejudice me as much in making me lose the time, as if you refused me that which so earnestly I desire, and which as a Christian you are obliged to grant me, as the Almighty Lord of heaven and earth doth well know, whom I take to witness of this my request.*

---

## CHAPTER XII.

The Queen of Aaru's departure from Malaca; her going to the King of Jantana; his summoning the Tyrant of Achem to restore the kingdom of Aaru, and that which past between them thereupon.

*P*EDRO DE FARIA, having heard what this desolate Queen said openly unto him, convinced by his own conscience, and even ashamed of having delayed her in that

fashion, answered her, that in truth, and by the faith of a
Christian, he had recommended this affair unto the Vice-roy,
and that doubtless there would some succour come for her ere
it were long, if so be there were no trouble in the *Indies* that
might hinder it; wherefore he advised and prayed her to stay
still at *Malaca*, and that shortly she should see the verity of
his speeches.   Thereunto this Princess having replyed upon
the uncertainty of such succour, *Pedro de Faria* grew into
choler, because he thought she did not believe him, so that in
the heat of his passion he lashed out some words that were
more rude than was fit.   Whereupon the desolate Queen with
tears in her eyes, and beholding the church gate, which was
just against her, and sobbing in such manner as she could
scarcely speak.   *The clear Fountain, said she, is the God which
is adored in that house out of whose mouth proceeds all truth
but the men of the earth are sinks of troubled water, wherein
change and faults are by nature continually remaining; wherefore accursed is he that trusts to the opening of their lips; for I
assure you, captain, that ever since I knew my self to this present
I have neither heard nor seen ought, but that the more such
unhappy wretches, as my late husband was, and my self now am
do for you* Portugals, *the less you regard them; and the more
you are obliged, the less you acknowledge; whence I may well
conclude that the recompence of the* Portugal *nation consists
more in favour, then in the merits of persons: and would to God
my deceased husband had nine and twenty years ago but known
what now for my sins I perceive too well; for then he had not
been so deceived by you as he was : but since it is so, I have this
onely left to comfort me in my misery; that I see many others
scandalized with your amity as well as my self : for if you had
neither the power nor the will to succour me, why would you so
far engage your self to me, a poor desolate widow, concerning
that which I hoped to obtain from you, and so beguile me with
your large promises ?*   Having spoken thus, she turned her
back to the Captain, and without harkning to what he might
say, she instantly returned to her lodging; then caused her
vessels, wherein she came thither, to be made ready, and the
next day set sail for *Bintan*, where the King of *Jantana* was
at that time, who, according to the report was made of it to

us afterward, received her with great honour at her arrival.
To him she recounted all that had past betwixt her and *Pedro
de Faria*, and how she had lost all hope of our friendship.
Unto whom, it is said, the King made this answer, *That he did
not marvel at the little faith she had found in us, for that we
had shewed it but too much upon sundry occasions unto all the
world.* Now the better to confirm his saying, he recited some
particular examples of matters, which he said had befaln us
conformable to his purpose; and like a *Mahometan*, and our
enemy, he made them appear more enormous then they were;
so after he had recounted many things of us very ill done,
amongst the which he interlaced divers treacheries, robberies,
and tyrannies, at length he told her, that as a good King, and
a good *Mahometan*, he would promise her, that ere it were
long she should see her self by his means restored again to
every foot of her kingdom ; and to the end she might be the
more assured of his promise he told her that he was content
to take her for his wife, if so she pleased, for that thereby he
should have the greater cause to become the King of *Achems*
enemy, upon whom, for her sake, he should be constrained
to make war, if he would not by fair means be perswaded to
abandon that which he had unjustly taken from her. Whereunto she made answer, that albeit the honour he did her was
very great, yet she should never accept of it, unless he would
first promise, as in way of a dowry, to revenge the death of
her former husband ; saying, it was a thing she so much
desired, as without it she would not accept of the sovereignty
of the whole world. The King condescended to her request,
and by a solemn oath taken on a book of their sect confirmed
the promise which to that effect he made her.

After that the King of *Jantana* had taken that oath before
a great *Cacis* of his, called *Rain Moulana*, upon a festival day
when as they solemnized their *Ramadan*, he went to the Isle
of *Compar*, where immediately upon the celebration of their
nuptials he called a councel for to advise of the course he was
to hold for the performance of that whereunto he had engaged
himself, for he knew it was a matter of great difficulty, and
wherein he should be forced to hazard much of his estate.
The resolution that he took hereupon was, before he enter-

prized any thing, to send to summon the Tyrant of *Achem* to surrender the kingdom of *Aaru*, which in the right of his new wife belonged now unto him, and then according to the answer he should receive to govern himself. This counsel seemed so good to the King, that he presently dispatched an embassadour to the Tyrant, with a rich present of jewels and silks, together with a letter [*to that effect*]. This embassadour being come to *Achem*, the Tyrant received him very honourably, and took his letter; but after he had opened it, and read the contents, he would presently have put him to death, had he not been diverted by his councel, who told him, that in so doing he would incur great infamy: whereupon he instantly dismissed the embassadour with his present, which in contempt of him he would not accept of; and in answer of that he brought him, he returned him a letter, wherein it was thus written : *I* Sultan Aaradin, *King of* Achem, Baarros, Pedir, Paacem, *and of the Signiories of* Dayaa, *and* Batas, *Prince of all the Land of the two Seas, both Mediterranean and Ocean, and of the mynes of* Menencabo, *and of the kingdome of* Aaru, *newly conquered upon just cause ; to thee King, replenished with joy, and desirous of a doubtful heritage. I have seen thy letter, written at the table of thy nuptials, and by the inconsiderate words thereof have discerned the drunkenness of thy councellours and secretaries, whereunto I would not have vouchsafed an answer, had it not been for the humble prayers of my servants. As touching the kingdom of* Aaru, *do not thou dare to speak of it, if thou desirest to live; sufficeth it that I have caused it to be taken in, and that it is mine, as thine also shall be ere long, if thou hast married* Anchesiny *with a purpose upon that occasion to make claim to a kingdome that now is none of hers ; wherefore live with her as other husbands do with their wives, that tilling the ground are contented with the labour of their hands. Recover first thy* Malaca, *since it was once thine, and then thou mayest think of that which never belonged to thee. I will favour thee as a vassal, and not as a brother, as thou qualifiest thy self. From my great and Royal House of rich* Achem, *the very day of this thy embassadours arrival, whom I have presently sent away without further seeing or hearing of him, as he may tell thee upon his return to thy presence.*

The King of *Jatana's* embassadour being dismissed with this answer the very same day that he arrived, which amongst them they hold for a mighty affront, carried back the present, which the Tyrant would not accept of, in the greater contempt both of him that sent, and he that brought it, and arrived at *Compar*, where the King of *Jantana* was at that instant, who upon the understanding of all that had past, grew by report so sad and vext, that his servants have vowed they have divers times seen him weep for very grief that the Tyrant should make so little reckoning of him; howbeit he held a councel there upon the second time, where it was concluded, that at any hand he should make war upon him, as on his mortal enemy, and that the first thing he should undertake should be the recovery of the kingdom of *Aaru*, and the fort of *Panetican*, before it was further fortified. The King accordingly set forth a fleet, of 200 sails, whereof the most part were *Lanchares*, *Calaluses*, and 15 tall *juncks*, furnished with munition necessary for the enterprize; and of this navy he made general the great *Laque Xemena*, his admiral, of whose valour the history of the *Indies* hath spoken in divers places. To him he gave 2000 souldiers, as also 4000 mariners and gally slaves, all choice and trained men. This general departed immediately with his fleet, and arrived at the river of *Panetican*, close by the enemies fort, which he assaulted several times, both with scaling ladders, and divers artificial fires; but perceiving he could not prevail that way, he began to batter it with 400 great pieces of ordnance, which shot continually for the space of 7 whole dayes together, at the end whereof the most part of the fort was ruined, and overthrown to the ground; whereupon he presently caused his men to give an assault to it, who performed it so valiantly, that they entred it, and slew 140 *Achems*, the most of which came thither but the day before the fleet arrived under the conduct of a *Turkish* captain, nephew to the *Bassa* of *Caire*, named *Mora do Arraiz*, who was also slain there with 400 *Turks* he had brought along with him, whereof *Laque Xemena* would not spare so much as one. After this he used such diligence in repairing that which was fallen, wherein most of the souldiers laboured, that in twelve dayes the fort was rebuilt, and made as strong as before, with the augmen-

tation of two bulwarks. The news of this fleet, which the
King of *Jantana* prepared in the ports of *Bintan* and *Compar*,
came to the Tyrants ears, who fearing to lose that which he
had gotten, put instantly to sea another fleet of 140 and
twenty sails, foists, lanchares, galiots, and 15 galleys, of 25
banks of oars a piece, wherein he caused fifteen thousand
men to be imbarqued; namely, twelve thousand souldiers,
and the rest mariners and such as were for the service of the
sea; of this army he made the same *Heredin Mahomet* general,
who had before (as I have already declared) conquered the
kingdom of *Aaru*, in regard he knew him to be a man of a
great spirit, and fortunate in war, who departing with his
army arrived at a place called *Aupessumhee*, within four
leagues of the river of *Panetican*, where he learnt of certain
fishermen, whom he took and put to torture, all that had past
concerning the fort and the kingdom, and how *Laque Xemena*
had made himself master both of the land and sea in expectation of him. At this news, it is said, that *Heredin Mahomet*
was much perplexed, because in truth he did not believe the
enemy could do so much in so little time : by reason whereof
he assembled his councel, where it was concluded, that since
both the fort and kingdom were regained, all the men he
had left there cut in pieces, as likewise for that the enemy was
very strong, both at sea and land, and the season very unfit
for their design, therefore they were to return back: never-
theles *Heredin Mahomet* was of a contrary opinion, saying,
that he would rather dye like a man of courage, then live in
dishonour ; and that seeing the king had made choice of him
for that purpose, by the help of God he would not lose one jot
of the reputation he had gotten; wherefore he vowed and swore
by the bones of *Mahomet*, and all the lamps that perpetually
burn in his chappel, to put all those to death as traytours that
should go about to oppose this intent of his, and that they
should be boyled alive in a cauldron of pitch, in such manner
as he meant to deal with *Laque Xemena* himself; and with
this boyling resolution he parted from the place where he rode
at anchor, with great cries, and noise of drums, and bells, as
they are accustomed to do upon like occasions. In this sort,
by force of oars and sails, they got into the entry of the river;

and coming in sight of *Laque Xemena's* navy, who was ready
waiting for him, and well reinforced with a great number of
souldiers, that were newly come to him from *Pera, Bintan,
Saca,* and many other places thereabout, he made towards
him; and after the discharging of their ordnance afar off, they
joyned together with as much violence as might be. The fight
was such, that during the space of an hour and a half there
could no advantage be discern'd on either part, until such time
as *Heredin Mahomet,* General of the *Achems,* was slain with a
great shot, that hit him just in the brest, and battered him to
pieces. The death of this chieftain discouraged his people in
such manner, as labouring to return unto a point, named
*Baroquirin,* with a purpose there to unite and fortifie themselves until night, and then by the favour thereof to fly away;
they could not execute their design, in regard of the great
currant of the water, which separated and dispersed them
sundry ways, by which means the Tyrants army fell into the
power of *Laque Xemena,* who defeated it, so that but fourteen
sails of them escaped, and the other 166 were taken, and in
them were 13000 and 500 men killed, besides the fourteen
hundred that were slain in the trench. These fourteen sails
that so escaped returned to *Achem,* where they gave the Tyrant
to understand how all had past, at which, it is reported he took
such grief, that he shut up himself for twenty dayes without
seeing any body; at the end whereof, he struck off the heads
of all the captains of the 14 sails, and commanded all the souldiers beards that were in them to be shaved off, enjoyning
them expresly upon pain of being sawed asunder alive, to go
ever after attired in womens apparel, playing on timbrels in
all places where they went; and that whensoever they made
any protestation, it should be in saying, *So may God bring me
back to my husband again, as this is true;* or, *So may I have
joy of the Children I have brought into the world.* Most of these
men seeing themselves inforced to undergo a chastisement so
scandalous to them, fled their country and many made themselves away; some with poyson, some with halters, and some
with the sword. A relation altogether true, without any
addition of mine. Thus was the kingdom of *Aaru* recovered
from the Tyrant of *Achem,* and remained in the hands of the

King of *Jantana*, until the year 1574.  At which time, the said
Tyrant with a fleet of two hundred sails, feigning as though
he would go to take in *Patava*, fell cunningly one night on
*Jantana*, where the king was at that time, whom together
with his wife, children, and many others, he took prisoners,
and carried into his country, where he put them all to most
cruel deaths, and for the king himself, he caused his brains to
be beaten out of his head with a great club.  After these bloody
executions he possest the kingdom of *Aaru*, whereof he presently made his eldest son king, the same that was afterwards
slain at *Malaca*, coming to besiege it in the time of *Don Lionis
Pereyra*, son to the Earl of *Feyra*, captain of the fortress, who
defended it so valiantly, that it seemed to be rather a miracle
then any natural work, by reason the power of that enemy
was so great, and ours so little in comparison of theirs, as it
may be truly spoken how they were two hundred *Mahometans*
against one *Christian*.

[*Here follows an account of Pinto's voyage to Pan, and his adventures until his return to Malaca,* omitted.]

---

## CHAPTER XIII.

Antonio de Faria's setting forth for the Isle of Ainan ; his arrival at the river
of Tinacorem ; and that which befel us in this voyage.

AS soon as *Antonio de Faria* was ready, he departed from
*Patana* on a Saturday the 9 of *May*, 1540, and steered
north north-west, towards the kingdom of *Champaa*, with an
intent to discover the ports and havens thereof, as also by the
of some good booty to furnish himself with such things as he
wanted ; for his haste to part from *Patana* was such, as he
had not time to furnish himself with that which was necessary
for him, no not with victual and warlike ammunition enough.
After we had sailed three dayes, we had sight of an island,
called *Pullo Condor*, at the height of eight degrees and three
quarters on the north coast, and almost north-west towards
the mouth of the river of *Camboia* ; so that having rounded all

the coast, we discovered a good haven eastward where in the Island of *Camboia*, distant some six leagues from the firm land, we met with a junk of *Lequios*, that was going to the kingdom of *Siam*, with an embassadour from the *Nautauquim* of *Lindau*, who was Prince of the Island of *Tosa*, and that had no sooner discovered us, but he sent a message by a *Chinese* pilot to *Antonio de Faria*, full of complements, whereunto was added these words from them all: *That the time would come when as they should communicate with us in the true love of the Law of God, and of His infinite clemency ; who by His death had given life to all men, and a perpetual inheritance in the house of the good, and that they believed this should be so, after the half of the half time was past.* With this complement they sent him a courtelas of great value, whose handle and scabbard was of gold, as also six and twenty pearls in a little box likewise of gold, made after the fashion of a salt-seller, whereat *Antonio de Faria* was very much grieved, by reason he was not able to render the like unto this prince as he was obliged to do, for when the *Chinese* arrived with this message, they were distant above a league at sea from us. Hereupon we went ashore, where we spent 3 dayes in taking in fresh water, and fishing. Then we put to sea again, labouring to get to the firm land, there to seek out a river named *Pullo Cambin*, which divides the State of *Camboia* from the kingdom of *Champaa*; in the height of nine degrees, where arriving on a Sunday, the last of *May*, we went up three leagues in this river, and anchored just against a great town called *Catimparu*, there we remained 12 dayes in peace, during the which we made our provision of all things necessary. Now because *Antonio de Faria* was naturally curious, he endeavoured to understand from the people of the country what nation inhabited beyond them, and whence that mighty river took its source; whereunto he was answered, that it was derived from a lake, named *Pinator*, distant from them eastward two hundred and sixty leagues in the kingdom of *Quitirvan*, and that it was environed with high mountains, at the foot whereof, upon the brink of the water, were eight and thirty villages, of which thirteen were very great, and the rest small, and that only in one of the great ones, called *Xinca-leu*, there was such a huge myne of gold, as by the report of those that lived thereabout, there was every day a bar and a half drawn out of it, which according to the value of our mony, makes two and twenty millions in a year ; and that four lords had share in it, who continually were in war together, each one striving to make himself master of it; I, and that one of them, named *Raiahitau*, had in an inner yard of his house in pots under ground, that were full to the very brims, above six hundred bars of gold in powder like to that of *Menancabo* of the Island of *Samatra*; and that if three hundred harquebusiers of our nation should go and assault it, without doubt they would carry it : moreover, that in another of these villages, called *Buaquirim*, there was a quarry, where out of an old rock they digged a great quantity of diamonds, that were very fine, and of greater value then those of *Lava* and *Taniampura* in the Isle of *Jaoa*.   Whereupon *Antonio de Faria*, having questioned them about many other particularities, they made him a relation of the fertility of the country which was further up this river, no less fit to be desired, then easie to be conquered, and that with little charge.

Being departed from this river of *Pullo Cambim*, we sailed along the coast of the kingdom of *Champaa*, till we came to an haven, called *Saleyzacau*, 17 leagues farther on towards the north, whereinto we entred.   Now because there was nothing to be gotten there, we went out of this place about sun-setting, and the next morning we came to a river named *Toobasoy*, without the which *Antonio de Faria* cast anchor, because the pilot would not venture to enter into it, for that he had never been there before, and therefore knew not the depth of it.   As we were contesting hereabout, some for to enter, and others gainsaying it, we discerned a great sail making towards the port from the main sea.   Hereupon without stirring from the place where we were, we prepared to receive them in a peaceful manner ; so that as soon as they came near us, we saluted them, and hung up the flag of the country, called *Charachina*, which is a sign of friendship, used among them in such like occasions. They of the ship, instead of answering us in the same manner, as in reason it seemed they should have done, and knowing that we were *Portugals*, to whom they wished not well, gave us very vile and base words, with a mighty noise and din of trumpets, drums, and bells, by way of scorn and derision of us. Whereat *Antonio de Faria* was so offended, that he gave them a whole broad side, to see if that would make them more courteous : to this shot of ours they returned us an answer of five pieces of ordnance, namely three faulcons, and two little field-pieces ; whereupon consulting together what we should do, we resolved to abide where we were, for we held it not fit to undertake so doubtful an enterprize, until such time as the next days light might discover the forces of this vessel unto us, that so we might afterwards either set upon her with the more security, or let her pass by : this counsel was approved both by *Antonia de Faria*, and us all ; so that keeping good watch, and giving order for all that was necessary, we continued in that place expecting day ; now about 2 of the clock in the morning we perceived 3 black things close to the water coming towards us, which we could not well discern, whereupon we wakned *Antonio de Faria*, who was then asleep on the hatches, and shewed him what we had discovered, being by that time not far from us : he fearing, as we did, lest they were enemies, cried out presently, *Arm, Arm, Arm*, wherein he was straightway obeyed ; for now plainly perceiving that they were vessels rowing towards us, we betook us to our arms, and were bestowed by our captain in places most necessary to defend our selves. We conceived by their silent approaching to us, that they were the enemies we had seen over night, so that *Antonio de Faria* said unto us, *My masters, this is some pyrate coming to set upon us, who thinks we are not above six or seven at the most, as the manner is in such kind of vessels ; wherefore let every man stoop down, so as they may not see any of us, and then we shall soon know their design ; in the mean time let the pots of powder be made ready, with which, and our swords, I hope we shall give a good end to this adventure : let every one also hide his match in such sort, as they may not be discovered, whereby they may be perswaded that we are asleep.* All which, as he had prudently ordained, was incontinently executed. These 3 vessels, being within a flight shot of ours, went round about her,. and after they had

viewed her well, they joyned all close together, as if they
had entred into some new consultation, continuing so about
a quarter of an hour; that done, they separated themselves
into two parts, namely the two lesser went together to our
poup, and the third that was greater, and better armed,
made to the starboard of us; hereupon they entred our lorch
where most conveniently they could, so that in less then
half a quarter of an hour above forty men were gotten in,
which seen by *Antonio de Faria*, he issued out from under the
hatches with some forty souldiers, and invoking Saint *James*
our patron, he fell so couragiously upon them, that in a short
time he killed them almost all; then with aid of the pots
of powders, that he caused to be cast in amongst those that
were remaining in the 3 vessels, which he presently took,
he made an end of defeating them, the most of them being
constraind to leap into the sea, where they were all drowned
but five, whom we took up alive, whereof one was a capher
slave and the other four were, one *Turk*, two *Achems*, and the
captain of the junk, named *Similau*, a notorious pyrat, and
our mortal enemy.  *Antonio de Faria* commanded them
instantly to be put to torture, for to draw out of them who
they were, from whence they came, and what they would
have had of us, whereunto the two *Achems* answered most
bruitishly; and when as we were going about to torment
the slave in like manner, he began with tears to beseech us
to spare him, for that he was a Christian as we were, and that
without torture he would answer truly to all our demands;
whereupon *Antonio de Faria* caused him to be unbound, and
setting him by him, gave him a piece of bisket, and a glass of
wine, then with fair words he perswaded him to declare the
truth of every thing to him, since he was a Christian, as he
affirmed; to which he replied in this sort, *If I do not speak
the truth unto you, then take me not for such as I am*; *my
name is* Sebastian, *and I was slave to* Gaspar de Melo, *whom
this dog* Similau, *here present, slew about two years ago in*
Liampao, *with five and twenty other* Portugals *that were in his
ship*.  *Antonio de Faria* hearing this, cryed out, like a man
amazed, and said, Nay now I care not for knowing any more;
is this then that dog *Similau*, that slew thy master; *Yes*,

answered he, *it is he, and that meant likewise to have done as much to you, thinking that ye were not above six or seven, for which effect he came away in haste with a purpose, as he said, to take you alive, for to make your brains flye out of your heads with a frontal of cord, as he did to my master; but God I hope will pay him for all the mischief he hath committed.* Antonio de Faria being also advertised by this slave, that this dog *Similau* had brought all his men of war along with him, and left none in his junk, but some *Chinese* mariners; he resolved to make use of this good fortune, after he had put *Similau* and his companions to death, by making their brains flye out of their heads with a cord, as *Similau* had done to *Gaspar de Mello,* and the other *Portugals* in *Liampao :* wherefore he presently imbarqued himself with thirty souldiers in his boat, and the three *Machnas* wherein the enemies came, and by means of the flood and a favourable wind, he arrived within less then an hour, where the junk rode at anchour within the river, about a league from us, whereupon he presently boarded her, and made himself master of the poup, from whence, with only four pots of powder, which he cast in among the rascals that were asleep upon the hatches, he made them all leap into the sea, where 9 or 10 of them were drowned, the rest crying out for help were taken up and saved, because we stood in need of them for the navigation of the junk, that was a great tall vessel. Thus you see how it pleased God out of His Divine justice to make the arrogant confidence of this cursed dog a means to chastise him for his cruelties, and to give him by the hands of *Portugals* a just punishment for that which he had done unto him. The next morning taking an inventory of this prize, we found six and thirty thousand *Taeis* in silver of *Japan,* which amounts in our mony to fifty four thousand ducates, besides divers other good commodities, that were not then praised for want of time, because the country was all in an uproar, and fires every where kindled, whereby they use to give warning one to another upon any alarm or doubt of enemies, which constrained us to make away with all speed.

[*Antonio de Faria coasts the Kingdom of Champaa, till he reaches the river Tinacoreu.*]

7

The Friday following we left this river of *Tinacoreu*, and by our pilots advice we went to find out *Pullo Champeiloo*, which is an inhabited island, scituate in the entrance to the bay of *Cauchenchina* in forty degrees, and a third to the northward; being come to it, we cast anchor in an haven, where there was good and safe riding, and there we remained three dayes, accommodating our artillery in the best manner we could; that done, we set sail towards the Isle of *Ainan*, hoping to meet with the pyrat *Coia Acem* there whom we sought for, and arriving at *Pullo Capas*, which was the first land that we saw of it, we sailed close to the shoar, the better to discover the ports and rivers on that side, and the entries into them. Now because the lorch, wherein *Antonio de Faria* came from *Patana*, leaked very much, he commanded all his souldiers to pass into another better vessel, which was immediately performed, and arriving at a river, that about evening we found towards the east, he cast anchor a league out at sea, by reason his junk was great, and drew much water, so that fearing the sands; which he had often met withall in this voyage, he sent *Christovano Borralho* with fourteen souldiers in the lorch up the river to discover what fires those might be that he saw.   Being gone then about a league in the river, he incountred a fleet of forty very great junks, whereupon fearing lest it was the *Mandarins* army, whereof we had heard much talk, he kept aloof off from them, and anchored close by the shoar; now about midnight the tyde began to come in, which *Borralho* no sooner perceived, but he presently without noise weighed anchor, and declining the junks he went on to that part where he had seen the fires, that by this time were almost all out, there being not above two or three that gave any light, and which served to guide him. So continuing his course very discreetly, he came to a place where he beheld a mighty company of great and small ships, to the number, as he guessed, of thousand sails, passing through the which very stilly he arrived at a town of above ten thousand housholds, enclosed with a strong wall of brick, with towers and bulwarks after our manner, and with curtains full of water. Here five of the fourteen souldiers, that were in the lorch, went on shoar with two of those *Chineses*, that were saved out of *Similaus* junk, who had left their wives as hostages with us for their return; these having spent three hours in viewing and surveying the town on the outside, reimbarqued themselves without any notice taken of them at all, and so went back very quietly as they came to the mouth of the river, where they found a junk riding at anchor, that was come thither since their departure in the evening. Being returned to *Antonio de Faria*, they related unto him what they had seen, particularly the great army that lay up in the river, as also the junk, which they had left riding at anchor at the entrance into it, telling him that it might well be the dog *Coia Acem* whom he sought for. These news so rejoyced him, that instantly he weighed anchor, and set sail, saying, his mind gave him that it was undoubtedly he; and if it proved so, he assured us all that he was contented to lose his life in fighting with him, for to be revenged of such a rogue as had done him so much wrong. Approaching within sight of the junk, he commanded the lorch to passe unto the other side of her, to the end they might board her both together at once, and charged that not a piece should be shot off, for fear they should be heard of the army that lay up in the river, who might thereupon come to discover them. As soon as we were come to the junk, she was presently invested by us, and twenty of our souldiers leaping in made themselves masters of her without any resistance, for the most of her men threw themselves into the sea, the rest that were more couragious valiantly made head against our people; but *Antonio de Faria* presently getting in with twenty souldiers more made an end of defeating them, killing above thirty of theirs, so as there remained none alive but those which voluntarily cast themselves into the sea, whom he caused to be drawn up to serve for the navigation of his vessels, and for to learn who they were, and from whence they came, to which purpose he commanded four of them to be put to torture, whereof two chose rather to dye then confess any thing; and as they were about to do the like to a little boy, an old man, his father, that was laid on the deck, cryed out with tears in his eyes for to give him the hearing before they did any hurt to the child;

*Antonio de Faria* made the executioner stay, and bad the
old man say what he would, provided he spake truth, for
otherwise he vowed, that both he and the boy should be
thrown alive into the sea; whereas on the contrary, if he
dealt truly, he promised to set them both at liberty on shoar,
and restore unto him whatsoever he would take his oath did
appertain unto him: whereunto the old *Mahometan* answered,
*I accept of the promise which thou makest me, and I very much
thank thee for sparing the life of this child, for as for mine, as a
thing unprofitable, I make no reckoning of it, and I will rely
on thy word, although the course thou holdest may well divert
me from it, in regard it is no way conformable to the Christian
law, which thou hast profest in thy baptism :* an answer, that
rendred *Antonio de Faria* so confounded and amazed, as he
knew not what to reply; howbeit he caused him to come
nearer unto him, and questioned him gently without any
further threatening.

This old man then sat him down by *Antonio de Faria*, who
seeing him white like unto us, asked him whether he were a
*Turk*, or a *Persian?* whereunto he answered, that he was
neither, but that he was a Christian, born at Mount *Sinai*.
*Antonio de Faria* thereupon replyed, how he wondred much,
being a Christiań, as he said, that he lived not amongst Christians. To which the old man answered, that he was a merchant of a good family, named *Tome Mostanguo*, and that
riding one day at anchor in a ship of his in the port of *Judaa*,
in the year one thousand five hundred thirty and eight, *Soliman* the Bassa, Vice-roy of *Cairo*, took his, and seven other
ships, to carry victual and munition for his army of threescore
gallies, wherewith he went by the command of the grand
*Seignior* to restore *Sultan Bandur* to his kingdom of *Cambaya*,
which the great *Mogul* had deprived him of; and that at the
end of the voyage going to demand the freight which they had
promised him, the *Turks*, that were ever cruel and faithless,
took his wife, and a young daughter he had, and forced them
before his face, and because his son wept at the sight of this
injury, they threw him bound hand and foot into the sea; as
for himself, they laid him in irons, and continually scourging
him they stript him of all his goods, to the value of six

thousand ducates and better, saying, that it was not lawful for
any to enjoy the blessings of God, but the holy and just
*Musselimians*, such as they were: and that his wife and
daughter dying not long after, he found means one night to
cast himself into the sea with that little boy, which was his
son, at the mouth of the river of *Diu*, from whence he went by
land to *Surrat*, and so to *Malaca* in a ship of *Carcia de Saas*,
captain of *Bacaim*; then how by the commandment of *Estevano de Gama*, going to *China* with *Christovano Sardinha*,
which had been factor at the *Molucques*, one night as they rode
at anchor in *Cincaapura*, *Quiay Taijano*, master of the junk,
surprized them, and killed the said *Sardinha* together with six
and twenty *Portugals* more; as for him, because he was a
gunner, they saved his life.  At this report *Antonio de Faria*
striking himself on the breast, as a man amazed at this discourse, *Lord, Lord,* said he, *this seems to be a dream that I
hear*; then turning himself to his souldiers that stood about
him, he related the life of this *Quiay* unto them, and further
affirmed, that he had slain at times in strayed vessels above an
hundred *Portugals*, and dispoiled them of an hundred thousand
ducates at least; and though his name was such as this
*Armenian* delivered, to wit, *Quiay Taijano*, yet after he had
killed *Christovano Sardinha* in *Cincaapura*, in a vain glory of
that which he had done he caused himself to be called Captain
*Sardinha*.    Whereupon having demanded of the *Armenian*
where he was, he told us, that he was very sore hurt, and
hidden in the hold of the junk amongst the cables, with five or
six others.    Hereat *Antonio de Faria* arose, and went directly
to the place where this dog was hidden, followed by the
greatest part of his souldiers, which opened the scuttle where
the cables lay, to see whether the *Armenian* spake true or no;
in the mean time the dog, and the six others that were with
him, got out at another scuttle, and most desperately fell upon
our men, who were about thirty in number, besides fourteen
boys.    Then began there so furious and bloody a fight, that in
less then a quarter of an hour we made a clean dispatch of
them all; but in the mean while two *Portugals*, and seven boys
were slain, besides I know not how many hurt, whereof
*Antonia de Faria* received two downright blowes on his head,

and one on his arm, which put him to very much pain.   After
this defeat, and that the wounded men were drest, he set sail,
for fear of the junks that were in the river: so getting far
from land, about evening we went and anchored on the other
side of *Cauchenchina*, where *Antonia de Faria* causing an
inventory to be taken of all that was in the pyrats junk, there
was found in her five hundred bars of pepper, after twenty
quintals to the bar, forty of nutmegs and mace, fourscore of
tin, thirty of ivory, twelve of wax, and five of wood of fine
aloes, which might be worth, according to the rate of the
country, seventy thousand ducates; besides a little fieldpiece,
four falcons, and thirty bases of brass, the greatest part of
which artillery had been ours, for this *Mahometan* had taken
them in the ships of *Sardinha*, *Oliveyra*, and *Bartholemew de
Matos*: there was also found three coffers covered with leather,
full of silk quilts, and the apparel of *Portugals*, with a great
bason and ewer silver and gilt, and a salt-seller of the same,
two and twenty spoones, three candlesticks, five gilt cups, eight
and fifty harquebuzes, twelve hundred twenty and two pieces
of *Bengala* cloth, all which were *Portugals* goods, eighteen
quintals of powder, and nine children about seven or eight
years of age, chained together by the hands and the feet, most
lamentable to behold, for that they were so weak and lean,
that one might easily through their skins have counted all the
bones in their bodies.

---

## CHAPTER XIV.

Antonio de Faria's arrival at the Bay of Camoy, where was the fishing
of pearles for the King of China; with that which happened to him
by the means of a renegado pyrat, and otherwise.

THE next day, after noon, *Antonio de Faria* parted from
the place where he rode at anchor, and returned towards
the coast of *Ainan*, by the which he kept all the rest of that
day, and the next night with five and twenty or thirty fathom
water.   In the morning he came to a bay, where there were
many great boats fishing for pearles, and being unresolved
what course to take, he bestowed all the forenoon in counsel

KING OF COCHIN

ON ELEPHANT

with his company thereabout, whereof some were of the
opinion that he should seize upon the boats that were fishing
for pearls ; and others opposed it, saying, it was a safer way
to treat with them as merchants, for that in exchange of the
great store of pearles, which were in that place, they might
easily put off the most part of their commodities.   This
appearing to be the best and safest advice, *Antonio de Faria*
caused the flag of trade to be hung out, according to the
custom of *China* ; so that instantly there came two lanteaas
from land to us, which are vessels like to foists, with great
abundance of refreshments, and those that were in them
having saluted us after their manner, went aboard the great
junk, wherein *Antonio de Faria* was ; but when they beheld
men, such as we were, having never seen the like before, they
were much amazed, and demanded what people we were, and
wherefore we came into their country.   Wherunto we answered
by an interpreter, that we were merchants born in the kingdom
of *Siam*, and were come thither to sell or barter our commodities with them, if so be they would permit us.   To this,
an old man, much respected of all the rest, replyed, that here
was no traffique used, but in another place further forward,
called *Guamboy*, where all strangers that came from *Cantan,
Chincheo, Lamau, Comhay, Sumbor, Liampau*, and other sea-
coast towns, did ordinarily trade : wherefore he counselled
him to get him suddenly from thence, in regard this was a
place destined only to the fishing of pearles for the treasure of
the house of the Son of the Sun, to the which, by the ordinance
of the *Tutan* of *Comhay*, who was the sovereign governor of
all the country of *Cauchenchina*, no vessel was permitted to
come, but only such as were appointed for that service, and
that all other ships, which were found there were by the law
to be burnt, and all that were in them ; but since he, as a
stranger, and ignorant of the laws of the country, had trans-
gressed the same, not out of contempt, but want of knowledge,
he thought fit to advertise him of it, to the end he might be
gone from thence before the arrival of the *Mandarin* of the
army, which we call general, to whom the government of that
fishing appertained, and that would be within three or four
dayes at the most, being gone not above six or seven leagues

from thence to a village, named *Buhaquirim*, for to take in
victual. *Antonio de Faria* thanking him for his good advice,
asked him how many sails, and what forces the *Mandarin* had
with him: whereunto the old man answered, that he was
accompanied with forty great junks, and twenty-five *Vancans*
with oars, wherein there were seven thousand men, namely,
five thousand souldiers, and the rest slaves and mariners; and
that he was there every year six months, during the which
time was the fishing for pearles, that is to say, from the 1st
of *March* to the last of *August*. Our captain desiring to know
what duties were paid out of this fishing, and what revenue it
yielded in those six months, the old man told him, that of
pearls which weighed above five carats they gave two thirds, of
the worser sort half less, and of seed pearl the third; and that
this revenue was not always alike, because the fishing was
sometimes better in one year, then in another, but that one
with another he thought it might yield annually four hundred
thousand *Taeis*. *Antonio de Faria* made very much of the old
man, and gave him two cakes of wax, a bag of pepper, and a
tooth of ivory, wherewith both he and the rest were exceedingly
well pleased. He also demanded of them, of what bignesse
this Isle of *Ainan* might be, whereof so many wonders were
spoken. Tell us first, replyed they, who you are, and wherefore you are come hither, then will we satisfie you in that you
desire of us; for we vow unto you, that in all of our lives we
never saw so many young fellows together in any merchants
ships, as we now see in this of yours, nor so spruce and neat;
and it seems that in their country *China* silks are so cheap
as they are of no esteem, or else that they have had them at
so easie a rate, as they have given nothing near the worth for
them, for we see them play away a piece of damask at one
cast at dice, as those that come lightly by them: a speech
that made *Antonio de Faria* secretly to smile, for that thereby
he well perceived how these fishermen had a shrewd guess
that the same were stolen, which made him tell them, that they
did this like young men, who were the sons of very rich merchants, and in that regard valued things far under that they
were worth, and had cost their fathers; dissembling them
what they thought, they answered in this manner, It may very

well be as you say. Whereupon *Antonio de Faria* gave a sign
to the souldiers to leave off their play, and to hide the pieces
of silk that they were playing for, to the end they might not
be suspected for robbers by these folks, which immediately
they did, and the better to assure these *Chineses* that we were
honest men, and merchants, our captain commanded the
scuttles of the junk to be opened, that we had taken the night
before from Captain *Sardinha*, which was laden with pepper,
whereby they were somewhat restored to a better opinion then
they had of us before, saying one to another, Since now we
find they are merchants indeed, let us freely answer to their
demand, so as they may not think, though we be rude, that
we know nothing but how to catch fish and oysters.

*[Here follows an account of the history of the Isle of Ainan,
omitted.]*

After *Antonio de Faria* had given him many thankes for
satisfying him so fully in his demands, he desired him to tell
him in what port he would advise him to go and sell his commodities, seeing the season was not proper to set sail for
*Liampoo.* Whereunto he answered, that we were not to go
into any port of that country, nor to put trust in any *Chinese*
whatsoever; for I assure you; said he, there is not one of
them will speak truth in any thing he sayes to you, and believe
me, for I am rich, and will not lye to you like a poor man,
besides, I would wish you to go in this streight always with
the plummet in your hand for to sound your way, because
there are very many dangerous shelves all along till you come
to a river called *Tanaquir*, and there is a port where is very
good anchoring, and where you may be as safe as you can
desire; as also you may there, in less then two dayes, put off
all your commodities, and much more if you had them. Nevertheless I will not counsel you to disimbarque your goods on
land, but to sell them in your vessels, in regard that many
times the sight causeth desire, and desire disorder amongst
peaceable persons, much more with them that are mutinous
and of an evil conscience, whose wicked inclination carries
them rather to take away another mans goods from him, then
give of their own to the needy for Gods sake. This said, both
he that spake, and those that accompanied him, took leave of

our captain, and us, with many complements and promises,
whereof they are not ordinarily very sparing in those parts,
bestowing on *Antonio de Faria*, in return of that he had given
them, a little box made of a tortoise shell, full of seed-pearl,
and twelve pearles of a pretty bigness, craving his pardon for
that they durst not traffique with him in this place, for fear
lest if they should do so, to be all put to death, conformable to
the law of the rigorous justice of the country; and they again
intreated him to make haste away before the *Mandarins* arrival
with his army; for if he found them there, he would burn both
his vessel, and him and all his company. *Antonio de Faria*
unwilling to neglect the counsel of this man, lest that which he
told him should prove true, he set sail immediately, and passed
to the other side towards the south, and in two days with a
westerly wind he arrived at the river of *Tanauquir*, where just
over against a little village, called *Neytor*, he cast anchor.

We remained all that day, and the next night, at the mouth
of the river of *Tanauquir*, intending the next morning to set
sail up to the town, which was some five leagues from thence
in the river, to see if by any means we might put off our commodities there, for our vessels were so heavy laden with them,
as there was scarce a day wherein we ran not twice or thrice
on some shelve or other, which in divers places were four or
five leagues long; wherefore it was concluded that before we
did any thing else we were to sell away our commodities, so
that we labored with all our might to get into the river, whose
current was so strong, that though we had all our sails up, yet
could we prevail but very little against it; as we were in this
pain we perceived two great junks in warlike manner come out
of the river upon us, which chaining themselves together for
the more strength, attaqued us so lively, as we had scarce the
leasure to defend our selves, so that we were constrained to
throw into the sea all that stood in our way to make room for
our artillery, being that we had then most need of. The
first salutation we had from them was a peal of six and twenty
pieces of ordnance, whereof nine were faulconets, and field-
pieces: *Antonio de Faria*, as a man verst in such affairs, seeing
them chained one to another, perceived their drift, and therefore made as though he fled, as well to win time to prepare

himself, as to make them believe that they were no Christians; whereupon they, like cunning thieves, desiring that the prey, which they held to be surely their own, should not escape out of their hands, loosed themselves the one from the other the better to set upon us, and approaching very near to us, they shot so many arrows and darts into our junk, as no man was able to appear upon the deck. *Antonio de Faria,* to avoid this storm, retired under the half deck, with five and twenty souldiers, and some ten or twelve others, slaves, and mariners; there he entertained the enemy with harquebuse shot the space of half an hour, in which time, having used all their munitions of war, some forty of them, that seemed to be more valiant then the rest, longing to finish their enterprize, leaped into our junk, with a purpose to make themselves masters of the prow ; but to hinder them from it, our captain was constrained to go and receive them, so that there began a most bloody fight, wherein it pleased God within an hour to give us the upper hand by the slaughter of four and twenty of their forty in the place. Thereupon twenty of ours, pursuing this good successe, boarded the enemies junk, where finding but small resistance, by reason the principals were already slain, all that were in her quickly rendred themselves unto us. That done, *Antonio de Faria* went with all speed to succour *Christovano Borallho,* who was boarded by the other junk, and very doubtful of the victory, in regard the greatest part of his men were hurt; but at our approach the enemies threw themselves all into the sea, where most of them were drowned, and so both the junks remained in our power. After this we took a survey of our company, the better to understand what this victory had cost us ; and we found there was one *Portugal,* five boyes, and nine mariners killed, besides those that were hurt; and on the enemies part fourscore were slain, and almost as many taken. Having given order then for the dressing and accommodating of our wounded men in the best manner that could be, *Antonio de Faria* caused as many mariners to be taken up as could be saved, and commanding them to be brought into the great junk where he was, he demanded of them what those junks were, how the captain of them was named, and whether he were alive or dead ; whereunto not one of them would make any answer, but chose rather to dye in torments like mad dogs, when as *Christovano Borralho* cryed out from the junk where he was, *Signior, Signior, come hither quickly, for we have more to do then we think of;* whereat *Antonio de Faria*, accompanied with fifteen or sixteen of his men, leapt into his junk, asking what the matter was ? *I hear a many talking together*, said he, *towards the prow, which I doubt are hidden there*; hereupon opening the scuttle, they heard divers cry out, *Lord Jesus, have mercy upon us*; and that in such a woful manner, as struck us all with pity: *Antonio de Faria* approaching to the scuttle, and looking down, could perceive some persons there shut up, but not able to discern what they might be, he made two of his boys to go down, who a little after brought up seventeen Christians, namely, two *Portugals*, five small children, two girls, and eight boys, which were in such a lamentable case, as would have grieved any heart to have beheld them; the first thing he did was to cause their irons to be strucken off, and then he enquired of one of the *Portugals* (for the other was like a man dead) unto whom those children appertained, and how they fell into the hands of this pyrat, as also what his name was. Whereunto he answered, that the pyrat had two names, the one Christian, the other Pagan, and that his Pagan name, wherewith he used to be called of late, was *Necoda Nicaulem*, and his Christian name *Francisco de Saa*, being christned at *Malaca*, at such time as *Garcia de Saa* was captain of the fortress, and for that he was his god-father, and had caused him to be baptized, he gave him that name, and married him to an orphan maid, a very handsome wench, the daughter of an honourable *Portugal*, to oblige him the more to our religion and country; but in the year 1534. setting sail for *China* in a great junk of his, wherein there accompanied him twenty of the wealthiest *Portugals* in *Malaca*, as also his wife, and arriving at the island of *Pullo Catan*, they staid two days to take in fresh water, during which time he and his company, who were all *Chineses* like himself, and no better Christians, conspired the death of the poor *Portugals* for to despoil them of their goods, so that one night whil'st the *Portugals* were asleep, and little dream'd of such treason, they killed them all with their hatchets, and their servants likewise, not sparing the life of any one that bore the name of a Christian ; after which, he perswaded with his wife, to turn Pagan, and adore an idol, that *Tucan*, captain of the junk, had concealed in his chest, and that then being free from the Christian religion he would marry her to *Tucan*, who in exchange would give him a sister of his to wife, that was a *Chinese*, and there with him. But in regard she would neither adore the idol, nor consent to the rest, the dog struck her over the head with a hatchet till her brains flew out, and then departing from thence went to the port of *Liampoo*, where the same year before he had traded ; and not daring to go to *Patana*, for fear of the *Portugals* that resided there, he wintred at *Siam*, and the year following he returned to the port of *Chincheo*, where he took a little junk that came from *Sunda*, with ten *Portugals* in her, all which he slew ; and because the wickedness that he had done us was known over all the country, doubting to encounter some *Portugal* forces, he had retired himself into this streight *Cauchenchina*, where as a merchant he traded, and as a pyrat robbed those he met with all that were weaker then himself. It being now three years since he had taken this river for a refuge of his robberies, thinking himself here secure from us *Portugals*, by reason we have not used to traffique in the ports of this streight, the island of *Ainan*. *Antonio de Faria* asked of him whether those children belonged to the *Portugals* he had mentioned before ; whereunto he answered, that they did not, but that both they, and the boys and girls, were the children of *Nuno Preto*, *Gian de Diaz*, and of *Pero Borges*, whom he had killed at *Mompollacota*, near the mouth of the river of *Siam* in *Joano Oliveyra's* junk, where he also put sixteen *Portugals* more to death, only he saved their two lives, because one was a shipwright, and the other a caulker, and had carried them along with him in this manner, continually whipping, and almost famishing of them ; further he said, that when he set upon us, he did not think we had been *Portugals*, but some *Chinese* merchant, like such as he had accustomed to rob when he found them at advantage, as he thought to have found us. *Antonio de Faria* demanded of him, whether he could know the pyrat amongst those other dead bodies ? Having replyed that he could, the captain presently arose, & taking him by the hand, went with him into the other junk, that was fastned to his, and having made him view all that lay dead upon the hatches, he said it was none of them.  Whereupon he commanded a manchuas, which is a little boat, to be made ready, wherein he and this man went and sought for him amongst the other dead bodies that floated on the water, where they found him with a great cut over his head, and thrust quite through the body ; so causing him to be taken up, and laid upon the hatches, he demanded of that man again, if he were sure that this was he, who answered, how without doubt it was he.  Whereunto *Antonio de Faria* gave the more credit, by reason of a great chain of gold he had about his neck, to which was fastned an idol of gold with two heads, made in the form of a lizard, having the tail and paws enamelled with green and black ; and commanding him to be drawn towards the prow, he caused his head to be chopt off, and the rest of the body to be cut in pieces, which were cast into the sea.

Having obtained this victory in the manner I have before declared, and caused our hurt men to be drest, and provided for the guard of our captains, we took an inventory of the goods that were in these two junks, and found that our prize was worth forty thousand *Taeis*, which was immediately committed to the charge of *Antonio Borges*, who was factor for the prizes. Both the junks were great and good, yet were we constrained to burn one of them for want of mariners to man it : there was in them besides seventeen pieces of brass ordnance, namely, four faulconets, and thirteen small pieces, the most part whereof had the royal arms of *Portugal* upon them, for the pyrat had taken them in the three ships where he killed the forty *Portugals*.  The next day *Antonio de Faria* went about once more to get into the river, but he was advised by fishermen, which he took a little before, that he should beware of going to the town, because they were advised there of all that had passed betwixt him and the renegado pyrat, for whose death the people were in an uproar ; in so much that if he would let them have his commodities for nothing, yet would they not take them, in regard that *Chileu*, the governor of that province, had contracted with him, to give him the third part of all the prizes he took, in lieu whereof he would render him

a safe retreat in his country; so that his loss being now great
by the death of the pyrat, he should be but badly welcomed by
him, and to that purpose had already commanded two great
rafts, covered with dry wood, barrels of pitch, and other combustible stuff, to be placed at the entring into the port, that
were to be kindled and sent down upon us, as soon as we had
cast anchor, for to fire us, besides two hundred proas, full of
shot, and men of war were also in readiness to assault us.
These news made *Antonio de Faria* conclude to make away unto
another port, named *Mutipinan*, distant from thence above forty
leagues towards the east, for that there were many rich merchants, as well natives as strangers, which came in great troops
from the countries of *Lauhos*, *Pafuaas*, and *Gueos*, with great
sums of mony. So we set sail with the three junks, and the
lorch, wherein we came from *Patana*, coasting the land from
one side to the other, by reason of a contrary wind, until we
arrived at a place called *Tilaumera*, where we anchored, for
that the current of the water ran very strong against us.
After we had continued so three dayes together, with a contrary
wind, and in great want of victual, our good fortune about evening brought four *Lanteaas* unto us, that are like unto foysts, in
one of the which was a bride, that was going to a village, named
*Pandurea*: now because they were all in a jollity, they had so
many drums beating aboard them, as it was almost impossible
to hear one another for the noise they made. Whereupon we
were in great doubt what this might be, and wherefore there
was such triumphing; some thought that they were spies sent
from the captain of *Tanauquir's* army, who insulting, for that
we were already in their power, gave this testimony thereof.
*Antonio de Faria* left his anchors in the sea, and preparing himself to sustain all that might happen unto him, he displayed all
his banners and flags, and with demonstration of joy attended
the arrival of these *Lanteaas*, who when they perceived us to
be all together, imagining it was the bridegroom that stay'd to
receive them, they came joyfully towards us. So after we had
saluted one another after the manner of the country, they went
and anchored by the shore. And because we could not comprehend the mystery of this affair, all our captains concluded
that they were spies from the enemies army, which forbore

assaulting us in expectation of some other vessels that were
also to come ; in this suspicion we spent the little remainder
of that evening, and almost two hours of the night : but when the
bride, seeing that her spouse sent not to visit her, as was his
part to do, to shew the love she bore him, she sent her uncle in
one of the *Lanteaas* with a letter to him, containing these
words. *If the feeble sex of a woman would permit me to go from
the place where I am for to see thy face, without reproach to mine
honour, assure thy self that to kiss thy tardy feet my body would
fly as doth the hungry falcon after the fearful heron : but since
I am parted from my fathers house for to seek thee out here, come
thy self hither to me, where indeed I am not, for I cannot see my
self, but in seeing thee. Now if thou dost not come to see me in
the obscuritie of this night, making it bright for me, I fear that
to morrow morning when thou arrivest here, thou shalt not find
me living. My uncle* Licorpinau *will more particularly acquaint
thee with what I keep concealed in my heart ; for I am not able
to say any more, such is my grief to be so long deprived of thy so
much desired sight : wherefore I pray thee come unto me, or permit me to come unto thee, as the greatness of my love to thee doth
deserve, and as thou art obliged to do unto her, whom now thou
art to possess in marriage until death, from which Almighty God
of His infinite goodness keep thee as many years, as the sunne and
moon have made turns about the world, since the beginning of
their birth.* This *Lanteaa* being arrived with the brides uncle
and letter, *Antonio de Faria* caused all the *Portugals* to hide
themselves, suffering none to appear but our *Chinese* mariners,
to the end they might not be afraid of us : to our junk then
they approached with confidence, and three of them coming
aboard us, asked where the bridegroom was ? All the answer
we made them was to lay hold of them, and clap them presently under hatches ; now because the most part of them were
drunk, those that were in the *Lanteaa* never heard our bustling
with them, nor if they had, could they have had time to
escape, for suddenly from the top of our poop we fastned a
cable to their mast, whereby they were so arrested, as it was
impossible for them to get loose of us ; whereupon casting in
some pots of powder amongst them, the most of them leapt
into the sea, by which time six or seven of our souldiers, and

as many mariners, got into the *Lanteaa*, and straight rendred themselves masters of her, where the next thing they did was to take up the poor wretches, who cried out that they drowned: having made them sure, *Antonio de Faria* went towards the other three *Lanteaas*, that anchored some quarter of a league from thence; and coming to the first, wherein was the bride, he entered her without any resistance, in regard there were none other in her but a few mariners, and six or seven men that seemed to be of good reckoning; all of kin to the bride, being there only to accompany her, together with two little boyes her brothers, that were very white, and certain ancient women, of such as in *China* are hired for money to dance, sing, and play of instruments upon like festival occasions. The other two *Lanteaas* beholding this bad success, left their anchors in the sea, and fled in such haste, as if the devil had been in them; but for all that we took one of them, so that we had three of the four: this done, we returned aboard our junk, and by reason it was now midnight, we did nothing for the present but take our prisoners, and shut them up under the hatches where they remained until day; that *Antonio de Faria* came to view them, and seeing they were most of them aged, full of sorrow, and fit for nothing, he caused them to be set on shore, retaining only the bride and her 2 brothers, because they were young, white, and well-favoured, and some 20 mariners, which afterwards were of great use to us for the navigation of our junks. This bride as since we learn'd, was daughter to the *Anchary* of *Colem* (which signifies governour) and betrothed to a youth, the son of *Chisuu*, captain of *Pandurea*, who had written unto her that he would attend her in this place with 3 or 4 junks of his fathers, who was very rich; but alas! we shamefully cozened him. After dinner, being departed from thence, the bride-groom arrived seeking for his bride, with five sail full of flags, streamers, and banners? Passing by us, he saluted us with great store of musick and shews of gladness, ignorant of his misfortune, and that we carried away his wife. In this jollity he doubled the Cape of *Tilaumera*, where the day before we took this prize, and there anchored attending his bride, according as he had written to her, whilest we sailing on arrived three days after at the port of *Mutipiman*, which was the place we aymed at, in regard of the advice that *Antonio de Faria* had, that there they might sell off his commodities.

---

## CHAPTER XV.

Antonio de Faria's arrival at the Port: the information that Antonio de
Faria had of the country; some passages between him and the
Nautarel of the town; his going to the river of Madel; with his
incountring a pyrat there, and that which passed betwixt them.

BEING arrived at this port we anchored in a rode, which the land makes near to a little island on the south side of the mouth of the river, at the entry whereinto we remained without saluting the port, or making any noise, intending as soon as it was night to send for to sound the river, and to be informed of that we desired to know. Upon the appearing of the moon, which was about 11 of the clock, *Antonio de Faria* sent away one of his *Lanteaas*, well furnished, and 12 souldiers in her, besides the captain named *Valentino Martins Dalpoem*, a discreet man, and of great courage, that at other times had given good proof of himself in like occasions, who departing went alwayes sounding the depth of the river, until he arrived where divers vessels rode at anchor; there he took two men that were sleeping in a barque laden with earthen ware, and returning aboard undiscovered, he rendred *Antonio de Faria* an accompt of what he had found touching the greatness of the place, and the fewness of the ships that were in the port, wherefore his opinion was, that he might boldly enter into it, and if it happened he could not trade there as he desired, no ·body could hinder him from issuing forth whensoever he pleased, by reason the river was very large, clean, and without any shelves, sands or other things that might endanger him. Having consulted then with his company, he concluded by their advice, not to put the two *Mahometans*, that were taken, to torture as was before ordained, because there was no need of it; day being come, *Antonio de Faria*, desiring before he stirred to be informed from those two *Mahometans* of some particulars he would fain know, and thinking he might sooner prevail with them by fair means, then by menaces and torment, he made very much of them, and then declared his mind : whereupon both of them with one accord said, that touching the entrance of the river there was nothing to be feared, in regard it was one of the best in all that bay, and that ordinarily far greater vessels then his went in and out there, for that the shallowest place was 15 fathom at the least ; and as for the people of the country he was not to stand in any doubt of them, by reason they were naturally weak, and without arms ; and that the strangers which were at that instant there, arrived some 9 days before from the kingdom of *Benan* in 2 companies of fifty oxen a piece, laden with store of silver, wood of aloes, cloth, silk, linnen, ivory, wax, lacre, benjamin, camphire, and gold in powder, like to that of the island of *Samatra*, who were come with this merchandise to buy pepper, drugs, and pearls of the Isle of *Ainan*. Being demanded whether there was any army in those parts, they answered No, because most of the wars, which the *Prechau*, that is, the Emperour of the *Cauchins*, made, or were made against him, were by land ; and that when any was made upon the rivers, it was always with little vessels, and not with such great ships as his, for that they were not deep enough for them : further being asked, whether the *Prechau* was near to that place, they replyed, that he was 12 days journey from thence, at the city of *Quangepaaru*, where most commonly he with his court resided, governing the kingdom in peace and justice, and that the mynes, reserved for his Crown, rendred him in yearly rent fifteen thousand *Picos* of silver, every *Pico* weighing five quintals, the moyety whereof by the Divine law, inviolably observed in his countries, was for the poor labourers, that tilled the ground, to sustain their families withal ; but that all his people by a general consent had freely relinquished that right unto him, upon condition that from thence-forward he should not constrain them to pay tribute, or any other thing that might concern them, and that the ancient *Prechaus* had protested to accomplish it as long as the sun should give light to the earth. *Antonio de Faria* further demanded of them, what belief they were of ; where-unto they answered, that they held the very verity of all

verities, and that they believed there was but one God
Almighty, who as He had created all, so He preserved all;
howbeit if at any time our understandings were intangled
with the disorder and discord of our desires, that no way
proceeded from the sovereign Creator, in whom was no im-
perfection, but only from the sinner himself, that out of his
impatience judged according to the wicked inclination of his
heart. Moreover, asking of them, whether in their law they
believed, that the great God, which governeth this all, came
at any time into the world, clothed with a humane form, they
said No, because there could be nothing that might oblige Him
to so great an extremity, in regard He was through the
excellency of the Divine nature delivered from our miseries,
and far esloigned from the treasures of the earth, all things
being more then base in the presence of his splendor. By
these answers of theirs, we perceived that these people had
never attained to any knowledge of our truth, more then their
eyes made them to see in the picture of heaven, and in the
beauty of the day; for continually in their *Combayes*, which
are their prayers, lifting up their hands they say, *By Thy
works, Lord, we confess Thy greatness*. After this *Antonio de
Faria* set them at liberty, and having given them certain
presents, wherewith they were very well pleased, he caused
them to be conveyed to land; that done, the wind beginning a
little to rise he set sail, having all his vessels adorned with
divers coloured silks, their banners, flags and streamers,
displayed, and a standard of trade hung out after the manner
of the country, to the end they might be taken for merchants,
and not for pyrats, and so an hour after he anchored just
against the key of the town, which he saluted with a little
peal of ordnance, whereupon ten or eleven *Almadiaes* came
presently to us with good store of refreshments; howbeit
finding us to be strangers, and discerning by our habits that
we were neither *Siams*, *Jaos*, nor *Malayos*, nor yet of any
other nation that ever they had seen, they said one to another,
*Please Heaven, that the dew of the fresh morning may be as
profitable to us all, as this evening seems fair with the presence
of these whom our eyes behold*. Having said thus, one of the
*Almadiaes* asked leave to come aboard us, which they were

told they might do, because we were all their brothers; so
that three of nine, which were in that *Almadia*, entered into
our junk, whom *Antonio de Faria* received very kindly; and
causing them to sit down upon a Turky carpet by him, he
told them, that he was a merchant of the kingdom of *Siam*,
and going with his goods towards the Isle of *Ainan*, he had
been advertised, that he might better and more securely sell
off his commodities in this town, then in any other place,
because the merchants thereof were juster and truer of their
word, then the *Chineses* of the coast of *Ainan*; whereunto
they thus answered, *Thou art not deceived in that which thou
sayest, for if thou be a merchant, as thou affirmest, believe it,
that in every thing and every where thou shalt be honoured in this
place, wherefore thou mayest sleep without fear.*

*Antonio de Faria* mistrusting some intelligence might come
over land concerning that which he had done to the pyrat
upon the river of *Tanauquir*, and so might work him some
prejudice, would not dis-imbarque his goods, as the officers of
the Custom-house would have had, which was the cause of
much displeasure and vexation to him afterward, so that his
business was twice interrupted by that means, wherefore
perceiving that good words would not serve to make them
consent to his propositions, he sent them word by a merchant,
who dealt between them, that he knew well enough they had
a great deal of reason to require the landing of his goods,
because it was the usual course for every one so to do; but he
assured them that he could not possibly do it, in regard the
season was almost past, and therefore he was of necessity to
hasten his departure as soon as might be, the rather too for
the accommodating of the junk wherein he came, for as much
as she took in so much water, that 60 mariners were alwayes
labouring at three pumps to clear her, whereby he ran a great
hazard of losing all his goods; and that touching the kings
customs, he was contented to pay them, not after thirty in the
hundred, as they demanded, but after ten, as they did in other
kingdoms, and so much he would pay presently and willingly.
To this offer they rendred no answer, but detained him that
carried the message prisoner; *Antonio de Faria* seeing that his
messenger returned not, set sail immediately, hanging forth a

number of flags, as one that cared not whether he sold or no ; whereupon the merchants strangers that were come thither to trade, perceiving the commodities, of which they hoped to make some profit, to be going out of the port, through the perversness and obstinacy of the *Nautarel* of the town, they went all to him, and desired him to recal *Antonio de Faria*, otherwise they protested to complain to the king of the injustice he did them, in being the cause of hindering their traffique.  The *Nautarel*, that is, the governour, with all the officers of the Custom-house, fearing lest they might upon this occasion be turned out of their places, condescended to their request, upon condition since we would pay but ten in the hundred, that they should pay five more, whereunto they agreed, and instantly sent away the merchant, whom they had detained prisoner, with a letter full of complements, wherein they declared the agreement they had made. *Antonio de Faria* answered them, that since he was out of the port, he would not re-enter it upon any terms, by reason he had not leasure to make any stay; howbeit if they would buy his commodities in gross, bringing lingots of silver with them for that purpose, he would sell them to them, and in no other manner would deal, for he was much distasted with the little respect the *Nautarel* of the town had carried towards him, by despising his messages ; and if they were contented to accept thereof, that then they should let him know so much within an hour at the farthest, otherwise he would sail away to *Ainan*, where he might put off his commodities far better then there. They finding him so resolved, and doubting to lose so fair an occasion, as this was, for them to return into their country, embarqued themselves in five great lighter with forty chests full of lingots of silver, and a many sacks to bring away the pepper : and arriving at *Antonio de Faria's* junk, they were very well received by him, unto whom they represented, anew, the agreement they had made with the *Nautarel* of the town, greatly complaining of his ill government and of some wrongs, which without all reason he had done them ; but since they had pacified him by consenting to give him 15 in the hundred, whereof they would pay five ; they desired him to pay the ten, as he had promised, for otherways they could not buy his

commodities. Whereunto *Antonio de Faria* answered, that he
was contented so to do, more for the love of them, then for
any profit he hoped to reap thereby, for which they gave him
many thanks, and so being on all sides agreed, they used such
diligence in discharging the goods, as in 3 days the most of it
was weighed and consigned into the hands of the owners
thereof; whereupon the accompts were made up, and the
lingots of silver received, amounting in all to an hundred and
thirty thousand *Taeis*, after the rate of 7 shillings and six
pence the *Taei*, as I have said elsewhere. And though all
possible speed was used herein, yet before all was finished,
news came of that which we had done to the pyrat in the
river of *Tanauquir*, in so much that not one of the inhabitants
would come near us afterward, by reason whereof *Antonio de
Faria* was constrained to set sail in all haste.

After we had quit the river of *Mutepinan*, directing our
course northward, *Antonio de Faria* thought good to make to
the coast of the island of *Ainan*, for to seek out a river named
*Madel*, with a purpose there to accommodate the great junk,
wherein he was, because it took in much water, or provide
himself of a better in exchange upon any tearms whatsoever;
so having saild for the space of 12 days, with a contrary wind,
at length he arrived at the cape of *Pullo Hinho*, which is the
island of *Cocos*; there hearing no news of the pyrat he sought
for, he returned towards the south coast, where he took
certain prizes, which were of good value, and well gotten as
we thought. For it was the main intention of this captain
to deal with the pyrats which frequented this coast of *Ainan*,
as they before had done with divers Christians, in depriving
them of their lives and goods; for as God doth ordinarily
draw good out of evil, so it pleased Him out of His divine
justice to permit, that *Antonio de Faria*, in revenge of the
robbery committed by *Coia Acem* upon us in the port of *Lugor*
should in the pursuit of him chastise other thieves that
deserved to be punished by the hands of the *Portugals*. Now
having for certain days together with much labour continued
our navigation within this bay of *Cauchenchina*, as we were
newly entred into a port, called *Madel*, upon the day of the
Nativity of our Lady, being the 8 of *Septem.* for the fear that

we were in of the new moon, during the which there oftentimes happens in this climate such a terrible storm of wind
and rain, as it is not possible for ships to withstand it, which
by the *Chineses* is named *Tufan*, and that the sky charged full
with clouds had 4 days together threatned that which we
feared, it pleased God amongst many other junks that fled
into this port for shelter, there came in one belonging to a
notorious *Chinese* pyrat, named *Hinimilau*, who of a Gentile,
that he had been, was not long before become a *Mahometan*,
induced thereunto (as it was said) by a *Cacis* of that accursed
sect, who had made him such an enemy to the Christian
name, as he vaunted publiquely, that God did owe heaven
unto him for the great service he had done Him upon earth,
in depopulating it by little and little of the *Portugal* nation,
who from their mothers wombs delighted in their offences, as
the very inhabitants of the smoaky house, a name which they
give to hell; and thus did he with such sayings, and other
like blasphemies, speak as villanously and abominably of us
as could be imagined. This pyrat, entring into the river in a
very great and tall junk, came up to us where we rode at
anchor, and saluted us after the custom of the country,
whereunto we returned the like, as it is the manner there to
do at the entry into any of the ports, they neither knowing us
to be *Portugals*, nor we what they were; for we thought they
had been *Chineses*, and that they came into the port to shroud
themselves from the storms as others did, whereupon, behold,
five young men, that were Christians, whom this robber held
as slaves in his junk, guessing us to be *Portugals*, fell a crying
out three or four times together, *Lord, have mercy upon us*.
At these words we all stood up to see who they were, and
perceiving them to be Christians, we called aloud to the
mariners for to stay their course, which they would not do,
but contrarily beating up a drum, as it were in contempt of
us, they gave three great shouts, and withal brandished their
naked scymitars in the ayr in a way of threatning us, and
then cast anchor some quarter of a league beyond us. *Antonio
de Faria* desiring to learn the reason hereof, sent a *Balon* to
them, which no sooner arrived near them, but the barbarous
rogues pelted them with so many stones, that the vessel was

almost overwhelmed, so that they were glad to return, both
mariners and souldiers being very sore hurt ; *Antonio de Faria*
seeing them come back all bloody, demanded the cause of it :
*Sir,* answered they, *we are not able to tell you, only you behold
in what plight we are* ; saying so, and shewing him the hurts
on their heads, they declared unto him in what manner they
had been entertained. At first this accident much troubled
*Antonio do Faria,* so that he stood musing a good while upon
it, but at length turning himself to them that were present,
*Let every one here,* said he, *prepare himself, for I cannot be
perswaded but this is that dog* Coia Acem, *who I hope this day
shall pay for all the wrong he hath done us.* Whereupon he
commanded presently to weigh anchor, and with all the speed
that might be he set sail with the three junks and *Lanteas.*
Being come within a musket shot of them, he saluted them
with six and thirty pieces of ordnance, whereof twelve were
faulconers, and other field-pieces, amongst the which was one
of battery, that carried cast bullets, wherewith the enemies
were so amazed, as all the resolution they could take for the
instant was to leave their anchors in the sea, not having
leasure to weigh them, and to make to the shoar, wherein also
they failed of their desire; for *Antonio de Faria* perceiving
their design got before them and boarded their junk with all
the forces of his vessels: hereupon began a most furious
combat both with pikes, darts, and pots full of powder thrown
from either side, so that for half an hour it could not be
discerned who had the better : but at length it pleased God to
favour us so much, that the enemies finding themselves weary,
wounded, and hurt, threw themselves into the sea. *Antonio
de Faria,* seeing these wretches ready to sink, by reason of
the impetuousness and strength of the current, he imbarqued
himself with some souldiers in two balons, and with much
ado saved 16 men, whereunto he was induced by the great
need he stood in of them for the manning of his *Lanteas,*
because he had lost a great many of his people in the former
fights.

## CHAPTER XVI.

What Antonio de Faria did with the Captain of the Pyrats Junk; that
which past between him and the people of the Country; with our
casting away upon the Island of Thieves.

ANTONIO DE FARIA having obtained this victory in the
manner I have related, the first thing he did was to see his
hurt men drest, as that which chiefly imported him ; then being
given to understand that the pyrat *Hinimilau*, the captain of the
junk he had taken, was one of the sixteen he had saved, he
commanded him to be brought before him, and after he had
caused him to be drest of two wounds that he had received,
he demanded of him what was become of the young *Portugals*
which he held as slaves ?  Whereunto the pyrat, being mad
with rage, having answered that he could not tell, upon the
second demand that was made him, with menaces, he said,
that if first they would give him a little water, in regard he
was so dry as he was not able to speak, that then he would
consider what answer to make.  Thereupon having water
brought him, which he drunk so greedily as he spilt the most
part of it without quenching his thirst, he desired to have
some more given him, protesting that if they would let him
drink his fill, they would oblige him by the law of *Mahomets
Alcoran* voluntarily to confess all that they desired to know of
him.  *Antonio de Fario*, having given him as much as he would
drink, questioned him again about the young Christians ;
whereto he replyed, that he should find them in the chamber
of the prow ; thereupon he commanded 3 souldiers to go thither
and fetch them, who had no sooner opened the scuttle to bid
them come up, but they saw them lie dead in the place, with
their throats cut; which made them cry out, *Jesus, Jesus,
come hither we beseech you, Sir, and behold a most lamentable
spectacle* ; hereat *Antonio de Faria*, and those that were with
him, ran thither, and beholding those youths lying so one upon
another, he could not forbear shedding of tears ; having caused
them then to be brought upon the deck, together with a woman
and two pretty children, about 7 or 8 years old, that had their
throats also cut; he demanded of the pyrat why he used such

cruelty to those poor innocents : whereunto he answered, that
it was because they were traytours, in discovering themselves
to those, which were such great enemies to him as the *Portugals* were, and also for that having heard them call upon their
Christ for help, he desired to see whether he would deliver
them ; as for the two infants, there was cause enough to kill
them, for that they were the children of *Portugals*, whom he
ever hated : with the like extravagancy he answered to many
other questions which were propounded to him, and that with
so much obstinacy as if he had been a very devil. Afterwards
being asked whether he were a Christian, he answered, no ;
but that he had been one at such time as *Don Paulo de
Gama* was captain of *Malaca*. Whereunto *Antonio de Faria*
demanded of him, what moved him since he had been a
Christian, to forsake the law of *Jesus Christ*, wherein he was
assured of his salvation, for to embrace that of the false
prophet *Mahomet*, from whence he could hope for nothing but
the loss of his soul. Thereunto he answered, that he was
induced so to do, for that so long as he was a Christian, the
*Portugals* had alwayes contemned him, whereas before when
he was a *Gentile*, they called him *Quiay Necoda*, that is to say,
*Signior* captain ; but that respect immediately upon his baptism forsook him, which he verily believed did arrive to him by
*Mahomets* express permission, to the end it should open his eyes
to turn *Mahometan*, as after he did at *Bintan*, where the King
of *Jantana* was in person present at the ceremony, and that
ever since he had much honoured him, and that all the *Mandarins* called him brother, in regard of the vow he had made
upon the Holy Book of Flowers, that as long as he lived he
would be a sworn enemy to the *Portugals*, and of all others
that profest the name of Christ, for which both the King and
*Cacis Moulana* had exceedingly commended him, promising
that his soul should be most blessed if he performed that vow.
Being likewise demanded how long ago it was since he revolted,
what *Portugal* vessels he had taken, how many men he had
put to death, and what merchandize he had despoyled them
of ? He answered, that it was 7 years since he became a
*Mahometan* ; that the first vessel he took was *Luiso de Pavia's*
junk, which he surprised in the River of *Liampoo* with 400

bars of pepper only, and no other spice, whereof having made himself master, that he had put to death 18 *Portugals*, besides their slaves, of whom he made no reckoning, because they were not such as could satisfie the oath he made.   That after this prize he had taken our ships, and in them had put to death above 100 persons, amongst whom there were some 70 *Portugals*, and that he thought the merchandize in them amounted to fifteen or sixteen hundred bars of pepper, whereof the King of *Pan* had the better moyity for to give him a safe retreat in his ports, and to secure him from the *Portugals*, giving him to that purpose 100 men, with commandment to obey him as their king.   Being further demanded, whether he had not killed any *Portugals*, or lent an hand for the doing thereof, he said no, but that some two years before, being in the River of *Choaboquec* on the coast of *China*, a great junk arrived there with a great many *Portugals* in her, whereof an intimate friend of his named *Ruy Lobo*, was captain, whom *Don Estevan de Cama*, then governour of the fortress of *Malaca*, had sent thither in the way of commerce, and that upon the sale of his commodities going out of the port, his junk about five dayes after took so great a leak, as not being able to clear her, he was constrained to return towards the same port from whence he parted ; but that by ill fortune clapping on all his sails to get the sooner to land was overset by the violence of the wind, so as all were cast away, saving *Ruy Lobo*, 17 *Portugals*, and some slaves, who in their skiff made for the island of *Lamau*, without sail, without water, or any manner of victuals ; that in this extremity *Ruy Lobo*, relying on the ancient friendship that was between them, came with tears in his eyes, and praid him on his knees to receive him and his into his junk, which was then ready to set sail for *Patana*, whereunto he agreed, upon condition that therefore he should give him two thousand ducates, for the performance whereof he bound himself by his oath of a Christian.   But that after he had taken them in, he counselled by the *Mahometans* not to trust unto the friendship of Christians, lest he might endanger his own life ; for when they had recovered strength, they would without doubt seize upon his junk, and all the goods that were in her, it being their usual custom so to do in all places where they found themselves the strongest : wherefore fearing lest that which the *Mahometans* suggested should befall him, he slew them all on a night as they slept, for the which notwithstanding he was sorry afterwards. This declaration so much incensed *Antonio de Faria*, and all that were about him, as indeed the enormity of so wicked a fact did require, that presently, without questioning or hearing of him further, he commanded him to be put to death with four more of his company ; and so they were all thrown into the sea.

This justice being executed on the pyrat and his four companions, *Antonio de Faria* caused an inventory to be taken of all that was in the junk, which was adjudged to mount unto forty thousand *Taeis* in raw and twisted silk, pieces of sattin, damask, musk, fine pourcelains, and other less valuable commodities, which with the junk we were constrained to burn, because we wanted mariners for our navigation. With those valorous exploits the *Chineses* were so amazed, as they stood in dread of the very mention of the name of the *Portugals*, in so much that the *Necodaes*, or masters of the junks that were in the port, fearing the like might be done to them assembled all together in councel ; and there making election of two of the principal amongst them, whom they held most capable of performing their charge, they sent them as embassadours unto *Antonio de Faria*, desiring him, that as King of the Sea, he would protect them, upon the assurance of his word, so as they might pass safely out of the place where they were for to make their voyage whil'st the season served ; in consideration whereof, as his tributary subjects and slaves, they would give him twenty thousand *Taeis* in ingots of silver, whereof payment should be made out of hand, by way of acknowledging him to be their lord. *Antonio de Faria* received them very courteously, and granting their request, protested and sware to perform the same, and upon his word to protect them for the future, from having any of their goods taken from them by any pyrat ; whereupon one of the embassadours remained as surety for the twenty thousand *Taeis*, and the other went to fetch the ingots which he brought an hour after, together with a rich present of many several things sent him over and above by the *Necodaes*. This done, *Antonio de Faria* desiring to

advance a servant of his, named *Costa*, made him clark of the
patents that were to be granted to the *Necodaes*, whereof he
presently set a rate, namely five *Taeis* for a junk, and two
*Taeis* for a *Vanco*, *Lantea*, and small barque, which proved so
beneficial to him, that in the space of thirteen days, wherein
these patents we dispatched, he got (according to the report
of those that envyed him) above four thousand *Taeis* in silver,
besides many good gratuities that were given him for expedition.   The form of these patents was thus : *I give assurance
upon my word to* Necoda *such a one, that he shall sail safely all
about the coast of* China *without any disturbance, of any that
belongs to me, upon condition that wheresoever he meets with any*
Portugals, *he shall entreat them as brethren* : and underneath
he signed, *Antonio de Faria* : All which patents were most
exactly observed, and by that means he was redoubted all
along the coast, as the *Chaem* himself of the island of *Ainan*,
who is the Vice-roy thereof, upon the report which he heard
of him, sent to visit him by his embassadour, with a rich
present of pearls and jewels ; as also a letter, whereby he
desired him to take entertainment from the Son of the Sun, a
name which they give to the Emperour of this monarchy for
to serve him as Commander General of all the coast from
*Lamau* to *Liampoo*, with ten thousand *Taeis* pension yearly,
and that if he carried himself well, according to the renown went
of him, he assured him that upon the expiration of his three years
charge, he should be advanced into the rank of the *Chaems* of
the state, and that such men as he if they were faithful, might
attain to be one of the twelve *Tutoens* of the Empire, whom
the sovereign Son of the Sun, being the Lion crowned on the
throne of the world, admitted to his bed and board, as members united to his person by means of the honour, power, and
command that he gave them with an annual pension of an
hundred thousand *Taeis*.   *Antonio de Faria* gave him many
thanks for this offer, and excused himself with complements,
after their manner ; saying, that he was not capable of so
great favour as he would honour him withal, but that without
any regard at all of mony he would be ready to serve him as
often as the *Tutoens* of *Pequin* would be pleased to command
him,   After this going out of the port of *Madel*, where he had

been fourteen days, he ran all along the coast of that country for to find out *Coia Acem*, it being the main design of all his voyage, as I have declared before. Imagining then that he might meet with him in some of these places, he stayed there above six months, with much pain and hazard of his person. At length he arrived at a very fair town, named *Quangiparu*, wherein were goodly buildings and temples. In 'this port he abode all that day and the night following, under colour of being a merchant, peaceably buying that which was brought him aboard ; and because it was a town of fifteen hundred fires, as we guessed, the next morning by break of day we set sail without any great notice taken of us. So returning to sea, although it were with a contrary wind, in 12 days with a troublesome navigation he visited the shores both of the south and north coasts, without incountring any thing worthy the observation, although they were replenished with a many of little villages, whereof divers were inclosed with walls of brick, but not strong enough to withstand the force of thirty good soldiers, the people of themselves being very weak, and having no other arms but staves hardned in the fire ; howsoever the scituation of this country was under one of the best and fertilest climates on the earth, abounding with great store of cattel, and many goodly large fields, sowed with wheat, rice, barly, millet, and sundry other kinds of grain ; as also replenished with many great groves of pine, and *Angeline* trees, as in the *Indies*, able to furnish a world of shipping. Moreover, by the relation of certain merchants *Antonio de Faria* was informed, that in this land there were many mynes of copper, silver, tin, saltpeter, sulphur, and an infinite deal of untilled, but excellently good ground, altogether neglected by this weak nation, which were it in our power, we might in all probability be more advanced in the *Indies*, then now we are through the unhappiness of our sins.

After we had been 7 months and an half in this country, somtimes on the one side, somtimes on the other, from river to river, and on both coasts, north and south ; as also in the Isle of *Ainan*, without hearing any news of *Coia Acem*, the souldiers weary of so long and tedious travel, assembled altogether, and desired *Antonio de Faria*, to make a partition of that which had

been gotten, according to a promise before made to them by a
note under his hand, saying, that thereupon they would return
unto the *Indies*, or where else they thought good, whereby a
great deal of stir arose amongst us. At length it was agreed,
that we should go and winter in *Siam*, where all the goods
which were in the junk should be sold, and being reduced into
gold, division should be made of it, as was desired. With this
accord, sworn and signed by all, we went and anchored in an
island, called the island of Thieves, in regard it was the outermost island of all that bay, to the end that from thence we
might make our voyage with the first fair wind that should
blow. So having continued there twelve dayes with an earnest
desire to effect the agreement we had made together ; it fortuned that by the conjunction of the new moon in *October*,
which we had alwayes feared, there arose such a tempest of
rain and wind, as seemed to be no natural thing, in so much
that lying open to the south wind, as we traverst the coast,
the waves went so high, that though we used all means possible
to save our selves, cutting down our masts, and all the dead
works from poup to prow ; as also casting into the sea even the
most part of our merchandize, reducing our great ordnance
into their places again out of which they had been toss'd, and
strengthning our cables that were half rotten with ropes ;
but all this was not able to preserve us, for the night was so
dark, the weather so cold, the sea so rough, the wind so high,
and the storm so horrible, that in these extremities nothing
could deliver us but the meer mercy of God, whom with continual cries and tears we called upon for help. But for as
much as in regard of our sins we did not deserve to receive
this grace at His hands, His Divine Justice ordained, that
about 2 hours after midnight there came such a fearful gust of
wind, as drove our 4 vessels foul of one another upon the
shore, where they were all broken to pieces, so that 400 and
80 men were drowned, amongst which were eight *Portugals*, and it pleased God that the remainder being 53 persons
were saved, whereof 23 were *Portugals*, the rest slaves and
mariners. After this lamentable shipwrack, we got half naked,
and most of us hurt into a marish hard by, where we stayed
till the next morning ; and as soon as it was day we returned

to the sea side, which we found all strewed with dead
bodies, a spectacle of that dread and horrour as scarce
any one of us could forbear swooning to behold it : over
them we stood lamenting a great while, till such time as
*Antonio de Faria*, who by the mercy of God was one of those
that remained alive, whereof we were all very glad, concealing
the grief which we could not dissemble, came where we were,
having on a scarlet coat that he had taken from one of the
dead, and with a joyful countenance, his eyes dry and void of
tears, he made a short speech unto us, wherein he remonstrated how variable and uncertain the things of this world
were, and therefore he desired us, as brethren, that we would
endeavour to forget them, seeing the remembrance of them
was but a means to grieve us; for considering the time and
miserable estate whereunto we were reduced, we saw how
necessary his counsel was : and how he hoped that God would
in this desolate place present us with some good opportunity to
save our selves, and how we might be assured that He never permitted any evil but for a greater good; moreover how he firmly
believed, that though we had now lost five hundred thousand
crowns, we should ere it were long get above six hundred thousand for them. This brief exhortation was heard by us all with
tears and discomfort enough; so we spent two days and an half
there in burying the dead; during which time we recovered
some wet victuals, and provisions to sustain us withal; but
they lasted not above five dayes of fifteen that we stayed there,
for by reason of their wetness they corrupted presently, and
did us little good. After these 15 days it pleased God, who
never forsakes them that truly put their trust in Him, miraculously to send us a remedy, whereby we escaped out of that
misery we were in, as I will declare hereafter.

## CHAPTER XVII.

In what sort we escaped miraculously out of this island; our passage
from thence to the river of Xingrau ; our incountring with a Chinese
pyrat, and the agreement we made with him.

BEING escaped from this miserable shipwrack, it was a
lamentable thing to see how we walked up and down
almost naked, enduring such cruel cold and hunger, that many
of us talking one to another, fell down suddenly dead with
very weakness, which proceeded not so much from want of
victuals, as from the eating of such things as were hurtful to
us, by reason they were all rotten, and stunk so vilely, that no
man could endure the taste of them in his mouth.   But as our
God is an infinite good, there is no place so remote, for desert,
where the misery of sinners can be hid from the assistance of
His infinite mercy, which I speak, in regard that on the day,
when as the feast of S. *Michael* is celebrated, as we were
drowned in tears, and without hope of any humane help,
according as it seemed to the weakness of our little faith, a kite
came unexpectedly flying over our heads from behinde a point
which the island made towards the south, and by chance let
fall a fish called a mullet, about a foot long.   This fish falling
close by *Antonio de Faria,* he took it and caused it to be broyled
upon coals, and given to such of the sick as had most need of
it ; then looking towards the point of the island from whence
the kite came, we perceived divers others that in their flying
made many stoopings, whence we concluded that there was
some kind of prey there whereon these fowls fed ; now all of
us being most desirous of relief, we went thither in all haste,
and coming to the top of the higher ground, we discovered a
low vally full of divers fruit trees, and in the middle a river of
fresh water, whereupon by good fortune before we went down
we saw a stag newly killed, and a tyger beginning to eat him,
therewith we made a great cry which frighted him away into
the wood, leaving us the stag as he was.   Then descended we
to the river, and by the bank of it staid all that night, making
a feast, as well with the stag, as with divers mullets that we
took there ; for there were a great number of kites, that from

the water catched a many of those fishes, and oftentimes let
them fall being scared with our cries. Thus continued we by
the rivers till Saturday following, when about the break of day
we discerned a sail making as we thought towards the island
where we were : the better to be assured whereof we returned
to the shoar where we were wracked, and there staying about
half an hour, we found it to be so indeed, in which regard we
got us presently into the wood to decline discovery from those
in the vessel; which arriving in the port we perceived it to be
a *Lamea*, and that those that were in her fastned her to the
shoar with 2 cables, at the beak and the stern the better to
accommodate a plank for to pass in and out of her. Being all
dis-imbarqued out of her to about the number of thirty persons,
more or less, they went presently, some to making provision of
water and wood, some to washing of their linnen, and dressing
of meat, and others to wrastling, and such like pastimes, little
thinking to find any body in that place which could any way
annoy them. *Antonio de Faria* seeing them altogether without
fear and order, and that there was none remaining in the vessel
able to resist us ; *My masters,* said he unto us, *you behold the
wretched estate whereinto our mis-fortune hath reduced us,
whereof I confess my sins are the cause; but the mercy of God
is so infinite, as I am verily perswaded He will not suffer us to
perish thus miserably here, and therefore hath as it were miraculously sent this vessel hither, by seizing whereupon we may
escape from hence, which before to humane reason seemed almost
impossible : wherefore I exhort you all to joyn with me in
making our selves masters suddenly of her ere ever we be heard
or seen, and having so done, let our onely care be to possess our
selves of the arms we shall find in her, that therewith we may
defend our selves, and make good our possession, upon which,
next under God, our safety depends ; and as soon as you shall
hear me say three times,* Jesus, *do as you shall see me do.*
Whereunto we answered, that we would diligently perform
what he had enjoyned us ; so that we standing all prepared to
execute his design, *Antonio de Faria* gave the signal which he
had spoken of, and withall ran as fast as ever he could, and we
along with him, till he arrived at the *Lantea*, whereinto we
suddenly entered without any contradiction ; then unloosing

the two cables with which she was fastned, we put out to sea about a cross-bow shot from land. The *Chineses* surprized in this manner, ran all to the sea side, upon the noise that they heard; and seeing their vessel taken, were much amazed, but knew not how to help it; for we shot at them with an iron base that was in the *Lantea*, which made them fly into the wood, where no doubt they passed the rest of that day in lamenting the sad success of their ill fortune, as we had done ours before.

After we were gotten into the *Lantea*, and that we were sure the deceived *Chineses* could no way hurt us, we sat us down to eat that at leasure, which they had caused to make ready for their dinner by an old man, that we found there, and it was a great skillet full of rice with hached lard, whereunto we fell with good stomacks, as being not a little hungry. Dinner done, and thanks rendred to God for His gracious mercy to us, an inventory was taken of the goods that were in the *Lantea*, which was raw silks, damasks, sattins, together with three great pots of musk, amounting in all to the value of four thousand crowns, beside good store of rice, sugar, gammons of bacon, and two coups full of poultry, whereof we had more need then of all the rest, for the recovery of our sick men, which were not a few amongst us. Hereupon we all began without fear to cut out pieces of silk, therewith to accommodate every one with clothes. *Antonio de Faria*, having found a pretty boy in the *Lantea*, about some twelve or thirteen years old, demanded of him from whence she came, and what she did in this place, as also to whom she belonged, and whither she was bound. *Alas!* answered the boy, *she not long since belonged to my unfortunate father, whose ill hap it is to have that taken from him by you in less then an hour, which he hath been above thirty years in getting. He came from a place called* Quoaman, *where in exchange of lingots of silver he bought all these commodities that you have, with a purpose to have gone and sold them to the junks of* Siam, *which are in the port of* Comhay; *and wanting fresh water, it was his ill hap to come hither for to take in some, where you have robbed him of all that he hath, without any fear at all of the Divine justice.* Whereupon *Antonio de Faria* bade him leave weeping, and making much

of him, promised to use him as his own son, and that he
would alwayes account him so ; hereat smiling as it were in
disdain, he answered, *Think not though I am but a childe, that
I am so foolish to believe, that having robbed my father, thou
canst ever use me like thy son ; but if thou wilt do as thou sayest,
I beseech thee for the love of thy God suffer me to swim unto
that sad land, where he remains that begot me, who indeed is my
true father, with whom I had rather dye where I see him lamenting,
then live with such wicked people as you are.* Then some of
them that were present, reprehending and telling him that it
was not well spoken. *Would you know,* replyed he, *why I said
so ? It was because I saw you after you had filled your bellies,
praise God with lifted up hands, and yet for all that like hypo-
crites never care for making restitution of that you have stollen ;
but be assured, that after death you shall feel the rigorous chastisement of the Lord Almighty for so unjustly taking mens goods
from them.* Antonio de Faria, admiring the childs speech,
asked him whether he would become a Christian? Whereunto, earnestly beholding him, he answered, *I understand not
what you say, nor that you propounded ; declare it first unto me,
and then you shall know my mind further.* Then *Antonio de
Faria* began to instruct him therein after the best manner he
could, but the boy would not answer him a word ; only lifting
up his hands and eyes to heaven, he said, weeping, *Blessed be
Thy power, O Lord, that permits such people to live on the
earth, that speak so well of Thee, and yet so ill observe Thy law,
as these blinded miscreants do, who think that robbing and
preaching are things acceptable to Thee.* Having said so, he
got him into a corner, and there remained weeping for three
dayes together, without eating any thing that was presented
unto him. Hereupon falling to consult whether it were the
best course for us to hold from this place, either northward, or
southward, much dispute arose thereabout, at length it was
concluded that we would go to *Liampoo,* a port distant from
thence northwards two hundred and threescore leagues; for
we hoped that along this coast we might happen to incounter
and seize on some other greater and more commodious vessel
then that we had, which was too little for so long a voyage, in
regard of the dangerous storms that are ordinarily caused by

the new moons on the coast of *China*, where dayly many ships
are cast away. With this design we put to sea about sun-set,
and so went on this night with a south-west wind, and before
day we discovered a little island, named *Quintoo*, where we
surprized a fisher-boat full of fresh fish, of which we took as
much as we had need of, as also 8. of 12. men that were in
her for the service of our *Lantea*, by reason our own were so
feeble as they were not able to hold out any longer. These 8.
fishermen, being demanded what ports there were on this
coast to *Chincheo*, where we thought we might meet with
some ship of *Malaca*, answered, that about 18. leagues from
thence there was a good river and a good rode called *Xingrau*,
much frequented with junks, where we might be easily and
throughly accommodated with all that we stand in need of;
that at the entring into it, there was a little village named
*Xamoy*, inhabited with poor fishermen, and 3. leagues beyond
that, the town where was great store of silks, musk, pourcelains, and many other sorts of commodities, which were
transported into divers parts. Upon this advice we steered
our course towards that river, where we arrived the next day
immediately after dinner, and cast anchor just against it about
a league in the sea, for fear lest our ill fortune should run us
into the same mischief we were in before. The night following we took a *Peroo* of fishermen, of whom we demanded
what junks there were in this river, and how they were
man'd, with divers other questions proper for our design.
Whereunto they answered, that at the town up the river there
was not above 200. junks, by reason the greatest part were
already gone to *Ainan*, *Sumbor*, *Lailoo*, and other ports of
*Cauchenchina;* moreover, that we might ride in safety at
*Xamoy*, and that there we might buy any thing we wanted.
Whereupon we entred into the river, and anchored close to the
village, where we continued the space of half an hour, being
much about midnight. But *Antonio de Faria* seeing that the
*Lantea* wherein we sailed could not carry us to *Liampoo*, where
we purposed to lie all the winter, he concluded by the advice
of his company to furnish himself with a better vessel; and
although we were not then in case to enterprise any thing, yet
necessity constrained us to undertake more then our forces

would permit. Now there being at that instant a little junk
riding at anchor fast by us alone, and no other near her,
having but few men in her, and those asleep, *Antonio de Faria*
thought he had a good opportunity to effect his purpose;
wherefore leaving his anchor in the sea, he got up close to this
junk, and with 27. souldiers and 8. boyes boarded her on a
sudden unespied, where finding 7. or 8. *Chinese* mariners fast
asleep, he caused them to be taken, and bound hand and foot,
threatning if they cryed out never so little to kill them all,
which put them in such a fear, as they durst not so much as
quetch. Then cutting her cables, he got him straight into the
river, and sayled away with all the speed he could. The next
day we arrived at an island, named *Pulio Quirim*, distant from
*Xamoy* not above nine leagues; there meeting with a favourable gale within 3 dayes we went and anchored at another
island, called *Luxitay*, where in regard the ayr was wholsom,
and the water good, we thought fit to stay some 15. days for
the recovery of our sick men. In this place we visited the junk,
but found no other commodity in her then rice, the greatest
part whereof we cast into the sea, to make her the lighter and
securer for our voyage; then we unladed all her furniture into
the *Lantea*, and set her on ground for to caulk her, so that in
doing thereof, and making our provision of water, we spent (as
I said before) fifteen days in this island, by which time our sick
men fully recovered their health; whereupon we departed for
*Liampoo*, being given to understand, that many *Portugals* were
come thither from *Malaca*, *Sunda*, *Siam*, and *Patana*, as they
used ordinarily to do about that time for to winter there.

We had sailed two days together along the coast of *Lamau*
with a favourable wind, when it pleased God to make us
encounter with a junk of *Patana*, that came from *Lequio*, which
was commanded by a *Chinese* pyrat, named *Quiay Panian*, a
great friend of the *Portugal* nation, and much addicted to our
fashions and manner of life, with him there were thirty
*Portugals*, choice and proper men, whom he kept in pay, and
advantaged more then the rest with gifts and presents, so that
they were all very rich. This pyrat had no sooner discovered
us but he resolved to attaque us, thinking nothing less then that
we were *Portugals*, so that endeavouring to invest us, like an

old souldier that he was, and verst in the trade of pyrat, he got
the wind of us; that done, falling down within a musket shot
of us, he saluted us with 15. pieces of ordnance, wherewith we
were much affrighted, because the most of them were faulconets; but *Antonio de Faria* encouraging his men, like a
valiant captain, and a good Christian, disposed them on the
hatches in places most convenient, as well in the prow as the
poop, reserving some to be afterwards fitted as need should
require.  Being thus resolved to see the end of that which
Fortune should present us, it pleased God that we descried a
cross in our enemies flag, and on the fore-deck a number of red
caps, which our men were wont to wear at sea in those times,
whereby we were perswaded that they might be *Portugals*
that were going from *Liampoo* to *Malaca*; whereupon we made
them a sign to make our selves known to them, who no sooner
perceived that we were *Portugals*, but in token of joy they gave
a great shout, and withal vailing their two top sails in shew of
obedience, they sent their long boat, called a balon, with 2.
*Portugals* in her, for to learn what we were, and from whence
we came.  At length having well observed and considered us,
they approached with some more confidence to our junk; and
having saluted us, and we them, they came aboard her, where
*Antonio de Faria* received them very courteously; and for that
they were known to some of our souldiers, they continued there
a good while, during the which they recounted divers particulars unto us necessary for our design.  That done, *Antonio de
Faria* sent *Christovano Borralho* to accompany them back, and
to visit *Quiay Panian* from him, as also to deliver him a letter
full of complements, and many other offers of friendship,
wherewith this pyrat *Panian* was so contented and proud, that
he seemed not to be himself (such was his vanity) and passing
close by our junk, he took in all his sails; then accompanied
with 20. *Portugals*, he came and visited *Antonio de Faria* with
a goodly rich present, worth about two thousand ducates, as
well in ambergreece and pearls, as jewels of gold and silver,
*Antonio de Faria*, and the rest of us, received him with great
demonstrations of love and honour.  After this he and all his
company were set, *Antonio de Faria* fell to discourse with them
of divers things according to the time and occasion, and then

recited unto them his unhappy voyage, and the loss he had sustained ; and acquainting them with his determination to go unto *Liampoo,* for to re-inforce himself with men, and make provision of vessels with oars, to the end he might return again to pass once more into the Streight of *Cauchenchina,* and so get to the mynes of *Quoaniaparu,* where he had been told there were six large houses full of lingots of silver, besides a far greater quantity that was continually melted all along the river, and that without any peril one might be wonderfully enriched. Where-unto the pyrat *Panian* made this answer, *For my own part, Signior Captain, I am not so rich as many think, though it is true I have been so heretofore ; but having been beaten with the same misfortune, which thou sayest has befallen thee, my riches have been taken from me.* Now to return to Patana, *where I have a wife and children, I dare not, by reason I am assured that the King will despoil me of all that I should bring thither, because I departed from thence without his permission, which he would make a most hainous crime, to the end he might seize upon my estate, as he has done to others for far lesser occasions then that wherewith he may charge me. Wherefore if thou canst be con-tented that I shall accompany thee in the voyage thou meanest to undertake, with an hundred men that I have in my junk ; fifteen pieces of ordnance, thirty muskets, and fourty harquebuses, which these signiors, the* Portugals *that are with me do carry, I shall most willingly do it, upon condition that thou wilt impart unto me a third part of that which shall be gotten, and to that effect I desire thee to give me an assurance under thy hand, as also to swear unto me by thy law to perform it accordingly.* Antonio de Faria accepted of this offer very gladly, and after he had ren-dred him many thanks for it, he swore unto him upon the holy evangelists fully and without all fail to eccomplish what he required, and thereof likewise made him a promise under his hand, to which divers of their company subscribed their names as witnesses. This accord past between them, they went both together into a river, called *Anay,* some 5. leagues from thence, where they furnished themselves with all that they stood in need of, by means of a present of an hundred ducates, which they gave to the *Mandarin,* captain of the town,

## CHAPTER XVIII.

Our encounter at sea with a little fisher-boat, wherein were eight Portugals very sore hurt; and Antonio de Faria's meeting and fighting with Coia Acem the pyrat.

BEING parted from this river of *Anay*, and well provided of all things necessary for the voyage we had undertaken, *Antonio de Faria* resolved by the advice and councel of *Quiay Panian*, whom he much respected, to go and anchor in the port of *Chincheo*, there to be informed by such *Portugals* as were come from *Sunda, Malaca, Timor,* and *Patana*, of certain matters requisite for his design, and whether they had any news from *Liampoo*, in regard the report went in the country, that the King of *China* had sent thither a fleet of 400. junks, wherein there were an hundred thousand men, for to take the *Portugals* that resided there, and to burn their houses, for that he would not endure them to be any longer in his dominions, because he had been lately advertised, that they were not a people so faithful and peaceable as he had been formerly given to understand. Arriving then in the port of *Chincheo*, we found five *Portugal* ships, that were come thither about a month before, from the places above mentioned. These ships received us with great joy, and after they had given us intelligence of the country, traffique, and tranquility of the ports, they told us they had no other news from *Liampoo*, but that it was said a great number of *Portugals* were come thither from many parts to winter there; and how that great army, which we so much feared, was not thereabout; but that it was suspected to be gone for the islands of *Goto*, to the succour of *Sucan de Pontir*, from whom the bruit went a brother-in-law of his had taken his kingdom, and that in regard *Sucan* had lately made himself subject to the King of *China*, and his tributary for an hundred thousand *Taeis* by the year, he had in compensation thereof given him this great army of 400. junks, with the forces aforesaid, for to restore him to his crown and signiories, whereof he had been despoyled. Being very glad of this news, after we had remained in this port of *Chincheo* the space of 9. days, we departed from thence for *Liampoo*, taking along with us five and thirty souldiers more out of the five ships we found there, to whom *Antonio de Faria* gave very good pay ; and after we had sailed five days with a contrary wind, coasting from one side to another, without advancing any whit at all, it happened that one night about the first watch, we met with a little fisher-boat, or *Paroo*, wherein there were eight *Portugals*, very sore hurt, two of the which were named *Mem Taborda*, and *Antonio Anriques*, men of honour, and very much renowned in those quarters, the cause why in particular I name them. These and the other six were in such a pitiful estate, and so hideous to see to, as they moved every one to compassion. This *Paroo* coming close to *Antonio de Faria*, he caused them to be taken up into his junk, where they presently cast themselves at his feet, from whence he raised them up, weeping for pity to behold them so naked, and all bathed in their own blood with the wounds they had received, and then demanded of them the occasion of their misfortune : whereunto one of the two made answer, that about 17 days before they set sail from *Liampoo* for *Malaca*, and that being advanced as far as the Isle of *Sumbor*, they had been set upon by a pyrat, a *Guzarat* by nation, called *Coia Acem*, who had three junks, and four *Lanteaas*, wherein were fifteen hundred men, namely an hundred and fifty *Mahometans*, the rest *Luzzons*, *Jaoas*, and *Champaas*, people of the other side of *Malaya*, and that after they had fought with them from one to four in the afternoon, they had been taken with the death of fourscore and two men, whereof 18. were *Portugals*, and as many made slaves; and that in their junk, what of his and of others, there was lost in merchandize above an hundred thousand *Taeis*. *Antonio de Faria* remaining a good while pensive at that which these men related unto him, at length said unto them ; I pray tell me how was it possible for you to escape more than the rest, the fight passing as you deliver ? *After we had been fought withal about an hour and an half, the three great junks boarded us five times, and with the force of their shot they so tore the prow of our vessel, that we were ready to sink ; wherefore to keep out the water, and lighten our ship, we were constrained to cast the most part of our goods into the sea; and whil'st our men were laboring to do so, our enemies layed so*

*close at us, as every one was fain to leave that he was about, for
to defend himselfe on the hatches.   But whil'st we were thus
troubled, most of our company being hurt, and many slain, it
pleased God that one of the enemies junks came to be so furiously
fired, as it caught hold likewise of another that was fastned unto
it, which made the pyrats souldiers leave the fight for to go and
save their vessels ; yet that they could not do so speedily, but that
one of them was burnt down even to the very water, so that they
of the junk were compelled to leap into the sea to save themselves
from burning, where most of them were drowned.   In the mean
time we made shift to get our junk close to a stock of piles, which
fishermen had planted there against a rock, hard by the mouth
of the river, where at this present is the temple of the* Siams *; but
the dog* Coia Acem *was instantly with us, and having fast
grapled us, he leapt into our vessel, being followed by a great
number of* Mahometans, *all armed with coats of mail, and buff
jerkins, who straight way killed above an hundred and fifty of
ours, whereof eighteen were* Portugals *; which we no sooner perceived, but all wounded as we were, and spoyled with the fire, as
you see, we sought for some way to save our selves, and to that
end we sped us into a* Manchua, *that was fastned to the stern of
our junk ; wherein it pleased God that fifteen of us escaped,
whereof two dyed yesterday ; and of the thirteen that remain yet
miraculously alive, there are eight* Portugals, *and five servants.
In this sort we got us with all speed between this pallisado and
the land amongst the rocks, the better to preserve us from being
boarded by their junk, but they were otherwise employed in seeking to save the men of their burnt vessel ; and afterwards they
entered into our junk, where they were so carried away with the
bootie, as they never thought of pursuing us ; so that the sun
being almost set, and they wonderful glad of their victorie over
us, they retired into the river with great acclamations.   Antonio
de Faria,* very joyful of this news, though he was sad again on
the other side, for the bad success of those that had made him
this relation, rendred thanks unto God for that he had found
his enemy, it being a matter so much desired of him and his.
Certainly, said he unto them then, by your report they must
needs be now in great disorder, and much spoyled in the river
where they are ; for I am perſwaded that neither your junk,

nor that of theirs, which was fastned to the burnt one, can do them any longer service, and that in the great junk which assaulted you, it is not possible but that you have hurt and killed a good many. Whereunto they answered, that without doubt they had killed and hurt a great number. Then *Antonio de Faria*, putting off his cap, fell down on his knees, and with his hands and eyes lifted up to heaven, he said weeping, *O Lord Jesus Christ, my God and Saviour, even as thou art the true hope of those that put their trust in thee; I, that am the greatest sinner of all men, do most humbly beseech thee, in the name of thy servants that are here present, whose souls thou hast bought with Thy precious blood, that Thou wilt give us strength and victory against this cruel enemy, the murtherer of so many* Portugals, *whom with Thy favour and aid, and for the honour of Thy holy name, I have resolved to seek out, as hitherto I have done, to the end he may pay to Thy souldiers and faithful servants what he hath so long owed them.* Whereunto all that were by answered with one cry, *To them, to them, in the name of Jesus Christ, that this dog may now render us that, which for so long together he hath taken, as well from us, as from our poor miserable companions.* Hereupon with marvellous ardor and great acclamations, we set sail for the port of *Lailoo*, which we had left eight leagues behind us, whither by the advice of some of his company *Antonio de Faria* went to furnish himself with all that was necessary for the fight he hoped to make with the pyrat, in the quest of whom (as I have already delivered) he had spent so much time, and yet could never till then hear any news of him in all the ports and places where he had been.

The next morning we arrived at the port of *Lailoo*, where *Quiay Panian* had much kindred and many friends, so that he wanted no credit in that place; wherefore he intreated the *Mandarin* (who is the captain of the town) to permit us to buy for our mony such things as we stood in need of, which he instantly granted, as well for fear lest some displeasure might be done him, as for the sum of 1000 duckets, presented unto him by *Antonio de Faria*, wherewith he rested very well satisfied. Hereupon some of our company went ashore, who with all diligence bought whatsoever we wanted, as saltpeter, and sulphur to make powder, lead, bullets, victual, cordage, oyl, pitch, rosin, ockam, timber, planks, arms, darts, staves hardened in the fire, masts, sails, sail-yards, targets, flints, pullies, and anchors; that done, we took in fresh water, and furnished our vessels with mariners. Now although that this place contained not above three or four hundred houses, yet was there both there, and in the villages adjoyning, such a quantity of the aforesaid things, that in truth it were hard to express it; for *China* is excellent in this, that it may vaunt to be the country in the world most abounding in all things that may be desired. Besides for that *Antonio de Faria* was exceeding liberal, in regard he spent out of the general booty, before the partitions were made, he paid for all that he bought at the price the sellers would set, by means whereof he had more brought him by far then he had use for; so that within 13 dayes he went out of this port wonderfully well accommodated, with two other new great junks, which he had exchanged for two little ones that he had, and 2 *Lanteaas* with oars, as also 160 mariners, both for rowing, and for governing the sails. After all these preparations were made, and we ready to weigh anchor, a general muster was taken of all that were in our army, which in number was found to be 500 persons, as well for fight, as for the service and navigation of our vessels, amongst whom were fourscore and fifteen *Portugals*, young and resolute, the rest were boys, and mariners, and men of the other coast, which *Quia Panian* kept in pay, and were well practised to sea-fight, as they that had been five years pyrats. Moreover, we had 160 harquebuses, forty pieces of brass ordnance, whereof twenty were field-pieces, that carried stone-bullets, threescore quintals of powder; namely, fifty-four for the great ordnance, and six for the harquebuses, besides what the harquebusiers had already delivered to them, nine hundred pots of artificial fire, whereof four hundred were of powder, and five hundred of unslaked lime after the *Chinese* manner, a great number of stones, arrows, half-pikes, four thousand small javelings, store of hatchets to serve at boarding, six boats full of flints, wherewith the sailors fought; twelve cramp-irons with their hooks fastned to great iron chains for to grapple vessels together, and many sorts of fire-works, which an

engineer of the *Levant* made for us. With all this equipage
we departed from this port of *Lailoo*, and within 3 days after
it pleased God that we arrived at the fishing place, where *Coia
Acem* took the *Portugals* junk. There as soon as it was night,
*Antonio de Faria* sent spies into the river, for to learn where-
abouts he was, we took a *Paroo*, with six fishermen in her, that
gave us to understand how this pirat was some 2 leagues from
thence in a river called *Tinlau*, and that he was accommodating
the junk he had taken from the *Portugals*, for to go in her,
with two others that he had, unto *Siam*, where he was born,
and that he was to depart within 2 days. Upon this news
*Antonio de Faria* called some of his company to councel, where
it was concluded that first of all the places and forces of our
enemy was to be visited and seen, because in a matter of so
much hazard, it was not safe to run as it were blindfold, unto
it, but to advise on it well beforehand; and that upon the certainty of that which should be known, such resolution might
afterwards be taken, as should seem good to all ; then drawing
the fishermen out of the *Paroo*, he put some of *Quiay Panians*
mariners into her, and sending her away only with the two of
those fishermen, keeping the rest as hostages, he committed
the charge of her to a valiant souldier, named *Vincentio Morosa*,
attired after the *Chinese* fashion, for fear of discovery ; who
arriving at the place where the enemy rode, made shew of
fishing, as others did; and by that means espied all that he
came for, whereupon returning, he gave an account of what he
had seen, and assured us that the enemies were so weak, as
upon boarding of them they might easily be taken. *Antonio
de Faria* caused the most experienced men of his company to be
assembled, to advise thereon, and that in *Quiay Panians* junk,
to honour him the more, as also to maintain his friendship,
which he much esteem'd. At this meeting it was resolved,
that as soon as it was night, they should go and anchor at the
mouth of the river where the enemy lay, for to set upon him
the next morning before day. This agreed unto by all, *Antonio
de Faria* set down what order and course should be held at the
entring into the river, and how the enemy should be assaulted:
then dividing his men, he placed thirty *Portugals* in *Quiay
Panians* junk, such as he pleased to choose, because he would

be sure to give him no distaste; likewise he disposed six *Portugals* into each of the *Lanteaas*, and into *Christovano Borralho's* junk twenty; the rest of the *Portugals*, being 33. he retained with himself, besides slaves and divers Christians, all valiant and trusty men. Thus accommodated and ordered for the execution of his enterprize, he set sail towards the river of *Tinlau*, where he arrived about sun-set; and there keeping good watch he past the night till three of the clock in the morning, at which time he made to the enemy, who rode some half a league up in the river.

It pleased God that the sea was calm, and the wind so favourable, as our fleet sailing up the river, arrived in less than an hour close to the enemy, unperceived of any; but because they were thieves, and feared the people of the country, in regard of the great mischiefs and robberies which they dayly committed, they stood so upon their guard, and so good watch, that as soon as they discerned us, in all haste they rung an alarum with a bell, the sound whereof caused such a rumor and disorder, as well amongst them that were ashore, as those aboard, that one could hardly hear one another, by reason of the great noise they made. Whereupon *Antonio de Faria*, seeing we were discovered, cried out to his company, *To them, my masters, to them in the name of God, before they be succoured by their Lorches*; wherewith discharging all his ordnance, it pleased heaven, that the shot light to such purpose, as it over-threw and tore in pieces the most part of the valiantest that then, were mounted and appeared on the deck even right as we could have wished. In the neck hereof our harquebusiers, which might be some hundred and threescore, failed not to shoot upon the signal that had formerly been ordained for it, so that the hatches of the junk were cleared of all those that were upon them, and that with such a slaughter, as not an enemy durst appear there afterwards; at which very instant our two junks boarded their two in the case they were in, where the fight grew so hot on either side, as I confess I am not able to relate in particular, what passed therein, though I was present at it; for when it began it was scarce day. Now that which rendred the conflict betwixt us and our enemies most dreadful was the noise of drums, basins and bells, accom-

panied with the report of the great ordnance, wherewith the
valleys and rocks thereabouts resounded again. This fight
continuing in this manner some quarter of an hour, their
*Lorches* and *Lanteas* came forth from the shore to assist them
with fresh men, which one named *Diego Meyrelez*, in *Quiay
Panians* junk, perceiving, and that a gunner employed not his
shot to any purpose, in regard he was so beside himself with
fear, that he knew not what he did, as he was ready to give
fire to a piece, he thrust him away so rudely, as he threw him
down into the scuttle, saying to him, *Away villain, thou canst
do nothing, this business belongs to men, such as I am, not to
thee*: whereupon pointing the gun with its wedges of level, as
he knew very well how to do, he gave fire to the piece which
was charged with bullets and stones, and hitting the *Lorch*
that came foremost, carried away the upper part of her from
poup to prow, so that she presently sank, and all that were in
her, not a man saved. The shot then having past so through
the first *Lorch*, fell on the hatches of another *Lorch* that came
a little behind, and killed the captain of her, with six or seven
more that were by him, wherewith the two other *Lorches* were
so terrified, that going about to fly back to land, they fell foul
one of another, so as they could not clear themselves, but
remained entangled together, and not able to go forward or
backward, which perceived by the captains of our two *Lorches*,
called *Gasparo d'Oliveyra*, and *Vincentio Morosa*, they presently
set upon them, casting a great many artificial pots into them,
wherewith they were so fired, that they burnt down to the
very water, which made the most of those that were in them
to leap into the sea, where our men killed them all with their
pikes, so that in those three *Lorches* alone, there dyed above
two hundred persons; and in the other, whereof the captain
was slain, there was not one escaped, for *Quiay Panian* pursued them in a *Champana*, which was the boat of his junk,
and dispatched most of them as they were getting to land, the
rest were all battered against the rocks that were by the shore:
which the enemies in the junks perceiving, being some hundred
and fifty *Mahometans*, *Luzzons*, *Borneos*, and *Jaos*, they began
to be so discouraged, that many of them threw themselves
into the sea; whereupon the dog *Coia Acem*, who yet was not

known, ran to this disorder, for to animate his men. He had on a coat of mail lined with crimson sattin, edged with gold fringe, that had formerly belonged to some *Portugal*; and crying out with a loud voyce, that every one might hear him, he said 3 times, *Lah hilah, hilah la Mahumed rocol halah, Massulmens, and true believers in the holy law of Mahomet, will you suffer your selves to be vanquished by such feeble slaves as these Christian dogs, who have no more heart then white pullets, or bearded women ? To them, to them, for we are assured by the Book of Flowers, wherein the Prophet* Noby *doth promise eternal delights to the* Daroezes *of the house of* Mecqua, *that he will keep his word both with you and me ; provided, that we bathe our selves in the blood of these dogs without law.* With these cursed words the devil so incouraged them, that rallying all into one body, they reinforced the fight, and so valiantly made head against us, as it was a dreadful thing to see how desperately they ran amongst our weapons. In the mean time *Antonio de Faria* thus exhorted his men : *Courage valiant Christians, and whilest these wicked miscreants fortifie themselves in their devilish sect, let us trust in our Lord Jesus Christ nailed on the Cross for us, who will never forsake us, how great sinners soever we be ; for after all we are His, which these dogs here are not.* With this fervour and zeal of faith flying upon *Coia Acem*, to whom he had most spleen, he discharged so great a blow on his head with a two-handed sword, that cutting through a cap of mail he wore, he laid him at his feet, then redoubling with another reverse stroke he lamed him of both his legs, as he could not rise, which his followers beholding, they gave a mighty cry, and assaulted *Antonio de Faria* with such fury and hardiness, as they made no reckning of a many of *Portugals*, by whom they were invironed, but gave him divers blows that had almost overthrown him to the ground. Our men seeing this ran presently to his aid, and behaved themselves so well, that in half a quarter of an hour fourty eight of our enemies, lay slaughtered on the dead body of *Coia Acem*, and but fourteen of ours, whereof there were not above five *Portugals*, the rest were servants and slaves, good and faithful Christians. The remainder of them, beginning to faint, retired in disorder towards the foredeck, with an intent to fortifie themselves there, for prevention whereof 20 souldiers of thirty that were in *Quiay Panians* junk, ran instantly and got before them ; so that ere they could render themselves masters of what they pretended unto, they were inforced to leap into the sea, where they fell one upon another, and were by our men quite made an end of, so that of all their number they remained but only five, whom they took alive, and cast into the hold bound hand and foot, to the end they might afterwards be forced by torments to confess certain matters that should be demanded of them ; but they fairly tore out one anothers throats with their teeth, for fear of the death they expected, which yet could not keep them from being dismembred by our servants, and after thrown into the sea, in the company of the dog; *Coia Acem* their captain, great *Cacis* of the King of *Bintan*, the Shedder and Drinker of the blood of *Portugals* ; titles which he ordinarily gave himself in his letters, and which he published openly to all *Mahometans*, by reason whereof, and for the superstition of his cursed sect, he was greatly honoured by them.

## CHAPTER XIX.

### What Antonio de Faria did after his victory.

THIS bloody battel finished with the honour of the victory, before mentioned, in the description whereof I have not used many words ; for if I should undertake to recount the particulars of it, and set forth all that was performed by ours, as also the valour wherewith the enemies defended themselves, besides that I am not able to do it, I should then be forced to make a far larger discourse, and more ample history then this is : but it being my intention to declare things *en passant*, I have laboured to speak succinctly in divers place, where possibly better wits then mine would amplifie matters in a more accomplished manner; and this is the reason that I have now delivered nothing but what was needful to be written. Returning then to my former discourse, I say, that the first thing *Antonio de*

*Faria* did after this victory was to see his hurt men looked unto, whereof there were about fourscore and twelve, the most part *Portugals*, our servants being included; as for the number of the dead there were on our side forty two, amongst which eight were *Portugals*, the loss of whom afflicted *Antonio de Faria* more then all the rest, and of the enemies three hundred and twenty, whereof an hundred and fifty fell by fire and sword, the remainder were drowned. Now albeit this victory brought a great deal of content to us all, yet were there many tears shed, both in general and particular for the slaughter of our companions, the most part of whose heads were cleft asunder with the enemies hatchets. After this *Antonio de Faria*, notwithstanding he was hurt in two or three places, went presently ashoar with those that were in case to accompany him, where the first thing he did was to give order for the burial of the dead; thereupon he surrounded the island for to see what he could discover. Compassing of it then in this sort he lighted upon a very pleasant valley, wherein were many gardens, replenished with sundry kinds of fruits; there also was a village of about forty or fifty very low houses, which the infamous *Coia Acem* had sacked, and in them slain many of the inhabitants, that had not the means to escape his hands. Further, in the said valley, and by a delicate river of fresh water, wherein were a number of mullets and trouts, he met with a very fair house, which seemed to be the *Pagode* of the village, that was full of sick and hurt persons, whom *Coia Acem* had put there to be cured; amongst these were divers *Mahometans* of his kindred, and others of his best souldiers, to the number of ninety six, who as soon as they perceived *Antonio de Faria* afar off cried out to him for mercy and forgiveness, but he would by no means hearken unto them, alledging that he could not spare those that had killed so many Christians; saying so, he caused the house to be fired in six or seven places, which in regard it was of wood, bepitched, and covered with dry palm-tree leaves, burned in such sort as it was dreadful to behold; in the mean time it would have moved any man to pity, to hear the lamentable cries made by these wretches within, and to see them cast themselves headlong out of the windows, where our men provoked with a desire for revenge, received them upon their pikes and halberds. This cruelty performed, *Antonio de Faria* returned to the sea side, where the junk lay that *Coia Acem* had taken a month before from the *Portugals* of *Liampoo*, and caused it to be lanched into the sea, having been formerly repaired and caulked, which being done, and he aboard again, he restored it to *Mem Tabordo*, and *Antonio Anriques*, to whom it belonged, as I have already declared.

[*Antonio de Faria departs from the river of Tinlau, is ship-wrecked on the point of Micuy, and loses his treasure-laden junk*, omitted.]

---

## CHAPTER XX.

Antonio de Faria hath news of the five Portugals that were made captives; his letter to the Mandarin of Nouday about them; and his assaulting the said town.

AFTER this furious tempest was wholly asswaged, *Antonio de Faria* incontinently imbarked himself in the other great junk, that he had taken from *Coia Acem*, whereof *Pedro de Silva* was captain, and setting sail, he departed with the rest of his company, which consisted of 3. junks, and 1. *Lorch* or *Lantea*, as the *Chineses* term them. The first thing he did then, was to go and anchor in the haven of *Nouday*, to the end, he might learn some news of the 13. captives that were carried thither; being arrived there about night he sent two small barques, called *Baloes*, well man'd, to spy the port, and sound the depth of the river; as also to observe the scituation of the country, and to learn by sunrise what ships were riding there; together with divers other matters answerable to his design; for which effect he commanded the mariners to endeavour all they could for to surprize some of the inhabitants of the town, that by them he might be truly informed what was become of the *Portugals*, by reason he was afraid they were already carried further up into the country. These *Baloes* went away about two hours after midnight, and arrived at a little village seated at the mouth of the river on a little stream of water, called *Nipaphau*: there it pleased God that they behaved themselves so well, as they returned before day aboard our junk, bringing along with them a barque laded with earthen vessels, and sugar canes, which they had found lying at anchor in the midst of the river: in this barque there were eight men, and two women, together with a little child some 6. or 7. years old, who seeing themselves thus in our power, became so transported with the fear of death, that they were in a manner besides themselves; which *Antonio de Faria* perceiving laboured all he could to comfort them, and began to speak them very fair; but to all his questions he could draw no other answer from them then these words following, *Do not kill us without cause, for God will require an account of our blood from you, because we are poor folks*, and saying thus, they wept and trembled in such sort, as they could scarce pronounce a word; whereupon *Antonio de Faria*, pitying their misery and simplicity, would importune them no further: howbeit, the better to compass his intent, he intreated a *Chinese* woman, that was a Christian, and came along with the pilot, to make much of them, and to assure them they should have no hurt, to the end, that being more confirmed by this means they might answer to that should be demanded of them: wherein the *Chinese* so well acquitted her self, and made them so tractable, as about an hour after they told her, that if the captain would let them freely return in their boat to the place from whence they were taken, they would willingly confess all that either they had heard or seen. *Antonio de Faria* having promised them to do so, and that with many words and protestations, one amongst them, that was ancienter, and that seemed to be of more authority then the rest, addressing himself to him: *Truly*, said he, *I do not rely much on thy words, because that by amplifying of them in such manner thou makest me afraid, that the effect will not be conformable to thy speech: wherefore I beseech thee to swear unto me by this element that bears thee, that thou wilt not fail to perform that which thou hast promised unto me: for otherwise perjuring thy self, be assured that the Lord, whose hand is Almighty, will be incensed against thee with such indignation, as the winds from above, and the seas from below, will never cease to oppose thy desires during thy voyages; for I vow unto thee by*

*the beauty of these stars, that lying is no less odious and abomin-
able in the sight of that Sovereign Lord, than the pride of those
judges on earth, that with scorn and contempt do answer those
which demand justice of them.* Antonio de Faria obliging himself by oath, as the old man required, to perform his word, the
*Chinese* said he was satisfied, and then he continued in this sort :
*About two dayes since I saw those men whom thou enquirest after,
laid in prison at* Nouday, *with great irons on their legs, because
it was believed they were notorious thieves, that made trade of
robbing such as they met upon the seas.* This relation very
much inraged and disquieted *Antonio de Faria,* who was perswaded that it might well be as the old man delivered ; so
that desiring to take some course for their deliverance as soon
as might be, he sent them a letter by one of the *Chineses,* retaining all the rest in hostage for him, who departed the next
morning by break of day ; and because it much imported the
*Chineses* to be delivered out of captivity, he that carried the
letter, and that was husband to one of the two women, which
had been taken in the boat of earthen vessels, and were now
aboard in our junk, made such speed, that he returned about noon,
with an answer endorsed on the letter we sent, and signed by all
the five *Portugals* ; thereby they gave *Antonio de Faria* to understand, that they were cruelly detained in prison, out of which
they did not think they should ever get, unless it were to go to
execution ; and therefore they besought him for the Passion of
our Lord Jesus Christ, that he would not suffer them to perish
there for want of succour, according as he had promised them
in their setting forth in that voyage ; and the rather in regard
it was only for his sake that they were reduced to that miserable estate ; hereunto they added many other very pitiful
intreaties as might well come from such poor wretches that
were captives under the tyranny of such fell and cruel people,
as the *Chineses* were. *Antonio de Faria,* having received this
letter, read it in the presence of all his company, of whom he
asked counsel thereupon ; but as they were many, so were
their opinions many and different, which was the occasion of
much contention amongst them ; whereby perceiving that
nothing would be concluded concerning this affair, he said to
them as it were in choler; *My masters and friends, I have*

*promised to God by a solemn oath that I have taken, never to part*
*from hence, till by some means or other I have recovered these*
*poor souldiers, my companions, though I should therefore venture*
*my life a thousand times, yea and all my estate, which I make*
*little reckoning of in regard of them. Wherefore my masters, I*
*earnestly desire you, that no man go about to oppose this resolu-*
*tion of mine, upon the execution whereof mine honour wholly*
*depends, for whosoever shall contrary me therein, I must take*
*him for mine enemy, as one that would seek the prejudice of my*
*soul.* To this speech all made answer, that he was in the
right, and for the discharge of his conscience nothing should
stay him from performing the same ; adding, moreover, that
all of them would stand to him in that behalf to the death.
The captain hereupon giving them many thanks, and with
tears in his eyes, and his hat in his hand, imbracing them, protested that he would when time should serve acknowledge this
good-will of theirs in such real manner as it deserved, wherewith they all remained very well satisfied.

This resolution being taken, they fell to councel concerning
the carriage of this affair, whereupon they concluded to treat
with the *Mandarin* in a gentle manner, and for that end to
send unto him to demand these prisoners, with promise to give
him for their ransom whatsoever should be thought reasonable,
and that according to his answer such further courses should
be taken therein as should seem requisite. A petition then was
presently drawn, answerable to the form that was usually
presented to the judges, which *Antonio de Faria* sent to the
*Mandarin* by 2. of the chiefest of the *Chineses* he had taken,
who also carried him a present worth 200. ducates, whereby he
hoped to induce him to restore the poor prisoners ; but it fell
out far otherwise then he expected : for as soon as the *Chineses*
had delivered the petition and the present, they returned the
next day with an answer written on the back of the petition,
the tenor whereof was this ; *Let thy mouth come and present*
*it self at my feet, and after I have heard thee, I will do thee*
*justice.* *Antonio de Faria* seeing what high words the *Mandarin*
gave, was exceedingly troubled, because he well perceiv'd by
this beginning that he should have much ado to deliver his
companions : wherefore having communicated this affair in

particular to some few, whom for that end he had called unto
him, they were of several opinions; nevertheless after good
deliberation, it was at length concluded to send another messenger, that should more effectually demand the prisoners of
him, and for their ransom offer the sum of 2000. *Taeis* in
lingots of silver and commodities, declaring unto him, that he
would not part from that place till he had return'd them; for
he made account that it might be this resolution would oblige
him to do that which he had refused him another way, or that
he would be carried to it by the consideration of his own gain
and interest.   So the 2. *Chineses* went again the second time
with a letter seal'd up, as from one person to another, without
any kind of ceremony or complement which these Gentiles so
much use amongst themselves; and this *Antonio de Faria* did
of purpose, to the end, that by the sharpness of this letter the
*Mandarin* might know he was displeased, and resolved to
execute what he had written.   But before I proceed any
further, I will only relate the two main points of the contents
of the letter, which were the cause of the utter ruine of this
business.   The first was, when *Antonio de Faria* said, that he
was a merchant stranger, *Portugal* by nation, that was going
by way of traffique towards the port of *Liampoo*, where there
were also many other merchants strangers like himself, who
duly paid the usual customs, without committing any manner
of ill, or injustice.   The second point was, where he said, that
the king of *Portugal* his master was allyed in a brotherly
amity with the king of *China*, by reason whereof they traded
in his country, as the *Chineses* used to do at *Malaca*, where
they were entertained with all favour and justice duly ministred
unto them.   Now though both these points were distasteful to
the *Mandarin*, yet the last wherein he mentioned the king of
*Portugal* to be brother to the king of *China*, was that which
put him so out of patience, that without any regard at all he
commanded them that brought the letter, not only to be
cruelly scourged, but to have their noses cut off, and in that
pickle he sent them back to *Antonio de Faria*, with an answer
written on a scurvie piece of torn paper; where these words were
written: *Stinking Carrion, begotten of vile flies in the filthiest
sink that ever was in any dungeon of a lothsome prison, what*

*hath made thy baseness so bold, as that thou darest undertake to*
*meddle with Heavenly things ?  Having caused thy petition to be*
*read, whereby like a Lord, as I am, thou prayest me to have pity*
*on thee, which art but a poor wretch, my greatness, out of its*
*generosity, was even deigning to accept of that little thou pre-*
*sentedst me withal, and was also inclining to grant thy request,*
*when as my ears were touched with the horrible blasphemy of*
*thy arrogance, which made thee term thy King brother to the Son*
*of the Sun, the Lion crowned by an incredible power in the throne*
*of the world, under whose feet all the diadems of those that*
*govern the Universe are subjected, nay all scepters do serve but*
*as latchets to his most rich sandals, as the writers of the*
*golden temple do certifie under the Law of their Verities, and*
*that through the whole habitable earth.   Know then, that for*
*the great heresie thou hast uttered, I have caused thy paper to*
*be burnt, thereby representing the vile effigies of thy person,*
*which I desire to use in like manner for the enormous crime thou*
*hast committed : wherefore I command thee to be speedily pack-*
*ing, that the river which bears thee may not be accursed.*   So
soon as the interpreter had read the letter, and expounded the
contents thereof; all that heard it were much vexed therewith,
but no man was so sensible of it as *Antonio de Faria*, who was
exceedingly grieved to see himself thus wholly deprived of all
hope of recovering his prisoners ; wherefore after they had well
considered the insolent words of the *Mandarins* letter, and his
great discourtesie, they in the end concluded to go ashoar, and
attaque the town, in hope that God would assist them, seeing
their intentions were good ; for this effect they instantly prepared vessels to land with, which were the four fishermens
great barques that they had taken the night before : whereupon taking a muster of the forces he could make for this
enterprize, he found the number to be 300. whereof 40. were
*Portugals*, the rest were slaves and mariners, besides *Quiay*
*Panians* men, amongst whom were an hundred and threescore
harquebusiers, the other were armed with pikes and lances ; he
had also some pieces of ordnance, and other things necessary
for his design.

  The next morning a little before day, *Antonio de Faria* sailed
up the river with three junks, the *Lorches,* and four barques he

had taken, and so went and anchored at, six fathom and an
half of water close by the walls of the town; then causing the
sails to be taken down without any noise, or discharge of
ordnance, he displayed the banner of trade according to the
fashion of *China,* to the end that by this demonstration of
peace, no complement should rest unperformed, although he
was persuaded that nothing would prevail with the *Mandarin :*
hereupon he sent another messenger unto him, never making
shew that he had received any ill usage from him, by whom
with a great deal of complement he demanded the prisoners,
and offered him a round sum of mony for their ransom, with a
promise of perpetual correspondence and amity; but so far
was this dog the *Mandarin* from hearkning thereunto, that contrariwise he made the poor *Chinese,* that carried the letter, to
be hewed in pieces, and so shewed him from the top of the wall
to the whole fleet, the more to despight us.  This tragical act
wholly deprived *Antonio de Faria* of that little hope which
some had given him for the deliverance of the prisoners ; hereupon the soldiers, being more incensed then before, said unto
him, that since he had resolved to land, he should no longer
defer it, because further delay would but give his enemies
leisure to gather more strength.  This counsel seeming good to
him, he presently imbarqued with them he had chosen for the
action, having first given order to shoot continually at the town,
and the enemy, wheresoever they perceivd any store of people
assembled ; howbeit, with this caution, to forbear till they saw
them together by the ears with them.  Having landed them
about a faulcon shot below the rode, he marched without any
let along the shoars side directly to the town : in the mean
time a number of people appeared upon the walls, with divers
ensigns of different colours, where these barbarians made a
mighty noise, with fifes, drums, and bells, and withal hooting at
us, made us signs with their caps to approach, thereby intima-
ting the little reckning they made of us.  Now by that time we
were come within a musket shot of the walls, we discerned
1000. or 1200. men, as we guessed, sally out at 2. several gates,
of which some 120. were mounted on horses, or to say better,
on lean carrion tits that were nothing but skin and bone,
wherewith they began to course up and down the field in a

skirmishing manner, wherein they shewed themselves so un-
toward, as they often ran one upon another, and tumbled down
together; which when *Antonio de Faria* saw he was exceeding
glad, and encouraged his men to fight.   He stood firm attending the enemy, who continued still wheeling about us, being
perswaded it seems, that that would suffice to skare us, and
make us retire to our vessels; but when they perceived us remain
unmoved, without turning our backs, as they believed, and as
it may be, they desired we would do, they closed themselves into
one body, and so in a very ill order they made a stand without
advancing on.   But then our captain, seeing them in this
posture, caused all his musketeers to discharge at one instant,
who till that time had not stirred, which such effect, as it
pleased God that the most part of this goodly cavalry fell to
the ground with fear; we taking this for a good presage ran
and lustily pursued them, invoking the name of Jesus, whose
good pleasure it was, through His Divine mercy, to make our
enemies flye before us so amazed, and in such disorder, as they
tumbled pell-mell one upon another, in which manner arriving
at a bridge that crost the town ditch, they were so pestered
together, as they could neither go forward nor backward: in
the mean time our forces coming up to them, discharged their
shot to such purpose amongst them, that we laid three hundred of them on the earth, which in truth was a pitiful sight
to behold, because there was not one of them that had the
heart so much as to draw a sword: whereupon hotly pursuing
the first point of this victory, we ran to the gate, where we
found the *Mandarin* in the front of six hundred men, mounted
upon a good horse, having on a cuirass lined with purple velvet,
which had belonged, as we knew afterwards to a *Portugal*,
named *Tome Perez*, whom King *Don Emanuel*, of glorious
memory had sent as Ambassadour to *China*, in *Fernando Perez*,
his ship, at such time as *Lopo Suarez d' Albergaria* governed
the *Indies*.   At the entrance into the gate, the *Mandarin* and
his people made head against us, so that there was a shrewd
bickering between us, this enemy shewing another manner of
courage then we had met with on the bridge.; but by good
hap it fortuned that one of our servants hit the *Mandarin* just
in the breast with an harquebuss shot, and overthrew him dead

from his horse, wherewith all the *Chinesses* were so terrified, as they presently turned their backs, and in great disorder retired within the gate, not one of them having the wit to shut it after them, so that we chased them before us with our lances, as if they had been a drove of cattel. In this sort they fled pell mell together quite through a great street, and issued out at another gate, which was on the lands, from whence they got all away, not so much as one remaining behinde. Thereupon *Antonio de Faria*, assembling his men into one body, for fear of some disorder, marched with them directly to the prison where our companions lay, who seeing us coming, gave a great cry; saying, *Lord have mercy upon us*; straightway the doors and iron-grates were broken up, and our poor fellows irons knocked off their legs; which being done, and they set at liberty, all our company had leave to make what purchase they could, to the end that without speaking afterwards of partition, every one might be master of what he had gotten. Howbeit *Antonio de Faria* desired them to perform it suddenly, and therefore he gave them but half an hours time for it; whereunto they all condescended very willingly, and so fell to ransaking the houses. In the meen space *Antonio de Faria* went to that of the *Mandarin*, which he took for his part, where he met with eight thousand *Taeis* in silver, together with eight great vessels full of musk, and that he caused to be reserved for himself; the rest he left to the servants that were with him, who moreover found there a great deal of raw silk, sattin, damask, and fine pourcelain, whereof every one took as much as he could carry; so as the four barques, and the three champanaes, that brought our men on shore, were four several times laden and unladen aboard the junks; insomuch that the meanest mariner amongst us spake not of this booty, but by whole cases, besides what each one concealed in his particular.

But when *Antonio de Faria* perceived that an hour and an half had been spent in pillaging, he commanded a surcease thereof, but his company were so hot upon the spoil, that by no means they would be drawn from it, wherein the persons of quality were most faulty; in which regard our captain, fearing lest some disaster might happen by reason the night ap-

proached, he caused the town to be set on fire in eleven or
twelve places; now for that most of it was built of firr, and
other wood, it was in such a flame within a quarter of an hour,
as to see it burn so; one would have taken it for a portraiture
of Hell. This done, and all our company retired, *Antonio de
Faria* embarqued without any impediment, every man being
well satisfied and contented, only it was great pity to behold a
number of handsome maids led away, tyed four and four, and
five and five together, with the matches of their muskets,
weeping and lamenting, whilest our people did nothing but
laugh and sing.

## CHAPTER XXI.

### Antonio de Faria's navigation till he came to the Port of Liampoo.

AFTER that *Antonio de Faria* had embarqued his men, the
first thing he did was to give order for the dressing of
those that were hurt, which were in number fifty, whereof eight
of them were *Portugals*, and the rest slaves and mariners. He
also took care for the burial of the dead, that were not above
nine, of which onely one was a *Portugal*. All that night we
kept good watch, and placed sentinels in sundry parts, for fear
of the junks that were upon the river; the next morning as
soon as it was day, our captain went to a little town that was
on the other side of the water, where he met not with any
inhabitant, they being all fled, howbeit he found a great deal of
merchandise in their houses, together with good store of
victuals, wherewith he had laded the junks, fearing lest that
which he had done in this place, should be the occasion of bar-
ring him from being furnished with any in the ports where he
should happen to arrive. Furthermore, by the advice of his
company, he resolved to go and winter, during the three
moneths he had yet to make his voyage in, at a certain desart
island, distant some fifteen leagues from the sea of *Liampoo*,
called *Pullo Hinhor*, where there was a good road, and good
water; whereunto he was chiefly induced, because he thought
that going directly to *Liampoo*, his voyage thither might bring

some prejudice to the traffique of the *Portugals*, who wintered there peaceably with their goods : and indeed this advice was so approved of every one, as it was generally applauded. Being departed then from *Nouday*, after we had sailed five days between the isles of *Comolem*, and the continent, we were set upon on *Saturday* about noone by a pirate, named *Premata Gundel*, a sworn enemy to the *Portugals*, unto whom he had oftentimes done much damage, as well at *Patana*, as at *Sunda*, *Siam*, and many other places, when he found himself the stronger. This rover believing that we were *Chineses* came and assailed us with 2 great junks, wherein there were two hundred fighting men, besides mariners : one of them being grappled to *Mem Taborda's* junk had almost made her self master of it, which *Quiay Panian* perceiving, who was a little before, he turned upon her, and with full sails running her on the starboard side gave her so terrible a shock, that they sank both together, whereby *Mem Taborda* was delivered from the danger he was in, howbeit *Quiay Panian* was instantly and opportunely succoured by three lorches, which *Antonio de Faria* had taken a little before at *Nouday*, that all his men in a manner were saved, but every one of the enemies were drowned. In the mean time the pirate *Premata Gundel* setting upon the great junk, wherein *Antonio de Faria* was, the first thing he did was to grapple her poop to prow with two great cramp-irons, fastened to long chains, whereupon began such a fight betwixt them, as deserved to be seen, which for half an hour was so couragiously maintained by the enemy, that *Antonio de Faria* and most of his men were hurt, and himself besides in danger twice to have been taken ; nevertheless it was his good hap to be relieved in time by three lorches, and a small junk, commanded by *Pedro de Sylva*, by which means it pleased God that ours not onely recovered what they had lost, but pressed the enemy in such sort, as the fight ended with the death of fourscore and six *Mahometans*, which were in *Antonio de Faria's* junk, and had held him up so strait, that our men had nothing left them but the fore-deck in her. After this we entred into the pirate's junk, and put all those to the edge of the sword that we found there, not sparing so much as one, all the mariners having cast themselves before

into the sea. Howbeit we got not this victory so cheap, but
that it cost seventeen mens lives, whereof five were *Portugals*, and of the best souldiers we had, besides three and forty
were hurt, *Antonio de Faria* being one of them, who had one
wound with a dart, and two with a sword. The fight being
ended in this sort, an inventory was taken of all that was
in the enemies junk, and this prize was estimated at fourscore thousand *Taeis*, the better part whereof consisted in
*Lingots* of silver of *Japan,* which the pirate had taken in
three merchants ships, that from *Firando* were bound for
*Chincheo,* so that the pirate had in this onely vessel to the
value of sixscore thousand crowns, and it was thought that
the other junk which was sunk was worth as much, to the
extreme grief of all our company. With this prize *Antonio
de Faria* retired to a little island, called *Buncalou,* which
was 3 or 4 leagues westward from thence, and much commended for good water, and safe riding. Having landed in
this place, we spent 18 days there, lodging in cabbins, that
were made for the accommodation of our hurt men. From
this island we sailed towards that part, whither we had
resolved before to go, namely, *Antonio de Faria* in the great
junk, *Mem Taborda,* and *Antonio Anriquez* in theirs, *Pedro de
Sylva* in the little junk, that was taken at *Nouday,* and *Quiay
Panian* with all his followers in the pirats, last taken, which
was given him in recompence of his that he had lost, together
with 20000 *Taeis* out of the general booty, wherewith he
rested very well contented, being done with consent of the
whole company at the request of *Antonio de Faria.* Sailing
in this manner we arrived 6 days after at the ports of *Liampoo,*
which are two islands, one just against another, distant 3
leagues from the place, where at that time the *Portugals*
used their commerce ; there they had built above a thousand
houses, that were governed by sheriffs, auditors, consuls,
judges, and 6 or 7 other kinde of officers, where the notaries
underneath the publick acts, which they made, wrote thus, *I,
such publick notary of this town of* Liampoo *for the King our
Sovereign Lord.* And this they did with as much confidence
and assurance, as if this place had been scituated between
*Santarem* and *Lisbon,* so that there were houses there which

cost three or four thousand ducates the building, but both they
and all the rest were afterwards demolished for our sins by the
*Chineses*, as I hope to relate more amply hereafter : whereby
one may see how uncertain our affairs are in *China*, whereof
the *Portugals* discourse with so much curiosity, and abused
with appearances make such account, never considering what
hazard they hourly run, and how they are exposed to infinite
disasters.

[*The Portuguese are received with much honour at Liampoo,
in which town they remain five months.*]

This term expired, *Antonio de Faria* made preparation of
vessels and men, for his voyage to the mines of *Quoaniaparu*;
for in regard the season was then proper for it, he resolved to
be gone as soon as possibly he could ; but in the mean time, it
happened that *Quiay Panian* fell into a dangerous sickness,
whereof not long after he died, to the extream grief of *Antonio
de Faria*, who exceedingly affected him for many good qualities
that were in him, worthy of his friendship, and therefore he
caused him to be honourably buried, as the last duty that he
could do for his friend. After the death of *Quiay Panian* he
was counselled not to hazard himself in that voyage, because
it was reported for a certainty, how all that countrey was
up in arms by reason of the wars which the *Prechau Muan*
had with the King of *Chamay*, and *Champaa*; and withall
he had information given him of a famous pirate, named
*Similau*, whom he went presently to seek out, and having
found him, the said *Similau* related strange wonders unto
him of an island, called *Calempluy*, where he assured him
there were 17 Kings of *China* interred in tombs of gold, as
also a great number of idols of the same metall, and such
other immense treasures, as I dare not deliver, for fear of not
being credited. Now *Antonio de Faria*, being naturally curious,
and carried with that ambition, whereunto souldiers are for
the most part inclined, lent so good ear to this *Chinese's*
report, as looking for no other assurance of it then what he
gave him, he presently resolved to undertake this voyage,
and expose himself to danger, without taking further counsel
of any man, whereat many of his friends were with reason
offended.

## CHAPTER XXII.

Antonio de Faria departs from Liampoo for to seek out the Island of
Calempluy, the strange things that we saw, and the hazard we ran in
our voyage thither.

THE season being now fit for navigation, and *Antonio de
Faria* furnished with all that was necessary for this new
voyage, which he had undertaken to make on *Munday* the 14th
of *May*, in the yeare 1542, he departed from this port to go to
the Island of *Calempluy* ; for which purpose he imbarqued in
two *Panoures*, resembling small gallies, but that they were a
little higher, by reason he was counselled not to use junks, as
well to avoid discovery, as in regard of the great currents of
water that descended from the Bay of *Nanquin*, which great
vessels with all their sails were not able to stem, especially at
the time wherein he set forth, for then the snows of *Tartaria*
and *Nixihumflao* dissolving ran all the months of *May, June,*
and *July*, into these seas with a most violent impetuosity.
In these two vessels were fifty *Portugals*, one priest to say
mass, and forty-eight mariners, all natives of *Patana*, as also
two and forty slaves, so that the whole number of our company
amounted to an hundred forty and one persons, for the Pirate
*Similau*, who was our pilot, would have no more men, nor
vessels, for fear of being known, because he was to traverse
the streight of *Nanquin*, and to enter into rivers that were
much frequented, whereby we might probably be subject to
great hazard. That day and all the night following we imployed in getting out from amongst the islands of *Angitur*, and
pursued our course through the seas, which the *Portugals* had
neither seen or sailed on till then. The first five days we had
the winde favourable enough, being still within sight of land
till we came to the mouth of the river of the fishings of *Nanquin* ; there we crost over a gulf of forty leagues, and discovered
a very high mountain, called *Nangofo*, towards the which
bending northwardly, we sailed fifty days ; at length the winde
abated somewhat, and because in that place the tides were
very great, *Similau* put into a little river, where was good
anchoring and riding, inhabited by men that were white and

handsome, having very little eyes like to the *Chineses*, but much different from them, both in language and attire. Now during the space of 3 days, that we continued there, the inhabitants would have no manner of communication with us, but contrari-wise they came in troops to the shore, by which we anchored, and running up and down like madmen they howled in a most hideous fashion, and shot at us with slings and cross-bows. As soon as the weather and the sea would permit us, *Similau*, by whom all was then governed, began to set sail, directing his course east north-east, and so proceeded 7 days in sight of land ; then traversing another gulf, and turning more directly to the east, he past through a streight, 10 leagues over, called *Sileupaquin* ; there he sailed 5 days more, still in view of many goodly cities and towns, this river being frequented with an infinite company of vessels ; where-upon *Antonio de Faria*, knowing that if he hapned to be discovered he should never escape with life, resolved to get from thence, and continue this course no longer, which *Similau* perceiving, and opposing the advice that every one gave him ; *Signior*, said he unto him, *I do not think that any of your company can accuse me for misperforming my duty hitherto, you know how at* Liampoo *I told you publickly in the General Council that was held in the church before an hundred* Portugals *at the least, that we were to expose our selves to great dangers, and chiefly my self, because I was a* Chinese *and a pilot, for all you could be made to endure but one death, whereas I should be made to endure two thousand if it were possible, whereby you may well conclude, that setting apart all treason, I must of necessity be faithful unto you, as I am, and ever will be, not onely in this voyage, but in all other enterprizes, in despight of those that murmur, and make false reports unto you of me ; howbeit if you fear the danger so much as you say, and are therefore pleased that we should take some other way less frequented with men and vessels ; and where we may sail without dread of any thing, then you must be contented to bestow a far longer time in this voyage, wherefore resolve with your company upon it with any further delay, or let us return back, for lo I am ready to do whatsoever you will.* Antonio de Faria, embracing, and giving him many thanks, fell to discourse with him about that other safer way of which he spake. Whereupon *Similau* told him, that some hundred and forty leagues further forwards to the north, there was a river somewhat larger by half a league, called *Sumhepadano*, where he should meet with no obstacle, for that it was not peopled like the streight of *Nanquin*, wherein they now were, but that then they should be retarded a moneth longer, by the exceeding much wynding of this river. *Antonio de Faria* thinking it far better to expose himself to a length of time, then to hazard his life for abridgement of way, followed the counsel that *Similau* gave him; so that going out of the streight of *Nanquin*, he coasted the land 5 days, at the end whereof we discovered a very high mountain towards the east, which *Similau* told us was called *Fanim*, approaching somewhat near unto it we entred into a very fair port, 40 fathom deep, that extending it self in the form of a crescent was sheltred from all sorts of windes, so spacious withall, as 2,000 vessels how great soever might ride there at ease. *Antonio de Faria* went ashore with some 10 or 11 souldiers, and rounded this haven, but could not meet with any one body, that could instruct him in the way he pretended to make, whereat he was very much vext, and greatly repented him for that without any kinde of consideration, or taking advice of any one, he had rashly, and out of a capricious humour, undertaken this voyage. Howbeit he dissembled this displeasure of his the best he could for fear lest his company should tax him with want of courage. In this haven he discoursed again with *Similau* before every one concerning this our navigation, which he told them was made but by guess; whereunto the *Chinese* answered, *Signior Captain, If I had any thing I could engage to you of more value then my head I protest unto you I would most willingly do it, for I am so sure of the course I hold, that I would not fear to give you my very children in hostage of the promise I made you at* Liampoo. *Nevertheless I advertise you again, that if repenting the undertaking of this enterprize you fear to proceed any further, in regard of the tales your people are ever tatling in your ear, as I have often observed, do but command, and you shall finde how ready I am to obey your pleasure. And whereas they would make you believe that I spin out this voyage longer then I promised you at* Liampoo, *the reason thereof you know well enough, which seemed*

*not amiss when I propounded it unto you, seeing then you once
allowed of it, let me intreat you to set your heart at rest for that
matter, and not to break off this design by returning back, whereby
at length you shall find how profitable this patience of yours
will prove.* This speech somewhat quieted *Antonio de Faria's*
minde, so that he bid him go on as he thought best, and never
trouble himself with the murmurings of the souldiers, whereof
he complained, saying, that it was ever the manner of such as
were idle, to finde fault with other mens actions, but if they
did not mend their errour the sooner, he would take a course
with them to make them to do it; wherewith *Similau* rested
very well satisfied and contented.

After we were gone from this haven, we sailed along the
coast above thirteen days together, always in sight of land, and
at length arrived at a port, called *Buxipalem,* in the height of
forty-nine degrees. We found this climate somewhat colder
then the rest, here we saw an infinite company of fishes and
serpents, of such strange forms, as I cannot speak of them
without fear; *Similau* told *Antonio de Faria* incredible things concerning them, as well of what he had seen himself; having been
there before, as of that had been reported unto him, especially
in the full moons of the moneths of *November, December,* and
*January,* when the storms reign there most, as indeed this
*Chinese* made it appear to our own eyes, whereby he justified
unto us the most of that which he had affirmed. For in this
place we saw fishes, in the shape of thornbacks, that were four
fathoms about, and had a muzzle like an ox; likewise we saw
others resembling great lizards, spotted all over with green and
black, having three rows of prickles on their backs, that were
very sharp, and of the bigness of an arrow; their bodies also
were full of the like, but they were neither so long, nor so
great as the others. These fishes would ever and anon bristle
up themselves like porcupines, which made them very dreadful
to behold; they had snouts that were very sharp and black,
with two crooked teeth out of each jaw-bone, two spans long,
like the tusks of a wild boar. We also saw fishes whose bodies
were exceeding black, so prodigious and great, that their heads
onely were above six spans broad. I will pass over in silence
many other fishes of sundry sorts, which we beheld in this

place, because I hold it not fit to stand upon things that were
out of our discourse ; let it suffice me to say, that during two
nights we stayed here we did not think ourselves safe, by
reason of lizards, whales, fishes and serpents, which in great
numbers shewed themselves to us.   Having left this haven of
*Buxipalem*, by us called the River of Serpents, which in great
numbers shewed themselves to us, *Similau* sailed fifteen leagues
further to another bay named *Calindano*, which was in form of
a crescent, six leagues in circuit, and invironed with high
mountains, and very thick woods, in the midst whereof divers
brooks of fresh water descended, which made up four great
rivers that fell all into this bay.   There *Similau* told us, that all
those prodigious creatures we had both seen and heard of, as
well in this bay, as in that where we were before, came thither
to feed upon such ordure and carrion, as the overflowing of
these rivers brought to this place.   *Antonio de Faria* demanding
of him, thereupon, whence those rivers should proceed, he
answered that he knew not, but it was said that the annals of
*China* affirmed, how two of those rivers took their beginnings
from a great lake, called *Moscombia*, and the other two from a
province, named *Alimania*, where there are high mountains,
that all the year long are covered with snow, so that the snow
coming to dissolve, these rivers swelled in that manner as we
then beheld them, for now they were bigger then at any other
time of the year.   Hereunto he added, that entring into the
mouth of the river, before the which we rode at anchor, we
should continue our course, steering eastward, for to find out
the port of *Nanquin* again, which we had left two hundred and
threescore leagues behind us, by reason that in all this distance
we had multiplied a greater height than that of the island was,
which we were in quest of.   Now although this was exceeding
grievous unto us, yet *Similau* desired *Antonio de Faria* to think
the time we had past well spent, because it was done for the
best, and for the better securing of our lives ; being asked then
by *Antonio de Faria* how long we should be in passing through
this river, he answered that we should be out of it in fourteen
or fifteen days, and that in five days after he would promise
to land him and his souldiers in the island of *Calempluy*, where
he hoped fully to content his desire, and to make him think

his pains well bestowed, whereof he now so complained. *Antonio de Faria*, having embraced him very lovingly thereupon, vowed to be his friend for ever, and reconciled him to his souldiers, who were very much out with him before. Being thus reconfirmed by *Similaus* speeches, and certified of this new course we were to take, he incouraged his company, and put all things in order convenient for his design, to that end preparing his ordnance which till then had never been charged; he caused also his arms to be made ready, ordained captains, and sentinels to keep good watch, together with all besides that he thought necessary for our defence, in case of any attempt upon us. That done, he spake unto *Diego Lobato*, who was the priest that we carried along with us, and one that we much respected, as a man of the church, to make a sermon unto his company for to animate them against all dangers that might happen, which he worthily performed, and by the efficacy of his words, full of sweetness, and excellent examples, he so revived our spirits, that before were much dejected through the apprehension of the dangers that menaced us; as there was not one amongst us but presently took fresh heart, boldly to excuse the enterprise we had undertaken. Whereupon with great devotion and zeal we sung a *Salvo*, before an image of our Lady, every man promising without any future fear to finish the voyage we had begun. That done, we joyfully hoysed sail, and entring into the mouth of the river, steering directly east, and with tears in our eyes, invoked from the bottome of our hearts, the assistance of that Sovereign Lord which sits at the right hand of the Father everlasting, to preserve us by His Almighty power.

Continuing on our course with the force of oars and sails, and steering divers ways, by reason of the many turnings of the river, the next day we arrived at a very high mountain called *Botinafau*, whence sundry rivers of fresh water ran down. In this mountain were a number tygers, rhinocerots, lyons, ounces, and such other creatures of several kinds, which running and roaring in their wilde manner, made cruel war upon other weaker beasts, as stags, boars, apes, monkeys, baboons, wolves, and foxes, wherein we took much delight, spending a great deal of time in beholding them; and ever and anon we

cryed out from our ships to fright them, but they were little
moved by it, in regard they were not used to be hunted. We
were about six days in passing this mountain, it being some
forty or fifty leagues long. Within a pretty while after we had
left this mountain we came to another, named *Gangitanon*, no
less wilde then the former, beyond the which all the country
was very stony, and almost inaccessible; moreover it was full
of such thick woods, as the sun could not possibly pierce them
with his beams. *Similau* told us, that in this mountain there
were ninety leagues of desart land, altogether unfit for tillage,
and the bottome thereof onely was inhabited by certain most
deformed men, called *Giganhos*, who lived after a most brutish
fashion, and fed on nothing but what they got in hunting, or
some rice, that the said merchants of *China* brought them to
*Catan* in exchange of Furs; which the said merchants carried
from thence to *Pocassor* and *Lantau*, amounting yearly as by
the books of the customs thereof appeared, to the number of
twenty thousand cates, each cate, or pack, containing threescore
skins, wherewith the people used in winter to line their gowns,
hang their houses, and make coverings for their beds, to withstand the cold of the climate, which is great there. *Antonio
de Faria* wondring at the relation this *Chinese* made of the
deformity of these *Giganhos*, desired him if it were possible to
let him see one of them, whereby he said he should more content him then if he should give him the treasures of *China*;
whereunto *Similau* made him this answer, *Signior Captain,
since it so much imports me, as well to maintain my credit
with you, as to stop their mouthes that murmur against me, and
that jogging one another scoff at me when I recount these things
unto you, which they account as so many fables, and to the end
that by the truth of the one, they may be ascertained of the
other, I will promise before sun-setting yet to shew you a
couple of these people, and that you shall also speak with them,
upon condition you do not go ashore, as you have still used
to do hitherto, for fear some mischance should happen to you, as
many times it doth to merchants in like cases: for I assure you,
that the* Giganhos *are of so savage and brutish a nature, as they
feed on nothing commonly but raw flesh and blood, like the wilde
beasts that live in this forrest.* So continuing our course all

along the side of this mountain, at length behind a little point
of land, we discovered a young youth, without ere an hair on
his face, driving six or seven cows before him, that pastured
there by. *Similau* making a sign to him with a napkin, he
presently stayed, whereupon coming a little neerer to him,
*Similau* shewed him a piece of green taffeta, which he told us
was a stuff very acceptable to these brutish men, and withal
by signs demanded of him whether he would buy it; this drew
him to the bank of the river, were he answered, with an hoarse
voice, some words that we could not comprehend, because
there was not one in all our vessels that understood this barbarous language, so that of necessity this commerce was to be
made by signs. *Antonio de Faria* commanded three or four
yards of the said piece of taffeta to be given him, as also six
pourcelains, wherewith this salvage seemed to be very well
pleased, for taking both the one and the other, transported
with joy he said something to us, which we could understand no better then the former, then making a sign with his
hand towards the place of his abode, he left his cows, and ran
away to the wood, clothed as he was with a tigers skin, his
arms and legs naked, bare-headed, and a staff hardned at one
end with the fire in his hand. For his person, he was well
proportioned of his limbs, his hair red and curled hanging
down on his shoulders; his stature by conjecture was above ten
foot high, but we were amazed to see him return about a quarter
of an hour to the very same place again, carrying a live stag
on his back, and having thirteen persons in his company,
namely eight men and five women, leading three cows tyed
together, and dancing as they went at the sound of a kind of
tabor, upon the which they beat five strokes at a time, and as
often clapped their hands together singing to it, with a very hoarse
voice in their language. Hereupon *Antonio de Faria* caused
five or six pieces of silk stuff, and a great many of pourcelains
to be shewed them, for to make them believe that we were merchants, at the sight whereof they very much rejoyced. These
persons, both men and women, were apparelled all after one
and the same fashion, without any kind of difference, saving
that the women wore great tinnen bracelets about the middle
of their arms, and their hair a great deal longer then the mens,

stuck all about with flowers, resembling our flower de luces;
they had chains also of red cockles about their necks, almost
as big as oyster-shels; as for the men, they carried great
staves in their hands, covered to the midst with the same
skins wherewith they were clothed; moreover they had all of
them fierce looks, great lips, flat noses, wide nostrils, and were
of stature very tall, but yet not so high as we thought they had
been; for *Antonio de Faria* having caused them to be measured,
he found that the tallest of them exceeded not ten spans and an
half, except one old man that reached to eleven. The womens
stature was not fully ten spans. Their very countenances
shewed them to be very rude and blockish, and less rational
then all the other people which we had seen in our conquests.
Now *Antonio de Faria* being glad that we had not altogether
lost our labour, bestowed on them threescore pourcelains, a
piece of green taffety, and a pannier full of pepper, wherewith
they seemed to be so contented, that prostrating themselves on
the ground, and lifting up their hands to heaven, they fell to
saying certain words which we took for a thanksgiving after
their manner, because they fell down three several times on the
earth, and gave us the three cows and the stag, as also a great
many of herbs. Having been talking about two hours with
them by signs, and no less wondring at us, then we at them,
they returned into the wood from whence they came, and we
pursued our course up the river by the space of five days,
during the which we saw more of them along by the water
side; after we had past all this distance of land, which might
be some forty leagues, or thereabouts, we navigated sixteen
days more with the force of oars and sails, without seeing any
person in that desart place, only for two nights together we
discerned certain fires a good way off at land. In the end, it
pleased God that we arrived at the Gulf of *Nanquin,* as *Similau*
had told us, with a hope in five or six days to see our desires
accomplished.

Being come into the gulf of *Nanquin, Similau* counselled
*Antonio de Faria,* that at any hand he should not suffer any
*Portugal* to be seen, because if such a thing should happen he
feared some uproar would follow amongst the *Chineses,* in
regard no strangers had ever been seen in those quarters;

adding withal, that it would be safer for them to keep still in
the middle of the gulf, then by the shore, by reason of the great
number of *Lorches* and *Lanteaas*, that incessantly sailed up and
down; this advice was approved of by every one; so that
having continued our course some six days east and east north-
east, we discovered a great town, called *Sileupamor*, whither
we directly went, and entred the haven about two hours
within night, where we found an infinite company of vessels
riding at anchor, to the number, according to our thinking, of
three thousand at the least, which gave us such an alarm, as
not daring scarce to wag we got out again with all the
secrecy that might be; crossing over the whole breadth of the
river then, which was some six or seven leagues, we prose-
cuted our course all the rest of that day, and coasted along by
a great plain, with a resolution to accommodate our selves
with victuals wheresoever we could first meet with any; for
we were in such scarcity, as for thirteen days together, no
man had more than three mouthfulls of boyled rice allowance.
Being in this extremity we arrived close to certain old buildings; there we went ashore one morning before day, and fell
upon a house, that stood a little way off from the rest, where
we found a great quantity of rice, some beans, divers pots full
of honey, poudred geese, onions, garlick, and sugar canes,
wherewith we thoroughly furnished our selves. Certain
*Chineses* told us afterwards, that this was the store-house of
an hospital, which was some two leagues off, where such
were entertained, as past that way in pilgrimage to the
sepulchres of the kings of *China*. Being reimbarqued, and
well provided of victual, we continued on our voyage seven
days more, which made up two moneths and an half, since we
put out of *Liampoo*. Then *Antonio de Faria* began to mistrust
the truth of what *Similau* had said, so that he repented the
undertaking of this voyage, as he confessed publiquely before
us all; nevertheless in regard there was no other remedy for
it but to recommend himself to God, and wisely to prepare
for all that might happen, he couragiously performed it.
Hereupon it fell out that *Antonio de Faria* having one morning
demanded of *Similau* in what part he thought they were, he
answered him so far from the purpose, and like a man that

had lost his judgement, or that knew not which way he had
gone, as put *Antonio de Faria* into such choler, that he was
going to stab him with a ponyard that he wore, which without
doubt he had done, had he not been diverted from it by some,
that counselled him to forbear, lest it should be the cause of his
utter ruine, whereupon moderating his anger he yielded to the
advice of his friends; nevertheless he was not for all that so
contained, but that taking him by the beard he swore, that if
within three days at the farthest, he did not let him see, either
the truth or the falshood of what he had told him, he would
ponyard him infallibly; wherewith *Similau* was so exceedingly terrified, that the night following as we were abiding by
the shore he slid down from the vessel into the river, and that
so closely, as he was never discovered by the sentinels or any
other until the end of the first watch, when as *Antonio de Faria*
was thereof advertised. This news put him so far besides himself, as he lost all patience, the rather for that he feared some
revolt upon it from his souldiers, who he saw were too much
disposed thereunto. But he presently went ashore with a
great many of his company, and spent the most part of the
night in seeking of *Similau*, without meeting him, or any other
living soul that was able to tell any news of him, but the worst
of it yet was, that upon his return into his junk, of forty six
*Chinese* mariners, that he had aboard him, he found six and
thirty fled away to prevent the danger they were afraid of,
whereat *Antonio de Faria* and all his company were so amazed,
that lifting up their hands and eyes to heaven, they stood a
long time mute, their tears supplying the defect of their speech,
thereby testifying the secret sorrow of their hearts, for considering well what had hapned unto them, and the great
peril they were in, the least that they could do in this confusion was to lose their courage and judgement, much more their
speech. Howbeit falling at length to consult what we should
do for the future, after much diversity of opinion, it was in the
end concluded, that we should pursue our design, and labour
to take some body that might inform us how far it was from
thence to the Island of *Calempluy*, and this to be done as
secretly as possible might be for fear the country should rise;
likewise that if upon the report should be made us we found it

would be easily taken, as *Similau* had assured us, we should then proceed on, otherwise, that we should return with the current of the water, which would bring us directly to the sea with its ordinary course. This resolution taken and approved of every one, we went on with no less confusion then fear, for in so manifest a danger we could not chuse but be very much perplexed; the night following about break of day we discovered a little barque ahead of us riding at anchor in the midst of the river; her we boarded with as little noise as might be, and took five men asleep in her, whom *Antonio de Faria* questioned each one apart by himself, to see how they would agree in that they said. To his demands they answered all of them, that the country wherein we were, was called *Temquilem*, from whence the Island of *Calempluy* was distant but ten leagues, and to many other questions propounded to them for our common security, they answered likewise separately one from the other to very good purpose, wherewith *Antonio de Faria* and his whole company, were exceedingly well satisfied, but yet it grieved us not a little, to think what an inconvenience the lack of *Similau* would prove to us in this attempt; however *Antonio de Faria* causing the five *Chineses* to be arrested, and chained to oars, continued his course two days and an half more, at the end whereof it pleased God that doubling a cape of land, called *Guimai Tarao*, we discovered this island of *Calempluy*, which we had been fourscore and three days seeking for, with extream confusion of pains and labour, as I have before related.

---

## CHAPTER XXIII.

Our arrival at Calempluy, and the description thereof; what hapned to Antonio de Faria in one of the hermitages thereof, and how we were discovered.

HAVING doubled the Cape of *Guimai Tarao*, two leagues beyond it, we discovered a goodly level of ground, scituated in the midst of a river, which to our seeming was not above a league in circuit, whereunto *Antonio de Faria* ap-

proached with exceeding great joy, which yet was intermingled
with much fear, because he knew not to what danger he and his
were exposed; about twelve of the clock at night he anchored
within a cannon shot of this island, and the next morning as
soon as it was day, he sate in councel with such of his company
as he had called to it, there it was concluded that it was not
possible so great and magnificent a thing should be without
some kind of guard, and therefore it was resolved that with the
greatest silence that might be, it should be rounded all about,
for to see what advenues it had, or what obstacles we might
meet with when there was question of landing, to the end that
accordingly we might deliberate more amply on that we had
to do. With this resolution, which was approved by every
one, *Antonio de Faria* weighed anchor, and without any noise
got close to the island, and compassing it about exactly
observed every particular that presented itself to his sight.
This island was all inclosed with a platform of jasper, six and
twenty spans high, the stones whereof were so neatly wrought,
and joyned together, that the wall seemed to be all of one
piece, at which every one greatly marvelled, as having never
seen any thing till then, either in the *Indiaes*, or elsewhere,
that merited comparison with it; this wall was six and
twenty spans deep from the bottom of the river to the super-
ficies of the water, so that the full height of it was two and
fifty spans. Furthermore the top of the platform was bordered
with the same stone, cut into great tower-work; upon this
wall, which invironed the whole island, was a gallery of
balisters of turn'd copper, that from six to six fathom joyned to
certain pillars of the same metal, upon each of the which was
the figure of a woman holding a bowl in her hand; within
this gallery were divers monsters cast in metal, standing all in
a row, which holding one another by the hand in manner of
a dance incompassed the whole island, being, as I have said, a
league about. Amidst these monstrous idols there was likewise another row of very rich arches, made of sundry coloured
pieces; a sumptuous work, and wherewith the eye might well
be entertained and contented. Within was a little wood of
orange trees, without any mixture of other plants, and in the
midst an hundred and threescore hermitages dedicated to the

gods of the year, of whom these Gentiles recount many pleasant
fables in their chronicles for the defence of their blindness in
their false belief. A quarter of a league beyond these hermitages, towards the east, divers goodly great edifices were seen,
separated the one from the other with seven fore-fronts of
houses, built after the manner of our churches, from the top to
the bottom as far as could be discerned, these buildings were
gilt all over, and annexed to very high towers, which in all
likelihood were steeples; their edifices were environed with
two great streets arched all along; like unto the frontispieces
of the houses; these arches were supported by very huge
pillars, on the top whereof, and between every arch was a
dainty prospective; now in regard these buildings, towers,
pillars and their chapiters, were so exceedingly gilt all over, as
one could discern nothing but gold, it perswaded us that this
temple must needs be wonderful sumptuous and rich, since such
cost had been bestowed on the very walls. After we had surrounded this whole island, and observed the advenues and
entries thereof, notwithstanding it was somewhat late, yet
would *Antonio de Faria* needs go ashore to see if he could get
any intelligence in one of those hermitages, to the end he
might thereupon resolve, either to prosecute his design, or
return back. So having left a guard sufficient for his two
vessels, and *Diego Lobato*, his chaplain, captain of them, he
landed with fourty souldiers, and twenty slaves, as well pikes,
as harquebuses. He also carried with him four of the
*Chineses*, which we took a while before, both for that they
knew the place well, as having been there at other times, and
likewise that they might serve us for truchmen and guides.
Being got to the shore unespied of any one, and without noise,
we entred the island by one of the eight advenues that it had,
and marching through the midst of the little wood of orange-
trees we arrived at the gate of the first hermitage, which might
be some two musket-shot from the place we dis-imbarqued,
where that hapned unto us which I will deliver hereafter.

*Antonio de Faria* went directly to the next hermitage he saw
before him with the greatest silence that might be, and
with no little fear, for that he knew not into what danger he
was going to ingage himself; which he found shut on the

inside, he commanded one of the *Chineses* to knock at it, as he
did two or three times, when at last he heard one speak in this
manner, *Praysed be the Creator, who hath enamelled the beauty
of the skies, let him that knocks at the gate go about, and he
shall find it open on the other side, where let me know what he
desires.*  The *Chinese* went presently about, and entring into
the hermitage by a back door, he opened the foregate to
*Antonio de Faria*, and let him in with all his followers; there
he found an old man, that seemed to be an hundred years old;
he was apparelled in a long violet coloured damask gown, and
by his countenance appeared to be a man of quality, as we
understood afterwards.  Being amazed to see so many men he
fell to the ground, where he lay a good while without speaking
a word, howbeit at length he began to be better confirmed, and
beholding us with a serious look, he gravely demanded of us
what we were, and what we would have; whereunto the interpreter answered by the express commandment of *Antonio de
Faria*, that he was a captain stranger, a native of the kingdom
of *Siam*, and that sayling in a junk of his, laden with merchandise, and bound for *Liampoo*, he had suffered shipwrack,
whence he had miraculously escaped with all his company:
and for that he had vowed to make a pilgrimage to this holy
place, to praise God for preserving him from so great a peril,
he was now come to perform his vow; also to crave somewhat
of him by way of alms, whereby his poverty might be relieved,
protesting within three years to render him twice as much as
he should then take from him: whereupon the hermit, named
*Hiticon*, having mused a little on the matter, and fixing his eye
on *Antonio de Faria : Whoever thou art*, said he unto him,
*know that I throughly understand what thou sayest, and that I
perceive but too well thy damnable intention, wherewith out of
the obscurity of thy blindness, like an infernal pilot, thou
carriest both thy self, and these others, into the profound abyss
of the lake of night : for instead of rendring thanks to God for
so great a favour as thou confessest He hath shewed thee, thou
comest hither to rob this holy house.  But let me ask thee, if thou
executest this mischievous design, what will the Divine Justice,
thinkest thou, do with thee at the last gasp of thy life ?  Change
then thy perverse inclination, and never suffer the imagination of*

*so great a sin to enter thy thoughts; give credit unto me that
tells thee nothing but the very truth, even as I hope to thrive by
it all the rest of my life.* Antonio de Faria seeming to approve
of the counsel which the old hermit gave him, earnestly desired
him not to be displeased, assuring him that he had no other
means or way left to relieve him and his, but what he could
find in that place. To which the hermit, wringing his hands,
and lifting up his eyes, said weeping. *Praised be Thou, O Lord,
that permittest men to live on the earth, who offend Thee under
pretext of seeking means to live, and that vouchsafe not to serve
Thee one hour, although they know how assured Thy glory is.*
After he had uttered these words, he remained very pensive
and much troubled to see the great disorder we used in breaking up the coffins, and flinging them out of their places; at
length looking upon *Antonio de Faria,* who stood leaning upon
his sword, he intreated him to sit down by him, which he did
with a great deal of complement, not desisting for all that
from making signs to his souldiers to persist as they had
begun, that was, to take the silver which was mingled amongst
the bones of the dead in the tombs that they brake up; whereat the hermit was so grieved as he fell down twice in a swoon
from his seat; but being come to himself, he spake thus to
*Antonio de Faria; I will declare unto thee, as to a man that
seems discreet, the means whereby thou mayst obtain pardon for
the sin which thou and thy people now commit, to the end that
thy soul may not perish eternally, when as the last breath of thy
mouth shall go out of thy body. Seeing then, as thou sayest,
that it is necessity constrains thee to offend in this grievous
manner, and that thou hast a purpose to make restitution before
thou diest, of that thou takest away from hence; if thou hast
time and power, thou must do these three things: First, thou
must render again what thou now carriest away, that the Sovereign Lord may not turn His mercy from thee. Secondly, thou
must with tears ask Him forgiveness for thy fault, which is so
odious unto Him, never ceasing to chastise thy flesh both day and
night. And thirdly, thou must distribute thy goods to the poor,
as liberally as to thy self, giving them alms with prudence and
discretion, to the end the servant of the night may have nothing
to accuse thee of at the last day. Now, for recompence of this*

12

*counsel, I desire thee to command thy followers to gather together
the bones of the saints, that they may not be dispersed on the
earth.*   Antonio de Faria promised him very courteously to
perform his request, wherewith the hermit was a little better
at quiet than before, but yet not fully satisfied; howbeit he
spake him very fair, and assured him that after he had once
seen him, he very much repented the undertaking of this enterprise, but his souldiers had threatned to kill him, if he
returned without executing of it, and this he told him as a very
great secret.   *God grant it be so,* replyed the hermit, *for that
thou shalt not be so blame worthy as these other monsters of the
night, which are so greedy, like to famished dogs, that it seems
all the silver in the world is not able to satiate them.*

After we had gathered all the silver together that was in the
graves amongst the dead mens bones, and carried it aboard
our ships, we were all of opinion not to go any farther to the
rest of the hermitages, as well because we knew not the
countrey, as for that it was almost night, upon hope that
the next day we might continue our enterprise more at leisure.
Now before he re-imbarqued himself, *Antonio de Faria* took
leave of the hermit, and giving him very good words, he
desired him for Gods sake not to be offended with that his
followers had done, being constrained thereunto by meer
necessity: for as for his particular he exceedingly abhorred
such like actions, adding withall, that at the first sight of him
he would have returned back, out of the remorse of conscience,
and true repentance; but that his company had hindred him,
saying, that if he did so, they would surely kill him; so that
for to save his life he was compelled to yield and consent
thereunto, though he plainly saw that it was a very great sin,
in regard whereof he was resolved, as soon as he could rid his
hands of them, to go up and down the world to perform such
penance as was requisite for the purging of him from so enormous a crime.   Hereunto the hermit answered, *Pleaseth the
Lord, who living, reigneth above the beauty of the stars, that
the knowledge which, by this discourse, thou showest to have, be
not prejudicial unto thee; for I be assured, that he who knows
these things, and doth them not, runs a far greater danger, than
he that sins through ignorance.*   Then one of ours, named *Nuno*

*Coelho*, who would needs have an oar in our talk, told him, that he was not to be angry for a matter of so small importance; whereunto the hermit beholding him with so stern a countenance, answered, *Certainly, the fear which thou hast of death is yet less, since thou imployest thy self in actions as infamous and black as the soul that is in thy body; and for my part, I cannot but be perswaded, that all thy ambition is wholly placed upon money, as but too well appears by the thirst of thy insatiable avarice, whereby thou wilt make an end of heaping up the measure of thine infernal appetite: continue then thy theeveries, for seeing then thou must go to hell for that which thou hast already taken out of this holy house, thou shalt also go thither for those things which thou shalt steal otherwise, so the heavier the burden shall be that thou bearest, the sooner shalt thou be precipitated into the bottom of hell, where already thy wicked works have prepared thee an everlasting abode.* Hereupon *Nuno de Coelho* prayed him to take all things patiently, affirming that the law of God commanded him so to do so. Then the hermit lift up his hand, by way of admiration, and as it were smiling at what the souldier had said, *Truly,* answered he, *I am come to see that I never thought to see or hear, namely, evil actions disguised with a specious pretext of vertue, which makes me believe that thy blindness is exceeding great, since trusting to good words thou spendest thy life so wickedly, wherefore it is not possible thou shouldest ever come to Heaven, or give any account to God at the last day, as of necessity thou must do.* Saying so, he turned him to *Antonio de Faria*, without attending further answer from him, and earnestly desired him not to suffer his company to spit upon and prophane the altar, which he vowed was more grievous to him, then the induring of a thousand deaths; whereupon to satisfie him, he presently commanded the forbearance of it; wherewith the hermit was somewhat comforted. Now because it grew late, *Antonio de Faria* resolved to leave the place, but before he departed he held it necessary to inform himself of certain other particulars, whereof he stood in some doubt, so that he inquired of the hermit how many persons there might be in all those hermitages: whereunto *Hiticon* answered, that there were about three hundred and threescore *Talagrepos*,

besides forty *Menigrepos*, appointed to furnish them with
things requisite for their maintenance, and to attend them
when they were sick : moreover he asked him, whether the
King of *China* came not sometimes thither; he told him, No,
for, said he, the King cannot be condemned by anybody, he is
the son of the Sun, but contrarily he had power to absolve
every one.   Then he enquired of him if there were any arms
in their, hermitages ?   O no, answered the hermit, *for all such
as pretend to go to heaven have more need of patience to indure
injuries, then of arms to revenge themselves* : being also desirous
to know of him the cause why so much silver was mingled
with the bones of the dead.   *This silver,* replied the hermit,
*comes of the alms that the deceased carry with them out of this
into the other life, for to serve them at their need in the heaven
of the moon, where they live eternally.   In conclusion,* having
demanded of him whether they had any women, he said, *That
they which would maintain the life of their souls, ought not to
taste the pleasures of the flesh, seeing experience made it apparent, that the bee which nourisheth herself in an honey-comb,
doth often sting such as offer to meddle with that sweetness.*
After *Antonio de Faria* had propounded all these questions, he
took his leave of him, and so went directly to his ships, with
an intention to return again the next day, for to set upon
the other hermitages, where, as he had been told, was great
abundance of silver, and certain idols of gold ; but our sins
would not permit us to see the effect of a business which we
had been two moneths and an half a purchasing with so much
labour and danger of our lives, as I will deliver hereafter.

At the clearing up of the day, *Antonio de Faria*, and all of
us, being embarqued, we went and anchored on the other side
of the island, about a faulcon shot from it, with an intent, as
I have before declared, to go ashore again the next morning,
and set upon the chappels where the kings of *China* were
interred, that so we might the more commodiously lade our
two vessels with such treasures ; which peradventure might
have succeeded according to our desires, if the business had
been well carried, and that *Antonio de Faria* had followed the
counsel was given him, which was, that since we had not been
as yet discovered, that he should have carried the hermit

away with him, to the end he might not acquaint the house
of the *Bonzoes* with what we had done; howbeit he would
never hearken to it, saying, that we were to fear nothing that
way, by reason the hermit was so old, and his legs so swoln
with the gout, as he was not able to stand, much less to go.
But it fell out clean contrary to his expectation, for the hermit
no sooner saw us imbarqued, as we understood afterwards,
but he presently crawled as well as he could to the next
hermitage, which was not above a flight shoot from his; and
giving intelligence of all that had past, he bad his companions,
because himself was not able, to go away with all speed to the
*Bonzoes* house to acquaint them with it, which the other
instantly performed; so that about midnight we saw a great
many of fires lighted on the top of the wall of the Temple,
where the kings were buried, being kindled to serve for a
signal to the countrey about, of some extraordinary danger
towards. This made us ask of our *Chineses*, what they might
mean; who answered, that assuredly we were discovered, in
regard whereof they advised us without any longer stay to set
sail immediately; herewith they acquainted *Antonio de Faria*,
who was fast asleep; but he straightway arose, and leaving
his anchor in the sea, rowed directly, afraid as he was, to the
island, for to learn what was done there. Being arrived near
to the key, he heard many bells ringing in each hermitage,
together with a noise of men talking; whereupon the *Chineses*
that accompanied him, said, Sir, never stand to hear or see
more, but retire, we beseech you, as fast as you may, and
cause us not to be all miserably slain with your further stay.
Howbeit little regarding, or afraid of their words, he went
ashore only with six souldiers, having no other arms but
swords and targets, and going up the stairs of the key, whether
it were that he was vext for having lost so fair an occasion, or
carried thereunto by his courage, he entred into the gallery,
that invironed the island, and ran up and down in it like a mad
man, without meeting any body; that done, and being returned
aboard his vessel, much grieved and ashamed, he consulted
with his company about what they should do, who were of
opinion that the best course we could take, was to depart, and
therefore they required him to put it accordingly in execution;

seeing them all so resolved, and fearing some tumults among
the souldiers, he was fain to answer, that he was also of their
mind; but first he thought it fit to know for what cause they
should fly away in that manner, and therefore he desired them
to stay for him a little in that place, because he would try
whether he could learn by some means or the other the truth
of the matter, whereof they had but a bare suspition; for
which, he told them, he would ask but half an hour at
the most, so that there would be time enough to take order
for any thing before day; some would have alledged reasons
against this, but he would not hear them; wherefore having
caused them all to take their oaths upon the holy Evangelists,
that they would stay for him, he returned to land with the
same souldiers that had accompanied him before, and entering
into the little wood he heard the sound of a bell, which addressed
him to another hermitage, far richer then that wherein we were
the day before.   There he met with two men, apparelled like
monks, with large hoods, which made him think they were hermits, of whom he presently laid hold; wherewith one of them
was so terrified, as he was not able to speak a good while after:
hereupon four of the six souldiers past into the hermitage, and
took an idol of silver from the altar, having a crown of gold on
its head, and a wheel in its hand; they also brought away
three candlesticks of silver, with long chains of the same
belonging to them.   This performed, *Antonio de Faria* carrying
the two hermits along with him, went aboard again, and sailing
away, he propounded divers questions to him, of the two, that
was least afraid, threatning to use him in a strange fashion
if he did not tell the truth.   This hermit seeing himself so
menaced, answered, That an holy man, named *Pilou Angiroo*
came about midnight to the house of the kings sepultures,
where knocking in haste at the gate, he cryed out, saying; *O
miserable men, buried in the drunkenness of carnal sleep, who
by a solemn vow have profest your selves to the honour of the
Goddess* Amida, *the rich reward of our labours, hear, hear, hear,
O the most wretched men that ever were born; there are
strangers come into our island, from the furthest end of the
world, which have long beards, and bodies of iron; these wicked
creatures have entered into the Holy House of the seven and*

*twenty Pillars, of whose sacred temple an holy man is keeper, that hath told me, where after they had ransacked the rich treasures of thy saints, they contemptuously threw their bones to the ground, which they prophaned with their stinking and infectious spitting, and made a mockery of them like devils, obstinate and hardned in their wretched sins; wherefore I advise you to look well to your selves; for it is said that they have sworn to kill us all as soon as it is day: fly away then, or call some people to your succour, since being religious men you are not permitted to meddle with any thing that may shed the blood of man.* Herewith they presently arose and ran to the gate, where they found the hermite laid on the ground, and half dead with grief and weariness through the imbecillity of his age; whereupon the *Grepos* and *Menigrepos* made those fires that you saw, and withall sent in all haste to the towns of *Corpilem,* and *Fonbana,* for to succour them speedily with the forces of the country; so that you may be assured it will not be long before they fall upon this place with all the fury that may be. *Now this is all that I am able to say concerning the truth of this affair; wherefore I desire you to return us both unto our hermitage with our lives saved; for if you do not so you will commit a greater sin, then you did yesterday: remember also that God, in regard of the continuall penance we perform, hath taken us so far into His protection, as He doth visit us almost every hour of the day; wherefore labour to save your selves as much as you will, yet shall you hardly do it; for be sure, that the earth, the air, the winds, the waters, the beasts, the fishes, the fowls, the trees, the plants, and all things created, will pursue and torment you so cruelly, as none but He that lives in heaven will be able to help you.* Antonio de *Faria* being hereby certainly informed of the truth of the business sailed instantly away, tearing his hair and beard for very rage, to see that through his negligence and indiscretion he had lost the fairest occasion that ever he should be able to meet withall.

## CHAPTER XXIV.

Our casting away in the Gulf of Nanquin, with all that befell us after this
lamentable shipwrack.

WE had already sailed seven days in the Gulf of *Nanquin*,
to the end that the force of the current might carry us
the more swiftly away, as men whose safety consisted wholly
in flight ; for we were so desolate and sad, that we scarce
spake one to another; in the mean time we arrived at a
village, called *Susequerim*, where no news being come either
of us, or what we had done, we furnished our selves with
some victual, and getting information very covertly of the
course we were to hold, we departed within two hours after,
and then, with the greatest speed we could make, we entred
into a streight, named *Xalingau*, much less frequented then
the gulf that we had past; here we navigated nine dayes
more, in which time we ran an hundred and forty leagues,
then entring again into the said Gulf of *Nanquin*, which in
that place was not above ten or eleven leagues broad, we
sailed for the space of thirteen dayes from one side to another
with a westerly winde, exceedingly afflicted, both with the
great labour we were fain to endure, and the cruel fear we
were in, besides the want we began to feel of victuals.  In this
case being come within sight of the mountains of *Conxinacau*,
which are in the height of forty and one degrees, there arose
so terrible a south winde, called by the *Chineses*, *Tufaon*, as it
could not possibly be thought a natural thing ; so that our
vessels being low built, weak, and without mariners, we were
reduced to such extremity, that out of all hope to escape we
suffered our selves to be driven along the coast, as the current
of the water would carry us ; for we held it more safe to
venture ourselves amongst the rocks, then to let us be swallowed up in the midst of the sea ; and though we had chosen
this design, as the better and less painful, yet did it not
succeed ; for after dinner the winde turned to the north-west,
whereby the waves became so high, that it was most dreadful
to behold ; our fear then was so extream, as we began to cast
all that we had into the sea, even to the chests full of silver,

That done, we cut down our two masts, and so without masts and sails we floated along all the rest of the day; at length about midnight we heard them in *Antonio de Faria's* vessel cry, *Lord have mercy upon us*, which perswaded us that they were cast away; the apprehension whereof put us in such a fright, as for an hour together no man spake a word. Having past all this sad night in so miserable a plight, about an hour before day our vessel opened about the keel, so that it was instantly full of water eight spans high, whereupon perceiving our selves to sink, we verily believed, it was the good pleasure of God that in this place we should finish both our lives and labours. As soon then as it was day we looked out to sea, as far as possibly we could discern, but could no way discover *Antonio de Faria*, which put us quite out of heart; and so continuing in this great affliction till about ten of. the clock, with so much terror and amazement, as words are not able to express; at last we ran against the coast, and even drowned as we were, the waves rolled us toward a point of rocks that stood out into the sea, where we were no sooner arrived but that all went to pieces, insomuch that of five and twenty *Portugals*, which we were, there were but fourteen saved, the other eleven being drowned, together with eighteen Christian servants, and seven *Chinese* mariners. This miserable disaster hapned on a Munday, the 5th of *August*, 1542, for which the Lord be praised everlastingly.

We fourteen *Portugals*, having escaped out of this shipwrack by the meer mercy of God, spent all that day, and the night following, in bewailing our mis-fortune, and the wretched estate whereunto we were reduced; but in the end consulting together, what course to take for to give some remedy thereunto; we concluded to enter into the country, hoping that far or neer we should not fail to meet with some body, that taking us for slaves would relieve us with meat, till such time as it should please Heaven to terminate our travels with the end of our lives. With this resolution we went some six or seven leagues over rocks and hills, and on the other side discovered a great marsh, so large and void, as it past the reach of our sight, there being no appearance of any land beyond it; which made us turn back again, towards the same

place where we were cast away; being arrived there the day
after about sun-set, we found upon the shore the bodies of our
men, which the sea had cast up, over whom we commenced
our sorrow and lamentations, and the next day we buried
them in the sand, to keep them from being devoured by the
tygers, whereof that country is full, which we performed with
much labour and pain, in regard we had no other tools
for that purpose but our hands and nails.   After these poor
bodies were interred we got us into a marsh, where we spent
all the night, as the safest place we could chuse to preserve
us from the tygers : from thence we continued our journey
towards the north, and that by such precipices and thick
woods, as we had much ado to pass through them.   Having
travelled in this manner three dayes, at length we arrived at
a little streight, without meeting anybody, over the which
resolving to swim, by ill fortune the four first that entred
into it, being three *Portugals* and a young youth, were
miserably drowned ; for being very feeble, and the streight
somewhat broad, and the current of the water very strong, they
were not able to hold out any longer when they came to the
midst; so we eleven, with three servants that remained, seeing
the infortunate success of our companions, could do nothing
but weep and lament, as men that hourly expected such or a
worse end.   Having spent all that dark night, exposed to the
winde, cold, and rain, it pleased our Lord that the next
morning before day we discovered a great fire towards the
east; whereupon as soon as the day broke, we marched
fair and softly that way, recommending our selves to that
Almighty God from whom alone we could hope for a remedy
to our miseries; and so continuing our journey all along the
river, the most part of that day, at last we came to a little
wood, where we found five men making of coals, whom on our
knees we besought for Gods sake to direct us to some place
where we might get some relief ; *I would,* said one of them
beholding us with an eye of pitie, *it lay in our power to help
you, but alas ! all the comfort we can give you is to bestow some
part of our supper on you, which is a little rice, wherewith you
may pass this night here with us if you will, though I hold it
better for you to proceed on your way, and recover the place*

*you see a little below, where you shall finde an hospital that serves to lodge such pilgrims as chance to come into these quarters.* Having thanked him for his good address, we fell to the rice they gave us, which came but to two mouthfuls apiece, and so took our leaves of them, going directly to the place they had shewed us, as well as our weakness would permit.

About an hour within night, we arrived at the hospital, where we met with four men, that had the charge of it, who received us very charitably. The next morning as soon as it was day, they demanded of us, what we were, and from whence we came? Thereunto we answered, that we were strangers, natives of the Kingdom of *Siam*, and that coming from the Port of *Liampoo* to go to the fishing of *Nanquin*, we were cast away at sea by the violence of a storm, having saved nothing out of this shipwrack, but those our miserable and naked bodies. Whereupon demanding of us again, what we intended to do, and whither we would go; we replyed, that we purposed to go to the city of *Nanquin*, there to imbarque our selves as rowers in the first *Lanteaa* that should put to sea, for to pass unto *Cantan*, where our countrymen, by the permission of the *Aitco* of *Panquin*, exercised their traffique under the protection of the son of the Sun, and *Lyon* crowned in the throne of the world; wherefore we desired them for Gods cause to let us stay in that hospital, until we had recovered our healths, and to bestow any poor clothes on us to cover our nakedness. After they had given good ear unto us; it were reason, answered they, to grant you that which you require with so much earnestness, and tears; but in regard the house is now very poor, we cannot so easily discharge our duties unto you as we should, howbeit, we will do what we may with a very good will. Then quite naked, as we were, they lead us all about the village, containing some forty or fifty fires, more or less; the inhabitants whereof were exceeding poor, having no other living but what they got by the labour of their hands, from whom they drew by way of alms some two *taeis* in money, half a sack of rice, a little meal, aricot beans, onions, and a few old rags, wherewith we made the best shift we could; over and above this they bestowed two *taeis* more on us out of the

stock of the hospital.   But whereas we desired that we might
be permitted to stay there, they excused themselves, saying,
that no poor might remain there above three days, or five at
the most, unless it were sick people, or women with child, of
whom special care was to be had, because in their extremities
they could not travel without endangering their lives, wherefore
they could for no other persons whatsoever transgress that
ordnance, which had of ancient time been instituted by the
advice of very learned and religious men ; nevertheless, that
three leagues from thence, we should in a great town, called
*Sileyiacau,* find a very rich hospital, where all sorts of poor
people were entertained, and that there we should be far better
looked unto then in their house, which was poor, and agreeable
to the place of its scituation ; to which end they would give us
a letter of recommendation, by means whereof we should incontinently be received.   For these good offices we rendred
them infinite thanks, and told them that God would reward
them for it, since they did it for His sake ; whereupon an old
man, one of those four, answered us fairly and gave us to the
brotherhood of the other hospital, whither we were to go, and
so we departed about noon, and arrived at the town an hour or
two before sun-set.   The first thing we did, was to go to the
house of the repose of the poor ; for so the *Chineses* call the
hospitals.   There we delivered our letters to the masters of
that Society, which they term *Tanigories,* whom we found
altogether in a chamber, where they were assembled about the
affairs of the poor.   After they had received the letter with a
kind of complement, that seemed very strange to us, they
commanded the Register to read it ; whereupon he stood up
and read it to them that were sitting at the table.   This letter
being read, they caused us presently to be lodged in a very
neat chamber, accomodated with a table, and divers chairs,
where after we had been served with good meat, we rested our
selves that night.   The next morning the Register came along
with the rest of the officers, and demanded of us who we
were, of what nation, and whereabout we had suffered shipwrack ; whereunto we answered, as we had done before, to
those of the village from whence we came, that we might not
be found in two tales, and convinced of lying ; whereupon

having further enquired of us what we meant to do ; we told them that our intention was to get our selves cured in that house, if it pleased them to permit us, in regard we were so weak and sickly as we could scarce stand upon our legs. To which they replyed that they would very willingly see that performed for us, as a thing that was ordinarily done there for the service of God ; for the which we thanked them weeping, with so much acknowledgement of their goodness and charity, as the tears stood in their eyes ; so that presently sending for a physician, they bid him look carefully to us, for that we were poor flocks, and had no other means but what we had from the house. That done, he took our names in writing, and set them down in a great book ; whereunto we all of us set our hands, saying, it was necessary it should be so, that an account might be rendred of the expence was to be made for us.

[*Pinto and his companions, being cured, continue their journey ; their further adventures, and hospitable reception by a gentleman at a country house ; omitted.*]

## CHAPTER XXV.

Our arrival at the town of Taypor, where we were made prisoners, and so sent to the city of Nanquin.

THE next morning by break of day parting from that place, we went to a village called *Finginilau,* which was some four leagues from the old gentlemans house, where we remained three dayes, and then continuing travelling from one place to another, and from village to village, ever declining the great towns, for fear lest the Justice of the country should call us in question in regard we were strangers ; in this manner we spent almost two moneths without receiving the least damage from any body. Now there is no doubt but we might easily have got to the city of *Nanquin* in that time if we had had a guide ; but for want of knowing the way we wandred we knew not whither, suffering much, and running many hazards. At length we arrived at a village, named *Chaucer,* at such a time as they were a solemnizing a sumptuous funeral of a very rich woman, that had disinherited her kindred, and left her estate to the *Pagode* of this village, where she was buried, as we understood by the inhabitants ; we were invited then to this funeral, as other poor people were, and according to the custom of the country we did eat on the grave of the deceased. At the end of three days that we stayed there, which was the time the funeral lasted, we had six *taeis* given us for an alms, conditionally that in all our oraisons we should pray unto God for the soul of the departed. Being gone from this place we continued on our journey to another village, called *Guinapalir*, from whence we were almost two moneths travelling from country to country, untill at last our ill fortune brought us to a town, named *Taypor*, where by chance there was at that time a *Chumbim*, that is to say, one of those super-intendents of Justice, that every three years are sent throughout the provinces for to make report unto the king of all that passeth there. This naughty man seeing us go begging from door to door, called to us from a window where he was, and would know of us who we were, and of what nation ; as also what obliged us to run up and down the world in that manner? Having asked us these questions in the presence of three Registers, and of many other persons, that were gathered together to behold us ; we answered him, that we were stangers, natives of the kingdom of *Siam*, who being cast away by a storm at sea went thus travelling and begging our living, to the end we might sustain our selves with the charity of good people, untill such time as we could arrive at *Nanquin*, whither we were going with an intent to imbarque our selves there in some of the merchants *Lanteaas* for *Canton*, where the shipping of our nation lay. This answer we made unto the *Chumbim*, who questionless had been well enough contented with it, and would have let us go, had it not been for one of his clerks ; for he told them that we were idle vagabonds, that spent our time in begging from door to door, and abusing the alms that were given us, and therefore he was at no hand to let us go free, for fear of incurring the punishment, ordained for such as offend in that sort, as is set forth in the seventh of the twelve books of the Statutes of the Realm ; wherefore as

his faithful servant he counselled him to lay us in good and
sure hold, that we might be forth-coming to answer the Law.
The *Chumbim* presently followed his clerks advice, and carried
himself toward us with as much barbarous cruelty, as could be
expected from a Pagan, such as he was, that lived without God
or religion ; to which effect after he had heard a number of
false witnesses, who charged us with many fowl crimes, whereof
we never so much as dream'd, he caused us to be put into a
deep dungeon, with irons on our hands and feet, and great
iron collars about our necks. In this miserable place we
endured such hunger, and were so fearfully whipped, that we
were in perpetual pain for six and twenty days together, at the
end whereof we were by the sentence of the same *Chumbim*
sent to the Parliament of the *Cheam* of *Nanquin*, because the
jurisdiction of this extended not to the condemnation of any
prisoner to death.

We remained six and twenty days in that cruel prison,
whereof I spake before ; and I vow we thought we had been
six and twenty thousand years there, in regard of the great
misery we suffered in it, which was such, as one of our companions called *Joano Roderiguez Bravo* died in our arms, being
eaten up with lice, we being no way able to help him ; and it
was almost a miracle, that the rest of us escaped alive from
that filthy vermine ; at length, one morning, when we thought
of nothing less, loaden with irons as we were, and so weak
that we could hardly speak, we were drawn out of that prison,
and then being chained one to another we were imbarqued
with many others, to the number of thirty or forty, that having
been convicted for sundry hainous crimes, were also sent to
the Parliament of *Nanquin*, where, as I have already declared,
is always residing a *Chaem* of Justice, which is like to the
sovereign title of the Vice-roy of *China*.

[*Here follows a relation of the Chinese Law.*]

After being reimbarqued, we sailed up a great river seven days
together, at the end whereof we arrived at *Nanquin*. As this
city is the second of all the empire, so is it also the capital of
the three kingdoms of *Liampoo*, *Fanius*, and *Sambor*. Here

we lay six weeks in prison, and suffered so much pain and misery, as reduced to the last extreamities, we died insensibly for want of succour, not able to do any thing, but look up to heaven with a pitiful eye ; for it was our ill fortune to have all that we had stoln from us the first night we came thither. This prison was so great, that there were four thousand prisoners in it at that time, as we were credibly informed, so that one should hardly sit down in any place without being robbed, and filled full of lice : having layn there a month and an half, as I said, the Anchacy, who was one of the judges before whom our cause was to be pleaded, pronounced our sentence at the suit of the Atturney General, the tenor whereof was : That having seen and considered our process, which the *Chumbim* of *Taypor* had sent him, it appeared by the accusations laid to our charge, that we were very hainous malefactors, and though we denied many things, yet in justice no credit was to be given unto us, and therfore that we were to be publickly whipped, for to teach us to live better in time to come, and that withal our two thumbs should be cut off, wherewith it was evident by manifest suspicions, that we used to commit robberies, and other vile crimes ; and furthermore, that for the remainder of the punishment we deserved, he referred us to the *Aytau* of *Bataupina*, unto whom it appertained to take cognisance of such causes, in regard of the jurisdiction that he had of life and death. This sentence was pronounced in the prison, where it had been better for us to have suffered death, then the stripes that we received, for all the ground round about us ran with blood upon our whiping, so that it was almost a miracle, that of the eleven which we were, nine escaped alive, for two of our company died three days after, besides one of our servants.

After we had been whipped in that manner, I have declared, we were carried into a great chamber, that was in the prison, where were a number of sick, and diseased persons, lying upon beds, and other ways ; there we had presently our stripes washed, and things applyed unto them, whereby we were somewhat eased of our pain, and that by men, much like unto the fraternity of mercy among the Papists, which onely out of charity, and for the honor of God, do tend those that are sick, and liberally furnish them with all things necessary. Hereafter some eleven or twelve days, we began to be prettily recovered, and as we were lamenting our ill fortune, for being so rigorously condemned to lose our thumbs, it pleased God one morning, when as we little dreamt of it, that we espied two men come into the chamber, of a good aspect, clothed in long gowns of violet coloured sattin, and carrying white rods in their hands; as soon as they arrived, all the sick persons in the chamber cried out, *Blessed be the ministers of the works of God :* whereunto they answered, holding up their rods, *May it please God to give you patience in your adversity :* whereupon having distributed clothes and money to those that were next to them, they came unto us, and after they had saluted us very courteously, with demonstration of being moved at our tears, they asked us who we were, and of what countrey, as also why we were imprisoned there : whereunto we answered weeping, that we were strangers, natives of the kingdom of *Siam*, and of a country called *Malaca ;* that being merchants and well to live, we had imbarqued our selves with our goods, and being bound for *Liampoo*, we had been cast away just against the Isles of *Laman*, having lost all that we had, and nothing left us but our miserable bodies in the case they now saw us; moreover we added, that being thus evil intreated by fortune, arriving at the city of *Taypor*, the *Chumbin* of Justice had caused us to be apprehended without any cause, laying to our charge, that we were thieves and vagabonds, who to avoid pains-taking went begging from door to door, entertaining our idle laziness with the alms that were given us unjustly, whereof the *Chumbin* having made informations at his pleasure, as being both judge and party, he had laid us in irons in the prison, where for two and forty days space, we had indured incredible pain and hunger, and no man would hear us in our justifications, as well because we had not wherewithal to give presents for to maintain our right, as for that we wanted the language of the country. In conclusion, we told them, how in the mean time, without any cognisance of the cause, we had been condemned to be whipped, as also to have our thumbs cut off, like thieves ; so that we had already suffered the first punishment, with so much rigour and cruelty, that the marks thereof remained but

*two* visibly upon our wretched bodies, and therefore we con-
jured them by the charge they had to serve God in assisting
the afflicted, that they would not abandon us in this need, the
rather for that our extream poverty rendred us odious to all
the world, and exposed us to the induring of all affronts. These
two men having heard us attentively, remained very pensive
and amazed at our speech; at length lifting up their eyes, all
bathed with tears, to heaven, and kneeling down on the
ground, *O Almighty Lord,* said they, *that governest in the
highest places, and whose patience is incomprehensible, be Thou
evermore blessed, for that Thou art pleased to hearken unto the
complaints of necessitous and miserable men, to the end that the
great offences committed against Thy Divine goodness by the
Ministers of Justice may not rest unpunished, as we hope that by
Thy holy Law they will be chastised at one time or other.*
Whereupon they informed themselves more amply by those
who were about us, of what we had told them, and presently
sending for the Register, in whose hands our sentence was,
they straitly commanded him, that upon pain of grievous
punishment he should forthwith bring them all the proceedings
which had been used against us, as instantly he did; now the
two officers, seeing there was no remedy for the whipping that
we had suffered, presented a petition in our behalf unto the
*Chaem,* whereunto this answer was returned by the Court:
*Mercy hath no place, where Justice loseth her name, in regard
whereof your request cannot be granted,* This answer was subscribed by the *Chaem,* and eight *Conchacis,* that are like
criminal judges. This hard proceeding much astonished these
two Proctors for the poor, so named from their office; wherefore, carried with an extream desire to draw us out of this
misery, they presently preferred another petition to the
Sovereign Court of Justice, of which I spake in the precedent
chapter, where the *Menigrepos* and *Talegrepos* were judges, an
assembly which in their language is called, *The breath of the
Creator of all things.* In this petition, as sinners, confessing
all that we were accused of, we had recourse to mercy, which
sorted well for us; for as soon as the petition was presented
unto them, they read the process quite through, and finding
that our right was over-born for want of succour, they instantly

dispatched away two of their Court, who with an express mandate under their hands and seals, went and prohibited the *Chaems* Court from intermedling with this cause, which they commanded away before them. In obedience to this prohibition the *Chaems* Court made this decree, *We, that are assembled in this Court of Justice of the Lyon crowned in the throne of the world, having perused the petition presented to the four and twenty judges of the austere life, do consent, that those nine strangers be sent by way of appeal to the Court of the Aytau of Aytaus in the City of* Pequin, *to the end that in mercy the sentence pronounced against them may be favourably moderated : Given the seventh day of the fourth Moon, in the three and twentieth year of the reign of the Son of the Sun.* This decree, being signed by the *Chaem*, and the eight *Conchacis*, was presently brought us by the two Proctors for the poor; upon the receit whereof we told them, that we could but pray unto God to reward them for the good they had done us for His sake; whereunto beholding us with an eye of pity, they answered, *May His Celestial goodness direct you in the knowledge of His works, that thereby you may with patience gather the fruit of your labours, as they which fear to offend His holy Name.*

After we had past all the adversities and miseries, whereof I have spoken before, we were imbarqued in the company of some other thirty or forty prisoners, that were sent, as we were, from this Court of Justice to that other Sovereign one by way of appeal, there to be either acquitted or condemned, according to the crimes they had committed, and the punishment they had deserved. Now a day before our departure, being imbarqued in a *Lanteaa*, and chained three and three together, the two Proctors for the poor came to us, and first of all furnishing us with all things needful, as clothes, and victuals, they asked us whether we wanted any thing else for our voyage. Whereunto we answered, that all we could desire of them was, that they would be pleased to convert that further good they intended to us into a letter of recommendation unto the officers of that holy fraternity of the city of *Pequin*, thereby to oblige them to maintain the right of our cause, in regard (as they very well knew) they should otherwise be sure to be utterly abandoned of every one, by reason they were

strangers and altogether unknown. The Proctors hearing us
speak in this manner : *Say not so,* replyed they, *for though
your ignorance discharges you before God, yet have you committed a great sin, because the more you are abased in the world
through poverty, the more shall you be exalted before the eyes of
His divine Majesty, if you patiently bear your crosses, whereunto
the flesh indeed doth always oppose it self, being evermore
rebellious against the spirit, but as a bird cannot fly without her
wings, no more can the soul meditate without works : As for the
letter you require of us ; we will give it you most willingly,
knowing it will be very necessary for you, to the end that the
favour of good people be not wanting to you in your need.* This
said, they gave us a sack full of rice, together with four *Taeis*
in silver, and a coverlet to lay upon us ; then having very
much recommended us unto the *Chifuu,* who was the officer of
justice that conducted us, they took their leaves of us in most
courteous manner. The next morning as soon as it was day
they sent us the letter, sealed with three seals in green wax,
the contents whereof were :—

[*A recital of the misfortunes of the Portuguese.*]

---

## CHAPTER XXVI.

The marvels of the city of Nanquin, our departure from thence towards
Pequin, and that which hapned unto us, till we arrived at the town of
Sempitay.

THIS letter being brought to us very early the next morning,
we departed in the manner before declared, and continued our voyage till sun-set, when as we anchord at a little
village, named *Minhacutem,* where the *Chifuu,* that conducted
us, was born, and where his wife and children were at that
time, which was the occasion that he remained there three
days ; at the end whereof he imbarqued himself with his
family, and so we passed on in the company of divers other
vessels, that went upon this river unto divers parts of this
empire : Now though we were all tyed together to the back

of the *Lanteaa,* where we rowed, yet did we not for all that
lose the view of many towns and villages that were scituated
along this river, whereof I hold it not amiss to make some
descriptions; to which effect, I will begin with the city of
*Nanquin,* from whence we last parted. This city . . . is seated
by the river of *Batampina,* upon a reasonable high hill, so as it
commands all the plains about it; the climate thereof is somewhat cold, but very healthy, and it is eight leagues about,
which way soever it is considered, three leagues broad, and one
long. The houses in it are not above two stories high, and
all built of wood; only those of the *Mandarins* are made of
hewed stone, and also invironed with walls and ditches, over
which are stone bridges, whereon they pass to the gates, that
have rich and costly arches, with divers sorts of inventions
upon the towers; all which put together make a pleasing
object to the eye, and represent a certain kind of I know not
what majesty. The houses of the *Chaems, Anchacys, Aytaus,*
*Tutons,* and *Chumbims,* which are all governours of provinces
or kingdoms, have stately towers, six or seven stories high,
and gilt all over, wherein they have their magazines for arms,
their wardrobes, their treasuries, and a world of rich household stuff, as also many other things of great value, together
with an infinite of delicate and most fine porcelain, which
amongst them is prized and esteemed as much as precious
stone; for this sort of porcelain never goes out of the kingdom, it being expressly forbidden by the laws of the country,
to be sold, upon pain of death, to any stranger, unless to the
*Xatamaas,* that is, the *Sophyes* of the *Persians,* who by a
particular permission buy of it at a very dear rate. The
*Chineses* assured us, that in this city there are eight hundred
thousand fires, four score thousand *Mandarins* houses, three
score and two great market-places, an hundred and thirty
butchers shambles, each of them containing four score shops,
and eight thousand streets, whereof six hundred that are
fairer and larger than the rest, are compassed about with
ballisters of copper; we were further assured, that there are
likewise two thousand and three hundred *Pagodes,* a thousand
of which were *Monasteries* of religious persons, professed in
their accursed sect, whose buildings were exceeding rich and

sumptuous, with very high steeples, wherein there were between sixty and seventy such mighty huge bells, that it was a dreadful thing to hear them rung; there are, moreover, in this city thirty great strong prisons, each whereof hath three or four thousand prisoners; and a charitable hospital, expressly established to supply the necessities of the poor, with proctors ordained for their defence, both in civil and criminal causes, as is before related. At the entrance into every principal street, there are arches and great gates, which for each mans security are shut every night, and in most of the streets are goodly fountains whose water is excellent to drink. Besides, at every full and new moon, open fairs are kept in several places, whither merchants resort from all parts, and where there is such abundance of all kind of victuall as cannot well be exprest, especially of flesh and fruit. It is not possible to deliver the great store of fish that is taken in this river, chiefly soles and mullets, which are all sold alive, besides a world of sea fish, both fresh, salted, and dried; we were told by certain *Chineses*, that in this city there are ten thousand trades for the working of silks, which from thence are sent all over the kingdom. The city it self is invironed with a very strong wall, made of fair hewed stone. The gates of are an hundred and thirty, at each of which there is porter, and two halberdiers, who are bound to give an account every day of all that passes in and out; there are also twelve forts or citadels, like unto ours, with bulwarks and very high towers, but without any ordnance at all. The same *Chineses* also affirmed unto us, that the city yielded the king daily two thousand *Taeis* of silver, which amount to three thousand ducates, as I have delivered heretofore. I will not speak of the palace royal, because I saw it but on the outside, howbeit the *Chineses* tell such wonders of it, as would amaze a man, for it is my intent to relate nothing save what we beheld here with our own eyes, and that was so much as I am afraid to write it; not that it would seem strange to those that have seen and read the marvels of the kingdom of *China*; but because I doubt that they, which would compare those wondrous things that are in the countrys, they have not seen, with that little they have seen in their own, will make some question of it, or, it may be, give no credit at all to these truthes, because they are not conformable to their understanding, and small experience.

Continuing our course up this river, the first two days we saw not any remarkable town or place, but onely a great number of villages, and little hamlets of two or three hundred fires apiece, which by their buildings seemed to be houses of fisher men, and poor people, that live by the labour of their hands. For the rest, all that was within view in the countrey was great woods of fir, groves, forests, and orange-trees, as also plains full of wheat, rice, beans, pease, millet, panick, barley, rye, flax, cotton-wool, with great inclosures of gardens, and goodly houses of pleasure, belonging to the *Mandarins,* and lords of the kingdom. There was likewise all along the river such an infinite number of cattel of all sorts, as I can assure you there is not more in *Æthiopia,* nor in all the dominions of *Prester John*; upon the top of the mountains many houses of their sects of *Gentiles* were to be seen, adorned with high steeples gilt all over, the glistering whereof was such, and so great, that to behold them afar off was an admirable sight. The fourth day of our voyage we arrived at a town, called *Pocasser,*twice as big as *Cantano,* compassed about with strong walls of hewed stone, and towers and bulwarks almost like ours, together with a key on the river side, twice as long as the shot of a falconet, and inclosed with two rows of iron grates, with very strong gates, where the junks and vessels that arrived there were unladen. This place abounds with all kinds of merchandise, which from thence is transported over all the kingdom, especially with copper, sugar, and allum, whereof there is very great store. Here also in the middest of a carrefour, that is almost at the end of the town, stands a mighty strong castle, having three bulwarks and five towers; in the highest of which the present kings father, as the *Chineses* told us, kept a king of *Tartaria* nine years prisoner, at the end whereof he killed himself with poyson, that his subjects sent him, because they would not be constrained to pay that ransom which the king of *China* demanded for his deliverance. In this town the *Chifuu* gave three of us leave to go up and down for to crave the alms of good people,

accompanied with four *Hupes*, that are as sergeants, or bailiffs
amongst us, who led us, chained together, as we were,
through six or seven streets, where we got in alms to the
value of above twenty ducates, as well in clothes, as money,
besides flesh, rice, meal, fruit, and other victuals, which was
bestowed on us; whereof we gave the one half to the *Hupes*
that conducted us, it being the custom so to do.  Afterwards
we were brought to a *Pagode*, whither the people flocked from
all parts that day, in regard of a very solemn feast that was
then celebrated there.  This temple, or *Pagode*, as we were
told, had sometime been a palace royal, where the king then
reigning was born; now because the queen his mother died
there in child-birth, she commanded her self to be buried in
the very same chamber where she was brought to bed; wherefore to honour her death the better, this temple was dedicated
to the invocation of *Tauhinaret*, which is one of the principal
sects of the *Pagans* in the kingdom of *China*, as I will more
amply declare, when as I shall speak of the *Labyrinth* of the
two and thirty laws that are in it.  All the buildings of this
temple, together with all the gardens, and walks, that belong
to it, are suspended in the air upon three hundred and threescore pillars, every one of the which is of one intire stone of a
very great bigness.  These three hundred and threescore
pillars are called by the names of three hundred and three
score days of the year, and in each of them is a particular
feast kept there with many alms, gifts, and bloody sacrifices,
accompanied with musick, dancing, and other sports.  Under
this *Pagode*, namely between those pillars, are eight very fair
streets, inclosed on every side with grates of copper, and gates
for the passage of pilgrims, and others, that run continually
to this feast, as it were to a jubilee; the chamber above,
where the queen lay, was made in the form of a chappel, but
round, and from the top to the bottom all garnished with
silver, the workmanship whereof was of greater cost then the
matter it self.  In the midst of it stood a kind of tribunal,
framed round, like the chamber, some fifteen steps high, compassed about with six gates of silver, on the top whereof was
a great bowl, and upon that a lion of silver, that with his
head supported a shrine of gold, three hand-breadths square,

wherein (they said) the bones of the queen were, which these
blinded ignorants reverenced as a great relique. Below this
tribunal, in equal proportion, were four bars of silver, that
traversed the chamber, whereon hung three and forty lamps
of the same metal, in memory of the three and forty years
that this queen lived, and seven lamps of gold in commemora-
tion of seven sons that she had; moreover, at the entry into
the chappel, just against the door, were eight other bars of
iron, whereon also hung a very great number of silver lamps,
which the *Chineses* told us were offered by some of the wives
of the *Chaems*, *Aytaos*, *Tutons*, and *Anchacys*, who were
assistant at the death of the queen, so that in acknowledgment of that honour they sent those lamps thither afterwards;
without the gates of the temple, and round about six ballisters
of copper that invironed it, were a great many statues of
giants, fifteen foot high, cast in brass, all well proportioned
with halberts or clubs in their hands, and some of them with
battle-axes on their shoulders, which made so brave and
majestical a shew, as one could never be satisfied enough with
looking on them.   Amongst these statues, which were in
number twelve hundred, as the *Chineses* affirmed, there were
four and twenty very great serpents also of brass, and under
every one of them a woman seated, with a sword in her hand,
and a silver crown on her head.  It was said, that those four
and twenty women carried the titles of queens, because they
sacrificed themselves to the death of this queen, to ·the end
their souls might serve hers in the other life, as in this their
bodies had served her body; a matter which the *Chineses*,
that draw their extraction from these men, hold for a very
great honour, insomuch as they inrich the crests of their coats
of arms with it; round about this row of giants was another
of triumphant arches, gilt all over, whereon a number of silver
bells hung by chains of the same metal, which moved with the
air kept such a continual ringing, as one could hardly hear one
another for the noise they made.   Without these arches there
were likewise at the same distance two rows of copper grates,
that inclosed all this huge work, and among them certain
pillars of the same metal, which supported lions rampant,
mounted upon bowls, being the arms of the kings of *China*, as

I have related elsewhere. At each corner of the carrefour was a monster of brass, of so strange and unmeasurable an heigth, and so deformed to behold, as it is not possible almost for a man to imagine; so that I think it best not to speak of them, the rather for that (I confess I) am not able in words to express the form wherein I saw their prodigies. Howbeit, as it is reasonable to conceal these things without giving some knowledge of them, I will say, as much as my weak understanding is able to deliver. One of these monsters which is on the right hand, as one comes into the carrefour, whom the *Chineses* call the Sergeant *Glutton* of the hollow or profound house of smoak, and that by their histories is held to be *Lucifer*, is represented under the figure of a serpent of an excessive heighth, with most hideous and deformed adders coming out of his stomack, covered all over with green and black scarrs, and a number of prickles on their backs above a span long, like unto porcupins quils; each of these adders had a woman between his jaws, with her hair all dishevelled, and standing on end, as one affrighted. The monster carried also in his mouth, which was unmeasurable great, a vizard that was above thirty foot long, and as big as a tun, with his nostrils and chaps so full of blood, that all the rest of his body was besmeared with it; this vizard held a great elephant between his paws, and seemed to gripe him so hard, as his very guts came out of his throat; and all this was done so proportionably, and to the life, that it made a man tremble to behold such a deformed figure, and which was scarce possible for one to imagine. His tail might be some twenty fathom long, and was entortilled about such another monster, that was the second of the four, whereof I spake, in the figure of a man, being an hundred foot high, and by the *Chineses* called *Turcamparoo*, who (they say) was the son of that serpent; besides that he was very ugly, he stood with both his hands in his mouth, that was as big as a great gate, with a row of horrible teeth, and a foul black tongue, hanging out two fathom long, most dreadful to behold. As for the other two monsters, one was in the form of a woman, named by the *Chineses*, *Magdelgau*, seventeen fathom high, and six thick. This same about the girdlesteed before had a face made proportionable to her body, above two fathom broad, and she breathed out of her mouth and nostrils great flakes, not of artificial, but true fire, which proceeded, as they told us, from her head, where fire was continually kept, that in like manner came out of the said face below. By this figure these idolaters would demonstrate that she was the queen of the fiery sphear, which according to their belief is to burn the earth at the end of the world. The fourth monster was a man, set stooping, which with great swoln cheeks, as big as the mainsail of a ship, seemed to blow extreamly; this monster was also of an unmeasurable height, and of such an hideous and ghastly aspect, that a man could hardly endure the sight of it; the *Chineses* called it *Vzanguenaboo*, and said, that it was he which raised tempests upon the sea, and demolished buildings; in regard whereof the people offered many things unto him, to the end he should do them no harm; and many presented him with a piece of money yearly, that he might not drown their junks, nor do any of theirs hurt that went by sea. I will omit many other abuses which their blindness makes them believe, and which they hold to be so true, as there is not one of them but would endure a thousand deaths for the maintenance thereof.

The next day, being gone from the town of *Pocasser*, we arrived at another fair and great town, called *Xinligau*; there we saw many buildings inclosed with walls of brick, and deep ditches about them, and at one end of the town two castles, very well fortified with towers and bulwarks after our fashion; at the gates were draw bridges, suspended in the air with great iron chains, and in the midst of them a tower five stories high, very curiously painted with several pictures; the *Chineses* assured us, that in those two castles there was as much treasure as amounted to fifteen thousand pieces of silver, which was the revenue of all this *Archipelage*, and laid up in this place by the King's grandfather now reigning, in memorial of a son of his that was born here, and named *Leuquinau*, that is to say, *The joy of all*; those of the country repute him for a saint, because he ended his days in religion, where also he was buried in a temple, dedicated to *Quiay Varatel*, the god of all the fishes of the sea, of whom these miserable ignorants recount a world of fooleries, as also the laws he invented, and the precepts which he left them, being able to astonish a man, as I will more amply declare when time shall serve. In this town and in another five leagues higher the most part of the silks of this kingdom are dyed, because they hold that the waters of these places make the colours far more lively then those of any other part; and these dyers, which are said to be thirteen thousand, pay unto the King yearly three hundred thousand *Taeis*. Continuing our course up the river the day after; about evening we arrived a certain great plains, where were great store of cattle, as horses, mares, colts, and cows, guarded by men on horsback, that make sale of them to butchers, who afterwards retale them indifferently as any other flesh. Having past these plains containing some ten or eleven leagues, we came to a town called *Junquileu*, walled with brick, but without battlements, bulwarks, or towers, as others had, whereof I have spoken before; at the end of the suburbs of this town we saw divers houses built in the water upon great piles, in the form of magazines. Before the gate of a little street stood a tomb made of stone, invironed with an iron grate, painted red and green, and over it a steeple framed of pieces of very fine pourcelain, sustained by four pillars of curious stone; upon the top of the tomb were five globes, and two others that seemed to be of cast iron, and on the one side thereof were graven in letters of gold, and in the *Chinese* language, words of this substance. *Here lyes* Trannocem Mudeliar, *uncle to the King of* Malaca, *whom death took out of the world before he could be revenged of Captain* Alphonso Albuquerque, *the lyon of the robberies of the sea.* We were much amazed to behold this inscription there; wherefore enquiring what it might mean, a *Chinese*, that seemed more honourable than the rest, told us; that about some forty years before, this man which lay buried there, came thither as ambassador from a prince, that stiled himself King of *Malaca*, to demand succour from the son of the Sun against men of a country that hath no name, which came by sea from the end of the world, and had taken *Malaca* from him; this man recounted many other incredible things concerning this matter, whereof mention is made in a printed book thereof; as also that this ambassador having continued three years at the kings court suing for this succour, just as it was granted him, and that preparations for it were a making, it was his ill-fortune to be surprised one night at supper with an apoplexie, whereof he died at the end of nine days ; so that extreamly afflicted to see himself carried away by a sudden death before he had accomplished his business, he expressed his earnest desire of revenge by the in-scription which he caused to be graven on his tomb, that posterity might know wherefore he was come thither. After-wards we departed from this place, and continued our voyage up the river, which thereabouts is not so large as towards the city of *Nanquin*; but the country is here better peopled with villages, boroughs, and gardens, than any other place, for every stones cast we met still with some *Pagode*, mansion of pleasure, or country house. Passing on about some two leagues further, we arrived at a place encompassed with great iron grates, in the midst whereof stood two mighty statues of brass upright, sus-tained by pillars of cast metal of the bigness of a bushel, and seven fathom high, the one of a man, and the other of a woman, both of them seventy-four spans in heighth, having their hands in their mouths, their cheeks horribly blown out, and their eyes so staring, as they affrighted all that looked upon them. That which represented a man, was called *Quiay Xingatalor*, and the other in the form of a woman was named *Apancapatur*. Having demanded of the *Chineses* the explication of these figures, they told us that the male was he, which with those mighty swoln cheeks blew the fire of hell for to torment all those miserable wretches that would not liberally bestow alms in this life ; and for the other monster, that she was porter of hell gate, where she would take notice of those that did her good in this world, and letting them fly away into a river of very cold water, called *Ochilenday*, would keep them hid there from being tormented by the devils, as other damned were. Upon this speech one of our company could not forbear laugh-ing at such a ridiculous and diabolical foolery, which three of their priests, or *Bonzoes* then present, observing, they were so exceedingly offended therewith, as they perswaded the *Chifuu*, which conducted us, that if he did not chastise us in such manner, as those gods might be well contented with the punishment inflicted on us for our mockery of them, both the one and the other would assuredly torment his soul, and never suffer it to go out of hell; which threatning so mightily terrified this dog, the *Chifuu*, that without further delay, or hearing us speak, he caused us all to be bound hand and foot, and commanded each of us to have an hundred lashes given him with a double cord, which was immediately executed with so much rigour, as we were all in a gore bloud, whereby we were taught not to jeer afterwards at anything we saw, or heard. At such time as we arrived here we found twelve *Bonzoes* upon the place, who with silver censers full of perfumes of aloes and benjamin, censed those two devilish monsters, and chanted out aloud, *Help us, even as we serve thee*; whereunto divers other priests answered in the name of the idol with a great noise, *So I promise to do like a good Lord*. In this sort they went as it were in procession round about the place, singing with an ill-tuned voice to the sound of a great many bells, that were in steeples thereabouts. In the mean time there were others, that with drums and basins made such a dinne, as I may truly say, put them all together, was most horrible to hear.

----

## CHAPTER XXVII.

Our arrival at Sempitay, our encounter there with a Christian woman, and an account of many things seen on the journey; with an account of Pequin.

FROM this place we continued our voyage eleven days more up the river, which in those parts is so peopled with cities, towns, villages, boroughs, forts and castles, that commonly they are not a flight shot distant one from another, besides a world of houses of pleasure, and temples, where steeples were all gilt; which made such a glorious show, as we were much amazed at it. In this manner we arrived at a town, named *Sempitay*, where we abode five days, by reason the *Chifuus* wife, that conducted us, was not well. Here by his permission we landed, and chained together as we were, we went up and down the streets craving of alms, which was very liberally given us by the inhabitants, who wondering to see such men as we,

demanded of us what kind of people we were, of what kingdom, and how our countrey was called ?  Hereunto we answered
conformably to that we had said before, namely that we were
natives of the kingdom of *Siam*, that going from *Liampoo* to
*Nanquin*, we had lost all our goods by shipwrack, and that
although they beheld us then in so poor a case, yet we had
been formerly very rich ; whereupon a woman who was come
thither amongst the rest to see us : it is very likely, said she,
speaking to then about her, that what these poor strangers
have related is most true, for daily experience doth shew how
those that trade by sea do oftentimes make it their grave,
wherefore it is best and surest to travel upon the earth, and to
esteem of it, as of that whereof it has pleased God to frame
us ; saying, so she gave us two Mazes, which amounts to
about sixteen pence of our money, advising us to make no
more such long voyages, since our lives were so short.   Hereupon she unbuttoned one of the sleeves of a red sattin gown
she had on, and baring her left arm, she showed us a cross imprinted on it, like the mark of a slave, *Do any of you know this
sign, which amongst those, that follow the way of truth, is called
a cross ? or have any of you heard it named ?*  To this falling
down on our knees, we answered, with tears in our eyes, that
we know exceeding well.   Then lifting up her hands, she cried
out, *Our Father, which art in Heaven, hallowed be Thy Name*,
speaking these words in the *Portugal* tongue, and because she
could speak no more of our language, she very earnestly
desired us in *Chinese* to tell her whether we were Christians ;
we replied that we were ; and for proof thereof, after we had
kissed that arm whereon the cross was, we repeated all the
rest of the Lord's Prayer, which she had left unsaid, wherewith
being assured that we were Christians indeed, she drew aside
from the rest there present, and weeping said to us, come along
Christians of the other end of the world, with her that is your
true sister in the faith of Jesus Christ, or peradventure a
kinswoman to one of you, by his side that begot me in this
miserable exile ; and so going to carry us to her house, the
*Hupes* which guarded us, would not suffer her, saying, that if
we would not continue our craving of alms, as the *Chifuu* had
permitted us, they would return us back to the ship ; but this

they spake in regard of their own interest, for that they were to have the moity of what was given us, as I have before declared, and accordingly they made as though they would have lead us thither again, which the woman perceiving, *I understand your meaning*, said she, *and indeed it is but reason you should make the best of your places, for thereby you live* ; so opening her purse, she gave them two *Taeis* in silver, wherewith they were very well satisfied; whereupon with the leave of the *Chifuu*, she carried us home to her house, and there kept us all the while we remained in that place, making exceeding much of us, and using us very charitably.  Here she shewed us an oratory, wherein she had a cross of wood gilt, as also candlesticks, and a lamp of silver.  Furthermore she told us, that she was named, *Inez de Leyria*, and her father *Tome Pirez*, who had been great ambassadour from *Portugal* to the King of *China*, and that in regard of an insurrection with a *Portugal* captain, made at *Canton*, the *Chineses* taking him for a spy, and not for an ambassador, as he termed himself, clapped him and all his followers up in prison, where by order of justice five of them were put to torture, receiving so many, and such cruel stripes on their bodies, as they died instantly, and the rest were all banished into several parts, together with her father into this place, where he married with her mother, that had some means, and how he made her a Christian, living so seven and twenty years together, and converting many *Gentiles* to the faith of Christ, whereof there were above three hundred then abiding in that town; which every *Sunday* assembled in her house to say the catechisme : whereupon demanding of her what were their accustomed prayers, she answered, that she used no other but these, which on their knees, with their eyes and hands lift up to Heaven, they pronounced in this manner, *O Lord Jesus Christ, as it is most true that Thou art the very Son of God, conceived by the Holy Ghost in the womb of the Virgine Mary for the salvation of sinners, so Thou wilt be pleased to forgive us our offences, that thereby we may become worthy to behold Thy face in the glory of Thy kingdom, where Thou art sitting at the right hand of the Almighty.  Our Father which art in Heaven, hallowed be Thy name.  In the name of the Father, the Son, and the Holy*

SHIP OF CHINA AND JAVA

WITH MAT SAILS.

*Ghost. Amen.* And so all of them kissing the cross, imbraced one another, and thereupon every one returned to his own home. Moreover she told us, that her father had left her many other prayers, which the *Chineses* had stollen from her, so that she had none left but those before recited; whereunto we replied, that those we had heard from her were very good, but before we went away we would leave her divers other good and wholsome prayers, *Do so then,* answered she, *for the respect you owe to so good a God, as yours is, and that hath done such things for you, for me, and all in general.* Then causing the cloth to be laid, she gave us a very good and plentifull dinner, and treated us in like sort every meal, during the five days we continued in her house, which (as I said before) was permitted by the *Chifuu,* in regard of a present that this good women sent his wife, whom she earnestly entreated so to deal with her husband, as we might be well intreated, for that we were men of whom God had a particular care, as the *Chifuu's* wife promised her to do with many thanks to her for the present she had received. In the mean space, during the five days we remained in her house, we read the catechism seven times to the Christians, wherewithall they were very much edified; beside, *Christophoro Borbalho* made them a little book in the *Chinese* tongue, containing the *Pater noster,* the *Creed,* the *Ten Commandments,* and many other good prayers. After these things we took our leaves of *Inez de Leyria,* and the Christians who gave us fifty *Taeis* in silver, which stood us since in good stead, as I shall declare hereafter; and withall *Inez de Leyria* gave us secretly fifty *Taeis* more, humbly desiring us to remember her in our prayers to God.

After our departure from the town of *Sempitay* we continued our course upon the river of *Batanpina,* unto a place, named *Lequinpau,* containing about eleven or twelve thousand fires, and very well built, at least we judged so by that we could discern, as also inclosed with good walls, and curtains round about it. Not far from it was an exceeding long house; having within it thirty fornaces on each side, where a great quantity of silver was melted, which was brought in carts from a mountain, some five leagues off, called *Tuxenguim.* The *Chineses* assured us, that above a thousand men wrought continually in that mine

14

to draw out the silver, and that the King of *China* had in
yearly revenue out of it above five thousand *Pico's*. This
place we left about sun-set, and the next day in the evening we
arrived just between two little towns, that stood opposite one
to another, the river onely between, the one named *Pacau*, and
the other *Nacau* ; which although they were little, yet were
they fairly built, and well walled with great hewed stone,
having a number of temples, which they call *Pagodes*, all gilt
over, and enriched with steeples and fanes of great price, very
pleasing and agreeable to the eye.

*[Here follows a legend of ¦the foundation of China, omitteb.]*

Now that I have spoken of the original and foundation of
this empire, together with the circuit of the great city of
*Pequin,* I hold it not amiss to intreat as succinctly as I may
of another particular, which is no less admirable then those
whereof I have made mention before. It is written in the fifth
book of the Scituation of all the remarkable places of this
empire, or rather monarchy, (for to speak truly, there is no
appellation so great but may be well attributed unto it) that a
king, named *Crisnagol Dicotay,* who according to the computation of that book, reigned in the year of our Lord 518,
happened to make war with the *Tartar,* about some difference
between them concerning the state of *Xenxinapau,* that borders
on the kingdom of *Lauhos,* and so valiantly demeaned himself
in a battel against him, that he defeated his army, and
remained master of the field ; whereupon the *Tartar* con-
federating himself with other kings, his friends, did by their
assistance assemble together greater forces than the former,
and therewith invaded the kingdom of *China,* where (it is said)
he took three and thirty very important towns, of which the
principal was *Panquilor,* insomuch that the *Chinese* fearing he
should not be well able to defend himself, concluded a peace
with him upon condition to relinquish his right, which he
pretended to that in question betwixt them, and to pay him
two thousand *Picos* of silver for to defray the charges of those
strangers the *Tartar* had entertained in this war ; by this
means *China* continued for a good while quiet, but the King
doubting lest the *Tartar* might in time to come return to annoy

him again, resolved to build a wall, that might serve for a
bulwark to his empire ; and to that end calling all his estates
together, he declared his determination unto them, which was
presently not onely well approved of, but held most necessary ;
so that to enable him for the performance of a business so
much concerning his state, they gave him ten thousand *Picos*
of silver, which amount, according to our account, unto fifteen
millions of gold, after the rate of fifteen hundred ducates each
*Pico* ; and moreover they entertained him two hundred and
fifty thousand men to labour in the work, whereof thirty
thousand were appointed for officers, and all the rest for
manual services. Order being taken then for whatsoever was
thought fit for so prodigious an enterprise, they fell to it in such
sort, as by the report of the history all that huge wall was in
seven and twenty years quite finished from one end to the
other ; which if credit may be given to the same chronicle is
seventy *Joas* in length, that is six hundred and fifteen miles
after nine miles every *Joa* ; wherein that which seemed most
wonderfull and most exceeding the belief of man, was that
seven hundred and fifty thousand men laboured incessantly for
so long a time in that great work, whereof the Commonalty,
as I delivered before, furnished one third part ; the priests, and
isles of *Aynen*, another third ; and the King assisted by the
princes, lords, *Chaems*, and *Anchacys* of the kingdom, the rest
of the building, which I have both seen and measured, being
thirty foot in height, and ten foot in breadth, where it is
thickest. It is made of lime and sand, and plaistered on the
outside with a kind of *Bitumen*, which renders it so strong,
that no cannon can demolish it : instead of bulwarks it hath
sentries, or watch-towers, two stages high, flanked with
buttresses of carpentry made of a certain black wood, which
they call *Caubesy*, that is to say, wood of iron, because it is
exceeding strong and hard, every buttress being as thick as an
hogshead, and very high, so that these sentries are far stronger
than if they were made of lime and stone. Now this wall,
by them termed *Chaufacan*, which signifies, *strong resistance*,
extends in height equal to the mountains, whereunto it is
joyned, and that those mountains also may serve for a wall
they are cut down very smooth and steep, which renders them

far stronger then the wall itself; but you must know that in
all this extent of land there is no wall, but in the void spaces
from hill to hill, so that the hills themselves make up the rest
of the wall and fence.　Further it is to be noted, that in this
whole length of a hundred and fifteen leagues, which this
fortification contains, there are but onely 5 entries whereby
the rivers of *Tartaria* do pass, which are derived from the
impetuous torrents that descend from these mountains, and
running above five hundred leagues in the country, render
themselves into the seas of *China* and *Caushenchina*; howbeit
one of these rivers, being greater then the rest, disembogues
by the Bay of *Cuy* in the kingdom of *Sournau*, commonly
called *Siam*.　Now in all these five passages both the King of
*China*, and the King of *Tartaria*, keep garrisons; the *Chinese*
in each of them entertains seven thousand men giving them
great pay, whereof six thousand are horse, the rest foot, being
for the most part strangers, as *Mogores, Pancrus, Champaas,
Corosones, Gizares* of *Persia*, and other different nations,
bordering upon this empire, and which in consideration of the
extraordinary pay they receive, serve the *Chinese*; who (to
speak truth) are nothing couragious, as being but little used to
the wars, and ill provided of arms and artillery.　In all this
length of wall there are three hundred and twenty companies,
each of them containing five hundred souldiers; so that there
are in all one hundred and threescore thousand men, besides
officers of justice, *Anchacis, Chaems*, and other such like
persons necessary for the government, and entertainment of
these forces; so that all joyned together make up the number
of two hundred thousand, which are all maintained at the
King's onely charge, by reason the most of them are male-
factours condemned to the reparations and labours of the wall,
as I shall more aptly declare when I come to speak of the
prison destined to this purpose, in the City of *Pequin*, which
is also another edifice, very remarkable, wherein there are
continually above thirty thousand prisoners, the most of them
from eighteen to forty-five years of age, appointed to work in
this wall.

Being departed from those two towns *Pacau* and *Nacau*, we
continued our course up the river, and arrived at another town

called *Mindoo,* somewhat bigger then those from whence we
parted, where about half a mile off was a great lake of salt
water, and a number of salt-houses round about it; The
*Chinese* assured us, that this lake did ebb and flow like the
sea, and that it extended above two hundred leagues into
the country, rendring the King of *China* in yearly revenue one
hundred thousand *Taeis,* onely for the third of the salt that
was drawn out of it; as also that the town yielded him other
one hundred thousand *Taeis* for the silk alone that was made
there, not speaking at all of the camphire, sugar, pourcelain,
vermilion, and quick-silver, whereof there was very great
plenty; moreover, that some two leagues from this town were
twelve exceeding long houses, like unto magazines, where a
world of people laboured in casting and purifying of copper
and the horrible din which the hammers made there was such
and so strange, as if there were anything on earth that could
represent hell, this was it; wherefore being desirous to understand the cause of this extraordinary noise, we would needs
go to see from whence it proceeded; and we found that there
were in each of these houses forty fornaces, that is twenty of
either side, with forty huge anvils, upon every of which eight
men beat in order, and so swiftly, as a mans eye could hardly
discern the blows, so as three hundred and twenty men wrought
in each of these twelve houses, which in all the twelve houses
made up three thousand eight hundred and forty workmen,
beside a great number of other persons that laboured in other
particular things; whereupon we demanded how much copper
might be wrought every year in each of these houses, and they
told us, one hundred and ten, or sixscore thousand *Pico's,*
whereof the King had two thirds, because the mines were his;
and that the mountain from whence it was drawn was called
*Corotum baya,* which signifies a river of copper, for that from
the time since it was discovered, being above two hundred
years, it never failed, but rather more and more was found.
Having past about a league beyond those twelve houses up the
river, we came to a place inclosed with three ranks of iron
grates, where we beheld thirty houses, divided into five rows,
six in each row, which were very long and complete, with
great towers full of bells of cast metall, and much carved

work, as also gilt pillars, and the frontispieces of fair hewed
stone, whereupon many inventions were engraved.  At this
place we went ashore by the *Chifuu's* permission, that carried
us, for that he had made a vow to this *Pagode*, which was
called *Bigay potim*, that is to say, *god of an hundred and ten
thousand gods, Corchoo fungane, ginaco ginaca*, which (according
to their report) signifies, *strong and great above all others*; for
some of the errours wherewith these wretched people are
blinded are, *that they believe every particular thing hath its
god, who hath created it, and preserves its natural being*; but
*that this* Bigay potim *brought them all forth from under his
arm-pits, and that from him as a father, they derive their being,
by a filial union, which they term* Bira Porentasay; *And in the
kingdom of* Pegu, *where I have often been, I have seen one like
unto this, named by those of the country,* Ginocoginans, *the god
of greatness, which temple was in times past built by the*
Chinese, *when as they commanded in the* India's, *being according to their supputation, from the year our Lord Jesus Christ*
1013, *to the year* 1072, *by which account it appears that the*
India's *were under the Empire of* China *but onely fifty and nine
years, from the successour of him that conquered it, called*
Exiragano, *voluntarily abandoned it in regard to the great
expence of money and bloud that the unprofitable keeping of it
cost him.*  In those thirty houses, whereof I formerly spake,
were a great number of idols of gilt wood; and a like number
of tin, latten, and pourcelain, being indeed so many, as I should
hardly be believed, to declare them.  Now we had not past
above five or six leagues from this place but we came to a
great town, about a league in circuit, quite destroyed and
ruinated.

[*Here follows a religious legend, omitted.*]

After our departure from the ruines of *Fiunganorsee*, we
arrived at a great town, called *Junquinalau*, which is very rich,
abounding with all kind of things, fortified with a strong
garrison of horse and foot, and having a number of junks and
vessels, riding before it.  Here we remained five days to
celebrate the funeral of our *Chifuu's* wife; for whose soul he
gave us by way of alms both meat and clothes, and withall

freeing us from the oar, permitted us to go ashore without irons, which was a very great ease unto us : Having left this place, we continued our course up the river, beholding still on either side a world of goodly great towns invironed with strong walls ; as also many fortresses and castles all along the waters side ; we saw likewise a great number of temples, whose steeples were all gilt, and in the fields such abundance of cattel that the ground was even covered over with them, so far as we could well discern. Moreover, there were so many vessels upon this river, especially in some parts, where fairs were kept, that at first sight one would have thought them to be populous towns; besides other lesser companies of three hundred, five hundred, six hundred, and a thousand boats, which continually we met withall on both sides of the river, wherein all things that one could imagine were sold ; Moreover, the *Chineses* assure us, that in this empire of *China*, the number of those which levied upon the rivers, was no less than those that dwelled in the towns, and that without the good order which is observed to make the common people work, and to constrain the meaner sort to supply themselves unto trades for to get their living, they would eat up one another. Now it is to be noted, that every kind of traffique and commerce is divided among them into three or four forms, as followeth : They which trade in ducks, whereof there are great quantities in this countrey, proceed therein diversly ; some cause their egs to be hatched for to sell the ducklings ; others fat them when they are great for to sell them dead after they are salted. These traffique only with the egs ; others with the feathers ; and some with the heads, feet, gizards, and intrails, no man being permitted to trench upon his companions sale, under the penalty of thirty lashes, which no priviledg can exempt them from. In the same manner, concerning hogs, some sell them alive, and by whole sale, others dead, and by retail ; some make bacon of them, others sell their pigs, and some again sell nothing but the chitterlings, the sweet-breads, the blood, and the haslets ; which is also observed for fish, for such a one sels it fresh, that cannot sell it either salted or dried ; and so of other provisions, as flesh, fruit, fowls, venison, pulse, and other things, wherein such rigour is used, as there are chambers expressly established, whose officers have commission and power to see, that they which trade in one particular may not do it in another, if it be not for just and lawful causes, and that on pain of thirty lashes. There be others likewise that get their living by selling fish alive, which to that purpose they keep in great well-boats, and so carry them into divers countries, where they know there is no other but salt fish. There are likewise all along this river of *Batampina*, whereon we went from *Nanquin* to *Pequin*, which is distant one from the other one hundred and fourscore leagues, such a number of engines for sugar, and presses for wine and oyl, made of divers sorts of pulse and fruit, as one could hardly see any other thing on either side of the water. In many other places also there were an infinite company of houses, and magazines full of all kinds of provision, that one could imagine, where all sorts of flesh are salted, dried, smoked, and piled up in great high heaps, as gammons of bacon, pork, lard, geese, ducks, cranes, bustards, ostriches, stags, cows, buffles, wild goats, rhinocerotes, horses, tygers, dogs, foxes, and almost all other creatures that one can name, so that we said many times amongst our selves, that it was not possible for all the people of the world to eat up all those provisions. We saw likewise upon the same river a number of vessels, which they call *Panouras*, covered from the poup to the prow with nets, in manner of a cage, three inches high, full of ducks and geese, that were carried from place to place to be sold; when the owners of those boats would have these fowl to feed, they approach to the land; and where there are rich medows, or marshes, they set forth planks; penning the doors of those cages, they beat three or four times upon a drum, which they have expressly for that perpose; whereupon all these fowl, being six or seven thousand at the least, go out of the boat with a mighty noise, and so fall to feeding all along the waters side. Now when the owner perceives, that these fowl have fed sufficiently, and that it is time to return them, he beats the drum the second time, at the sound whereof they gather all together, and re-enter with the same noise, as they went out; wherein it is strange to observe, that they return all in again, not so much as one missing. That done, the master of the

boat parts from that place, and afterwards when he thinks it
is time for them to lay, he repairs towards land, and where he
finds the grounds dry, and good grass, he opens the doors, and
beats the drum again, at which all the fowl of the boat came
forth to lay ; and then at such time as the master judges that
these fowl have laid, he beats his drum afresh, and suddenly
in haste they all throng in to the boat, not so much as one
remaining behind. Thereupon two or three men get ashore,
with baskets in their hands, whereinto they gather up the eggs,
till they have gotten eleven or twelve baskets full, and so they
proceed on their voyage to make sale of their ware ; which
being almost spent, to store themselves anew, they go for to
buy more unto them that breed them, whose trade it is to sell
them young ; for they are not suffered to keep them when they
are great, as the others do, by reason, as I have said before,
no man may deal in any commodity for which he hath not
permission from the governours of the towns. They that get
their living by breeding of ducks have neer to their houses
certain ponds, where many times they keep ten or eleven
thousand of these ducklings, some bigger, some lesser. Now
for to hatch the eggs, they have in very long galleries twenty
or thirty furnaces full of dung, wherein they bury two hundred,
three hundred, and five hundred eggs together, then stopping
the mouth of each furnace that the dung may become the
hotter, they leave the eggs there till they think the young
ones are disclosed ; whereupon putting into every several
furnace a capon half pulled, and the skin stript from off his
brest, they leave him shut up therein for the space of two days ;
at the end whereof being all come out of the shell, they carry
them into certain places under ground made for that purpose,
setting them bran soaked in liquor ; and so being left there
loose some ten or eleven dayes, they go afterwards of themselves into the ponds, where they feed and bring them up for
to sell them unto those former merchants, who trade with
them into divers parts, it being unlawfull for one to trench
upon anothers traffique, as I have before related ; so that in
the markets and publique places, where provisions for the
mouth are sold, if any that sell goose eggs do chance to be
taken siesed with hens eggs, and it is suspected that they sell

of them, they are presently punished with thirty lashes on the bare buttocks, without hearing any justification they can make for themselves, being as I have said, found siesed of them ; so that if they will have hens eggs for their own use, to avoid incurring the penalty of the law, they must be broken at one end ; whereby it may appear that they keep them not to sell, but to eat.    As for them that sell fish alive, if any of their fish chance to die, they cut them in pieces, and salting them sell them at the price of salt-fish, which is less then that of fresh-fish, wherein they proceed so exactly, that no man dares pass the limits which are prescribed and ordained by the *Conchalis* of the State, upon pain of most severe punishment ; for in all this county the King is so much respected, and justice so feared, as no kinde of person, how great soever, dares murmur, or look awry at an officer, no not at the very *Huppes*, which are as the bayliffs or beadles amongst us.

------

## CHAPTER XXVIII.

*The order which is observed in the removing towns that are made upon the rivers ; and that which further befell us.*

WE saw likewise all along this great river a number of hogs both wilde and domestick, that were kept by certain men on horseback, and many herds of tame red deer, which were driven from place to place like sheep, to feed, all lamed of their right legs, to hinder them from running away ; and they are lamed so, when they are but calves, to avoid the danger that otherwise they might incur of their lives : we saw also divers parks, wherein a world of dogs were kept to be sold to the butchers ; for in these countries they eat all manner of flesh, whereof they know the price, and of what creatures they are, by the choppings they make of them.    Moreover, we met with many small barques, whereof some were full of pigs, others of tortoises, frogs, otters, adders, eeles, snails, and lizards ; for (as I have said) they buy there of all that is judged good to eat ; now to the end that such provisions may pass at an easier rate, all that sell them are permitted to make traffique of them in several fashions ; true it is, that in some things they have greater franchises then in others, to the end that by means thereof no merchandise may want sale. We saw many boats likewise laden with dried orange pils, wherewith in victualling houses they boyl dogs flesh, for to take away the rank savour and humidity of it, as also to render it more firm. In brief, we saw so many *Vaucans*, *Lanteaas*, and *Barcasses*, in this river, laden with all kinds of provision, that either the sea or land produces, and that in such abundance, as I must confess, I am not able to express it in words; for it is not possible to imagine the infinite store of things that are in this country ; of each whereof you shall see two or three hundred vessels together at a time, all full, especially at the fairs, and markets, that are kept upon the solemn festival days of their *Pagodes*; for then all the fairs are free, and the *Pagodes* for the most part are scituated upon the banks of rivers, to the end all commodities may the more commodiously be brought thither by water. Now when all these vessels come to joyn together, during these fairs, they take such order, as they make, as it were, a great and fair town of them; so that sometimes you shall have of them a league in length, and three quarters of a league in bredth, being composed of above twenty thousand vessels; besides *Balons*, *Guedees*, and *Manchuas*, which are small boats, whose number is infinite; for the government hereof there are threescore captains appointed, of which thirty are to see good order kept, and the other thirty are for the guard of the merchants that come thither, to the end they may sail in safety. Moreover, there is above them a *Chaem*, who hath absolute power, both in civil and criminal causes, without any appeal or opposition whatsoever, during the fifteen days that this fair lasts, which is from the new to the full moon; and indeed more come to see the policy, order, and beauty of this kind of town, then otherwise; for (to speak the truth, the framing of it in that manner with vessels) makes it more to be admired then all the edifices that can be seen upon the land. There are in this moving town two thousand streets, exceeding long, and very strait, inclosed on either side with ships, most of which are covered with silks, and adorned with a world of banners, flags, and streamers, wherein all kinds of commodities

that can be desired are to be sold. In other streets are as
many trades to be seen, as in any town on the land; amidst
the which they that traffique, go up and down in little *Manchuas*, and that very quietly, and without any disorder. Now
if by chance any one is taken stealing, he is instantly punished
according to his offence. As soon as it is night, all these
streets are shut up with cords athwart them, to the end none
may pass after the retreat sounded; in each of these streets
there are at least a dozen of lanthorns, with lights burning,
fastened a good heighth on the masts of the vessels, by means
whereof all that go in and out are seen, so that it may be
known who they are, from whence they come, and what they
would have, to the end the *Chaem* may the next morning
receive an account thereof. And truly, to behold all these
lights together in the night, is a sight scarce able to be
imagined; neither is there a street without a bell, and a sentinel; so as when that of the *Chaems* ship is heard to ring, all
the other bels answer it, with so great a noise of voices adjoyned thereunto, that we were almost beside our selves, at the
hearing of a thing which cannot be well conceived; and that
was ruled with such good order. In every of these streets,
even in the poorest of them, there is a chappel to pray in,
framed upon great *barcasses*, like to gallies, very neat, and so
well accommodated, that for the most part they are enriched
with silks, and cloth of gold. In these chappels are their idols,
and priests which administer their sacrifices, and receive the
offerings that are made them, wherewith they are abundantly
furnished for their living. Out of each street, one of the most
account, or chiefest merchant, is chosen to watch all night in
his turn with those of his squadron, besides the captains of the
government, who in ballons walk the round without, to the end
no thief may escape by any avenue whatsoever; and for that
purpose these guards cry as loud as they can, that they may
be heard. Amongst the most remarkable things, we saw one
street, where there were above an hundred vessels, laden with
idols of gilt wood, of divers fashions, which were sold for to be
offered to the *Pagodes*; together with a world of feet, thighs,
arms, and heads, that sick folks bought to offer in devotion.
There also we beheld other ships, covered with silk hangings,

where comedies and other plays were represented to entertain
the people withall, which in great numbers flocked together.
In other places, bills of exchange for Heaven were sold, whereby
these priests of the devil promised them many merits, with
great interest, affirming that without these bils they could not
possibly be saved; for that God, say they, is a mortal enemy
to all such as do not some good to the *Pagodes*; whereupon
they tell them such fables and lies, as these unhappy wretches
do often times take the very bread from their mouthes to give
it them. There were also other vessels all laden with dead
mens skuls, which divers men bought for to present as an
offering at the tombs of their friends, when they should happen
to die; for, say they, as the deceased is laid in the grave in the
company of these skuls, so shall his soul enter into Heaven,
attended by those unto whom those skuls belonged; wherefore
when the porter of Paradise shall see such a merchant, with
many followers, he will do him honour, as to a man that in
this life hath been a man of quality; for if he be poor, and
without a train, the porter will not open to him; whereas,
contrarily, the more dead mens skuls he hath buried with him,
the more happy he shall be esteemed. There were many boats
likewise, where there were men that had a great many of
cages, full of live birds, who playing on divers instruments of
musick, exhorted the people with a loud voice, to deliver those
poor creatures of God, that were there in captivity; whereupon
many came and gave them money for the redemption of those
prisoners, which presently they let out of the cages; and then
as they flew away, the redeemers of them cried out to the
birds, *Pichau pitanel catan vacaxi*, that is, *Go, and tell God,
how we serve him here below*. In imitation of these, there are
others also, who in their ships kept a great many of live fishes
in great pots of water, and like the sellers of birds invite the
people, for Gods cause, to free those poor innocent fishes, that
had never sinned; so that divers bought many of them, and
casting them into the river, said, *Get ye gone, and tell there
below the good I have done you for Gods sake*. To conclude all,
the vessels where these things are exposed to sale are seldom
less in number then two hundred, besides thousands of others,
which sell such like wares in a far greater quantity.

We saw likewise many *Barcasses* full of men and women, that played upon divers sorts of instruments, and for money gave them musick that desired it. There were other vessels laden with horns, which the priests sold, therewith to make feasts in Heaven; for they say, that those were the horns of several beasts, which were offered in sacrifice to the idols out of devotion, and for the performance of vows that men had made in divers kind of mis-fortunes, and sicknesses, wherein they had at other times been. And that as the flesh of those beasts had been given here below for the honour of God to the poor, so the souls of them for whom those horns were offered do in the other world eat the souls of those beasts to whom those horns belonged, and thereunto invite the souls of their friends, as men use to invite others here on earth. Other vessels we saw covered with blacks, and ful of tombs, torches, and great wax lights; as also women in them, that for money would be hired to weep and lament for the dead; others there were, called *Pitaleus*, that in great barques kept divers kinds of wild beasts to be shewed for money, most dreadful to behold as serpents, huge adders, monstrous lizards, tygers, and many others such like; we saw in like sort a great number of stationers, which sold all manner of books that could be desired, as well concerning the creation of the world, whereof they tell a thousand lies, as touching the states, kingdomes, islands, and provinces of the world, together with the laws and customs of nations; but especially of the kings of *China*, their number, brave acts, and of all things else that happened in each of their reigns. Moreover, we saw a great many of the light, swift foysts, wherein were men very well armed, who cried out with a loud voice, that if any one had received an affront, whereof he desired to be avenged, let him come unto them, and they would cause satisfaction to be made him. In other vessels there were old women, that served for midwives, and that would bring women speedily and easily abed; as also a many of nurses, ready to be entertained for to give children suck. There were barques likewise very well adorned, and set forth, that had in them divers reverend old men, and grave matrons, whose profession was to make marriages, and to comfort widows, or such as had lost their children, or suffered any other mis-fortune. In others there were a number of young men and maids, that lacked masters, and mistresses, which offered themselves to any that would hire them. There were other vessels that had in them such as undertook to tell fortunes, and to help folks to things lost. In a word, not to dwell any longer upon every particular that was to be seen in this moving town, (for then I should never have done) it shall suffice me to say, that nothing can be desired on land, which was not to be had in their vessels, and that in greater abundance than I have delivered, wherefore I will pass from it to shew you that one of the principal causes why this monarchy of *China*, that contains two and thirty kingdoms, is so mighty, rich, and of so great commerce, is, because it is exceedingly replenished with rivers, and a world of chanels that have been anciently made by the kings, great lords, and people thereof, for to render all the country navigable, and so communicate their labours with one another. The narrowest of these chanels have bridges of hewed stone over them, that are very high, long and broad, whereof some are of one stone, eighty, ninety, nay, an hundred spans long, and fifteen or twenty broad, which doubtless is very marvellous; for it is almost impossible to comprehend by what means so huge a mass of stone could be drawn out of the quarry without breaking, and how it should be transported to the place where it was to be set. All the ways and passages, from cities, towns, and villages, have very large causeys made of fair stone, at the ends whereof are costly pillars and arches, upon which are inscriptions with letters of gold, containing the prayses of them that erected them; moreover, there are handsome seats placed all along for poor passengers to rest themselves on. There are likewise innumerable aqueducts and fountains every where, whose water is most wholesom and excellent to drink. And in divers parts there are certain wenches of love, that out of charity prostitute themselves to travellers which have no money; and although amongst us this is held for a great abuse and abomination, yet with them it is accounted a work of mercy; so that many on their death-beds do by their testaments bequeathe great revenues, for the maintenance of this wickedness, as a thing very meritorious for the salvation of their souls; moreover, many others have left lands for the erecting and maintaining of houses, in desarts and uninhabited places, where great fires are kept all the night to guide such as have strayed out of their way; as also water for men to drink, and seats to repose them in; and that there may be no default herein, there are divers persons entertained with very good means, to see these things carefully continued, according to the institution of him that founded them for the health of his soul. By these marvels which are found in the particular towns of this empire may be concluded, what the greatness thereof might be, were they joyned all together; but for the better satisfaction of the reader, I dare boldly say, if my testimony may be worthy of credit, that in one and twenty years space (during which time, with a world of mis-fortune, labour and pain, I traversed the greatest part of *Asia*, as may appear by this my discourse) I had seen in some countries a wonderfull abundance of several sorts of victuals, and provisions, which we have not in our *Europe*; yet, without speaking what each of them might have in particular, I do not think there is in all *Europe* so much as there is in *China* alone. And the same may be said of all the rest, wherewith Heaven hath favoured this climate, as well for the temperature of the air, as for that which concerns the policy, and riches, the magnificence and greatness of their estate. Now that which gives the greatest lustre unto it, is, their exact observation of justice; for there is so well ruled a government in this country, as it may justly be envied of all others in the world. And to speak the truth, such as want this particular, have no gloss, be they otherways never so great and commendable. Verily, so often as I represent unto my self those great things which I have seen in this *China*, I am on the one side amazed to think how liberally it hath pleased God to heap upon this people the goods of the earth; and on the other side I am exceedingly grieved to consider how ungratefull they are in acknowledging such extraordinary favours; for they commit amongst themselves an infinite of most enormous sins, wherewithall they incessantly offend the Divine Goodness.

## CHAPTER XXIX.

Our arrival at the city of Pequin, together with our imprisonment, and that
which moreover happened unto us there ; as also the great majesty of
the officers of their Court of Justice.

AFTER we were departed from that rare and marvellous
town, whereof I have spoken, we continued our course up
the river, until at length, on *Tuesday*, the nineteenth of *October*,
in the year 1541, we arrived at the great city of *Pequin*,
whither, as I have said before, we had been remitted by appeal.
In this manner, chained three and three together, we were cast
into a prison, called *Gofaniauserca*, where for our welcom we
had at the first dash thirty lashes apiece given us, wherewith
some of us became very sick. Now as soon as the *Chifuu* who
conducted us thither had presented the process of our sentence,
sealed with twelve seals, to the justice of the *Aytao*, which is
their Parliament, the twelve *Chonchalis* of the criminal chamber, unto whom the cognisance of our cause appertained, commanded us presently away to prison ; whereupon one of those
twelve, assisted by two Registers, and six or seven officers,
whom they term *Hupes*, (and are much like our Catchpoles
here), terrified us not a little, as he was leading us thither ; for
giving us very threatning speeches, *Come*, said he unto us,
*By the power and authority which I have from the Aytao of*
Batampina, *chief president of the two and thirty judges of*
*strangers (within whose brest are the secrets of the lyon crowned*
*on the throne of the world inclosed) I enjoyn and command you*
*to tell me, what people you are, as also of what country, and*
*whether you have a king, who for the service of God, and for the*
*discharge of his dignity, is inclined to do good to the poor, and*
*to render them justice, to the end that with tears in their eyes,*
*and hands lifted up, they may not address their complaints to*
*that Sovereigne Lord which hath made the bright enamel of the*
*skies, and for whose holy feet all they that reign with Him,*
*serve but for sandals.* To this demand we answered him, that
we were poor strangers, natives of the kingdom of *Siam*, who
being imbarqued with our merchandise for *Liampoo* were cast
away in a great storm at sea, from whence we escaped naked

15

with the loss of all that we had ; and how in that deplorable
estate we were fain to get our living by begging from door to
door, till such time as at our arrival at the town of *Taypor*, the
*Chumbim*, then resident there, had arrested us for prisoners
without cause, and so sent us to the city of *Nanquin*, where by
his report we had been condemned to the whip, and to have
our thumbs cut off, without so much as once deigning to hear
us in our justifications ; by reason whereof, lifting up our eyes
to Heaven, we had been advised to have recourse, with our
tears, to the four and twenty judges of austere life, that
(through their zeal to God) they might take our cause in hand,
since by reason of our poverty we were altogether without support, and abandoned of all men, which with an holy zeal they
incontinently effected, by revoking the cause, and annulling the
judgment that had been given against us ; and that, these
things considered, we most instantly besought him, that for the
service of God he would be pleased to have regard to our
misery, and the great injustice that was done us, for that we
had no means in this country, nor person, that would speak
one word for us.   The judge remained sometime in suspence
upon that we had said to him ; at length he answered, that we
need say no more to him ; for it is sufficient that I know you
are poor, to the end this affair may go another way then
hitherto it hath done ; nevertheless, to acquit me of my charge,
I give you five days time, conformably to the law of the third
book, that within the said term you may retain a proctor to
undertake your cause ; but if you will be advised by me, you
shall present your request to the *Tanigores* of the sacred office,
to the end that they, carried by an holy zeal of the honour of
God, may out of compassion of your miseries take upon them
to defend your right.   Having spoken thus, he gave us a *Taeis*,
in way of alms, and said further to us, Beware of the prisoners
that are here ; for I assure you, that they make it their trade,
to steal all that they can from any one ; whereupon entering
into another chamber where there were a great number of
prisoners, he continued there above three hours in giving them
audience ; at the end whereof he sent seven and twenty men,
that the day before had received their judgement, to execution,
which was inflicted upon them by whipping to death ; a spec-

tacle so dreadful to us, and that put us in such a fright, as it
almost set us besides our selves. The next morning, as soon
as it was day, the jaylors clapt irons on our feet, and manacles
on our hands, and put us to exceeding great pain; but seven
days after we had endured such misery, being laid on the
ground one by another, and bewayling our disaster, for the
extream fear we were in of suffering a most cruel death, if that
which we had done at *Calempluy* should by any means chance
to be discovered, it pleased God that we were visited by the
*Tanigores* of the house of mercy, which is of the jurisdiction
of this prison, who are called in their language *Cofilem Gnaxy.*
At their arrival all the prisoners bowing themselves, said with
a lamentable tone, *Blessed be the day wherein God doth visit us
by the ministry of His servants* ; whereunto the *Tanigores* made
answer, with a grave and modest countenance, *The Almighty
and Divine hand of Him that hath formed the beauty of the stars
keep and preserve you.* Then approaching to us, they very
courteously demanded of us what people we were, and whence
it proceeded that our imprisonment was more sensible to us
then to others? To this speech we replyed, with tears in our
eyes, that we were poor strangers, so abandoned of men, as in
all the country there was not one that knew our names, and
that all we could in our poverty say, to intreat them to think
of us for Gods sake, was contained in a letter, that we had
brought them from the chamber of the society of the house of
*Quiay Hinarol,* in the city of *Nanquin* ; whereupon *Christophoro Borralho,* presenting them with the letter, they received
it with a new ceremony, full of all courtesie, saying, *Praised be
He who hath created all things, for that He is pleased to serve
Himself of sinners here below, whereby they may be recompensed
at the last day of all days, by satisfying them double their labour
with the riches of His holy treasures, which shall be done, as we
believe, in as great abundance, as the drops of rain fall from the
clouds to the earth.* After this, one of the four, putting up the
letter, said unto us, that as soon as the chamber of justice for
the poor was open, they would all of them give an answer to
our business, and see us furnished with all that we had need
of, and so they departed from us. Three days after they
returned to visit us in the prison ; and in the next morning

coming to us again, they asked us many questions answerable
to a memorial which they had thereof; whereunto we replyed
in every point according as we were questioned by each of
them, so as they remained very well satisfied with our answers.
Then calling the Register to them, who had our papers in
charge, they inquired very exactly of him, touching many
things that concerned us, and withall required his advice about
our affair; that done, having digested all that might make for
the conversation of our right into certain heads, they took our
process from him, saying, they would peruse it all of them
together in their Chambers of Justice with the proctors of the
house, and the next day return it him again, that he might
carry it to the *Chaem*, as he was resolved before to do.

Not to trouble my self with recounting in particular all that
occurred in this affair, untill such time as it was fully concluded, wherein six moneths and an half were imployed,
(during the which we continued still prisoners in such misery)
I will in few words relate all that befell us unto the end; when
as our business was come before the twelve *Conchalis* of the
criminal court, the two proctors of the house of mercy most
willingly took upon them to cause the unjust sentence which
had been given against us to be revoked. Having gotten then
all the proceedings to be disannulled, they by petition remonstrated unto the *Chaem*, who was the president of the court.
*How we could not for any cause whatsoever be condemned to
death, seeing there were no witnesses of any credit that could testifie that we had robbed any man, or had ever seen us carry any
offensive weapons contrary to the prohibition made against it by
the law of the first book; but that we were apprehended quite
naked, like wretched men, wandering after a lamentable shipwrack; and that therefore our poverty and misery was worthy
rather of a pitiful compassion, then of that rigour wherewith the
first minister of the arm of wrath had caused us to be whipt;
moreover, that God alone was the judge of our innocency; in
whose name they required him once, twice, nay many times, to
consider that he was mortal, and could not last long; for that
God had given him a perishable life, at the end whereof he was
to render an account of that which had been required of him,
since by a solemn oath he was obliged to do all that should be*

*manifest to his judgement, without any considerations of men of
the world; whose custom it was to make the ballance sway down,
which God would have to be upright, according to the integrity
of His Divine justice.*   To this petition the Kings proctor opposing himself, as he that was our adverse party, and that in
certain articles, which he framed against us, set forth, how he
would prove by ocular witnesses, as well of the country, as
strangers, that we were publique thieves, making a common
practice of robbing, and not merchants, such as we pretended
to be; whereunto he added, that if we had come to the coast
of *China* with a good design, and with an intent to pay the
King his due in his custom-houses, we would have repaired to
the ports, where they were established by the ordinance of the
*Aytan* of the Government; but for a punishment, because we
went from isle to isle, like pirats, Almighty God, that detests
sin and robbery, had permitted us to suffer shipwrack, that so
falling into the hands of the ministers of His justice we might
receive the guerdon of our wicked works, namely, the pains of
death, whereof our crimes rendred us most worthy. In regard
of all which, he desired we might be condemned according to
the law of the second book, that commanded it in express
terms.   And that if for other considerations, no way remarkable in us, we could by any law be exempted from death, yet
nevertheless, for that we were strangers, and vagabonds, without either faith, or knowledg of God, that alone would suffice,
at leastwise to condemn us to have our hands and noses cut off,
and so to be banished for ever into the country of *Ponxileytay*,
whither such people as we, were wont to be exiled, as might be
verified by divers sentences given and executed in like cases;
and to that effect, he desired the admittance of his articles,
which he promised to prove within the time, that should be
prescribed him. These articles were presently excepted against
by the proctor of the Court of Justice, established for the poor,
who offered to make the contrary appear within a certain term,
which to that end, and for many other reasons alledged by him
in our favour, was granted him; wherefore he required that the
said articles might not be admitted, especially for that they were
infamous, and directly contrary to the ordinances of justice.
Whereupon the *Chaem* ordered, that his articles should not be

admitted, unless he did prove them by evident testimonies, and such as were conformable to the divine law, within six days next ensuing, and that upon pain in case of contravention not to be admitted to any demand of a longer delay. The said term of six days being prescribed the Kings proctor, he, in the mean time, producing no one proof against us, nor any person that so much as knew us, came and demanded a delay of other six days, which was flatly denied him, in regard it but too well appeared, that all he did was only to win time, and therefore he would by no means consent unto it; but contrarily, he gave the proctor for the poor five days respit to alledge all that further he could in our defence. In the mean time, the Kings proctor declaimed against us in such foul and opprobrious terms, as the *Chaem* was much offended thereat; so that he condemned him to pay us twenty *Taeis* of silver, both for his want of charity, and for that he could not prove any one of the obligations which he had exhibited against us. Three days being spent herein, four *Tanigores* of the house of the poor, coming very early in the morning to the prison, sent for us into the *Infirmirie*, where they told us that our business went very well, and how we might hope that our sentence would have a good issue; whereupon we cast our selves at their feet, and with abundance of tears desired God to reward them for the pains they had taken in our behalf. Thereunto one of them replyed, *And we also most humbly beseech Him to keep you in the knowledge of His law, wherein all the happiness of good men consists*; and so they caused two coverlets to be given us, for to lay upon our beds in the night, because the weather was cold, and withall bid us, that we should not stick to ask any thing we wanted, for that God Almighty did not love a sparing hand in the distributing of alms for His sake. A little after their departure came the Register, and shewing us the *Chaems* order, whereby the Kings proctor was condemned to pay us twenty *Taeis*, gave us the money, and took an acquittance under our hands for the receipt of it. For which giving him a world of thanks, we intreated him for his pains to take as much thereof as he pleased; but he would not touch a peny, saying, I will not for so small a matter lose the recompence which I hope to gain from God, for the consideration of you.

We past nine days in great fear, still expecting to have our sentence pronounced, when as on *Saturday* morning two *Chumbims* of Justice came to the prison for us, accompanied with twenty officers, by them called *Huppes*, carrying halberts, portisans, and other arms, which made them very dreadful to the beholders. These men tying us all nine together in a long iron chain, lead us to the *Caladigan*, which was the place where audience was given, and where execution was done on delinquents. Now how we got thither, to confess the truth, I am not able to relate; for we where at that instant so far besides our selves, as we knew not what we did, or which way we went; so as in that extremity all our thought was how to conform our selves to the will of God, and beg of Him with tears, that for the merit of His sacred passion, He would be pleased to receive the punishment that should be inflicted on us for the satisfaction of our sins. At length after much pain, and many affronts, that were done us by many which followed after us, with loud cries, we arrived at the first hall of the *Caladigan*, where were four and twenty executioners, whom they call, *The Ministers of the arm of justice*, with a great many of other people, that were there about their affairs. Here we remained a long time, till at length upon the ringing of a bell, other doors were opened, that stood under a great arch of architecture, very artificially wrought, and whereon were a number of rich figures. On the top a monstrous lion of silver was seen, with his fore and hind feet upon a mighty great bowl, made of the same metal, whereby the arms of the King of *China* are represented, which are ordinarily placed on the fore-front of all the sovereign courts, where the *Chaems* preside, who are as vice-roys amongst us. Those doors being opened, as I said before, all that were there present entred into a very great hall, like the body of a church, hung from the top to the bottom with divers pictures, wherein strange kinds of execution done upon persons of all conditions, after a most dreadful manner were constrained; and under every picture was this inscription, *Such a one was executed with this kind of death for committing such a crime*; so that in beholding the diversity of these fearful pourtraitures one might see in it, as it were, a declaration of the kind of death that was ordained

for each crime, as also the extream rigour which the justice
there observed in such executions. From this hall we went
into another room far richer, and more costly, for it was gilt
all over, so that one could not have a more pleasing object,
at least wise, if we could have taken pleasure in any thing,
considering the misery we were in. In the midst of this
room there was a Tribunal, whereunto one ascended by seven
steps, invironed with three rows of ballisters of iron, copper,
and ebony; the tops whereof were beautified with mother of
pearl. At the upper end of all was a cloth of state of white
damask, frenged about with a deep cawl frenge of green silk
and gold; under this state sat the *Chaem* with a world of
greatness and majesty; he was seated in a very rich chair
of silver, having before him a little table, and about him three
boys on their knees, sumptuously apparelled, with chains of
gold; one of the which (namely, he in the middle) served to
give the *Chaem* the pen wherewithal he signed; the other
two took the petitions that were preferred, and presented
them on the table, that they might be signed; on the right
hand, in another place somewhat higher, and almost equal
with the *Chaem*, stood a boy, some ten or eleven years old,
attired in a rich robe of white satin, imbroidered with roses
of gold, having a chain of pearl three double about his neck,
and hair as long as a womans, most neatly plaited with a
fillet of gold, all enamelled with green, and powdered over
with great seed pearl. In his hand he held, as a mark of that
which he represented, a little branch of roses, made of silk,
gold thread, and rich pearls, very curiously intermixed. And
in this manner he appeared so gentle, handsome, and beautiful,
as no woman, how fair soever, could overmatch him; this boy
leaned on his elbow upon the *Chaems* chair, and figured mercy.
In the like manner, on the left hand was another goodly boy,
richly apparelled in a coat of carnation satin, all set with roses
of gold, having his right arm bared up to the elbow, and died
with a vermilion as red as blood, and in that hand holding a
naked sword, which seemed also to be bloody: moreover, on
his head he wore a crown, in fashion like to a myter, hung all
with little razors, like unto lancets, wherewith Chirurgions
let men blood; being thus gallantly set forth, and of most

beautiful presence, yet he struck all that beheld him with
fear, in regard of that he represented, which was justice. For
they say, that the judge, who holds the place of the King,
who presents God on earth, ought necessarily to have those
two qualities, *justice*, and *mercy*; and that he which doth not
use them is a tyrant, acknowledging no law, and usurping the
power that he hath. The *Chaem* was apparelled in a long
gown of violet satin, frenged with green silk and gold, with a
kind of scapulair about his neck, in the midst of which was
a great plate of gold, wherein an hand holding a very even
pair of ballance was engraven, and the inscription about it :
*It is the nature of the Lord Almighty, to observe in His justice,
weight, measure, and true account; therefore take heed to what
thou doest, for if thou comest to sin thou shalt suffer for it
eternally.* Upon his head he had a kind of round bonnet,
bordered about with small sprigs of gold, all enamelled violet
and green, and on the top of it was a little crowned lion of
gold, upon a round bowl of the same metal ; by which lion
crowned, as I have delivered heretofore, is the King signified,
and by the bowl, the world ; as if by these devices they would
denote, that the King is the Lion crowned on the throne of
the world. In his right hand he held a little rod of ivory,
some three spans long, in manner of a scepter ; upon the top
of the 3 first steps of this tribunal stood eight ushers with
silver maces on their shoulders, and below were threescore
*Mogors* on their knees, disposed into three ranks, carrying
halberds in their hands, that were neatly damasked with gold.
In the vantgard of these same stood, like as if they had been,
the commanders or captains of this squadron, the statues of
two giants, of a most gallant aspect, and very richly attired,
with their swords hanging in scarfs, and mighty great halberds
in their hands, and these the *Chineses* in their language call
*Gigaes* ; on the two sides of this Tribunal, below in the room,
were two very long tables, at each of which sat twelve men,
whereof four were presidents, or judges, two registers, four
solicitors, and two *Conchalis*, which are (as it were) assistants
to the Court, one of these tables was for criminal, and the
other for civil causes, and all the officers of both these tables
were apparelled in the gowns of white satin, that were very

long, and had large slieves, thereby demonstrating the latitude and purity of justice; the tables were covered with carpets of violet damask, and richly bordered about with gold, the *Chaems* table, because it was of silver, had no carpet on it, nor any thing else, but a cushion of cloth of gold, and a standith. Now all these things put together, as we saw them, carried a wonderful shew of state and majesty; but to proceed, upon the fourth ringing of a bell, one of the *Conchalis* stood up, and after a low obeysance made to the *Chaem*, with a very loud voice, that he might be heard of every one, he said, *Peace there, and with all submission hearken, on pain of incurring the punishment, ordained by the* Chaems *of the Government for those, that interrupt the silence of sacred justice.* Whereupon this same sitting down again, another arose, and with the like reverence, mounting up to the Tribunal, where the *Chaem* sat, he took the sentences from him that held them in his hand, and published them aloud one after another, with so many ceremonies, and compliments, as he employed above an hour therein. At length coming to pronounce our judgment, they caused us to kneel down, with our eyes fixed on the ground, and our hands lifted up, as if we were praying unto heaven, to the end that in all humility we might hear the publication thereof, which was thus:

[*A portion only of the judgment is here given.*]

*I do ordain, and decree, that these nine strangers shall be clearly quit and absolved of all that which the Kings proctor hath laid to their charge, as also of all the punishment belonging thereunto, condemning them only to a years exile, during which time they shall work for their living in the reparations of* Quansy; *and when as eight moneths of the said year shall be accomplished, then I expresly enjoyn all the* Chumbims, Conchalis, Monteos, *and other ministers of their government, that immediately upon their presenting of this my decree unto them, they give them a pass-port and safe conduct, to the end they may freely and securely return into their country, or to any other place they shall think fit.* After this sentence was thus published in our hearing, we all cried out with a loud voice, *The sentence of thy clear judgement is confirmed in us, even as the purity of thy heart is agreeable to the Son of the Sun.* This said, one of the *Conchalis*, that sate at one of the tables, stood up, and having made a very low obeisance to the *Chaem*, he said aloud five times one after another, to all that press of people which were there in great number; *Is there any one in this court, in this city, or in this kingdom, that will oppose this decree, or the deliverance of these nine prisoners ?* Whereunto no answer being made, the two boys, that represented justice and mercy, touched the ensigns which they held in their hands together, and said aloud, *Let them be freed and discharged according to the sentence very justly pronounced for it* ; whereupon one of those ministers, whom they call *Huppes*, having rung a bell thrice, the two *Chumbims* of execution, that had formerly bound us, unloosed us from our chain, and withal took off our manacles, collers, and the other irons from our legs, so that we were quite delivered, for which we gave infinite thanks to our Lord Jesus Christ, because we always thought, that for the ill conceit men had of us we should be condemned to death. From thence, so delivered as we were, they led us back to the prison, where the two *Chumbims* signed our enlargment in the jaylors book ; nevertheless that we might be altogether discharged, we were to go two months after to serve a year according to our sentence, upon pain of becoming slaves for ever to the King, conformable to his ordinances. Now because we would presently have gone about to demand the alms of good people in the city, the *Chifuu*, who was as Grand Provost of that prison, perswaded us to stay till the next day, that he might first recommend us to the *Tanigores* of mercy, that they might do something for us.

## CHAPTER XXX.

What past betwixt us and the Tanigores of mercy, with the great favors
they did us ; and a brief relation of the city of Pequin, where the King
of China kept his Court.

THE next morning the four *Tanigores* of mercy came to
visit the infirmity of this prison, as they used to do ;
where they rejoyced with us for the good success of our sentence, giving us great testimony, how well contented they
were with it, for which we returned them many thanks, not
without shedding abundance of tears, whereat they seemed
to be not a little pleased, and willed us not to be troubled
with the term we were condemned to serve in, for they told
us that in stead of a year we should continue but eight
months there, and that the other four moneths, which made
the third part of our punishment, the King remitted it by
way of alms for Gods sake, in consideration that we were
poor ; for otherwise, if we had been rich, and of ability, we
should have had no favour at all, promising to cause this
diminution of punishment to be endorsed on our sentence,
and besides that they would· go, and speak to a very honourable man for us, that was appointed to be the chief Marshal,
or Monteo, of *Quansy*, the place where we were to serve, to
the end he might shew us favour, and cause us to be truly
paid for the time we should remain there.   Now because this
man was naturally a friend to the poor, and inclined to do
them good, they thought it would be fit to carry us along with
them to his house, the rather for that it might be he would
take us into his charge ; we gave them all very humble thanks
for this good offer of theirs, and told them that God would
reward this charity they shewed us for His sake ; whereupon
we accompanied them to the *Monteos* house, who came forth
to receive us in his outward Court, leading his wife by the
hand ; which he did, either out of a greater form of complement, or to do the more honour to the *Tanigores*, and coming
neer them he prostrated himself at their feet, and said : *It is
now, my lord, and holy brethren, that I have cause to rejoyce
for that it hath pleased God to permit, that you His holy servants*

*should come unto my house, being that which I could not hope for, in regard I held my self unworthy of such favour.* After the *Tanigores* had used many complements and ceremonies to him, as is usual in that country, they answered him thus, *May God, our Sovereign Lord, the infinite source of mercy, recompense the good thou dost for the poor with blessing in this life; for believe it, dear brother, the strongest staff whereon the soul doth lean to keep her from falling so often as she happens to stumble, is the charity which we use towards our neighbour, when as the vain glory of this world doth not blind the good zeal whereunto His holy law doth oblige us; and that thou mayst merit the blessed felicity of beholding His face, we have brought thee here these nine* Portugals, *who are so poor, as none in this kingdom are like to them; wherefore we pray thee, that in the place whither thou art going now, as* Monteo, *thou wilt do for them all that thou thinkest will be acceptable to the Lord above, in whose behalf we crave this of thee.* To this speech the *Monteo*, and his wife, replyed in such courteous and remarkable terms, as we were almost besides our selves to hear in what manner they attributed the success of their affairs to the principal cause of all goodness, even as though they had had the light of faith, or the knowledge of the Christian verity. Hereupon they withdrew into a chamber, into which we went not, and continued there about half an hour; then as they were about to take leave of one another, they commanded us to come in to them, where the *Tanigores* spake to them again about us, and recommending us unto them more then before, the *Monteo* caused our names to be written down in a book that lay before him, and said unto us, *I do this, because I am not so good a man, as to give you something of mine own, nor so bad as to deprive you of the sweat of your labour, whereunto the King hath bound you; wherefore even at this instant you shall begin to get your living, although you do not serve as yet, for the desire I have that this may be accounted to me for an alms, so that now you have nothing to do, but to be merry in my house, where I will give order that you shall be provided of all that is necessary for you. Besides this, I will not promise you any thing, for the fear I am in of the shewing some vanity by my promise, and so the divel may make use thereof as of an advantage, to lay hold on me, a matter that often arrives through the weakness of our nature ; wherefore let it suffice you for the present to know, that I will be mindful of you for the love of these holy brethren here, who have spoken to me for you.* The four *Tanigores* thereupon taking their leave, gave us four *Taeis*, and said unto us, *Forget not to render thanks unto God for the good success you have had in your business ; for it would be a grievous sin in you not to acknowledge so great a grace.* Thus were we very well entertained in the house of this captain for the space of two months, that we remained there ; at the end whereof we parted from thence, for to go to *Quansy*, where we were to make up our time, under the conduct of this captain, who ever after used us very kindly, and shewed us many favours, until that the *Tartars* entred into the town, who did a world of mischief there, as I will more amply declare hereafter.

Before I recount that which happened unto us, after we were imbarqued with those *Chineses* that conducted us, and that gave us great hope of setting us at liberty, I think it not amiss to make a brief relation here of the city of *Pequin*, which may truly be termed the capital of the monarchy of the world ; as also of some particulars I observed there, as well for its arches and policy, as for that which concerns its extent, its government, the laws of the countrey, and the admirable manner of providing for the good of the whole state, together in what sort they are paid that serve in the time of war, according to the ordinances of the kingdom, and many other things like unto these ; though I must needs confess that herein I shall want the best part, namely, wit, and capacity, to render a reason in what clymate it is scituated, and in the height of how many degrees, which is a matter the learned and curious most desire to be satisfied in. But my design having never been other (as I have said heretofore) then to leave this my book unto my children, that therein they may see the sufferings I have undergone, it little imports me to write otherwise then I do, that is, in a gross and rude manner ; for I hold it better to treat of these things in such sort as nature hath taught me, then to use hyperboles, and speeches from the purpose, whereby the weakness of my poor understanding may be made more evident. Howbeit, since I am obliged to make mention of this matter, by the promise I have made of it heretofore, I say, that this city, which we call *Pequin*, and they of the country *Pequin*, is scituated in the height of forty and one degrees of northerly latitude; the walls of it are in circuit (by the report of the *Chineses* themselves, and as I have read in a little book, treating of the greatness thereof, and intituled *Aquisendan*, which I brought since along with me into *Portugal*) thirty large leagues, namely ten long, and five broad; some others hold, that it is fifty, namely seventeen in length, and eight in bredth: and forasmuch as they that treat of it are of different opinions, in that the one make the extent of it thirty leagues, as I have said before, and others fifty, I will render a reason of this doubt, comformable to that which I have seen my self. It is true, that in the manner it is now built, it is thirty leagues in circuit, as they say; for it is invironed with two rows of strong walls, where there are a number of towers and bulwarks after our fashion; but without this circuit, which is of the city it self, there is another far greater, both in length and breadth, that the *Chineses* affirm was anciently all inhabited, but at this present there are only some boroughs and villages, as also a many of fair houses, or castles, about it, amongst the which there are sixteen hundred that have great advantages over the rest, and are the houses of the proctors of the sixteen hundred cities, and most remarkable towns of the two and thirty kingdoms of this monarchy, who repair into this city at the general assembly of the estates, which is held every three years for the publique good. Without this great inclosure, which (as I have said) is not comprehended in the city, there is in a distance of three leagues broad, and seven long, fourscore thousand tombs of the *Mandarins*, which are little chappels all gilded within, and compassed about with ballisters of iron and lattin, the entries whereinto are through very rich and sumptuous arches: near to these chappels there are also very great houses, with gardens and tufted woods of high trees, as also many inventions of ponds, fountains, and aquæducts; whereunto may be added, that the walls of the inclosure are on the inside covered with fine porcelain, and on

the fanes above are many lions pourtrayed in gold, as also in
the squares of the steeples, which are likewise very high, and
embellished with pictures. It hath also five hundred very
great palaces, which are called *the houses of the son of the
sun*, whither all those retire that have been hurt in the wars
for the service of the King, as also many other souldiers, who
in regard of age or sickness are no longer able to bear arms,
and to the end that during the rest of their days they may be
exempted from incommodity, each of them receives monethly
a certain pay to find himself withal, and to live upon. Now
all these men of war, as we learned of the *Chineses*, are
ordinarily an hundred thousand, there being in each of those
houses two hundred men according to their report. We saw
also another long street of low houses, where there were four
and twenty thousand oar-men, belonging to the King *Panoures*;
and another of the same structure a good league in length,
where fourteen thousand taverners that followed the Court
dwelt; as also a third street like unto the other two, where
live a great number of light women, exempted from the
tribute which they of the city pay, for that they are curti-
sans, whereof the most part had quitted their husbands for
to follow that wretched trade; and if for that cause they
come to receive any hurt, their husbands are grievously
punished for it, because they are there as in a place of
freedom, and under the protection of the *Tutan* of the Court,
lord steward of the Kings house. In this inclosure do
likewise remain all the landresses, by them called *Maynates*,
which wash the linnen of the city, who as we were told, are
above an hundred thousand, and live in this quarter, for that
there are divers rivers there, together with a number of wells,
and deep pools of water, compassed about with good walls.
Within this same inclosure, as the said *Aquisendan* relates,
there are thirteen hundred gallant and very sumptuous houses
of religious men and women, who make profession of the four
principal laws of those two and thirty which are in the empire
of *China*; and it is thought that in some of these houses there
are above a thousand persons, besides the servants, that from
abroad do furnish them with victuals, and other necessary
provisions. We saw also a great many houses, which have

fair buildings of a large extent, with spacious inclosures, wherein there are gardens, and very thick woods, full of any kind of game, either for hawking, or hunting, that may be desired; and these houses are as it were inns, whither come continually in great number people of all ages and sexes, as to see comedies, plays, combates, bull-baitings, wrastlings, and magnificent feast, which the *Tutons, Chaems, Conchacys, Aytaos, Bracalons, Chumbims, Monteos, Lauteas,* lords, *gentlemen, captains, merchants,* and other rich men, do make for to give content to their kindred and friends; these houses are bravely furnished with rich hangings, beds, chairs, and stools, as likewise with huge cupbords of plate, not onely of silver, but of gold also; and the attendants that wait at the table, are maids ready to be married, very beautiful, and gallantly attired; howbeit all this is nothing in comparison of the sumptuousness, and other magnificences that we saw there. Now the *Chineses* assured us, there were some feasts that lasted ten days after the *Carachina,* or *Chinese* manner, which in regard of the state, pomp, and charge thereof, as well in the attendance of servants and wayters, as in the costly fare of all kind of flesh, fowl, fish, and all delicacies in musick, in sports of hunting, and hawking, in plays, comedies, jilts, turnayes, and in shews both of horse and foot, fighting and skirmishing together, do cost above twenty thousand *Taeis.* These inns do stand in at least a million of gold, and are maintained by certain companies of very rich merchants, who in way of commerce and traffique employ their mony therein, whereby it is thought they gain far more, then if they should venture it to sea. It is said also, that there is so good and exact an order observed there, that whensoever any one will be at a charge that way, he goes to the *Xipaton* of the house, who is the superintendent thereof, and declares unto him what his design is; whereupon he shews him a book, all divided into chapters, which treats of the ordering and sumptuousness of feasts, as also the rates of them, and how they shall be served in, to the end, that he who will be at the charge, may chuse which he pleases. This book, called *Pinetoreu,* I have seen, and heard it read; so that I remember now in the three first chapters thereof, it speaks of the feasts,

16

whereunto God is to be invited, and of what price they are; and then it descends to the King of *China*, of whom it says, *That by a special grace of Heaven, and right of sovereignty, he hath the government of the whole earth, and of all the kings that inhabit it.* After it hath done with the King of *China*, it speaks of the feasts of the *Tutons*, which are the ten sovereign dignities, that command over the forty *Chaems*, who are as the vice-roys of the state. These *Tutons* also are termed the beams of the sun, for, say they, as the King of *China* is the son of the sun, so the *Tutons*, who represent him, may rightly be termed his beams, for that they proceed from him, even as the rays do from the sun.

[*Here follows a description of the inns and universities of Pequin, omitted.*]

------

## CHAPTER XXXI.

The Prison of Xinanguibaleu, wherein those are kept, which have been condemned to serve at the reparations of the wall of Tartaria; and another inclosure, called the Treasure of the Dead, with the revenues wherewith the prison is maintained.

DESISTING now from speaking in particular of the great number of the rich and magnificent buildings, which we saw in the city of *Pequin*, I will only insist on some of the edifices thereof, that seemed more remarkable to me then the rest, whence it may be easie to infer, what all those might be, whereof I will not make any mention here, to avoid prolixity. The first building which I saw of those that were most remarkable, was a prison, which they call *Xinanguibaleu*, that is to say, *the inclosure of the Epiles*; the circuit of this prison is two leagues square, or little less, both in length and bredth: it is inclosed with a very high wall without any battlements; the wall on the outside is invironed with a great deep ditch full of water, over the which are a many of draw bridges, that are drawn up in the night with certain iron chains, and so hang suspended on huge cast pillars; in this prison is an arch

)f strong hewed stone, abutting in 2 towers, in the tops whereof are 6 great sentinel-bells, which are never rung but ill the rest within the said inclosure do answer them, which :he *Chineses* affirm to be above a hundred, and indeed they nake a most horrible din. In this place there are ordinarily :hree hundred thousand prisoners, between 17 and 50, whereat we were much amazed; and indeed we had good cause, in :egard it is a thing so unusual and extraordinary. Now lesiring to know of the *Chineses* the occasion of so marvellous i building, and of the great number of prisoners that were in t; they answered us, that after the King of *China*, named *Crisnago Docotay*, had finished a wall of 300 leagues space )etwixt the kingdom of *China*, and that of *Tartaria*, as I have leclared other where, he ordained by the advice of his people, for to that effect he caused an assembly of his estates to be 1eld) that all those which should be condemned to banishment ihould be sent to work in the repairing of this wall, and that ifter they had served 6 years together therein, they might ïreely depart, though they were sentenced to serve for a onger time, because the king pardoned them the remainder )f the term by way of charity and alms; but if during those years they should happen to perform any remarkable act, or )ther thing, where it appeared they had advantage over others, )r if they were 3 times wounded in the sallies they should nake, or if they killed some of their enemies, they were then o be dispensed with for all the rest of their time, and that :he *Chaem* should grant them a certificate thereof, where it ihould be declared why he had delivered them, and how he 1ad thereby satisfied the ordinances of war. Two hundred ind ten thousand men are to be continually entertained in the vork of the wall, by the first institution, whereof defalcation s made of a third part, for such as are dead, maimed, and lelivered, either for their notable actions, or for that they had ,ccomplished their time: and likewise when as the *Chaem*, vho is the chief of all those, sent to the *Pitaucamay*, which s the highest court of justice, to furnish him with that 1umber of men, they could not assemble them together so oon as was necessary, for that they were divided in so many everal places of that empire, which is prodigiously great, as

I have delivered before, and that withall a long time was
required for the assembling them together, another king
named *Gopiley Apirau*, who succeeded to that *Crisnago
Docotay*, ordained that the great inclosure should be made in
the city of *Pequin*, to the end that as soon as any were
condemned to the work of this wall, they should be carried
to *Xinanguibaleu*, for to be there altogether, by which means
they might be sent away without any delay, as now is done.
So soon as the court of justice hath committed the prisoners
to this prison, whereof he that brings them hath a certificate,
they are immediately left at liberty, so that they may walk at
their pleasure within this great inclosure, having nothing but
a little plate of a span long, and 4 fingers broad, wherein
these words are engraven, *such a one of such a place hath been
condemned to the general exile for such a cause ; he entred such
a day, such a moneth, such a year*.   Now the reason why they
make every prisoner to carry this plate for a testimony of their
evil actions, is, to manifest for what crime he was condemned,
and at what time he entred, because every one goes forth
conformably to the length of time that shall be since he
entred in.   These prisoners are held for duly delivered when
they are drawne out of captivity for to go and work at the
wall, for they cannot upon any cause whatsoever be exempted
from the prison of *Xinanguibaleu*, and the time they are there
is counted to them for nothing, in regard they have no hope
of liberty but at that instant when their term permits them to
work in the reparations ; for then they may be sure to be
delivered, according to the ordinance whereof I have made
mention before.   Having now delivered the occasion wherefore
so great a prison was made, before I leave it, I hold it not
amiss to speak of a fair we saw there, of two that are
usually kept every year ; which those of the country call
*Gunxinem, Apparau, Xinanguibaleu*, that is to say, *The
rich fair of the prison of the condemned*.   These fairs are
kept in the moneths of *July* and *January*, with very
magnificent feasts, solemnized for the invocation of their
idols, and even, there they have their plenary indulgences,
by means whereof great riches of gold and silver are promised
them in the other world.   They are both of them frank and

ree, so as the merchants pay no duties, which is the cause
hat they flock thither in such great number, as they assured
ıs that there were three millions of persons there; and for
ıs much as I said before, that the three hundred thousand that
ıre imprisoned there are at liberty, as well as those that go
n and out, you shall see what course they hold to keep the
)risoners from getting forth amongst others. Every one that
s free and comes in hath a mark set on the wrist of his right
ırm with a certain confection made of oyl, bitumen, lacre,
:hubarb, and alum, which being once dry cannot be any ways
lefaced, but by the means of vinegar and salt mingled together
rery hot: and to the end that so great a number of people
nay be marked, on both sides of the gates stand a many of
*Jhainpatoens*, who with stamps of lead, dipt in this bitumen,
mprints a mark on every one that presents himself unto them.
ınd so they let him enter; which is onely practised on men,
ıot upon women, because none of that sex are ever condemned
ıo the labour of the wall. When therefore they come to go
)ut of the gates, they must all have their arms bared where
:his mark is, that the said *Chainpatoens*, who are the porters
ınd ministers of this affair, may know them, and let them
)ass; and if by chance any one be so unhappy as to have that
nark defaced by any accident, he must even have patience,
ınd remain with the other prisoners, in regard there is no way
ıo get him out of this place if he be found without that mark.
Now those *Chainpatoens* are so dextrous and well versed in it,
:hat an hundred thousand men may in an hour go in and out
without trouble, so that by this means the three hundred
:housand prisoners continue in their captivity, and none of
:hem can slip away amongst others to get out. There are in
:his prison 3 great inclosures like great towns, where there are
ı number of houses, and very long streets, without any lanes;
ınd at the entrance into each street there are good gates, with
:heir sentinel bells aloft, together with a *Chumbim*, and 20
nen for a guard; within a flight-shoot of those inclosures are
:he lodgings of the *Chaem*, who commands all this prison, and
:hose lodgings are composed of a number of fair houses, where-
n are many out-courts, gardens, ponds, halls, and chambers,
ınriched with excellent inventions, able to lodge a king at his

ease, how great a court soever he have. In the 2 principal
of these towns there are 2 streets, each of them about a
flight-shoot long, which abut upon the *Chaem's* lodgings,
arched all along with stone, and covered over head like the
hospital at *Lisbon*, but that they far surpass it. Here are all
things to be sold that one can desire, as well for victual, and
other kind of provisions, as for all sorts of merchandise, and
rich wares. In those arched streets, which are very spacious
and long, are these 2 fairs kept every year, whither such a
multitude of people resort, as I have declared before. Moreover within the inclosure of this prison are divers woods of
tall and high trees, with many small streams, and ponds of
clear sweet water for the use of the prisoners, and to wash
their linnen, as also sundry hermitages, and hospitals, together
with 12 very sumptuous and rich monasteries, so that whatsoever is to be had in a great town, may in great abundance be
found within the inclosure, and with advantage in many
things, because the most part of these prisoners have their
wives and children there, to whom the king gives a lodging
answerable to the household or family, which each one hath.

The second of those things, which I have undertaken to
relate, is another inclosure we saw almost as big as the former,
compassed about with strong walls, and great ditches. This
place is called the *Muxiparan*, which signifies, *The treasure of
the dead*; where are many towers of hewed carved stone, and
steeples diversly painted. The walls on the top are instead
of battlements environed with iron gates, where there are a
number of idols of different figures, as of men, serpents,
horses, oxen, elephants, fishes, adders, and many other monstrous forms of creatures (which were never seen) some of
brass, and iron, and others of tin and copper; so that this
infinite company of several figures joyned together is one of
the most remarkable and pleasantest things that can be
imagined. Having passed over the bridge of the ditch we
arrived at a great court that was at the first entrance, inclosed
round about with huge gates, and paved all over with white
and black stones in chequer-work, so polished and bright, as
one might see himself in them as in a looking-glass. In the
midst of this court was a pillar of jasper six and thirty spans

high, and as it seemed all one piece, on the top whereof was an idol of silver in the figure of a woman, which with her hands strangled a serpent, that was excellently enamelled with black and green. A little further at the entrance of another gate, which stood between two very high towers, and accompanied with four and twenty pillars of huge great stone, there were two figures of men, each of them with an iron club in his hand, as if they had served to guard that passage, being an hundred and forty spans high, with such hideous and ugly visages, as make them even to tremble that behold them. The *Chineses* called them *Xixipatan Xalican*, that is to say, *The blowers of the house of smoke*. At the entring into this gate there were twelve men with halberds, and two registers, set at a table, who enrolled all that entered there, unto whom every one paid a matter of a groat; when we were entered within this gate, we met with a very large street, closed on both sides with goodly arches, as well in regard of the workmanship, as the rest, round about the which hung an infinite company of little bells of Lattin, by chains of the same metall, that moved by the air, made such a noise as one could not without much ado hear one another. The street might be about half a league long, and within these arches, on both sides of the way, were two rows of low houses, like unto great churches, with steeples gilt, and divers inventions of painting. Of these houses the *Chineses* assured us there was in that place three thousand, all which (from the very top to the bottom) were full of dead men's skulls, a thing so strange, that in every mans judgment a thousand great shops could hardly contain them. Behind these houses, both on the one side and the other, were two great mounts of dead mens bones, reaching far above the ridges of the houses, full as long as the street, and of a mighty bredth. These bones were ordered and disposed one upon another so curiously and aptly, that they seemed to grow there. Having demanded of the *Chineses* whether any register was kept of these bones; they answered, there was; for the *Talagrepos*, unto whose charge the administration of these three thousand houses was committed, enrolled them all; and that none of the houses yielded less than two thousand *Taeis* revenue out of such lands, as the

owners of these bones had bequeathed to them for their souls
health; and that the rent of these three thousand houses
together amounted unto five millions of gold yearly, whereof
the King had four, and the *Talagrepos* the other, for to defray
the expences of this fabrick, and that the four appertained to
the King, as their support, who dispenced them in the maintenance of the three hundred thousand prisoners of *Xinanguibaleu*. Being amazed at this marvel, we began to go along
this street, in the midst whereof we found a great *Piazza*,
compassed about with two huge grates of Lattin, and within
it was an adder of brass, infolded into I don't know how
many boughts, and so big that it contained thirty fathom in
circuit, being withall so ugly and dreadfull, as no words are
able to describe it. Some of us would estimate the weight of
it, and the least opinions reached to a thousand quintals, were
it hollow within, as I believe it was. Now although it was
of an unmeasurable greatness, yet was it in every part so well
proportioned, as nothing could be amended, whereunto also
the workmanship thereof is so correspondent, that all the
perfection that can be desired from a good workman is observed in it. This monstrous serpent, which the *Chineses*
call, *the gluttonous Serpent of the house of smoke*, had on the
top of his head a bowl of iron, two and fifty foot in circumference, as if it had been thrown at him from some other
place; twenty paces further was the figure of a man of the
same brass in the form of a giant, in like manner very strange
and extraordinary, as well for the greatness of the body, as
the hugeness of the limbs. This monster held an iron bowl
just as big as the other aloft in both his hands, and beholding
the serpent with a frowning and angry countenance, he
seemed as though he would throw his bowl at him. Round
about this figure was a number of little idols all gilt on their
knees, with their hands lifted up to him, as if they would
adore him. All this great edifice was consecrated to the
honour of this idol, called *Mucluparon*, whom the *Chineses*
affirmed to be treasurer of all the dead bones, and that when
the gluttonous serpent before mentioned came to steal them
away, he made at him with the bowl which he held in his
hands, whereupon the serpent in great fear fled immediately

away to the bottom of the profound house of smoke, whither God had precipitated him for his great wickedness ; and further that he had maintained a combat with him three thousand years already, and was to continue the same three thousand years more, so that from three thousand to three thousand years he was to imploy five bowls, wherewith he was to make an end of killing him. Hereunto they added, that as soon as this serpent should be dead, the bones that were there assembled, would return to their bodies, to which they appertained formerly, and so should go and remain for ever in the House of the Moon. To these brutish opinions they joyn many others such like, unto which they give so much faith, that nothing can be able to remove them from it, for it is the doctrine that is preached unto them by their *Bonzes*, who also tell them that the true way to make a soul happy, is to gather these bones together into this place, by means whereof there is not a day passes but that a thousand or two of these wretches bones are brought thither. Now if some for their far distance cannot bring all the bones whole thither, they will at leastwise bring a tooth or two, and so they say that by way of an alms they make as good satisfaction as if they brought all the rest ; which is the reason that in all these charnel houses there is such an infinite multitude of these teeth, that one might lade many ships with them.

[*Here follows an account of the chapels of the Kings of China, and other matters, omitted.*]

---

## CHAPTER XXXII.

### Of our going to Quincay to accomplish the time of our exile ; and what befell us there.

WE had been now two moneths and an half in this city of *Pequin*, when as on *Saturday*, the 13th of *July*, 1554. we were carried away to the town of *Quancy*, there to serve all the time that we were condemned unto. Now as soon as we arrived there, the *Chaem* caused us to be brought before him, and after he had asked us some questions, he appointed us to be of the number of fourscore halberdiers, which the King assigned him for his guard. This we took as a special favour from God, both in regard this imployment was not very painful, as also because the entertainment was good, and the pay of it better, being assured besides that at the time we should recover our liberty. Thus lived we almost a moneth very peaceably, and well contented for that we met with a better fortune then we expected, when as the devil, seeing how well all we nine agreed together (for all that we had was in common amongst us, and whatsoever misery any one had, we shared it with him like true brethren), he so wrought that two of our company fell into a quarrel, which proved very prejudicial to us all. This division sprung from a certain vanity too familiar with the *Portugal* nation, whereof I can render no other reason, but that they are naturally sensible of any thing that touches upon honour. Now see what the difference was; two of us nine falling by chance in contest about the extraction of the *Madureyras* and the *Fonsecas*, for to know which of these two houses was in most esteem at the King of *Portugals* Court, the matter went so far, that from one word to another they came at length to terms of oyster-wives, saying one to the other, Who are you? and again, who are you? so that thereupon they suffered themselves to be so transported with choler, that one of them gave the other a great box on the ear, who instantly returned him a blow with his sword, which cut away almost half his cheek; this same feeling himself hurt caught up an halberd, and therewith ran the other through the arm; this disaster begot such part-taking amongst us, as of nine that we were seven of us found our selves grievously wounded. In the mean time, the *Chaem* came running in person to this tumult with all the *Anchacys* of Justice, who laying hold of us gave us presently thirty lashes apiece, which drew more blood from us than our hurts. This done, they shut us up in a dungeon under ground, where they kept us six and forty days with heavy iron collars about our necks, manacles on our hands, and irons on our legs, so that we suffered exceedingly in this deplorable estate. This while our business was brought before

the Kings atturney, who having seen our accusations, and that
one of the articles made faith, that there were sixteen witnesses against us, he stuck not to say, *That we were people
without the fear or knowledge of God, who did not confess him
otherwise with our mouthes, then as any wild beast might do if
he could speak ; that these things presupposed it was to be
believed, that we were men of blood, of a language, of a law,
of a nation, of a country, and of a kingdom, the inhabitants
whereof wounded and killed one another most cruelly without
any reason or cause, and therefore no other judgment could be
made of us, but that we were the servants of the most gluttonous
serpent of the profound pit of smoak, as appeared by our
works, since they were no better then such as that accursed
serpent had accustomed to do ; so that according to the law of
the third Book of the will of the Son of the Sun, called* Mileterau,
*we were to be condemned to a banishment from all commerce of
people, as a venemous and contagious plague ; so that we deserved
to be confined to the mountains of* Chabaguay, Sumbor, *or*
Lamau, *whither such as we were used to be exiled, to the end
they might in that place hear the wild beasts howl in the night,
which were of as vile a breed and nature as we.* From this
prison we were one morning led to a place, called by
them *Pitau Calidan,* where the *Anchacy* sat in judgement with a majestical and dreadful greatness. He was
accompanied by divers *Chumbims, Huppes, Lanteas,* and
*Cypatons,* besides a number of other persons ; there each
of us had 30 lashes apiece more given us, and then by
publick sentence we were removed to another prison, where
we were in better case yet then in that out of which we came,
howbeit for all that we did not a little detest amongst our
selves both the *Fonseca's,* and the *Madureyra's,* but much
more the devil, that wrought us this mischief. In this prison
we continued almost 2 moneths, during which time our stripes
were throughly healed, howbeit we were exceedingly afflicted
with hunger, and thirst. At length it pleased God that the
*Chaem* took compassion of us ; for on a certain day, wherein
they use to do works of charity for the dead, coming to
review our sentence he ordained, *That in regard we were
strangers, and of a country so far distant from theirs, as no man*

*had knowledge of us, nor that there was any book or writing which made mention of our name, and that none understood our language; as also that we were accustomed, and even hardned to misery and poverty, which many times puts the best and most peaceable persons into disorder, and therefore might well trouble such, as made no profession of patience in their adversities; whence it followed, that our discord proceeded rather from the effects of our misery, then from any inclination unto mutiny and tumult, wherewith the Kings atturny charged us; and further- more representing unto himself what great need there was of men for the ordinary service of the state, and of the officers of justice, for which provision necessarily was to be made, he thought fit, that the punishment for the crimes we had committed, should in the way of an alms bestowed in the Kings name be moderated, and reduced to the whipping which we twice already had, upon condition nevertheless that we should be detained there as slaves for ever, unless it should please the* Tuton *otherwise to ordain of us.* This sentence was pronounced against us, and though we shed a many of tears to see our selves reduced unto this miserable condition, wherein we were, yet this seemed not so bad unto us as the former. After the publication of this decree we were presently drawn out of prison, and tied 3 and 3 together, then led to certain iron forges, where we past 6 whole moneths in strange labours, and great necessities, being in a manner quite naked, without any bed to lie on, and almost famished. At last after the enduring of so many evils, we fell sick of a lethargy, which was the cause, in regard it was a contagious disease, that they turned us out of doors for to go and seek our living, untill we became well again. Being thus set at liberty we continued 4 moneths sick, and begging the alms of good people from door to door, which was given us but sparingly, by reason of the great dearth that then reigned over all the country, so as we were constrained to agree better together, and to promise one another by a solemn oath, that we took, to live lovingly, for the future, as good Christians should do, and that every moneth one should be chosen from amongst us to be as it were a kinde of chief, whom, by the oath we had taken, all the rest of us were to obey, as their superiour, so that none of us was to dispose of himself, or do any thing, without his command, or appointment; and those rules were put into writing by us, that they might be the better observed; as indeed God gave us the grace to live ever afterward in good peace and concord, though it were in great pain, and extreme necessity of all things.

[*Pinto meets a certain Portuguese, one Vasco Calvo, settled in China many years, omitted.*]

---

## CHAPTER XXXIII.

A Tartar commander enters with his army into the town of Quinsay, and that which followed thereupon; with the Nauticor's besieging the Castle of Nixiamcoo, and the taking of it by the means of some Portugals.

WE had been now 8 moneths and an half in this captivity, wherein we endured much misery and many incommodities, for that we had nothing to live upon but that we got by begging up and down the town, when as one *Wednesday*, the 3rd of *July*, in the year 1544. a little after midnight there was such a hurly burly amongst the people, that to hear the noises and cries which was made in every part, one would have thought the earth would have come over and over, which caused us to go in haste to *Vasco Calvo* his house, of whom we demanded the occasion of so great a tumult, whereunto with tears in his eyes he answered us, that certain news were come how the King of *Tartary* was fallen upon the city of *Pequin* with so great an army, as the like had never been seen since *Adam's* time. In this army, according to report, were seven and twenty kings, under whom marched eighteen hundred thousand men, whereof six hundred thousand were horse, which were come by land from the cities of *Luamsama*, *Famstir*, and *Mecuy*, with fourscore thousand *Rhinocerots*, that drew the waggons, wherein was all the baggage of the army, as for the other twelve hundred thousand, which were foot, it was said that they arrived by sea in seventeen thousand vessels, down through the river of *Batampina*; by reason whereof the King of *China* finding himself too weak for the resisting of such great forces, had with a few retired himself to the city of

*Nanquin.* And that also it was reported for certain, that a *Nanticor*, one of the chiefest *Tartar* commanders, was come to the forrest of *Malincataran*, not above a league and a half from *Quinsay*, with an army of threescore and two thousand horse, wherewith he marched against the town, that in all likelihood he would be there within two hours at the furthest. These news so troubled us, that we did nothing but look one upon another, without being able to speak a word to any purpose, howbeit desiring to save our selves, we prayed *Vasco Calvo* to shew us what means he thought we might use to effect it, who sad and full of grief thus answered us; O that we were in our countrey between *Laura* and *Carucha*, where I have often been, and should be there now in safety, but since it cannot be so, all that we can do for the present, is to recommend our selves to God, and to pray unto Him to assist us; for I assure you that an hour ago I would have given a thousand *Taeis* in silver to any one, that could have got me from hence, and saved me with my wife and children, but there was no possibility for it, because the gates were then all shut up, and the walls round about invironed with armed men, which the *Chaem* had placed there to withstand the enemy. So my fellows and I, that were nine in number, past the rest of the night in much affliction and unquietness, without any means of counselling one another, or resolving on what we were to do, continually weeping for the extreme fear we were in of what should become of us. The next morning a little before sun-rising the enemy appeared in a most dreadful manner, they were divided into 7 very great battalions, having their ensigns quartered with green and white, which are the colours of the King of *Tartaria*; marching in this order to the sound of their trumpets, they arrived at a *Pagode*, called *Petilau Nameioo*, a place of good receit, in regard of the many lodgings it had, which was not much distant from the walls. In their vantguard they had a number of light-horse, who ran confusedly up and down with their lances in their rests. Being in this sort come to the *Pagode*, they staid there about half an hour, and then marching on till they were within an harquebuse-shot of the walls, they suddenly ran to them with such hideous cries, as one would have thought that heaven and earth would have come together, and rearing up above two thousand ladders, which for that purpose they had brought along with them, they assaulted the town on every side with a most invincible courage. Now though the besieged at the beginning made some resistance, yet was it not able to hinder the enemy from effecting his design, for by the means of certain iron rams breaking up the 4 principal gates, they rendred themselves masters of the town after they had slain the *Chaem,* together with a great number of *Mandarins,* and gentlemen, that were run thither to keep them from entring. Thus did these barbarians possess themselves of this miserable town, whereof they put all the inhabitants they could meet withall to the sword, without sparing any; and it was said that the number of the slain amounted to threescore thousand persons, amongst whom were many women and maids of very great beauty, which appertained to the chiefest lords of the place. After the bloudy massacre of so much people, and that the town was fired, the principal houses overthrown, and the most sumptuous temples laid level with the ground, nothing remaining on foot during the disorder, the *Tartars* continued there 7 days, at the end whereof they returned towards *Pequin,* where the King was, and from whence he had sent them to this execution, carrying with them a world of gold and silver onely, having burnt all the merchandize they found there, as well because they knew not how to transport it away, as for that the *Chineses* should not make any benefit of it. Two days after their departure they arrived at a castle, named *Nixiamcoo,* where the *Nauticor* of *Luansama,* their general, pitched his camp, and intrenched himself on all sides with an intention to take it by assault the next day to be revenged on the *Chineses* there, for that upon his passing by them towards *Quinsay,* they had cut off an hundred of his men by an ambuscado.

After the army was encamped, and intrenched, and that the general had placed 4 guards and sentinels in all places, he retired to his tent, whither he sent for 70 captains that commanded his army, unto whom upon their arrival he discovered his resolution, which being well approved of, they fell into deliberation in what manner the castle should be assaulted the day following, which concluded on, the next morning as soon

as it was light the souldiers began to march towards the castle,
divided into 14 battalions; being come within a flight-shoot of
it with the sound of trumpets, and most hideous cries, they
reared up their ladders against the walls, and couragiously
mounted up; but in the heat of this assault, where every one
showed his valour, the one in bravely attempting, and the
other in well defending, the *Tartar* in less then 2 hours lost
above three thousand of his men, which made him sound a
retreat in great disorder, and he past the rest of that day in
burying the dead, and curing of the wounded, whereof, there
being a great number, the most part died not long after, for
that the arrows wherewith they were hurt had been smeared
by the *Chineses* with so strange and deadly poison, as there
was no remedy found for it. In the mean time the *Tartar*
commanders seeing the ill success of this assault, and fearing
the King would be offended at so great a loss for so small
an occasion, perswaded the general to call another council,
wherein it might be considered, whether it would be most
expedient for the Kings honour to persist in the siege of
that place, or to give it over, whereupon this affair coming
accordingly into deliberation it was a long time debated
with such diversity of opinions, as they were not able to
conclude upon any thing; so that it was thought fit, in regard
it was then late, to put off the assembly till the next day. This
resolution taken, every man retired to his quarter. Now we
being led away amidst a great many of other slaves, with whom
we had escaped out of the fire of the town, it fell out, (whether
for our good, or for our greater mis-fortune, we could not then
tell) that we were under the guard, as prisoners of war, of one
of that assembly, a rich and honourable man; who returning
to his tent with three other persons, of like quality to himself,
whom he had invited to supper, it chanced after they were risen
from table that one of them espied us, where we stood chained
in a corner of the tent, and perceiving us to weep, was so moved,
that he demanded of us what people we were? what the name
of our country was? and how we came to be slaves to the
*Chineses*? whereunto we gave such an answer, as the *Tartar*
ingaging himself further in this discourse, enquired of us whether
our king was inclined to the wars, and whether we did use to

fight in our country ? to whom one of our companions, named *Jorge Mendez*, replyed that we did, and that we had been trained up from our infancy in a military course of life; which so pleased the *Tartar*, that calling his two friends unto him, Come hither, said he, and have the patience to hear what these prisoners can say; for, believe me, they seem to be men of understanding; whereupon the other two came near, and hearing us relate some part of our mis-fortunes, it begat a desire in them to ask us other questions; wherein having satisfied them the best that we could, one of them that seemed more curious then the rest, addressing himself to *Jorge Mendez*, spake thus; *Since you have seen so much of the world, as you say, if there were any one amongst you that could find out any device, or stratagem of war, whereby the* Mitaquer *(for so was the* Nauticor *called) might take this castle, I vow to you that he would become your prisoner, whereas you are his.* Then *Jorge Mendez*, never considering with what imprudence he spake, nor understanding what he said, nor into what danger he was putting himself, boldly answered him; *If my Lord* Mitaquer *will in the name of the King give it us under his hand, that we shall have a safe conduct to convey us by sea to the Isle of* Ainan, *from whence we may safely return into our country, possibly I may be the man that will shew him how he shall take the castle with little ado.* This speech being heard, and maturely considered by one of the three, a man in years, and of great authority, as having the honour to be much esteemed and beloved of the *Mitaquer*; *Think well of what thou sayest,* replyed he to Jorge Mendez; *for I assure thee if thou doest it, that whatsoever thou demandest shall be granted thee, aye, and more too.* Hereupon the rest of us seeing what *Jorge Mendez* was going to undertake, as also how far he ingaged himself in his promise, and that the *Tartars* began already to ground some hope thereupon, we thought fit to reprehend him for it, and to tell him, that he was not to hazard himself, so at random, by promising a thing that might bring us into the danger of our lives. *I fear nothing less,* said he unto us; *for as for my life in the estate where now I am, I make so little account of it, that if any of these* Barbarians *would play for it at* Primero, *I would with three of the worst cards in the pack venture it upon the first encounter; for I am confident that all the benefit they can expect*

17

*from us will never oblige them to grant us either life or liberty;
so that, for my particular, I had as lief die to day as to morrow ·
judge you only by that which you saw them do at* Quincay,
*whether you are likely to be better dealt withall now.* The *Tartars*
were much abashed to see us thus in contestation one with
another, and to hear us talk so loud, which is not usual amongst
them ; wherefore they reprehended us very seriously, saying ;
*That it was for women to speak aloud, who could not put a bridle
to their tongue, nor a key to their mouthes, and not for men, that
carry a sword, and are made for the wars ; Howbeit, if it were
so that* Jorge Mendez *could execute what he had propounded, the*
Mitaquer *could not refuse him any thing he could demand.* This
said, the *Tartars* retired every one to his lodging, for that it was
eleven of the clock at night, the first watch being newly past,
and the captains of the guard beginning then to walk the round
about the camp, at the sound of divers instruments, as is the
custom in semblable occasions.

The same of the three *Tartar*-commanders, which I said before
was so esteemed of by the *Mitaquer*, had no sooner learnt of
*Jorge Mendez*, that he could tell how to take the castle of
*Nixiamcoo*, but that he went presently to acquaint the general
with it, and making the matter greater then it was, he told him,
that he could do no less then send for him to hear his reasons,
which peradventure would perswade him to give credit unto
him ; and in case it proved not so, yet was there nothing lost
thereby. The *Mitaquer* being well pleased with this advice, sent
incontinently a command to *Tileymay*, which was the captain
under whose guard we were, for to bring us unto him, as
presently he did. Being then arrived, chained as we were, at
the *Mitaquer's* tent, we found him set in councel with the
seventy commanders of the army about two hours after midnight.
At our coming, he received us with an affable countenance, yet
grave and severe ; and causing us to approach nearer unto him,
he commanded part of our chains to be undone ; then asked us
if we would eat, whereunto we answered, most willingly ; for
that in three days together we had not so much as tasted a bit
of any thing; whereat the *Mitaquer* was very much offended,
and sharply reproving the *Tileymay* for it, willed two great
platters of sodden rice, and ducks cut in small pieces, to be set

before us, whereto we fell with such an appetite, like men that
were almost famished, as those of the company, who took great
pleasure to see us feed so, said to the *Mitaquer, When as you
had nothing else, my Lord, but to cause these to come before you
for to slack their hunger, verily you had done very much for them,
by saving them from a languishing death, which otherwise they
could not have avoided ; and so you might have lost these slaves,
of whom the service or sale might have been some way profitable
unto you ; for if you will not make use of them at* Lancama, *you
may sell them for a thousand* Taeis *at least.* Here some began
to laugh, but the *Mitaquer* commanded more rice to be given us,
together with some apples, and other things, conjuring us again
to eat, as a thing which he took pleasure to see us do, wherein
we most willingly gave him satisfaction. After we had fed well,
he began to talk with *Jorge Mendez,* about that which had been
told him of him, and of the means that were to be used for
taking the castle, making him many great promises of honours,
pensions, favour with the King, and liberty for all the rest of his
fellows, with other such offers, as passed all measure : for he
swore unto him, that if by his means God should give him the
victory, whereby he sought nothing but to be revenged on his
enemies for the blood which they had shed of his men, he should
every way be like unto himself, or at least, to any of his children
which soever. Herewith *Jorge Mendez* found himself somewhat
perplexed, because he held it almost impossible for him to bring
it to effect ; howsoever he told him, that, not to hold him longer
in hand, he did not think but if he might view the castle with
his own eyes, he might then peradventure let him know how it
might be taken ; wherefore, if his lordship pleased, he would
the next morning consider it all about, and thereupon render
him an account what course was to be taken therein. The
*Mitaquer,* and all the rest, allowed very well of his answer, and
greatly commending him for it sent us to be lodged in a tent not
far from his, where we spent the rest of the night under a sure
guard ; you may judg now in what fear we were, knowing that
if the business did not succeed according to the desire of these
*Barbarians,* they would cut us all in pieces, for that they were
a people which for never so small a matter would not stick to
kill twenty or thirty men, without any regard either of God, or

any thing else. The next morning, about eight of the clock, *Jorge Mendez*, and two of us, that were appointed to accompany him, went to survey the place with thirty horse for our safe-guard; when as *Jorge Mendez* had well observed the situation thereof, as also that part whereby it might most commodiously be assaulted, he returned to the *Mitaquer*, that expected him with impatience, to whom he gave an account of what he had seen, and facilitated the taking of the castle with little hazard; whereat the *Mitaquer* was so overjoyed, that he presently caused the rest of our irons, and the chains, wherewith we were fastened by the neck and feet to be taken off, swearing to us by the rice he did eat, that as soon as he came to *Pequin*, he would present us to the king, and infallibly accomplish all that he had promised us; for the more assurance whereof he confirmed it by a deed under his hand, that was written in letters of gold, to make it more authentical. That done, he sent for us to dinner, and would needs have us to sit with him at table, doing us many other honours according their manner, which greatly contented us; but on the other side, we were in no little fear, lest this affair should not for our sins have a success answerable to that hope the *Mitaquer* had already conceived of it. The rest of this day the commanders spent in resolving upon the order that was to be observed for assaulting the castle, wherein *Jorge Mendez* was the sole director. First of all then, an infinite company of bavins and fagots was gotten together for to fill up the ditches; there were also three hundred ladders made, very strong, and so large, that three men might easily mount up on them afront without incombring one another; likewise there was a world of paniers, dossers, and baskets provided, together with a great multitude of mattocks, and spades, that were found in the villages and burroughs thereabout, which the inhabitants had deserted upon the bruit of this war; and all the souldiers of the army made preparation of such things as they should need the next day when the assault was to be given. In the mean time *Jorge Mendez* rode always by the *Mitaquers* side, who shewed him many great favours, which we perceived had begotten in him a stately carriage, far different from that he was wont to have; whereat we wondering, some of us (who envious of anothers good fortune, and out of an ill nature) could not chuse but murmur, saying one to another, as it were in disdain, and in a kind of jeering, *What think you of this dog ? verily he will be the cause that either to morrow morning we shall be all cut in pieces, or if the business he hath undertaken succeed as we desire, it is probable that he will be in such credit with these* Barbarians, *that we shall account it for a happiness to be his servants*; and this was the talk which we had amongst us.   The next day all the army was put into order, and divided into twelve battalions, whereof they made twelve files, and one counterfile in the vantguard, that incompassed the whole camp, in manner of an half moon : upon the wings were the foremost, with all that mass of bavins, ladders, baskets, mattocks, spades, and other materials, to fill up the ditch, and make it equal with the rest of the ground.   Marching in this manner they arrived at the castle, which they found strongly mann'd, and with a number of flags and streamers waving upon the battlements.   The first salutation between the besiegers and the besieged was with arrows, darts, stones, and pots of wild-fire, which continued about half an hour ; then the *Tartars* presently filled the ditch with bavins and earth, and so reared up their ladders against the wall, that now by reason of the filling up of the ditch, was not very high.   The first that mounted up was *Jorge Mendez*, accompanied with two of ours, who as men resolved had made up their mind, either to die there, or to render their valour remarkable by some memorable act ; as in effect it pleased our Lord that their resolution had a good success ; for they not only entred first, but also planted the first colours upon the wall, whereat the *Mitaquer*, and all that were with him, were so amazed, as they said one to another, Doubtless if these people did besiege *Pequin*, as we do, the *Chineses*, which defend that city, would sooner lose their honour, then we shall make them to do it with all the forces we have ; in the mean time all the *Tartars*, that were at the foot of the ladders, followed the three *Portugals*, and carried themselves so valiantly, what with the example of a captain that had shewed them the way, as out of their own natural disposition, almost as resolute as those of *Japan*, that in a very short space above 5000 of them were got upon the walls, from whence with great violence they made the *Chineses* to retire ; whereupon so furious and bloody a fight ensued between either party, that in less then half an hour the business was fully decided, and the castle taken, with the death of two thousand *Chineses* and *Mogores* that were in it, there being not above sixscore of the *Tartars* slain. That done, the gates being opened, the *Mitaquer* with great acclamations of joy entred, and causing the *Chineses* colours to be taken down, and his own to be advanced in their places, he with a new ceremony of rejoycing at the sound of many instruments of war, after the manner of the *Tartars*, gave rewards to the wounded, and made divers of the most valiant of his followers knights, by putting bracelets of gold about their right arms ; and then about noon he with the chief commanders of his army, for the greater triumph, dined in the castle, where he also bestowed bracelets of gold upon *Jorge Mendez*, and the other *Portugals*, whom he made to sit down at table with him. After the cloth was taken away, he went out of the castle with all his company, and then causing all the walls of it to be dismantled, he razed the place quite to the ground, setting on fire all that remained, with a number of ceremonies, which was performed with great cries and acclamations, to the sound of divers instruments of war. Moreover he commanded the ruines of this castle to be sprinkled with the blood of his enemies, and the heads of all of them that lay dead there to be cut off ; as for his own souldiers that were slain, he caused them to be triumphantly buried, and such as were hurt to be carefully looked unto ; this done, he retired, with a huge train, and in great pomp, to his tent, having *Jorge Mendez* close by him on horsback. As for the other eight of us, together with many brave noblemen and captains, we followed him on foot. Being arrived at his tent, which was richly hung, he sent *Jorge Mendez* a thousand *Taeis* for a reward, and to us but an hundred apiece ; whereat some of us, that thought themselves to be better qualified, were very much discontented, for that he was more respected then they, by whose means, as well as his, the enterprise had been so happily achieved, though by the good success thereof we had all obtained honour and liberty.

## CHAPTER XXXIV.

The Mitaquer departs from the castle of Nixiancoo, and goes to the King of Tartary his camp before Pequin ; with the Mitaquers presenting us unto the King.

THE next day the *Mitaquer* having nothing more to do where he was, resolved to take his way towards the city of *Pequin*, before which the King lay, as I have delivered before ; to this effect having put his army into battle aray, he departed from thence at eight of the clock in the morning, and marching leasurely to the sound of his warlike instruments, he made his first station about noon on the bank of a river, whose scituation was very pleasant, being all about invironed with a company of fruit trees, and a many goodly houses, but wholly deserted, and bereaved of all things which the *Barbarians* might any way have made booty of. Having past the greatest heat of the day there, he arose and marched on until about an hour in the night that he took up his lodgings at a pretty good town, called *Lantimay*, which likewise we found deserted, for all this whole country was quite dispeopled for fear of the *Barbarians*, who spared no kind of person, but wheresoever they came put all to fire and sword, as the next day they did by this place, and many other along this river, which they burnt down to the ground ; and that which yet was more lamentable, they set on fire, and clean consumed to ashes a great large plain, being about six leagues about, and full of corn ready to be reaped, This cruelty executed, the army began again to move, composed, as it was, of some three-score and five thousand horse, (for as touching the rest they were all slain, as well at the taking of *Quincay*, as in that of the castle of *Nixiancoo*,) and went on to a mountain, named *Pommitay*, where they remained that night ; the next morning dislodging from thence, they marched on somewhat faster then before, that they might arrive by day at the city of *Pequin*, which was distant about seven leagues from that mountain. At three of the clock in the afternoon we came to the river of *Palamxitan*, where a *Tartar* captain, accompanied with an hundred horse, came to receive us, having waited

there two days for that purpose.  The first thing that he did,
was the delivering of a letter from the King to our general,
who received it with a great deal of ceremony.  From this
river to the Kings quarter, which might be some two leagues,
the army marched without order, as being unable to do otherwise, partly as well in regard of the great concourse of people,
wherewith the ways were full in coming to see the generals
arrival, as for the great train which the lords brought along
with them, that overspread all the fields.  In this order, or rather
disorder, we arrived at the castle of *Lautir*, which was the first
fort of nine that the camp had for the retreat of the spies ;
there we found a young prince, whom the *Tartar*, had sent
thither to accompany the general, who alighting from his
horse took his scymitar from his side, and on his knees offered
it unto him, after he had kissed the ground five times, being the
ceremony or complement ordinarily used amongst them.   The
Prince was exceedingly pleased with this honour done unto him,
which with a smiling countenance, and much acknowledgment
of words he testified unto him.   This past, the Prince with a
new ceremony stept two or three paces back, and lifting up his
voice with more gravity then before, as he that represented
the person of the King, in whose name he came, said unto him,
*He, the border of whose rich vesture my mouth kisseth, and that
out of an incredible greatness mastereth the ·scepters of the
earth, and of the Isles of the Sea, sends thee word by me, who am
his slave, that thy honourable arrival is no less agreeable unto
him, then the summers sweet morning is to the ground, when as
the dew doth comfort and refresh our bodies, and therefore would
have thee without further delay to come and hear his voice
mounted on his horse, whose trappings are garnished with jewels
taken out of his treasury, to the end, that riding by my side, thou
mayest be made equal in honour to the greatest of his Court, and
that they which behold thee marching in this sort, may acknowledge that the right hand of him is mighty and valiant unto whom
the labours of war giveth this recompence.*   Hereupon the
*Mitaquer* prostrating himself on the earth, with his hands lifted
up, answered him thus ; *Let my head be an hundred times
trampled on by the sole of his feet, that all those of my race may
be sensible of so great a favour, and that my eldest son may ever*

*carry it for a mark of honour.* Then mounting on the horse
which the Prince had given him, trapped with gold and
precious stones, being one of those that the King used to ride
on himself, they marched on with a great deal of state and
majesty. In this pomp were many spare horses led richly
harnessed; there were also a number of ushers, carrying
silver maces on their shoulders, and six hundred halberdiers
on horsback, together with fifteen chariots, full of silver
cymbals, and many other ill-tuned barbarous instruments,
that made so great a din, as it was not possible to hear one
another. Moreover, in all this distance of way, which was a
league and a half, there were so many men on horsback, as one
could hardly pass through the crowd in any part thereof. The
*Mitaquer*, being thus in triumph arrived at the first trenches
of the camp, he sent us by one of his servants to his quarter,
where we were very well received, and abundantly furnished
with all things necessary for us.

*[Pinto and his companions are called before the King.]*

Fourteen days after we arrived at this camp, the *Mitaquer*,
our general sent us nine horses, upon which we mounted,
and, attending him in a litter drawn by two horses, we
went to the tent of the King. The King was set on his
throne under a rich cloth of state, and had about him 12
young boys kneeling on their knees, with little maces of gold
sceptres, which they carried on their shoulders; close behinde
was a young lady extremely beautiful, and wonderfully richly
attired, with a ventiloe in her hand, wherewith she ever and
anon fanned him. The same was the sister of the *Mitaquer*,
our general, and infinitely beloved of the King, for whose sake
therefore it was that he was in such credit and reputation
throughout the whole army. The King was much about 40
years of age, full stature, somewhat lean, and of a good aspect;
his beard was very short, his mustaches, after the *Turkish*
manner, his eyes like to the *Chineses*, and his countenance severe
and majestical. As for his vesture, it was violet-colour, in
fashion like to a *Turkish* robe, imbroidered with pearl, upon
his feet he had green sandals wrought all over with gold-purl,
and great pearls among it, and on his head a sattin cap of the

colour of his habit, with a rich band of diamonds and rubies
intermingled together.  Before we past any farther, after we
had gone ten or eleven steps in the room, we made our complement by kissing of the ground three several times, and
performing other ceremonies, which the Truch-men taught us.
In the mean time the King commanded the musick to cease,
and addressing himself to the *Mitaquer*; ask these men of the
other end of the world, said he unto him, whether they have
a king, what is the name of their country, and how far distant
it is from this kingdom of *China* where now I am?  Thereupon
one of ours, speaking for all the rest, answered.  That our
country was called *Portugal*, that the king thereof was exceeding rich and mighty, and that from thence to the city of
*Pequin* was at the least three years voyage.  This answer
much amazed the King, because he did not think the world
had been so large, so that striking his thigh with a wand that
he had in his hand, and lifting up his eyes to heaven, as though
he would render thanks unto God; he said aloud, so as every
one might hear him :  *O Creator of all things ! are we able to
comprehend the marvels of Thy greatness, we that at the best are
but poor worms of the earth ?*  Fuxiquidane, fuxiquidane, *let
them approach, let them approach.*  Thereupon beckning to us
with his hand, he caused us to come even to the first degree
of the throne, where the fourteen kings sate, and demanded of
him again, as a man astonished, *Pucan, pucan*, that is to say,
*how far, how far ?* whereunto he answered as before, that we
should be at least three years in returning to our country.
Then he asked, why we came not rather by land, then by sea,
where so many labours and dangers were to be undergone?
Thereunto he replied, that there was too great an extent of
land, through which we were not assured to pass, for that it
was commanded by kings of several nations.  *What come you
for to seek for then*, added the King, *and wherefore do you expose
your selves to such dangers ?*  Then having rendred him a
reason to this last demand, with all the submission that might
be, he stayed a pretty while without speaking; and then
shaking his head three or four times, he addressed himself to
an old man that was not far from him, and said, *Certainly we
must needs conclude, that there is either much ambition, or little*

*justice in the country of these people, seeing they come so far to* *conquer other lands.* To this speech the old man, named *Raia Benan,* made no other answer, but that it must needs be so; for men, said he, who have recourse unto their industry and invention to run over the sea for to get that which God hath not given them, are necessarily carried thereunto, either by extreme poverty, or by an excess of blindness and vanity, derived from much covetousness, which is the cause why they renounce God, and those that brought them into the world. This reply of the old man was seconded by many jeering words by the other courtiers, who made great sport upon this occasion, that very much pleased the King; in the mean time the women fell to their musick again, and so continued, till the King withdrew into another chamber in the company of these fair musicians, and that young lady that fanned him, not so much as one of those great personages daring to enter besides. Not long after one of those twelve boys that carried the scepters before mentioned, came to the *Mitaquer,* and told him from his sister, that the King commanded him to depart away, which he held for a singular favour, by reason this message was delivered to him in the presence of those kings and lords that were in the room, so that he stirred not, but sent us word, that we should go unto our tent with this assurance, that he would take care the Son of the Sun should be mindful of us.

---

## CHAPTER XXXV.

The King of Tartaria's raising of his siege from before Pequin, for to return to his country.

WE had been now full three and forty days in this camp, during which time there past many fights and skirmishes between the besiegers and the besieged, as also two assaults in the open day, which were resisted by them within with an invincible courage, like resolute men as they were. In the mean time the King of *Tartaria,* seeing how contrary to his hope so great an enterprise had been, wherein he had consumed so much treasure, caused his council of war

to be assembled, in the which were present the seven and
twenty kings that accompanied him, and likewise many
princes, and lords, and the most part of the chief commanders
of the army.    In this council it was resolved, that in regard
winter was at hand, and that the rivers had already overflowed
their banks with such force and violence, as they had ravaged
and carried away most of the trenches and pallisadoes of the
camp, and that moreover great numbers of the souldiers died
daily of sickness, and for want of victuals, that therefore the
King could not do better then to raise his siege, and be gone
before winter came, for fear lest staying longer, he should run
the hazard of losing himself, and his army.    All these reasons
seemed so good to the King, that without further delay he
resolved to follow this counsel, and to obey the present
necessity, though it were to his great grief; so that incontinently he caused all his infantry and ammunition to be
imbarqued; then having commanded his camp to be set on
fire, he himself went away by land with three hundred thousand horse, and twenty thousand rhinocerots.    Now after
they had taken an account of all the dead, they appeared to
be four hundred and fifty thousand, the most of whom died of
sickness, as also an hundred thousand horses, and threescore
thousand rhinocerots, which were eaten in the space of two
moneths and an half, wherein they wanted victual; so that of
eighteen hundred thousand men wherewith the King of
*Tartaria*, came out of his country to besiege the city of
*Pequin*, before the which he lay six moneths and a half, he
carried home some seven hundred and fifty thousand less then
he brought forth, whereof four and fifty thousand died of
sickness, famine, and war, and three hundred thousand went
and rendred themselves unto the *Chineses*, drawn thereunto
by the great pay which they gave them, and other advantages
of honor and presents which they continually bestowed on
them; whereat we are not to marvel, seeing experience doth
show, how that alone is of far more power to oblige men, then
all other things in the world.    After the King of *Tartaria* was
gone from this city of *Pequin*, upon a *Munday*, the 17th
of *October*, with three hundred thousand horse, as I have
related before, the same day about evening he went and lodged

near to a river, called *Quatragun*, and the next morning, an
hour before day, the army began to march at the sound of
the drums, fifes, and other instruments of war, according to
the order prescribed them. In this manner he arrived a
little before night, at a town named *Guiiampea*, which he
found altogether depopulated. After his army had réposed
there about an hour and an half, he set forth again, and
marching somewhat fast he came to lodge at the foot of a
great mountain, called *Liampeu*, from whence he departed
towards morning. Thus marched he eight leagues a day for
fourteen day together, at the end whereof he arrived at a
good town, named *Guauxitim*, which might contain about
eleven or twelve thousand fires. There he was counselled to
furnish himself with victuals, whereof he had great need, for
which purpose therefore he begirt it round, and skaling
it in the open day he quickly made himself master of it,
and put it to the sack with so cruel a massacre of the
inhabitants, as my fellows and I were ready to swoond for
very astonishment. Now after that the sword and fire had
consumed all things, and that the army was abundantly
provided of ammunition and victual, he departed at the break
of day; and though he past the next morning in the view of
*Caixiloo*, yet would not he attaque it, for that it was a great
and strong town and by scituation impregnable, having heard
besides that there were fifty thousand men within it, whereof
ten thousand were *Mogores, Cauchins,* and *Champaas,* resolute
souldiers, and much more warlike then the *Chineses.* From
thence passing on he arrived at the walls of *Singrachirau*,
which are the very same that, as I have said heretofore, do
divide those two empires of *China* and *Tartaria.* There meeting
with no resistance he went and lodged on the further side of it
at *Panquinor*, which was the first of his own towns, and seated
some three leagues from the said wall, and the next day he
marched to *Psipator*, where he dismissed the most part of his
people. In this place he stayed not above seven days, which
he spent in providing pay for his souldiers, and in the execution of certain prisoners he had taken in that war, and brought
along with him. These things thus expedited, he, as a man
not very well pleased, imbarqued himself for *Lancame*, in

sixscore *Lanlees*, with no more then ten or eleven thousand
men. So in six days after his imbarquing, he arrived at
*Lancame*, where not permitting any reception to be made him,
he landed about two hours within night.

------

## CHAPTER XXXVI.

In what manner we were brought again before the King of Tartaria; with
our departure from that kingdom; and our adventures after quitting
the city of Uzamguee in Cochin-China, till our arrival at the Isle of
Tanixumaa in Japan.

AFTER some time had been spent in the celebration of
certain remarkable feasts, that were made for joy of the
conclusion of a marriage betwixt the Princess *Meica vidan*, the
Kings sister, and the Emperour of *Caran*, the *Tartar*, by the
advice of his captains, resolved to return anew to the siege of
*Pequin*, which he had formerly quitted, taking the ill success
that he had there as a great affront to his person. To this
effect then he caused all the estates of his kingdom to be
assembled, and also made a league with all the kings and
princes bordering in his dominions : whereupon considering
with our selves how prejudicial this might prove to the promise
had been made us for the setting of us at liberty, we repaired
to the *Mitaquer*, and represented unto him many things that
made for our purpose, and obliged him to keep his word with
us. To which he returned us this answer: Certainly you have
a great deal of reason for that you say, and I have yet more,
not to refuse you that which you demand of me with so much
justice ; wherefore I resolve to put the King in minde of you,
that you may enjoy your liberty ; and the sooner you shall be
gone from hence, the sooner you shall be freed from the labors
which the time begins to prepare for us in the enterprise that
his Majesty hath newly undertaken by the counsel of some
particulars, who for that they know not how to govern themselves have more need to be counselled, then the earth hath
need of water to produce the fruits that are sowed in her ; but
to morrow morning I shall put the King in minde of you, and

your poverty, and withall I shall present unto him how you
have poor fatherless children, as you have heretofore told me,
to the end he may be thereby incited to cast his eyes upon
you, as he is accustomed to do in like cases, which is none of
the least marks of his greatness. Hereupon he dismissed us
for that day, and the next morning he went to *Pontiveu,* which
is a place where the King useth to give audience to all such as
have any suit to him. There beseeching his Majesty to think
of us, he answered him, that as soon as he had dispatched
away an ambassador to the King of *Cauchenchina,* he would
send us along with him, for so he had resolved to do. With
this answer the *Mitaquer* returned to his house, where we
were ready attending his coming, and told us what the King
had promised him, wherewithall not a little contented we went
back to our lodging. There in the expectation of the good
success of this promise we continued 10 days with some
impatience ; at the end whereof the *Mitaquer* by the Kings
express command carried us with him to the Court, where
causing us to approach near to his Majesty, with those ceremonies of greatness which are observed in coming before him,
being the same we used at *Pequin,* after he had beheld us with
a gentle eye, he bid the *Mitaquer* ask of us whether we would
serve him, and in case we would, he should not onely be very
well pleased with it, but he would also give us better entertainment, and more advantageous conditions then all the
strangers that should follow him in this war. To this demand
the *Mitaquer* answered very favourably for us, how he had
often heard us say, that we were maried in our country, and
had a great charge of children, who had no other means to
maintain them, but what we got with our labor, which was
poorly enough, God knows. The King heard this speech with
some demonstration of pity, so that looking on the *Mitaquer* ;
*I am glad,* said he, *to know that they have such good cause to
return home as they speak of, that I may with the more contentment acquit me of that which thou hast promised them in my
name.* At these words the *Mitaquer* and all we that were with
him, lifting up our hands, as a testimony of our thankfulness
unto him, we kissed the ground 3 times and said, *May thy feet
rest themselves upon a thousand generations, to the end that thou*

*mayst be Lord of the inhabitants of the earth.* Hereat the King
began to smile, and said to a prince that was near him, *These
men speak as if they had been bred amongst us.* Then casting
his eyes on *Jorge Mendez,* who stood before us all next to the
*Mitaquer, And thou,* said he unto him, *in what condition art
thou, wilt thou go, or stay ?* whereupon *Mendez,* who had long
before premeditated his answer, *Sir,* replied he, *for me, that
have neither wife nor children to bewail my absence, the thing I
most desire in the world is to serve your Majesty, since you are
pleased therewith, whereunto I have more affection then to be
Chaem of* Pequin *one thousand years together.* At this the
King smiled again, and then dismissed us, so that we returned
very well satisfied to our lodging, where we continued 3 days
in a readiness to depart, at the end of which, by the mediation
of the *Mitaquer,* and means of his sister, who, as I have said
before, was wonderfully beloved of the King, his Majesty sent
us, for the eight that we were 2000 *Taeis,* and gave us in
charge to his ambassador, whom he sent to the city of *Uzamguee* in *Cauchenchina,* in the company of the same King of
*Cauchenchina's* ambassador. With him we departed from
thence 5 days after, being imbarqued in the vessel wherein he
went himself. But before our departure *Jorge Mendez* gave us
1000 duckets, which was easie for him to do, for that he had
already 6000 of yearly rent, withall he kept us company all
that day, and at the length took his leave of us, not without
shedding many a tear for grief that he had so exposed himself
to a voluntary exile.

[*Here follows an account of Pinto's journey with the Ambassador to the city of Uzamguee in Cochin-China,* omitted.]

Upon the 12 of *January* we departed from the city of
*Uzamguee,* exceedingly rejoycing at our escape from so many
labors and crosses, which we before had sustained, and imbarqued our selves upon a river, that was above a league
broad, down the which we went 7 days together, beholding in
the mean time on either side thereof many fair towns, and
goodly boroughs, which by the outward appearance we believed
were inhabited by very rich people, in regard of the sumptuous-

less of the buildings, not onely of particular houses, but much
more of the temples, whose steeples were all covered over with
gold ; as likewise in regard of the great number of barques and
vessels that were on this river, abundantly fraught with all
sorts of provisions and merchandise. Now when we were
come to a very fair town called *Quangeparuu*, containing some
18 or 2000 fires, the *Naudelum*, who was he that conducted us
by the express commandment from the King, stayed there
12 days to trade in exchange of silver and pearl; whereby he
confessed to us that he had gained 14 for 1, and that if he had
been so advised as to have brought salt thither, he had doubled
his money above thirty times : we were assured that in this
town the King had yearly out of the silver mines above 1500
*Picos*, which are 40000 *Quintals* of our weight, besides the huge
revenue that he drew out of many other different things. This
town had no other fortification then a weak brick wall, 8 foot
high, and a shallow ditch some 30 foot broad. The inhabitants
are weak and unarmed, having neither artillery, nor any thing
for their defence, so that 500 resolute souldiers might easily
take it. We parted from this place on *Tuesday* morning, and
continued our course 13 days, at the end whereof we got to
the port of *Sanchan*, in the kingdom of *China*. Now because
there was no shipping of *Malaca* there, for they were gone
from thence 9 days before, we went 7 leagues further to
another port, named *Lampacau*, where we found 2 juncks of
*Malaya*, one of *Patana*, and another of *Lugor*. And whereas
it is the quality of us *Portugals* to abound in our own sense,
and to be obstinate in our opinions, there arose amongst us eight
so great a contrariety of judgement about a thing, (wherein
nothing was so necessary for us, as to maintain our selves in
peace and unity) that we were even upon the point of killing
one another. But because the matter would be too shamefull
to recount in the manner as it past, I will say no more, but
that the *Necoda* of the *Lorche*, which had brought us thither
from *Uzamguee*, amazed at this so great barbarousness of ours,
separated himself from us in such displeasure, that he would
not charge himself either with our messages of letters, saying,
that he had rather the King should command his head to be
cut off, than to offend God in carrying with him any thing

18

whatsoever that belonged to us. Thus different as we were in opinions, and in very bad terms amongst our selves, we lingred above 9 days in this little island, during which time the juncks departed without vouchsafing to take us in, so that we were constrained to remain in these solitudes, exposed to many great dangers, out of which I did not think that ever we could have escaped, if God had not been extraordinarily mercifull unto us ; for having been there 17 days in great misery and want ; it happened that a pyrat, named *Samipocheca*, arrived in this place, who having been defeated, went flying from the fleet of *Aytao* of *Chincheo*, that of eight and twenty sail, which this pyrat had, had taken six and twenty of them from him, so that he had with much ado escaped with those onely two remaining, wherein the most part of his men were hurt, for which cause he was constrained to stay there 7 days to have them cured. Now the present necessity enforcing us to take some course, whatsoever it were, we were glad to agree to serve under him untill such time as we might meet with some good opportunity to get unto *Malaca*. Those 20 days ended, wherein yet there was no manner of reconciliation between us, but still continuing in discord we imbarqued our selves with the pyrat, namely, 3 in the junck where he himself was, and 5 in the other, whereof he had made a nephew of his captain. Having left this island with an intent to sail unto a port, called *Lailoo*, some 7 leagues from *Chincheo*, we continued our voyage with a good winde all along the coast of *Lamau* for the space nine days, untill that one morning when we were near to the River of Salt, which is about five leagues from *Chabaquea*, it was our ill fortune to be assailed by a pirate, who with seven great juncks fell to fighting with us from six in the morning till ten of the clock before noon, in which conflict we were so entertained with shot, and pots full of artificiall fire, that at last there were three sail burnt, to wit, two of the pirats, and one of ours, which was the junck, wherein the five *Portugals* were, whom we could by no means succour, for that then most of our men were hurt. But at length towards night being well refreshed by the afternoons gale, it pleased our Lord that we escaped out of this pirats hands. In this ill equipage wherein we were, we continued our course for three days together, at the end whereof we were invironed by so great and impetuous a tempest, that the same night in which it seized us we lost the coast; and because the violence of the storm would never suffer us after to recover it again, we were forced to make with full sail towards the islands of the *Lequios*, where the pirate, with whom we went, was well known, both to the King, and those of the country; with this resolution we set our selves to sail through the Archipelage of these islands, where notwithstanding we could not make land, as well for that we wanted a pilot to steer the vessel, ours being slain in the last fight, as also because the wind and tide was against us. Amidst so many crosses we beat up and down with labour enough from one rhomb to another for three and twenty dayes together, at the end whereof it pleased God that we discovered land, whereunto approaching to see if we could descry any appearance of a port, or good anchorage, we perceived on the south-coast near to the horizon of the sea a great fire, which perswaded us that there we might peradventure find some borough, where we might furnish our selves with fresh water, whereof we had very great need. So we went and rode just before the island in seventy fathom, and presently we beheld two *Almedias* come towards us from the land with six men in them, who being come close to the side of our junck, and having complemented with us according to their manner, demanded of us from whence we came? whereunto having answered, that we came from *China*, with merchandize, intending to trade in this place if we might be suffered, one of the six replyed; That the *Nautaquim*, lord of that island, called *Tanixumaa*, would very willingly permit it upon payment of such customs as are usual in *Jappan*, which is, continued he, this great country that you see here before you. At these news, and many other things which they told us, we were exceeding glad; so that after they had shewed us the port, we weighed anchor, and went and put our selves under the lee-shore of a creek, which was on the south-side, and where stood a great town, named *Miay-gimaa*, from whence there came instantly aboard of us divers *Paroos* with refreshments, which we bought.

We had not been two hours in this creek of *Miay-gimaa*,

when as the *Nautaquim*, Prince of this island of *Tanixumaa*, came directly to our junck, attended by divers gentlemen and merchants, who had brought with them many chests full of silver ingots, therewith to barter for our commodities; so after ordinary complements past on either side, and that we had given our word for his easiest coming aboard of us; he no sooner perceived us three *Portugals*, but he demanded what people we were, saying, that by our beards and faces we could not be *Chineses :* hereunto the pirate answered, That we were of a country called *Malaca*, whither many years before we were come from another land, named *Portugal*, which was at the further end of the world. At these words the *Nautaquim* remained much amazed, and turning himself to his followers; *Let me not live*, said he unto them, *if these men here be not the* Cheuchicogis, *of whom it is written in our books, That flying on the top of the waters they shall from thence subdue the inhabitants of the earth, where God hath created the riches of the world, wherefore it will be a good fortune for us if they come into our country as good friends.* Thereupon having called a woman of *Lequia*, whom he had brought to serve as an interpreter between him and the *Chinese*, captain of the junck; *Ask the Necoda*, said he unto her, *where he met with these men, and upon what occasion he had brought them hither with him into our country of* Jappan? The captain thereunto replied, That we were honest men and merchants, and that having found us at *Lampacau*, where we had been cast away, he had out of charity taken us in, as he used to do unto all such as he met withall in the like case, to the end that God might out of His gracious goodness be thereby moved to deliver him from the danger of such violent tempests, as commonly such as sail on the sea are subject to perish in. This saying of the pirate seemed so reasonable to the *Nautaquim*, that he presently came aboard of us, and because those of his train were very many, he commanded that none but such as he named should enter in. After he had seen all the commodities in the junck, he sate him down in a chair upon the deck, and began to question us about certain things which he desired to know, to the which we answered him in such sort, as we thought would be most agreeable to his humour, so that he seemed to be exceedingly satisfied therewith; in this manner he entertained us a good while together, making it apparent by his demands that he was a man very curious, and much inclined to hear of novelties and rare things. That done, he took his leave of us, and the *Necoda*, little regarding the rest, saying, *Come and see me at my house to morrow, and for a present bring me an ample relation of the strange things of that great world through which you have travelled, as also of the countries that you have seen, and withall remember to tell me how they are called; for I swear unto you that I would far more willingly buy this commodity then any that you can sell me.* This said, he returned to land, and the next morning, as soon as it was day, he sent us to our junck a great *Parao*, full of divers sorts of refreshments, as raysins, pears, melons, and other kinds of fruits of that country; in exchange of this present the *Necoda* returned him, by the same messenger, divers rich pieces of stuff, together with certain knacks and rarities of *China*, and withall sent him word, that as soon as his junck should be at anchor, and out of danger of the weather, he would come and wait on him ashore, and bring him some patterns of the commodities which we had to sell; as indeed the next morning he went on land, and carried us three along with him, as also some ten or eleven of the chiefest of the *Chineses* of his company, to the end that at this first sight he might settle a good opinion of himself in this people for the better satisfaction of that vanity whereunto they are naturally inclined; we went then to the *Nautaquims* house, where we were very well entertained, and the *Necoda* having given him a rich present, shewed him the patterns of all the commodities he had, wherewith he rested so contented, that he sent presently for the principal merchants of the place, with whom the *Necoda* having agreed upon a price for his commodities, it was resolved that the next day they should be transported from the junck into a certain house, which was appointed for the *Necoda* and his people to remain in till such time as he should set sail for *China*. After all this was concluded, the *Nautaquim* fell again to questioning of us about many several matters, whereunto we rendred him such answers as might rather fit his humour, then agree with the truth indeed, which yet we did not observe but in some certain demands that he made us, where we thought it necessary to make use of certain particulars altogether fained by us, that so we might not derogate from the great opinion he had conceived of our country. The first thing he propounded was, how he had learned from the *Chineses* and *Lequois*, that *Portugal* was far richer and of a larger extent, then the whole empire of *China*, which we confirmed unto him. The second, how he had likewise been assured, that our king had upon the sea conquered the greatest part of the world, which also we averred to be so; the third, that our king was so rich in gold and silver, as it was held for most certain, that he had above two thousand houses full of it even to the very tops; but thereunto we answered, that we could not truly say the number of the houses, because the kingdom of *Portugal* was so spacious, so abounding with treasure, and so populous, as it was impossible to specifie the same. So after the *Nautaquim* had entertained us above two hours with such and the like discourse, he turned him to those of his train, and said, *Assuredly not one of those kings, which at this present we know to be on the earth, is to be esteemed happy, if he be not the vassal of so great a monarch as the emperour of this people here.* Whereupon having dismissed the *Necoda* and his company, he intreated us to passe that night on shore with him, for to satisfie the extream desire that he had to be informed from us of many things of the world, whereunto he was exceedingly carried by his own inclination; withall he told us, that the next day he would assigne us a lodging next to his own palace, which was in the most commodious place of the town, and for that instant he sent us to lie at a very rich merchant's house, who entertained us very bountifully that night.

———

## CHAPTER XXXVII.

The great honour which the Nautaquim, Lord of the Isle, did to one of us for having seen him shoot with an harquebuse ; and his sending me to the King of Bungo ; and that which passed till my arrival at his Court.

THE next day the *Chinese Necoda* disimbarqued all his commodities, as the *Nautaquim* had enjoyed him, and put them into sure rooms, which were given him for that purpose, and in three days he sold them all, as well for that he had not many, as because his good fortune was such, that the country was at that time utterly unfurnished thereof, by which means this pirate profited so much, that by this sale he wholly recovered himself of the loss of the six and twenty saile which the *Chinese* pirate had taken from him; for they gave him any price he demanded, so that he confessed unto us, that of the value of some five and twenty hundred *Taeis* which he might have in goods, he made above thirty thousand. Now as for us three *Portugals*, having nothing to sell, we imployed our time either in fishing, hunting, or seeing the temples of these *Gentiles*, which were very sumptuous and rich, whereinto the *Bonzes*, who are their priests, received us very courteously, for indeed it is the custome of those of *Jappan* to be exceeding kind and courteous. Thus we having little to do, one of us, called *Diego Zeimoto*, went many times a shooting for his pleasure in an *harquebuse* that he had, wherein he was very expert, so that going one day by chance to a certain marsh, where there was a great store of fowl, he killed at that time about six and twenty wild ducks. In the mean time these people beholding this manner of shooting, which they had never seen before, were much amazed at it, insomuch that it came to the notice of the *Nautaquim*, who was at that instant riding of horses, and not knowing what to think of this novelty, sent presently for *Zeimoto*, just as he was shooting in the marsh, but when he saw him come with his *harquebuse* on his shoulder, and two *Chineses* with him carrying the fowl, he was so mightily taken with the matter, as he could not sufficiently admire it: for whereas they had never seen any gun before in that country, they could not comprehend what

it might be, so that for want of understanding the secret of
the powder, they all concluded that of necessity it must be
some sorcery; thereupon *Zeimoto* seeing them so astonished,
and the *Nautaquim* so contented, made three shoots before
them, whereof the effect was such, that he killed one kite, and
two turtle doves; in a word then, and not to lose time, by
endearing the matter with much speech, I will say no more,
but that the *Nautaquim* caused *Zeimoto* to get up on the
horses crupper behind him, and so accompanied with a great
croud of people, and four *Ushers*, who with battoons headed
with iron went before him, crying all along the streets, *Know
all men, that the* Nautaquim, *Prince of this island of*
Tanixumaa, *and lord of our heads, enjoyns and expresly
commands, That all persons whatsoever, which inhabit the land
that lies between the two seas, do honour this* Chenchicogim, *of
the further end of the world, for even at this present and for
hereafter he makes him his kinsman, in such manner as the*
Jacharons *are, who sit next his person; and whosoever shall
not do so willingly, he shall be sure to lose his head.* Whereupon all the people answered with a great noise; *We will do
so for ever.* In this pomp *Zeimoto* being come to the palace
gate, the *Nautaquim* alighted from his horse, and taking him
by the hand, whilest we two followed on foot a pretty way
after, he led him into his court, where he made him sit with
him at his own table, and to honour him the more, he would
needs have him lodge there that night, showing many other
favours to him afterwards, and to us also for his sake. Now
*Zeimoto* conceiving, that he could not better acknowledge the
honour which the *Nautaquim* did him, then by giving him his
*harquebuse* which he thought would be a most acceptable
present unto him; on a day when he came home from
shooting, he tendred it unto him with a number of pigeons
and turtle-doves, which he received very kindly, as a thing of
great value, assuring him that he esteemed of it more, then of
all the treasures of *China*, and giving him withall in recompence
thereof a thousand *Taeis* in silver, he desired him to teach him
how to make the powder, saying, that without that the *harquebuse* would be of no use to him, as being but a piece of
unprofitable iron, which *Zeimoto* promised him to do, and

accordingly performed the same. Now the *Nautaquim* taking pleasure in nothing so much as shooting in this *harquebuse*, and his subjects perceiving that they could not content him better in any thing, then in this, wherewith he was so much delighted, they took a pattern of the said *harquebuse* to make others by it, and the effect thereof was such, that before our departure (which was five moneths and an half after) there was six hundred of them made in the country; nay I will say more, that afterwards, namely, the last time that the Vice-roy *Don Alphonso de Noronha* sent me thither with a present to the King of *Bungo*, which happened in the year 1556. those of *Jappan* affirmed, that in the city of *Fucheo*, being the chief of that kingdom, there were above thirty thousand; whereat finding my self to be much amazed, for that it seemed impossible unto me, that this invention should multiply in such sort, certain merchants of good credit assured me that in the whole island of *Jappan* there were above three hundred thousand *harquebuses*, and that they alone had transported of them in the way of trade to the country of the *Lequios*, at six several times, to the number of five and twenty hundred; so that by the means of that one, which *Zeimoto* presented to the *Nautaquim* in acknowledgment of the honour and good offices that he had done him, as I have declared before, the country was filled with such abundance of them, as at this day there is not so small an hamlet but hath an hundred at the least; for as for cities and great towns, they have them by thousands, whereby one may perceive, what the inclination of this people is, and how much they are naturally addicted to the wars, wherein they take more delight, then any other nation that we know.

We had been now three and twenty days in the Island of *Tanixumaa*, where very contentedly we past away the time, either in fishing, fowling, or hunting, whereunto these people of *Jappan* are much addicted, when as a vessel belonging to the King of *Bungo* arriving in that port, in the which were divers men of quality, and certain merchants, who as soon as they were landed went to wait upon the *Nautaquim* with their presents, according to the usual custom of the country. Amongst them there was an ancient man, very well attended,

and unto whom the rest carried much respect, that falling on
his knees before the *Nautaquim*, presented him with a letter,
and a rich courtelass garnished with gold, together with a box
full of ventiloes, which the *Nautaquim* received with a great
deal of ceremony. Then having spent some time with him in
asking of certain questions, he read the letter to himself, and
thereupon having remained a pretty while as it were in suspence,
and dismissed the bearer thereof from his presence, with an
express charge to those about him to see him honourably entertained, he called us unto him, and commanded the truchman
that was thereby, to use these words unto us, *My good friends,
I intreat you that you will hear this letter read, which is sent
me from my lord and uncle, and then I will let you know what
I desire of you*; so giving it to a treasurer of his, he commanded
him to read it, which instantly he did, and these were the
contents of it, *Thou right eye of my face,* Hynscarangoxo,
Nautiquim *of* Tanixumaa, *I* Orgemdoo, *who am your father
in the true love of my bowels, as he from whom you have taken
the name and being of your person, King of* Bungo *and* Fatacaa,
*Lord of the great House of* Fiancima, Tosa, *and* Bandou, *chief
soveraign of the petty kings of the Islands of* Goto *and* Xaman-
axequa, *I give you to understand, my son, by the words of my
mouth, which are spoken of your person, that some days since
certain men, coming from your country, have assured me, that
you have in your town three* Chenchicogims *of the other end of
the world, men that accommodate themselves very well with those
of* Jappan, *are clothed in silk, and usually wear swords by their
sides, not like merchants that use traffique, but in the quality of
persons that make profession of honour, and which by that only
mean pretend to render their names immortal; moreover, I have
heard for a truth, that these same men have entertained you at
large with all matters of the whole universe, and have assured
unto you on their faith, that there is another world greater then
ours, inhabited with black and tawny people, of whom they have
told you things most incredible to our judgement, for which cause
I infinitely desire you, as if you were my son, that by* Fiangean-
dono, *whom I have despatched from hence to visit my daughter,
you will send me one of those three strangers, which I am told
you have in your house; the rather for that you know my long*

*indisposition, accompanied with so much pain and grief, hath
great need of some diversion: now if it should happen that they
would not be willing thereunto, you may then assure them, as
well on your own faith, as on mine, that I will not fail to return
them back in all safety; whereupon, like a good son that desires
to°please his father, so order the matter that I may rejoyce my
self in the sight of them, and so have my desire accomplished.
What I have further to say unto you, my ambassadour* Fingeandono *shall acquaint you with, by whom I pray you liberally
impart to me the good news of your person, and that of my
daughter, seeing she is, as you know, the apple of my right eye,
whereof the sight is all the joy of my face. From the house of*
Fucheo *the seventh Mamoque of the Moon.* After that the
*Nautaquim* had heard this letter read; the King of *Bungo*, said
he unto us, is my lord, and my *uncle*, the brother of my mother,
and (above all) he is my good father, for I call him by that
name, because he is so to my wife, which is the reason that he
loves me no less then his own children; wherefore I count my
self exceedingly bound unto him, and do so much desire to
please him that I could now find in my heart to give the best
part of my estate for to be transformed into one of you, as well for
to go unto him, as to give him the content of seeing you, which
out of the knowledge I have of his disposition, I am assured he
will value more then all the treasures of *China*. Now having thus
acquainted you with his desire, I earnestly intreat you to render
your selves conformable thereunto, and that one of you two
will take the pains to go to *Bungo*, there to see the King whom
I hold for my father and my lord; for as for this other, to
whom I have given the name and being of a kinsman, I am
not willing to part with him till he hath taught me to shoot
as well as himself. Hereupon *Christovano Borralho*, and I,
greatly satisfied with the *Nautaquim's* courtesie, answered
him, that we kissed his Highness hands for the exceeding
honor he did us in vouchsafing to make use of us; and seeing
it was his pleasure so to do, that he should for that effect
make choice of which of us two he thought best, and he should
not fail to be suddenly ready for the voyage. At these words
standing a while in musing to himself, he looked on me, and
said, I am resolved to send him there, because he seems not

so solemn, but is of a more lively humour, wherewith those of *Jappan* are infinitely delighted, and may thereby chear up the sick man, whereas the too serious gravity of this other, said he, turning him to *Borralho*, though very commendable for more important matters, would serve but to entertain his melancholy instead of diverting it.   Thereupon falling into merry discourse, and jesting with those about him, whereunto the people of *Jappan* are much inclined, the *Fingeandono* arrived, unto whom he presented me, with a special and particular recommendation touching the assurance of my person, wherewith I was not onely well satisfied, but had my minde also cleared from certain doubts, which out of the little knowledge I had of these peoples humors, had formerly troubled me. This done, the *Nautaquim* commanded 200 *Taeis* to be given me for the expence of my voyage, whereupon the *Fingeandono* and I imbarqued our selves in a vessel with oars, called a Funce, and in one night having traversed all this island of *Tanixumaa*, the next morning we cast anchor in an haven, named *Hiamangoo*, from whence we went to a good town, called *Quanquixumaa*, and so continuing our course afore the winde, with a very fair gale, we arrived the day ensuing at a very sweet place, named *Tanaro*, whence the morrow after we went to *Minato*, and so forward to a fortress of the King of *Bungoes*, called *Osquy*, where the *Fingeandono* stayed some time, by reason that the captain of the place (who was his brother in law) found himself much indisposed in his health. There we left the vessel in which we came, and so went by land directly to the city, where being arrived about noon, the *Fingeandono*, because it was not at a time fit to wait upon the King, went to his own house.   After dinner having rested a little, and shifted himself into a better habit, he mounted on horsback, and with certain of his friends rode to the court, carrying me along with him, where the King was no sooner advertised of his coming, but he sent a son of his about nine or ten years of age to receive him, who accompanied with a number of noblemen, richly apparelled, and his ushers with their maces going before him, took the *Fingeandono* by the hand, and beholding him with a smiling countenance ; *May thy entrance*, said he unto him, *into the house of the King my lord, bring thee as much content and honour as thy children deserve, and are worthy, being thine, to sit at table with me in the solemn feasts.* At these words the *Fingeandono* prostrating himself on the ground; *My lord,* answered he, *I most humbly beseech them that are in heaven above, which have taught thee to be so courteous and so good, either to answer for me, or to give me a tongue so voluble, as may express my thankfulness in terms agreeable to thy ears for the great honour thou art pleased to do me at this present; for in doing otherwise I should offend no less, then those ungratefull wretches which inhabit the lowest pit of the profound and obscure house of smoak.* This said, he offered to kiss the curtelass which the young prince wore by his side, which he would by no means permit, but taking him by the hand, he led him to the King his father, unto whom, lying sick in his bed, he delivered a letter from the *Nautaquim,* which after he had read, he commanded him to call me in from the next room where I staid attending, which instantly he did, and presented me to the King, who entertaining me very graciously; *Thy arrival,* said he unto me, *in this my country is no less pleasing to me, then the rain which falls from heaven is profitable to our fields that are sowed with rice.* Finding my self somewhat perplexed with the novelty of these terms, and this manner of salutation, I made him no answer for the instant, which made the King say to the lords that were about him, I imagine that this stranger is daunted with seeing so much company here, for that peradventure he hath not been accustomed unto it, wherefore I hold it fit to remit him unto some other time, when as he may be better acquainted, and not be so abashed at the sight of the people. Upon this speech of the Kings I answered by my truchman, that whereas his Highness had said that I was daunted, I confessed that it was true, not in regard of so many folks as were about me, because I had seen far many more, but that my amazement proceeded from the consideration that I was now before the feet of so great a king, which was sufficient to make me mute an hundred thousand years, if I could live so long. I added further, that those which were present there seemed to me but men, as I my self was, but as for his Highness, that God had given him such great advantages above all, as it was His pleasure he should be lord, and that others should be mere servants, yea, and that I my self was but a silly ant, in comparison of his greatness, so that his Majesty could not see me in regard of my smalness, nor I in respect thereof be able to answer unto his demands. All the assistants much such account of this mad answer of mine, as clapping their hands by way of astonishment, they said unto the King, Mark, I beseech your Highness, how he speaks to purpose; verily it seems that this man is not a merchant, which meddles with base things, as buying and selling, but rather a *Bonze*, that offer sacrifices for the people; or if not so, surely he is some great captain that hath a long time scoured the seas. Truly, said the King, I am of the same opinion, now that I see him so resolute; but let every man be silent, because I purpose that none shall speak to him but my self alone; for I assure you that I take so much delight in hearing him talk, that at this instant I feel no pain. At those words the Queen and her daughters, which were set by him, were not a little glad, and falling on their knees, with their hands lifted up to heaven, they thanked God for this His goodness unto them.

-----

## CHAPTER XXXVIII.

The great mishap that befell the King of Bungo's son, with the extreme danger that I was in for the same; and what followed thereupon.

A LITTLE after the King caused me to approach unto his bed, where he lay sick of the gout, when I was near him. *I prithee*, said he unto me, *be not unwilling to stay here by me, for it does me much good to look on thee, and talk with thee; thou shalt also oblige me to let me know whether in thy country, which is at the further end of the world, thou hast not learn'd any remedy for this disease wherewith I am tormented, or for the lack of appetite, which hath continued with me now almost these two moneths without eating any thing to speak of.* Hereunto I answered, that I made no profession of physick, for that I had never learn'd that art, but that in the junk, wherein I came from *China*, there was a certain wood, which

infused in water healed far greater sicknesses then that whereof he complained, and that if he took of it, it would assuredly
help him.  To hear of this he was very glad, insomuch that
transported with an extreme desire to be healed, he sent
away for it in all haste to *Tanixumaa*, where the junck
lay, and having used of it 30 days together, he perfectly
recovered of his disease, which had held him so for 2 years
together, as he was not able to stir from one place to another.
Now during the time that I remained with much content in
this city of *Fuchea*, being some 20 days, I wanted not occasions
to entertain my self withall; for sometimes I was imployed
in answering the questions, which the King, Queen, princes,
and lords asked of me, wherein I easily satisfied them, for
that the matters they demanded of me were of very little
consequence.   Other-whiles I bestowed my self in beholding
their solemnities, the temples where they offered up their
prayers, their warlike exercises, their naval fleets, as also their
fishing and hunting, wherein they greatly delight, especially in
the high-flying of falcons and vultures.   Oftentimes I past
away the time with my harquebuse in killing of turtles and
quails, whereof there is great abundance in the country.   In
the mean season this new manner of shooting seemed no less
marvellous and strange to the inhabitants of this land, then
to them of *Tanixumaa*; so that beholding a thing which they
had never seen before, they made more reckoning of it than I
am able to express, which was the cause that the Kings second
son, named *Arichaudono*, of the age of 16 or 17 years, and
whom the King wonderfully loved, intreated me one day to
teach him to shoot; but I put him off, by saying that there
needed a far longer time for it then he imagined, wherewith
not well pleased he complained to his father of me, who to
content the prince desired me to give him a couple of charges
for the satisfying of his minde; whereunto I answered that I
would give him as many as his Highness would be pleased to
command me.   Now because he was that day to dine with
his father, the matter was referred to the afternoon, howbeit
then too there was nothing done, for that he waited on his
mother to a village adjoyning, whither they came from all
parts on pilgrimage by reason of a certain feast, which was

celebrated there for the health of the King. The next day
this young prince came with onely 2 young gentlemen waiting
on him to my lodging, where finding me asleep on a mat, and
my *harquebuse* hanging on a hook by, he would not wake me
till he had shot off a couple of charges, intending, as he told
me afterwards himself, that these two shoots should not be
comprised in them I had promised him. Having then commanded one of the young gentlemen that attended him, to go
softly and kindle the match, he took down the *harquebuse* from
the place where it hung, and going to charge it, as he had
seen me do, not knowing how much powder he should put in,
he charged the piece almost two spans deep, then putting in
the bullet, he set himself with it to shoot at an orange tree
that was not far off; but fire being given, it was his ill hap
that the *harquebuse* brake into 3 pieces, and gave him 2 hurts,
by one of the which his right hand thumb was in a manner
lost; instantly whereupon the prince fell down as one dead,
which the 2 gentlemen perceiving, they ran away towards the
court, crying along in the streets that the strangers *harquebuse*
had killed the prince. At these sad news the people flocked
in all haste with weapons and great cries to the house where
I was. Now God knows whether I was not a little amazed
when coming to awake I saw this tumult, as also the young
prince lying along upon the floor by me weltring in his own
bloud without stirring either hand or foot. All that I could
do then was to imbrace him in my arms, so besides my self, as
I knew not where I was. In the mean time, behold the King
comes in a chair carried upon 4 mens shoulders, and so sad
and pale, as he seemed more dead then alive; after him
followed the Queen on foot leaning upon 2 ladies, with her 2
daughters, and a many of women all weeping. As soon as
they were entred into the chamber, and beheld the young
prince extended on the ground, as if he had been dead,
imbraced in my arms, and both of us wallowing in bloud,
they all concluded that I had killed him; so that 2 of the
company drawing out their scymitars, would have slain me;
which the King perceiving, *Stay, stay,* cried he, *let us know
first how the matter goes, for I fear it comes further off, and
that this fellow here hath been corrupted by some of those*

*traitors kinred, whom I caused to be last executed.* Thereupon
commanding the 2 young gentlemen to be called which had
accompanied the prince, his son, thither, he questioned them
exactly. Their answer was, that my *harquebuse* with the
inchantments in it had killed him. This deposition served
but to incense the assistants the more, who in a rage addressing themselves to the King. What need, sir, have you to hear
more, cried they? Here is but too much, let him be put to a
cruel death. Therewith they sent in all haste for the *Jarabuca,*
who was my interpreter, to them; now for that upon the
arrival of this disaster he was out of extreme fear fled away,
they brought him straight to the King; but before they fell to
examining of him, they mightily threatned him, in case he
did not confess the truth; whereunto he answered trembling,
and with tears in his eyes,that he would reveal all that he knew.
In the mean time being on my knees, with my hands bound,
a *Bonzo,* that was President of their Justice, having his arms
bared up to the shoulders, and a poiniard in his hand dipped
in the bloud of the young prince, said thus unto me, *I conjure
thee, thou son of some devil, and culpable of the same crime for
which they are damned that inhabit in the house of smoak,
where they lie buried in the obscure and deep pit of the centre
of the earth, that thou confess unto me with a voice so loud that
every one may hear thee, for what cause thou hast with these
sorceries and inchantments killed this young innocent, whom we
hold for the hairs, and chief ornaments of our heads.* To this
demand I knew not what to answer upon the sudden, for that
I was so far besides my self, as if one had taken away my
life, I believe I should not have felt it; which the president
perceiving, and beholding me with a terrible countenance,
*Seest thou not,* continued he, *that if thou doest not answer to
the questions I ask thee, that thou mayest hold thy self for condemned to a death of bloud, of fire, of water, and of the blasts
of the winde; for thou shalt be dismembred into air, like the
feathers of dead fowl, which the winde carries from one place
to another, separated from the body with which they were joyned
whilest they lived.* This said, he gave me a great kick with
his foot for to rowse up my spirits, and cried out again, *Speak,
confess who they are that have corrupted thee? what sum of*
19

*money have they given thee ? how are they called ? and where are they at this present ?* At these words being somewhat come again to my self, I answered him, that God knew my innocence, and that I took him for witness thereof. But he not contented with what he had done began to menace me more than before, and set before mine eyes an infinite of torments and terrible things ; wherein a long time being spent, it pleased God at length that the young prince came to himself, who no sooner saw the King his father, as also his mother and sisters dissolved into tears, but that he desired them not to weep ; and that if he chanced to die, they would attribute his death to none but himself, who was the onely cause thereof, conjuring them moreover by the bloud, wherein they beheld him weltring, to cause me to be unbound without all delay, if they desired not to make him die anew. The King much amazed with this language, commanded the manacles to be taken off which they had put upon me ; whereupon came in 4 *Bonzoes* to apply remedies unto him, but when they saw in what manner he was wounded, and that his thumb hung in a sort but by the skin, they were so troubled at it, as they knew not what to do ; which the poor prince observing, Away, away, said he, send hence these devils, and let others come that have more heart to judge of my hurt, since it hath pleased God to send it me. Therewith the 4 *Bonzoes* were sent away, and other 4 came in their stead, who likewise wanted the courage to dress him ; which the King perceiving was so much troubled as he knew not what to do ; howbeit he resolved at length to be advised therein by them that were about him, who counselled him to send for a *Bonzo*, called *Teixeandono*, a man of great reputation amongst them, and that lived then at the city of *Facataa*, some 70 leagues from that place ; but the wounded prince not able to brook these delays ; *I know not,* answered he, *what you mean by this counsel which you give my father, seeing me in the deplorable estate wherein I am ; for whereas I ought to have been drest already, you would have me stay for an old rotten man, who cannot be here untill one hath made a journey of an hundred and forty leagues, both in going and coming, so that it must be a moneth at least before he can arrive ; wherefore speak no more of it, but if you desire to do me a pleasure, free this stranger a little from the fear you have put him in, and clear the room of all this throng, he that you believe hath hurt me will help me, as he may, for I had rather die under the hands of this poor wretch; that hath wept so much for me, then be touched by* Bonzo *of* Facataa, *who at the age he is of, of ninety and two years, can see no further then his nose.*

---

## CHAPTER XXXIX.

My curing the young Prince of Bungo; with my return to Tanixumaa, and imbarquing there for Liampoo; and also that which happened to us on land, after the shipwrack we suffered by the way.

THE King of *Bungo* being extremely grieved to see the disaster of his son, turned himself to me, and beholding me with a very gentle countenance; *Stranger,* said he unto me, *try I pray thee, if thou canst assist my son in this peril of his life, for I swear unto thee, if thou canst do it, I will make no less esteem of thee, then of him himself, and will give thee whatsoever thou wilt demand of me.* Hereunto I answered the King, that I desired his Majesty to command all those people away, because the coyl that they kept confounded me, and that then I would see whether his hurts were dangerous; for if I found that I was able to cure them, I would do it most willingly. Presently the King willed every one to be gone; whereupon approaching unto the prince, I perceived that he had but two hurts; one on the top of his forehead, which was no great matter; and the other on his right hand thumb, that was almost cut off. So that our Lord inspiring me, as it were, with new courage, I besought the King not to be grieved, for I hoped in less then a month to render him his son perfectly recovered. Having comforted him in this manner, I began to prepare my self for the dressing of the prince; but in the mean time the King was very much reprehended by the *Bonzoes,* who told him, that his son would assuredly die that night, and therefore it was better for him to put me to death presently, then to suffer me to kill the prince outright, adding further, that if it should happen to prove so, as it was very likely, it would not only be a great scandal unto him, but also much alienate his peoples affections from him.  To these speeches of the *Bonzoes* the King replied, that he thought they had reason for that they said, and therefore he desired them to let him know how he should govern himself in this extremity.  You must, said they, stay the coming of the *Bonzo Teixeandono*, and never think of any other course; for we assure you, in regard he is the holiest man living, he will no sooner lay his hand on him but he will heal him strait, as he hath healed many others in our sight. As the King was even resolved to follow the cursed counsel of these servants of the devil, the prince complained that his wounds pained him in such sort that he was not able to endure it, and therefore prayed that any handsome remedy might be instantly applied to them; whereupon the King, much distracted between the opinion of the *Bonzoes*, and the danger that his son was in of his life, together with the extreme pain that he suffered, desiring those about him to advise him what he should resolve on, in that exigent; not one of them but was of the mind, that it was far more expedient to have the prince drest out of hand, then to stay the time which the *Bonzoes* spake of.  This counsel being approved of the King, he came again to me, and making very much of me, he promised me mighty matters if I could recover his son; I answered him with tears in my eyes, that by the help of God I would do it, and that he himself should be witness of my care therein.  So recommending my self to God, and taking a good heart unto me, for I saw there was no other way to save my life, but that, I perpared all things necessary to perform the cure.  Now because the hurt of the right hand thumb was most dangerous, I began with that, and gave it seven stitches, whereas peradventure if a chirurgion had drest him, he would have given it fewer; as for that of the forehead, I gave it but four, in regard it was much slighter then the other; that done, I applyed to them tow wet in the whites of eggs, and so bound them up very close, as I had seen others done in the *Indiaes*. Five days after I cut the stitches, and continued dressing him as before, until that at the end of twenty days it pleased God he was throughly cured, without any other inconvenience remaining in him than a little weakness in his thumb. For this cause after that time the King and his lords did me much honour; the Queen also, and the princesses her daughters presented me with a great many sutes of silks, and the chiefest of the court with cymitars, and other things, besides all which the King gave me six hundred *Taeis;* so that after this sort I received in recompence of this my cure above fifteen hundred ducates, that I carried with me from this place. After things were past in this manner, being advertised by letters from my two companions at *Tanixumaa,* that the *Chinese* pirate, with whom we came thither, was preparing for his return to *China,* I besought the King of *Bungo* to give me leave to go back, which he readily granted me, and with much acknowledgment of the curing of his son he willed a *Funce* to be made ready for me, furnished with all things necessary, wherein commanded a man of quality, that was attended by twenty of the Kings servants, with whom I departed on *Saturday* morning for the city of *Fucheo,* and the *Friday* following about sun-set I arrived at *Tanixumaa,* where I found my two camrades, who received me with much joy. Here we continued fifteen days longer, till such time as the junck was quite ready, and then we set sail for *Liampoo,* which is a sea-port of the kingdom of *China,* whereof I have spoken at large heretofore, and where at that time the *Portugals* traded. Having continued our voyage with a prosperous wind, it pleased God that we arrived safe at our desired port, where it is not to believed how much we were welcomed by the inhabitants of the place.

[*Pinto sets sail with the Portuguese from Liampoo, and is shipwrecked on the Island of the Lequios; his imprisonment in the town of Pungor, and other adventures, till his safe return to Liampoo,* omitted.]

## CHAPTER XL.

My sayling from Liampoo to Malaca, from whence the captain of the fortress
sent me to the Chaubainhaa at Martabano; and all that befel us in our
voyage thither.

BEING arrived at *Liampoo*, we were very well received by
the *Portugals*, that lived there. From whence within a
while after I imbarqued my self in the ship of a *Portugal*,
named *Tristano de Gaa*, for to return unto *Malaca*, with an
intention once more to try my fortune, which had so often
been contrary to me, as may appear by that which I have
delivered before. This ship being safely arrived at *Malaca*, I
went presently unto *Pedro de Faria*, Governour of the fortress,
who desiring to benefit me somewhat before the time of his
Government was expired, he caused me to undertake the
voyage of *Martaban*, which was usually very profitable, and
that in the junck of a *Mahometan*, named *Necoda Mamude*,
who had wife and children at *Malaca*. Now the principal
designe of this voyage was, to conclude a peace with the
*Chaubainhaa*, King of *Martabano ;* as also to continue the
commerce of those of that country with us, because their
juncks did greatly serve for the provisions of our fortress,
which at that time was unfurnished thereof by reason of the
success of the wars of *Jaoa*. Besides I had a designe in this
my voyage of no less consequence, then the rest, which was to
get one, called *Lancarote Guerreyro*, to come thither, who was
then on the coast of *Tanaucarim*, with an hundred men in four
foists, under the name of a rebel or mutiner ; I was to require
him to come to the succour of the fortress, in regard it was
held for certain, that the King of *Achem* was suddainly to fall
upon it; so that *Petro de Faria*, seeing himself destitute of all
that was necessary for him to sustain a siege, and of men likewise, found it fit to make use of these hundred men, the
rather for that they were nearest, and so might be the sooner
with him. In the third place, he sent me upon another
important occasion, namely, to give advice to the ships of
*Bengala*, that they should come all carefully in consort

together, lest their negligence in their navigation should be the
cause of some disaster. This voyage then I undertook very
unwillingly, and parted from *Malaca* upon a *Wednesday*, the
9th day of *January*, in the year 1545; being under sail I
continued my course with a good wind to *Pullo Pracelar*,
where the pilot was a little retarded by means of the shelves,
which cross all that channel of the firm land, even unto the
island of *Sumatra*. When we were got forth with much
labour, we passed on to the islands of *Pullo Sambillam*, where
I put my self into a *Manchua*, which I had very well equipped;
and sailing in it the space of twelve days, I observed, according to the order *Pedro de Faria* had given me for it, all the
coast of that country of *Malaya*, which unto *Juncalan* contains an hundred and thirty leagues, entring by all the rivers
of *Bartuhaas*, *Salangor*, *Panaagim*, *Quedam*, *Parles*, *Pendan*,
and *Sambilan*, *Siam*, without so much as hearing any news at
all of his enemies in any of them. So continuing the same
course nine days more, being the three and twentieth of our
voyage, we went and cast anchor at a little island, called
*Pisandurea*, where the *Necoda*, the *Mahumetan* captain of the
junck, was of necessity to make a cable, and furnish himself
with wood and water. With this resolution going on shore
every man applyed himself to the labour he was appointed
unto, and therein spent most part of the day. Now whilest
they were thus at work the son of this *Mahumetan* captain
came and asked me whither I would go with him, and see if
we could kill a stag, whereof there was great plenty in that
island; I answered him that I would accompany him with all
my heart, so that having taken my *Harquebuse*, I went along
with him athwart the wood, where we had not walked above
an hundred spaces, but that we espied a many of wild boars,
that were rooting in the earth near to a pond. Having discovered this game, we got as near to them as we could, and
discharging amongst them, we carried two of them to the
ground. Being very glad of this good success we presently
gave a great shout, and ran straight to the place we had seen
them rooting. But (O dreadful to behold) in this place we
found above a dozen bodies of men digged out of the earth,
and some nine or ten others half eaten. Being much amazed

at this object, we withdrew a little aside by reason of the great stench which proceeded from these dead bodies. Hereupon the *Saracen* told me, that he thought we should do well to advertise his father of this, to the end we might instantly surround this island all about for to see whether we could discover any vessels with pirats; for, said he, there may be some lie hidden behind yonder poynt, whereby we may very well run the hazard of our lives, as it hath often befallen other ships, where many men have been lost by the carelessness of their captains. This advice of the *Saracen* seemed so good unto me, that we presently returned back unto the rode, where he gave an account to his father of that we had seen. Now for that the *Necoda* was a very prudent man, and scalded (as one may say) with the like inconveniences, he straight way gave order to have the island surrounded; then causing the women, children, and linnen, although it were but half washed, to be imbarqued, he himself being followed by forty men, armed with harquebuses and lances, went directly to the place where we had discovered those bodies, and viewing them one after another, with stopping our noses by reason of the stench, which was insupportable, he was so moved with compassion, that he commanded the mariners to dig a great pit for to bury them in. But as they were about to render them this last duty, and looking over them again, there was found upon some of them little daggers garnished with gold, and on others bracelets. Whereupon the *Necoda*, understanding well this mystery, wished me with all speed to dispatch away the rowing vessel that I had to the captain of *Malaca*, for that, as he assured me, those dead men, which they saw there, were *Achems*, who had been defeated near to *Tanaucarim*, whither their armies ordinarily retired because of the war which they had with the King of *Siam*. The reason he alledged to us for this was, that those which we saw there lying dead, having golden bracelets about them, were captains of *Achem*, who had caused themselves to be buried without permitting them to be taken away, and that he would lose his head if it were not so. For a greater proof whereof, he further added, that he would make some more of them to be dis-enterred, as incontinently he did; and having digged some seven and thirty of them out of the earth, there was found about them sixteen bracelets of gold, twelve very rich daggers, and many jewels, so that thinking of no other but hunting, we got a booty worth above a thousand ducates, which the *Necoda* had, besides what was concealed; but the truth is, this was not altogether to our advantage, for the most part of our men became sick with the extream stench of those bodies. At the very instant I dispatched away the rowing vessel that we had to *Malaca*, and advertised *Pedro de Faria* of the whole success of our voyage. Withall I certified him what course we had held; as also into what ports, and into what rivers we had entred, without hearing any other news of his enemies, then that it was suspected they had been at *Tanaucarim*, where by the appearances of those dead bodies, it was to be believed that they had been defeated; whereunto I added, for a conclusion, that if I could light on any more assured news concerning them, I would presently acquaint him with it, in what part soever I were.

After I had dispatched away the rowing vessel to *Malaca*, with the letters which I had directed to *Pedro de Faria*, and that our junck was furnished with all things necessary for her, we sayled towards the coast of *Tanaucarim*, where, as I said before, I had order to land for to treat with *Lancerote Gurerreyro*, that he, and the rest of the *Portugals* of his company, might come to the succour of *Malaca*, which the *Achems* intended to besiege, according to the report that went of it. Being under sail then we arrived at a little island, a league in circuit, called *Pulho Hinhor*, where a *Parao* came unto us, in the which were six tawny Moors, poorly clad, with red bonnets on their heads; their boat being close to our junck, which was then under sail, they saluted us in the way of peace, whereunto we answered in the like manner. That done, they demanded of us if there were any *Portugals* amongst us? We told them that there were, but mistrusting it, they desired to see one or two of them upon the hatches, because, added they, it imports much that it should be so. Whereupon the *Necoda* prayed me to come up, which incontinently I did, though at that time I was shut up in my cabbin below somewhat indisposed in my health; when I was on the deck I

called to them that were in the *Parao*, who had no sooner seen
me, and known me to be a *Portugal*, but they gave a great
shout; and clapping their hands for joy, they came aboard
our junck.  Then one of them, who by his countenance seemed
to have more authority then the rest, began to say unto me :
*Seignior, before I crave leave of thee to speak, I desire thee to
read this letter, to the end it may induce thee the more readily
to believe that which I am to say unto thee.*  Thereupon, out of
an old filthy clout he took a letter, wherein (after I had opened
it) I found this written: *Signiors Portugals, which are true
Christians, this honourable man, that shall shew you this letter,
is king of this island, newly converted to the faith, and called
Dom Lancerote.  He hath rendred many good offices, not onely
to them who have subscribed this writing, but to us also who
have navigated on these coasts.  For he hath given us very
important advertisements of the treasons which the Achems and
Turks have plotted against us, so that by the means of this honest
man we have discovered all their designs : withall God hath
made use of him for to give us not long since a great victory
against them, wherein we have taken from them one gally, four
galliots, and five foists, with the death of above a thousand Sar-*
*razins.  Wherefore we intreat you, by the wounds of our Lord
Jesus Christ, and by the merits of His holy passion, not onely to
keep him from all wrong, but to assist him with all your power,
as the manner is of all good Portugals, that it may serve for an
example to those which shall know this, to do the like in imitation of you.  And so we kiss your hands, this 13th day of*
November, 1544.  This letter was signed by more then 50
*Portugals*, amongst whom were the 4 captains that I fought
for,- namely, *Lancerote Guerreyra, Antonie Gomez, Pedro Fer-
reyra,* and *Cosmo Bernaldes.*  When I had read this letter, I
made a tender of my person to this petty king, for otherways
my power was so small, as it could not reach further then to
the giving him a bad dinner, and a red bonnet I had on, which
all worn as it was, was yet better then his own.  Now after
this poor king had made some declaration to me of himself,
and of his miseries, lifting up his hands to heaven, and shedding abundance of tears.  *Our Lord Jesus Christ,* said he unto
me, *whose slave I am, doth know what great need I have now of*

*the favour and succour of some Christians; for because I am a*
*Christian, as they are, a* Mahometan *slave of mine, about four*
*monthes ago, reduced me to that extremity wherein I behold my*
*self at this instant, being not able in the state I am in to do any*
*other then cast up mine eyes to heaven, and lament my mis-*
*fortune, with much sorrow, and little remedy. And I assure*
*thee, by the verity of that holy and new law, whereof I now make*
*profession, that not onely for being a Christian, and a friend of*
*the* Portugals, *I am persecuted in this sort. Now for that being*
*alone, as thou art, it is not possible for thee to assist me. I*
*beseech thee,* Signior, *to take me along with thee, to the end that*
*this soul which God hath put into me may not perish, and in*
*recompence thereof I promise to serve thee as a slave all the days*
*of my life.* Lo this is that which this poor king said with so
many tears, as it was great pity to behold it; in the mean
time the *Necoda,* who was of a good disposition, and charitably
inclined, was very much moved with the disaster of the unfortunate king, so that he gave him a little rice, and some linnen
to cover him withall, for he was so ragged, that one might see
his naked skin every where about him. After he had informed
himself from him of certain particulars, the knowledge whereof concerned him, he demanded him where his enemy was, and
what forces he had? Whereunto he answered, that he was a
quarter of a league from thence, in a cabbin covered with
straw, having not above thirty fishermen with him, who were
most of them without arms. Hereupon the *Necoda* cast his
eye upon me, and seeing me sad, for that I was not able of
my self to succour this poor Christian, thinking withall that
he should much oblige me thereby, *Signior,* said he unto me,
*if thou wert now captain of my junck, as I am, what remedy*
*wouldst thou give to the tears of this poor man, wherewith also*
*thy eyes do participate?* I knew not what reply to make him,
for that I was greatly moved to behold my neighbour, a
Christian like my self, to suffer in that manner, which the
*Necoda's* son perceiving, who was, as I have said, a young man
of a good spirit, and brought up amongst the *Portugals,* and
guessing at the shame and sorrow I was in, he desired his
father to lend him 20 mariners of his junck, that by their
means he might re-establish this poor King, and chase the

thief out of the island. To this the *Necoda* answered, that if I would demand so much of him, he would do it very willingly; whereupon casting my self at his feet, and embracing him, which is the humblest complement used amongst them, I told him with tears in my eyes, that if he would do me this favour I would be his slave whilest I lived, and that both he and his children should finde how ready I would be always to acknowledge the same. He presently granted my request, so that causing the junck to approach near the shoar, he prepared himself in 3 boats with one faulcon, 3 bases, and 60 men, *Jaos* and *Lesons*, all well armed, for 30 of them carried *Harquebuses*, the rest lances, and bowes and arrows, besides granadoes, and other such like fire-works, as we thought were convenient for our design.

It was about 2 of the clock in the afternoon when we landed, and so we went directly to the trench where the enemies were. The *Necoda's* son led the vanguard, consisting of 40 men, whereof 20 were armed with *Harquebuses*, and the rest with bowes and arrows. The *Necoda* himself brought on the rear; wherein were 30 souldiers, carrying a banner, which *Pedro de Faria* had given him at his parting from *Malaca*, with a cross painted in it, to the end that he might be known for a vassal to our king, in case he should encounter any of our ships. Marching in this order by the guiding of this petty king, we arrived where the rebell was with his men set in order, who by the shouting and cries seemed in shew not to make any reckoning of us. There were in number about 50, but weak, unarmed, and utterly destitute of all things necessary for their defence, having for all their arms but staves, 10 or 11 lances, and 1 *Harquebuse*. As soon as we had discovered them we gave fire to the faulcon and bases, discharging withall 20 *Harquebuses*, whereupon the thieves betook themselves presently to flight, being in great disorder, and most of them hurt. We pursued them then so close, that we overtook them on the top of a little hill, where they were defeated in the space of 2 *Credo's*, not one of them escaping with life save onely 3, whom we spared for that they said they were Christians. That done, we went to a village, where there were not above 20 poor low cabbins, covered with straw;

in it were found some threescore and four women, with a many
of little children, who no sooner perceived us, but all of them
with tears fell a crying out, *Christian, Christian, Jesus, Jesus.*
At these words being fully perswaded that they were Christians,
I desired the *Necoda* that he would cause his son to retire, and
not to suffer any of them to be killed, because they were not
*Gentiles*, which he presently yielded unto, and yet for all that
he could not keep the cabbins from sacking, though in them all
there was not found the value of 5 ducates. For the people
of this island are so poor, that scarce one of them is worth a
groat; they feed on nothing but a little fish, which they take
with angling, and eat it broiled on the coals without salt; yet
are they so vain and presumptuous, that not one almost
amongst them but terms himself a king of some vile piece of
ground, wherein there is little more then one poor cabbin;
besides, neither the men nor the women have wherewithall to
cover their nakedness. After the slaughter of the rebellious
*Saracen* and his followers, and the re-establishment of the poor
Christian king, putting him in possession of his wife and
children, whom his enemy had made slaves, together with
above threescore and three Christian souls, we ordained a
kinde of church amongst them, for the instruction of those
that were newly converted. And then returning to our junck,
we presently set sail, and continued our course towards
*Taunacarim*, where I was perswaded I should finde *Lancerote
Guerreyra*, and his companions, for to treat with them about
the business, whereof I have formerly spoken. But for as
much as in the letter, which the petty king shewed me, the
*Portugals* made mention of a victory which God had given
them against the *Turks* and *Achems* of this coast, I hold it not
amiss to relate here how that hapned, as well for the content
the reader may take therein, as to shew that there is no
enterprise which valiant souldiers at a need may not bring to
pass, in regard whereof it imports much to cherish, and make
esteem of them. For eight moneths and more our hundred
*Portugals* had scoured up and down this coast in four well
rigg'd foists, wherewith they had taken three and twenty rich
ships, and many other lesser vessels, so that they which used
to sail in those parts were so terrified with the sole name of the

*Portugals*, as they quitted their commerce without making any
further use of their shipping: by this surcease of trade the
custom-houses of the ports of *Tanaucarim, Juncalan, Merguim,
Vagaruu*, and *Tavay*, fell much in their revenue, in so much
that those people were constrained to give notice of it to the
Emperor of *Sornau*, King of *Siam*, and soveraign lord of all
that country, beseeching him to give a remedy to this mischief,
whereof every one complained. Instantly whereupon, being
then at the city of *Odiaa*, he sent with all speed to the frontire
of *Lauhos* for a Turkish captain of his, named *Heredrin
Mahomet*, the same who in the year 1538 came from *Suez* to
the army of *Soliman* the *Bashaw*, Vice-roy of *Cairo*, when as the
great *Turk* sent him to invade the *Indies*; but it fell out that
this man slipping from the body of the army arrived in a gally
on the coast of *Tanaucarim*, where he was entertained by the
*Sornau* King of *Siam*, and for a pension of twelve thousand
ducates by the year served him as a general of that frontire.
Now for that the King held this *Turk* for invincible, and made
more account of him then of all others, he commanded him
from the place where he was, with three hundred *Janizaries*
that he had with him, and giving him a great sum of money
he made him General of all the coast of this sea, to the end
that he might free those people from our incursions; withal
he promised to make him Duke of *Banchaa*, which is an estate
of great extent, if he could bring him the heads of four
*Portugal* captains. This proud *Turk*, becoming more insolent
by the reward and promises which the King made him posted
presently away to *Tanaucarim*, where being arrived he rigged
forth a fleet of ten sails for to fight with us, being so confident
of vanquishing us, as in answer of certain letters, which the
*Sornau* had written unto him from *Odiaa*, these words were
found in one of them. *From the time that my head was
esloigned from the feet of your Highness for to execute this small
enterprize, wherein it seems you are pleased I should serve you,
I continued my voyage till at the end of nine days I arrived at*
Tanaucarim, *where I presently provided my self of such vessels
as were necessary for me, and indeed would have had but only
two, for I hold it most infallible that those would suffice to chase
away these petty thieves; howbeit not to disobey the commission,*

*which* Combracalon *the Governor of the Empire hath given me under your great seal, I have made ready the great gally, as also the four little ones, and the five Foists, with which I purpose to set forth with all speed ; for I fear lest these dogs should have news of my coming, and that for my sins God should be so much their friend, as to give them leasure to fly, which would be so great a grief unto me, that the very imagination thereof might be my death, or through an excess of despair render me like unto them ; but I hope that the Prophet* Mahomet, *of whose law I have made profession from mine infancy, will not permit that it should so happen for my sins.* This *Heredrin Mahomet* being arrived at *Tanaucarim,* as I have delivered before, presently made ready his fleet, which was composed of five foists, four galliots, and one gally royal: within these vessels he imbarqued eight hundred *Mahometans,* men of combat (besides the mariners), amongst the which were three hundred *Janizaries,* as for the rest they were *Turks, Greeks, Malabares, Achems,* and *Msgores,* all choyce men, and so disciplined, that their captain held the victory already for most assured ; assisted with these forces he parted from the port of *Tanaucarim* for to go in the quest of our men, who at that time were in this island of *Pulho Hinhor,* whereof the foresaid Christian was king. Now during those levies of men of war, this petty king going to the town for to sell some dryed fish there, as soon as he perceived what was intended against us, he left all his commodities behind him, and in all haste returned to this island of his ; where finding our men in great security, as little dreaming of that which was in hand against us, he related it all unto them, whereat they remained so much amazed, as the importance of the matter did require ; in so much that the same night and the next day having well caulked their vessels which they had drawn ashore, they lanched them into the sea, after they had imbarqued their provisions, their water, their artillery, and ammunition. So falling to their oars, with a purpose (as I have heard them say since) to get to *Bengala,* or to *Racan,* for that they durst not withstand so great an army ; but as they were unresolved thereupon, and divided in opinion, behold they saw all the ten sails appearing together, and behind them five great ships of

*Guzarates*, whose masters had given *Heredrin Mahomet* thirty
thousand ducates for to secure them against our *Portugals*.
The sight of these fifteen sails put our men into a very great
confusion; and because they were not able at that time to
make to sea for that the wind was contrary, they put themselves into a creek, which was on the south-side of the island
and invironned by a down, or hill, where they resolved to
attend what God would send them. In the mean time the
five *Guzarat* ships shewed themselves with full sails at sea,
and the ten sails with oars went directly to the island, where
they arrived about sun-set. Presently thereupon the *Turkish*
captain sent out spies to the ports, where he was advertised
that they had been, and entered by little and little into the
mouth of the haven, that so he might render himself more
assured of the prize which he pretended to make, with hope
that as soon as it was day he should take them all, and so
bound hand and foot present them to the *Sornau* of *Siam*, who
in recompence thereof had promised him the state of *Banchaa*,
as I have said before. The *Manchua*, which had been at the
port to spy them out, returned to the fleet about two hours
within night, and told *Heredrin* for news, that they were fled
and gone; wherewith it is said this barbarian was so afflicted,
that tearing his hair, *I always feared*, said he weeping, *my sins
would be the cause that in the execution of this enterprize God
would shew Himself more a Christian, then a* Sarazin, *and that*
Mahomet *would be like to these dogs, of whom I go in quest.*
This said, he fell down all along in the place, and so continued
a good while without speaking a word. Nevertheless being
come again to himself he gave order, like a good captain, to
all that was necessary. First of all then he sent the four
galliots in quest of them to an island, called *Tanbasoy*, distant
from that of *Pulho Hinhor* about seven leagues, for he was
perswaded that our men were retired thither, because this was
a better harbor then that of the island from whence they were
gone. As for the five foists he divided them into three,
whereof he sent two to another island, named *Sambilan*, and
other two to those which were nearest to the firm land, for
that all these places were very proper to shelter one in; as for
the fifth foist, in regard she was flatter then the rest, he sent

her along with the four galliots, that she might before it was
day bring him news of that which should happen, with
promise of great reward for the same ; but during these things
our men, who had always a watchful eye, seeing the *Turk* had
rid himself of his greatest forces, and that there was no more
remaining with him but the gally wherein he was, they
resolved to fight with him ; and so sailing out of the creek,
where they had shrouded themselves, they rowed directly to
her. Now in regard it was past midnight, and that the
enemies had but weak sentinels, for that they thought themselves most secure, and never dreamt of any body lying in
wait to attaque them there, our four foists had the opportunity
to board her all together, and threescore of their lustiest men
leaping suddenly into her, in less then a quarter of an hour,
and before the enemies knew where they were for to make use
of their arms, they killed above fourscore *Turks* ; as for the
rest they cast themselves all into the sea, not one man remaining alive : the dog *Heredrin Mahomet* was slain amongst
the rest, and in this great action God was so gracious to our
men, and gave them this victory at so cheap a rate, that they
had but one young man killed, and nine *Portugals* hurt.
They assured me since, that in this gally, in so short a time,
what by water, and the sword, above three hundred *Mahometans* lost their lives, whereof the most part were *Janizaries*
of the Gold Chain, which among the *Turks* is a mark of honour.
Our *Portugals* having past the rest of the night with much
contentment, and always keeping good watch, it pleased God
that the next morning the two foists arrived from the island
whither they had been sent; who altogether ignorant of that
which had past, came carelessly doubling the point of the
haven, where the gally lay, so that the four foists made
themselves masters of them in a little space, and with the
loss of but a few men. After so good a success they fell
diligently to work in fortifying the gally and the two foists,
which they had taken, and then flanked the south-side of the
island with five great pieces of ordnance to defend the entry
into the haven. Now about evening the other two foists
arrived, making to land with the same indiscretion as the
others ; and although they had much ado to reach them, yet

were they constrained at length to render themselves, with the loss onely of two *Portugals*. Hereupon our men resolved to attend the four galliots that remained, and which had been sent to the next island, but the next day so great a wind arose from the north, that two of them were cast away upon the coast, not one that was in them escaping. As for the other two, about evening they discovered them very much in disorder, destitute of oars, and separated above three leagues the one from the other; but at last about sun-set one of them came to the port, and ran the same fortune as the former, without saving any one of the *Sarazins* lives. The next morning an hour before day, the wind being very calm, our men discovered the other galliot, which for want of oars was not able to recover the port, in regard whereof our men resolved to go and fetch her in, as accordingly they did, and coming somewhat near her with two cannon shot, they killed the most part of them that were in her, and boarding her took her very easily; now because all her men were either slain, or hurt, they drew her to land by force of other boats; so that of the ten sail of this fleet, our men had the gally, two galliots, and four foysts; as for the other two galliots, they were cast away on the Isle of *Taubasoy*, as I have delivered before; and touching the fift foyst, no news could be heard of her, which made it credible that she also suffered shipwrack, or that the wind had cast her upon some of the other islands. This glorious victory, which it pleased God to give us, was obtained in the month of *September*, 1544, on *Michaelmas* Eve, which rendred the name of the *Portugals* so famous through all those coasts, that for three years after there was nothing else spoken of; so that the *Chaubainhaa*, King of *Martabano*, hearing of it, sent presently to seek them out, and promised them great advantages if they would succour him against the King of *Bramaa*, who at that time was making preparation in his city of *Pegu*, for to go and besiege *Martabano*, with an army of seven hundred thousand men.

———

## CHAPTER XLI.

The continuance of our voyage to the Bar of Martabano; and certain
memorable particularities hapning there.

BEING departed, as I said, from the Island of *Pulho Hinhor,*
we continued our course towards the port of *Tarnassery,*
for the affair of which I have spoken; but upon the approach
of the night, the pilot desiring to avoid certain sands that
were to the prow-ward of him, put forth to sea, with an
intention as soon as it was day to return tówards land with
the westerly wind, which at the instant blew from the *Indiaes*
by reason of the season. We had now held this course five
days, running with much labour by many different rhombs,
when as it pleased God that we accidently discovered a little
vessel; and for as much as we thought it to be a fisher-boat,
we made to it, for to be informed from them in her where-
abouts we were, and how many leagues it was from thence to
*Tarnassery*; but having passed close by her, and haled her
without receiving any answer, we sent off a shallop, well
furnished with men for to compel her to come aboard us: our
boat then going directly to the vessel, we entred her, but
were much amazed to find in her only five *Portugals,* two
dead, and three alive, with a coffer, and a sack full of *Tangues,*
and *Larius,* which is the mony of that country, and a fardle,
wherein there were basins and ewers of silver, and two other
very great basins. Having laid up all this safely, I caused the
*Portugals* to be brought into our junk; where looking very
carefully unto them, yet could I not in two days get one word
from them; but at length by the means of yelks of eggs, and
good broaths, which I made them take, they came again to
themselves; so that in six or seven days they were able to
render me a reason of their accident. One of those *Portugals*
was called *Christovano Doria,* who was since sent into this
country for a captain to Saint *Tome*; the other *Luys Tabonda,*
and the third *Simano de Brito,* all men of credit, and rich
merchants. These same recounted unto us, that coming from
the *Indies* in a vessel belonging to *Jorge Manhoz,* that was
married at *Goa,* with a purpose to go to the port of *Charingan,*

in the kingdom of *Bengala*, they were cast away in the sands
of *Rucano* for want of taking heed; so that of fourscore
persons, that they were in the vessel, onely seventeen being
saved, they had continued their course all along by the coast
for five days together, intending if possibly they could to
recover the river of *Cosmira* in the kingdom of *Pegu*, there to
ship themselves for the *Indiaes* in some vessel or other that
they should meet with in the port; but whilst they were in
this resolution, they were so driven by a most impetuous
westerly wind, that in one day and a night they lost the sight
of land, finding themselves in the main sea without oars,
without sayls, and all knowledge of the winds, they continued
in that state sixteen days together, at the end whereof their
water coming to fail, all died but those three he saw before
him.   Upon the finishing of this relation we proceeded on in
our course, and within four days after we met with five
*Portugal* vessels, which were sayling from *Bengala* to *Malaca*.
Having shewed them *Pedro de Faria's* order, I desired them
to keep in consort together for fear of the *Achems* army, that
ranged all over the coast, lest through their imprudence they
should fall into any mischief, and thereof I demanded a
certificate from them, which they willingly granted, as also
furnished me very plentifully with all things necessary.
Having made this dispatch we continued our course, and nine
days after we arrived at the bar of *Martabano*, on a *Friday*, the
27th of *March*, 1545, having past by *Tarnassey, Tovay, Merguin,
Juncay, Pullo, Camuda*, and *Vagaruu*, without hearing any
tidings of those hundred *Portugals*, in search of whom I went,
because before that they had taken pay in the service of the
*Chaubainhaa*, King of *Martabano*, who, according to report,
had sent for them to assist him against the King of *Bramaa*,
that held him besieged with an army of seven hundred
thousand men, as I have declared before; howbeit they were
not at this time in his service; as we shall see presently.

It was almost two hours within night, when we arrived at
the mouth of the river; where we cast anchor with a resolution to go up the next day to the city. Having continued sometime very quiet, we ever and anon heard many cannon shot,
whereat we were so troubled, as we knew not what to resolve

on ; as soon as the sun rose, the *Necoda* assembled his men to
councel ; for in semblable occasions he always used so to do,
and told them, that as sure as they were all to have a share
in the peril, so it was fit that every one should give his advice
about it ; then he made a speech, wherein he represented unto
them that which they had heard that night, and how in regard
thereof he feared to go unto the city. Their opinions upon it
were very different, howbeit at length they concluded, that
their eyes were to be witnesses of that whereof they stood in
such doubt. To this end we set sail, having both wind and
tyde, and doubled a point, called *Mounay*, from whence we
discovered the city, invironed with a world of men, and upon
the river almost as many vessels, and although we suspected
what this might be, because we had heard something of it, yet
left we not off from sayling to the port, where we arrived with
a great deal of care, and having discharged our ordnance
according to the usual manner, in sign of peace, we perceived
a vessel very well furnished came directly to us from the shore,
wherein there was six *Portugals*, at which we exceedingly
rejoyced ; these presently came aboard our junck, where they
were very well entertained ; and having declared unto us what
we were to do for the safety of our persons, they counselled
us not to budge from thence for any thing in the world, as
we had told them our resolution was to have fled that night
to *Bengala*; because if we had followed that design, we had
assuredly been lost, and taken by the fleet which the King of
*Bramaa* had in that place, consisting of seventeen hundred
sayls, wherein were comprised an hundred gallies very well
furnished with strangers. They added withal, that they were
of opinion I should go ashore with them to *Joano Cayeyro*,
who was captain of the *Portugals*, for to give him an account
of the cause that brought me thither, the rather for that he
was a man of sweet disposition, and a great friend of *Pedro de
Faria's*, to whom they had often heard him give much com-
mendation, as well for his noble extraction, as for the goodly
qualities that were in him ; besides they told me that I should
find *Lancarote Gueyreyo*, and the rest of the captains with
him, unto whom my aforesaid letters were directed, and that
I should do nothing therein prejudicial to the service of God.

and the King. This counsel seeming good unto me, I went
presently to land with the *Portugals* to wait on *Joano Cayeyro*,
to whom I was exceeding welcome, as likewise to all the rest
that were in his quarters, to the number of seven hundred
*Portugals*, all rich men, and of good esteem. Then I shewed
*Joano Cayeyro* my letters, and the order that *Pedro de Faria*
had given me; moreover I treated with him about the affair
that led me thither : whereupon I observed that he was very
instant with the captains, to whom I was addrest, who
answered him that they were ready to serve the King in all
occasions that should be presented; howbeit since the letter
of *Pedro de Faria*, Governour of *Malaca*, was grounded on the
fear that he was in of the army of the *Achems*, composed of
an hundred and thirty sayl, whereof *Bijaya Sora* King of
*Pedir* was General; and it having fallen out, that his Admiral
had been defeated at *Tarnasery* by those of the country,
with the loss of seventy *Lanchares*, and six thousand men,
it was not needful they should stir for that occasion; for
according to what they had seen with their own eyes, the
forces of that enemy were so mightily weakned, as they did
not think he could in ten years space recover again the loss
he had sustained. To this they added many other reasons,
which made them all to agree, that it was not necessary they
should go to *Malaca*. After these things I desired *Joano
Cayeyro* to make me a declaration of all that had past in this
business, that it might serve me, as it were, for a certificate at
my return to our fortress, determining as soon as I had it to
get me from this place, for that I had nothing more to do there.
With this resolution I stayed there with *Joano Cáyeyro*, in
continual expectation to be gone when the season should serve
for the junck to depart, and remained with him at this siege
the space of six and forty days, which was the chief time
of the King of *Bramaa* his abode there; of whom I will say
something here in a few words, because I conceive the curious
would be well content to know what success the *Chaubainhaa*,
King of *Martabano*, had in this war. This siege had lasted
now six months and thirteen days, in which space the city
had been assaulted five times in plain day, but the besieged
defended themselves always very valiantly, and like men of

great courage. Howbeit in regard they were insensibly consumed with length of time, and the success of war, that no
succour came to them from any part, their enemies were
without comparison far more in number then they, in such
sort as the *Chaubainhaa*, found himself so destitute of men, as
it was thought he had not above five thousand soldiers left in
the city, the hundred and thirty thousand which were said to
be there at the beginning of the siege, being consumed by
famine, or the sword, by reason whereof the Council assembling
for to deliberate what was to be done thereupon, it was resolved
that the king should sound his enemy by his interest, which he
presently put in execution. For that effect he sent to tell him,
that if he would raise the siege he would give him thirty thousand bisses of silver, which is in value a million of gold, and would
become his tributary at threescore thousand ducates by the year.
The answer made by the King of *Bramaa*, hereunto was, that
he could accept of no conditions from him, if he did not first
yield himself to his mercy. The second time he propounded
unto him, that if he would suffer him to depart away with two
ships, in one of which should be his treasure, and in the other
his wife and children, that then he would deliver him the city,
and all that was in it. But the King of *Bramaa* would hearken
no more to that then the former. The third proposition which
he made him was this, that he should retire with his army to
*Tagalaa*, some six leagues off, that so he might have liberty to
go away freely with all his, and thereupon he would deliver
him the city, and the kingdom, together with all the treasure
belonging to the king his predecessor, or that in lieu thereof he
would give him three millions of gold. But he also refused this
last offer, insomuch that the *Chaubainhaa* utterly dispairing
of ever making his peace with so cruel an enemy, began to
meditate with himself what means he might use to save himself
from him. Having long thought upon it he found no better
an expedient then therein to serve himself of the succour of the
*Portugals*, for he was perswaded that by their means he might
escape the present danger. He sent then secretly to tell *Joano
Cayeyro*, that if he would imbarque himself in the night in
his four ships, and take him in with his wife and children, and
so save them, he would give him half his treasure. In this

affair he very closely imployed a certain *Portugal*, named *Paulo de Seixas*, born in the town of *Obidos*, who at that time was with him in the city.  This same having disguised himself in a *Pegu* habit, that he might not be known, stole one night to *Cayeyro's* tent and delivered him a letter from the *Chaubainhaa*, wherein this was contained.  *Valiant and faithful Commander of the* Portugals, *through the grace of the King of the other end of the world, the strong and mighty Lion, dreadfully roaring, with a crown of majesty in the House of the Sun, I the unhappy* Chaubainha's, *heretofore a prince, but now no longer so, finding my self besieged in this wretched and infortunate city, do give thee to understand by the words pronounced out of my mouth, with an assurance no less faithful then true, that I now render my self the vassal of the great king of* Portugal, *soveraign lord of me, and my children, with an acknowledgement of homage, and such tribute as he at his pleasure shall impose on me : wherefore I require thee on his behalf, that as soon as* Paulo Seixas *shall present this my letter unto thee, thou come speedily with thy ships to the bulwark of the* Chappel-key, *where thou shalt find me ready attending thee, and then without taking further counsel, I will deliver my self up to thy mercy, with all the treasures that I have in gold, and precious stones, whereof I will most willingly give the one half to the King of* Portugal, *upon condition that he shall permit me with the remainder to levy in his kingdom, or in the fortresses which he hath in the* Indiaes, *two thousand* Portugals, *to whom I will give extraordinary great pay that by their means I may be re-established in this state, which now I am constrained to abandon ; since my ill fortune will have it so.  As for that which concerns thee, and thy men, I do promise them, by the faith of my verity, that in case they do help to save me, I will divide my treasure so liberally among them, that all of them shall be very well satisfied and contented ; and for that time will not suffer me to enlarge any further,* Paulo de Seixas, *by whom I send this unto thee, shall assure thee both of that which he hath seen, and of the rest which I have communicated unto him.  Joano Cayeyro* had no sooner received this letter, but he presently caused the chief of his followers secretly to assemble together in Councel. Having shewed them the letter, he represented unto them how important and profitable it would be for the service of God, and the King, to accept of the offer, which the *Chaubainhaa* had made them. Whereupon causing an oath to be given to *Paulo de Seixas*, he willed him freely to declare all his knowledge of the matter, and whether it were true that the *Chaubainhaa* his treasure was so great, as it was reported to be. Thereunto he answered by the oath what he had taken, that he knew not certainly how great his treasure was, but that he was well assured how he had often seen, with his own eyes, an house in form of a church, and a reasonable bigness, all full up to the very tyles of bars and wedges of gold, which might very well lade two great ships. He further said, that he had more-over seen six and twenty chests bound about with strong cords, wherein according to the *Chaubainhaa* his own report was the treasure of the deceased *Presaguean* King of *Pegu*, which said treasure containing an hundred and thirty thousand bisses, and every biss in value five hundred ducates, made up all together the sum of threescore millions of gold. He said also, that he knew not certainly the number of wedges of gold which he had seen in the Temple of the God of Thunder, but he was most assured notwithstanding that they would fully lade four good vessels. And for a conclusion, he told them, that the said *Chaubainhaa* had shewed him the golden image of *Quiay Frigau*, which was taken at *Degum*, all full of such rich and resplendent stones as it was thought the like again were not in the whole world. So that this declaration which this man made upon oath astonished them so that heard it, as they could not possibly believe it to be true. Howbeit after they had sent him out of the tent, they entered into consultation about this affair, wherein nothing was resolved, of which I verily believe our sins were the cause; for there were in this assembly as many different opinions, as *Babel* had diversities of languages, which proceeded especially from the envy of six or seven men there present, who would needs perswade the rest, that if this affair should happen to have such success as was hoped for, *Joano Cayeyro* (unto whom they all bore no good will) would go then into *Portugal* with so much honor and reputation, as it would be a small matter for the King to make him an earl, or a marquis, or at least recom-pence him with the government of the *Indies*; so that after these ministers of the devil had alledged many reasons where-

fore it might not be done, which I think was but the mask of
their weakness and ill nature, though it may be they did it
out of the fear they were in of losing both their goods and lives
if this matter should come to be discovered to the King of
*Bramaa*; howsoever they would not agree to accept of this offer,
but contrariwise they threatened *Joano Cayeyro*, that if he
desisted not from his purpose, which was to comply with the
*Chaubainhaa*, they would disclose it to the *Bramaa*; so that
*Cayeyro* was constrained to abandon this business, lest if he
should persist therein the *Portugals* themselves would discover
him, as they threatened to do, without either fear of God, or
regard of men.

*Joano Cayeyro*, seeing he could not possibly bring his
desire to pass, wrote a letter to the *Caubainhaa*, wherein he
used many weak excuses for not performing that which he
demanded of him, and giving it to *Paulo de Seixas*, he speedily
dispatched him away with it; so that departing about three
hours after midnight he arrived safe at the city, where he
found the *Caubainhaa*, attending him in the same place which
he had named in his letter, unto whom he delivered the answer
he had brought. After he had read it, and thereby found
that he could not be succoured by our men, as he always
thought he should, it is said that he remained so confounded,
that for very grief and sorrow he sunk down to the ground
like a dead man, and continuing a pretty while in that manner,
at length he came again to himself, and then beting his brest,
and bewailing his miserable fortune. *Ah Portugals*, said he with
tears in his eyes, *how ill do you acknowledge that which I have
done for you, imagining that thereby I should make acquisition
of your friendship, as of a treasure, to the end that like faithful
men you would be assisting to me in so great a necessity as this
is which now I am in, whereby I desired no other thing then to
save my childrens lives, inrich your king, and state you in the
number of my chiefest friends ?    And would it had pleased him
who raigns in the beauty of these stars, that you had merited
before him the doing me this good office, which onely for my
sins you have refused me; for in so doing you had by my
means augmented his law, and I been saved in the promises of
his truth.* Thereupon sending away *Paulo de Seixas*, with a

young wench, by whom he had had two sons, he gave him a pair of bracelets, and said unto him, *I desire thee not to think of this little which now I give thee, but of the great love I have always born thee; above all, forget not to tell the* Portugals, *with how much cause and grief I complain of their extream ingratitude, whereof I will render them culpable before God at the last and dreadful day of judgement.* The night following *Paul de Seixas* came back to the *Portugals*, with two children, and a very fair young damosel their mother, with whom he married afterwards at *Coromandel*, and shewed to *Simon de Binto*, and *Pedro de Bruges*, lapidaries, the bracelets which the *Chaubainhaa* had given him, who buying them of him payd six and thirty thousand ducats for them, and had afterwards fourscore thousand for them of *Trimira Raia* Governour of *Narsingua*. Five days after *Paulo de Seixas* coming to the camp, where he recounted all that I have related before, the *Chaubainhaa*, seeing himself destitute of all humane remedy, advised with his Council what course he should take in so many misfortunes, that dayly in the neck of one another fell upon him; and it was resolved by them to put to the sword all things living that were not able to fight, and with the blood of them to make a sacrifice to *Quiay Nivandel*, God of Battels, then to cast all the treasure into the sea, that their enemies might make no benefit of it, afterward to set the whole city on fire, and lastly that all those which were able to bear arms should make themselves *Amoucos*, that is to say, men resolved either to dye, or vanquish, in fighting with the *Bramaas*. The *Chaubainhaa* very much approved this counsel, and concluding of it accordingly they fell presently to the demolishing of houses, and were preparing all other things for the effecting of their design, when as one of the three principal commanders of the city, apprehending that which was to follow the next day, fled the night ensuing to the enemies camp, and there rendered himself with four thousand men under his leading to the *Bramaa*. Hereupon the courages of all the rest were so abated by such a strange infidelity and flight, that not one of them cared afterwards either to keep watch, maintain the breaches, or do any other service whatsoever, but contrarily all that remained stuck not to say

publiquely, that if the *Chaubainhaa* would not suddenly resolve to yield himself to the *Bramaa*, they would open the
gates and let him in, for that it would be better for them to
dye so, then to languish and consume away like rotten beasts
as they did. The *Chaubainhaa* seeing them stifly bent thereunto, for to appease them, answered, that he would perform
their desire; howbeit withal he caused a review to be made
of those that would fight, but he found them to be not above
two thousand in all, and they too so destitute of courage, as
they could hardly have resisted feeble women. Beholding
himself then reduced to the last cast, he communicated his
mind to the Queen onely, as having no other at that time by
whom he might be advised, or that indeed could advise him.
The onely expedient then that he could rest on, was to render
himself into the hands of his enemy, and to stand to his
mercy, or his rigor. Wherefore the next day about six of
the clock in the morning he caused a white flag to be hung
out over the wall in sign of peace, whereunto they of the
camp answered with another like banner. Hereupon the
*Xenimbrum*, who was as it were marshal of the camp, sent
an horseman to the bulwark, where the flag stood, unto whom
it was delivered from the top of the wall. That the *Chaubainhaa* desired to send a letter to the King, so as he might
have a safe-conduct for it; which being signified to the
*Xenimbrum*, he instantly dispatched away two of good quality
in the army with a safe-conduct, and so these two *Bramaas*
remaining for hostages in the city, the *Chaubainhaa* sent the
King a letter by one of his priests, that was fourscore years of
age, and reputed for a saint amongst them. The contents
of this letter were these: *The love of children hath so much
power in this house of our weakness, that amongst us, who are
fathers, there is not so much as one that for their sakes would
not be well contented to descend a thousand times into the deep
pit of the house of the serpent, much more would expose his life
for them, and put himself into the hands of one that useth so
much clemency towards them that shall do so. For which
reason I resolved this night with my wife and children, contrary
to the opinions that would disswade me from this good, which I
hold the greatest of all others, to render my self unto your High*

*ness, that you may do with me as you think fit, and as shall be
most agreeable to your good pleasure. As for the fault wherewith I may be charged, and which I submit at your feet, I
humbly beseech you not to regard it, that so the merit of the
mercy, which you shall shew me, may be the greater before God
and men. May your Highness therefore be pleased to send some
presently for to take possession of my person, of my wife, of my
children, of the city, of the treasure, and of all the kingdom ; all
which I do even now yield up unto you, as to my sovereign lord,
and lawful king. All the request that I have to make unto you
hereupon with my knees on the ground, is, that we may all of us
with your permission finish our days in a cloister, where I have
already vowed continually to bewail and repent my faults past.
For as touching the honors and estates of the world, wherewith
your Highness might inrich me, as Lord of the most part of the
Earth, and of the Isles of the Sea, they are things which I
utterly renounce for evermore. In a word, I do solemnly swear
unto you before the greatest of all the gods, who with the gentle
touch of His Almighty hand makes the clouds of heaven to move,
never to leave that religion which by your pleasure I shall be
commanded to profess, where being freed from the vain hopes of
the world, my repentance may be the more pleasing to Him that
pardoneth all things. This holy Grepo, Dean of the Golden
House of Saint Quiay, who for his goodness and austerity of
life hath all power over me, will make a more ample relation
unto you of what I have omitted, and can more particularly tell
you that which concerns the offer I make you of rendring my
self ; that so relying on the reality of his speech, the unquietness
wherewith my soul is incessantly troubled may be appeased.*
The King of *Bramaa* having read this letter instantly returned
another in answer thereunto full of promises and oaths to this
effect, *That he would forget all that was past, and that for the
future he would provide him an estate of so great a revenue, as
should very well content him.* Which he but badly accomplished, as I shall declare hereafter. These news was published throughout all the camp with a great deal of joy, and
the next morning all the equipage and train that the King had
in his quarter was set forth to view. First of all there were
to be seen fourscore and six field-tents, wonderful rich, each

of them being invironed with thirty elephants, ranked in two
files, as if they had been ready to fight, with castles on their
backs full of banners, and their *Panores* fastened to their
trunks, the whole number of them amounted unto two
thousand, five hundred, and fourscore. Not far from them
were twelve thousand and five hundred *Bramaas*, all mounted
on horses, very richly accoustred ; with the order, which they
kept, they inclosed all the Kings quarter in four files, and
were all armed in corslets, or coats of mayl, with lances,
cymitars, and gilded bucklers. After these Horse followed
four files of Foot, all *Bramaas*, being in number above twenty
thousand. For all the other souldiers of the camp, there were
so many as they could not be counted, and they marched all
in order after their captains. In this publique muster were
to be seen a world of banners, and rich colours, and such a
number of instruments of war sounded, that the noise thereof,
together with that which the souldiers made, was most
dreadful, and so great as it was not possible to hear one
another. Now for that the King of *Bramaa* would this day
make shew of his greatness, in the reddition of the *Chaubainhaa*, he gave express command, that all the captains
which were strangers, with their men, should put on their
best clothes, and arms, and so ranged in two files, they
should make as it were a kind of street, through which the
*Chaubainhaa* might pass ; this accordingly was put in execution ; and this street took beginning from the city gate, and
reached as far as to the Kings tent, being in length about
three quarters of a league, or better. In this street there were
six and thirty thousand strangers, of two and forty different
nations, namely *Portugals, Grecians, Venetians, Turks, Janizaries, Jews, Armenians, Tartars, Mogores, Abyssins, Raiz-
butos, Nobins, Coracones, Persians, Tuparaas, Gizares, Tanacos,
Malabares, Jaos, Achems, Moens, Siams, Lussons* of the Island
*Borneo, Chacomas, Arracons, Predine, Papuaas, Selebres, Min-
dancas, Pegus, Bramaas*, and many others whose names I
know not. All these nations were ranked according to the
*Xemimbrums* order, whereby the *Portugals* were placed in the
vanguard, which was next to the gate of the city where the
*Chabainhaa* was to come. After them followed the *Armenians*,
then the *Janizaries* and *Turks*, and so the rest.

## CHAPTER XLII.

In what manner the Chaubainhaa rendred himself to the King of Bramaa, and the cruel proceeding against the Queen of Martabano, and the ladies, her attendants.

A BOUT one of the clock in the afternoon a cannon was shot off, which was the signal for the instant opening of the gates of the city; whereupon first of all issued out the souldiers, whom the King had sent thither for the guard of it, being 4000 *Siams* and *Bramaas*, all harquebusiers, halber-diers, and pikemen, with above 300 armed elephants; all which were commanded by a *Bramaa*, uncle to the King, named *Monpocasser Bainha*, of the city of *Melietay*. Ten or eleven paces after this guard of elephants marched divers princes, and great lords, whom the King had sent to receive the *Chaubainhaa*, all mounted on elephants, richly harnessed, with chairs upon their backs, plated over with gold, and collars of precious stones about their necks. Then followed at some 8 or 9 paces distance the *Rolim* of *Mounay*, Sovereign *Talapoy* of all the priests of the kingdom, and held in the reputation of a saint, who went alone with the *Chaubainhaa*, as a mediatour between the King and him; immediately after him came in a close chair, carried upon mens shoulders, *Nhay Canateo*, the daughter of the King of *Pegu*, from whom this *Bramaa* had taken his kingdom, and wife to the *Chaubainhaa*, having with her 4 small children, namely, 2 boys, and 2 girls, whereof the eldest was not 7 years old; round about her and them went some 30 or 40 young women of noble extraction, and wonderfull fair, with cast down looks, and tears in their eyes, leaning upon other women. After them marched in order certain *Talagrepos*, which were amongst them as the *Capuchins* with us, who bare-foot and bare-headed went alone praying, holding beads in their hands, and ever and anon comforting those ladies the best they could, and casting water in their faces for to bring them to themselves again, when as they fainted, which they did very often; a spectacle so lamentable, as it was not possible to behold it without shedding of tears. This desolate company was attended by another guard of Foot, and 500 *Bramaas* on horsback.  The *Chaubainhaa* was mounted on a little elephant, in sign of poverty and contempt of the world, conformable to the religion which he intended to enter into, being simply apparelled in a long cassock of black velvet, as a mark of his mourning, having his beard, head, and eye-brows shaven, with an old cord about his neck, so to render himself to the King.  In this equipage he appeared so sad and afflicted, that one could not forbear weeping to behold him.  As for his age, he was about threescore and two years old, tall of stature, with a grave and severe look, and the countenance of a generous prince.  As soon as he was arrived at a place which was near to the gate of the city, where a great throng of women, children, and old men, waited for him, when they saw him in so deplorable an estate, they all made (7 times one after another) so loud and dreadfull a cry, as if heaven and earth would have come together.  Now these lamentations and complaints were presently seconded with such terrible blows, that they gave themselves without pity on their faces with stones, as they were most of them all of a gore-bloud.  In the mean time things so horrible to behold, and mournfull to hear, so much afflicted all the assistants, that the very *Bramaas* of the Guard, though men of war, and consequently but little inclined to compassion, being also enemies to the *Chaubainhaa*, could not forbear weeping.  It was likewise in this place, where *Nhay Canatoo*, and all the other ladies that attended on her, fainted twice, by reason whereof they were fain to let the *Chaubainhaa* alight from his elephant for to go and comfort her; whereupon seeing her lying upon the ground in a swoon with her 4 children in her arms, he kneeled down on both his knees, and looking up to heaven with his eyes full of tears, *O mighty power of God*, cried he, *who is able to comprehend the righteous judgments of Thy divine justice, in that Thou, having no regard to the innocency of these poor creatures, givest way to Thy wrath, which passeth far beyond the reach of our weak capacities! but remember, O Lord, who Thou art, and not what I am.*  This said, he fell with his face on the ground, near to the Queen his wife, which caused all the assembly, who were without number, to make another such loud and horrible cry, as my words are not able to express it. The *Chaubainhaa* then took water in his mouth, and spurted it on his wife, by which means he brought her to her self again, and so taking her up in his arms, he fell a comforting her with speeches so full of zeal and devotion, as any one that heard him would have taken him rather for a Christian, then a *Gentile.* After he had employed about half an hours time therein, and that they had remounted him on his elephant, they proceed on their way in the same order as they held before, and as soon as the *Chaubainhaa* was out of the city gate, and came to the street which was formed of the several companies of the strangers, ranked in 2 files, he by chance cast his eye on that side where the 700 *Portugals* were, all of them in their best clothes, with their buff-coats, great feathers in their caps, and their harquebusiers on their shoulders, as also *Joano Cayeyro* in the midst of them, in a carnation sattin suit, and a gilt partisan in his hand, wherewith he made room; the afflicted prince no sooner knew him, but he presently fell down on the elephant; and there standing still without passing on, he said with tears in his eyes, to those that were about him; *My brethren, and good friends, I protest unto you, that it is a less grief unto me to make this sacrifice of my self, which the divine justice of God permits me to make him this day, then to look upon men so wicked and ingratefull as these same here are: either kill me then, or send these away, for otherwise I will not stir a foot further.* Having said so he turned away his face three times that he might not behold us, thereby shewing the great spleen that he bore us; and indeed all things well considered there was a great deal of reason that he should carry himself in that sort towards us, in regard of that which I have related before. In the mean time the captain of the guard seeing the stay which the *Chaubainhaa* had made, and understanding the cause why he would not go on, though he could not imagine wherefore he complained so of the *Portugals*, yet he hastily turned his elephant towards *Cayeyro*, and giving him a scurvy look; *Get you gone*, said he, *and that instantly, for such wicked men as you are do not deserve to stand on any ground that bears fruit; and I pray God to pardon him which hath put it into the Kings head that*

21

*you can be any ways profitable unto him. It were fitter for you therefore to shave away your beards, that you may not deceive the world as you do, and we will have women in your places that shall serve us for our money.* Whereupon the *Bramaas* of the guard, being incensed against us, drove us away from thence with a great deal of shame and contumely. And truly, not to lye, never was I so sensible of anything as this, in respect of the honour of my country-men. After this, the *Chaubainhaa* went on till he came to the tent of the King, who attended him with a royal pomp: for he was accompanied with a great number of lords, amongst the which there were 15 *Bainhaas*, who are as dukes with us, and of 6 or 7 others, that were of greater dignity then they. As soon as the *Chaubainhaa* came near him, he threw himself at his feet, and so prostrated on the ground he lay there a good while, as it were in a swoon, without speaking a word; but the *Rolim* of *Mounay*, that was close by him, supplied that defect, and like a religious man, as he was, spake for him to the King, saying; *Sir, here is a spectacle able to move thy heart to pity, though the crime be such as it is. Remember then that the thing most pleasing to God in this world, and whereunto the effects of His mercy is soonest communicated, is such an action, and voluntary submission, as this is, which here thou beholdest. It is for thee now to imitate His clemency, and so to do thou art most humbly intreated by the hearts of all them that are mollified by so great a misfortune as this is. Now if thou grantest them this their request, which with so much instance they beg of thee, be assured that God will take it in good part, and that at the hour of thy death He will stretch forth His mighty hand over thee, to the end thou mayst be exempted from all manner of faults.* Hereunto he added many other speeches, whereby he perswaded the King to pardon him ; at leastwise he promised so to do, wherewith the *Rolim*, and all the lords there present, shewed themselves very well contented, and commended him exceedingly for it, imagining that the effect would be answerable to that which he had engaged himself for before all. Now because it began to be night, he commanded the most of them that were about him to retire; as for the *Chaubainhaa*, he committed him into the hands of a

*Bramaa* commander, named *Xemin Commidau*; and the Queen
his wife, with his children, and the other ladies were put into
the custody of *Xemin Ansedaa*, as well because he had his
wife there, as for that he was an honourable old man, in
whom the King of *Bramaa* much confided.

The fear which the King of *Bramaa* was in lest the men of
war should enter into the city of *Martabano*, and should
pillage it now that it was night before he had done all that
which I am hereafter to relate, was the cause that he sent to
all the gates of the city, (being 24) *Bramaa* captains for to
guard them, with express commandment, that upon pain of
death no man should be suffered to enter in at any of them,
before he had taken order for the performance of the promise
which he had made to the strangers, to give them the
spoil of it; howbeit he took not that care, nor used such
diligence for the consideration he spake of, but onely that he
might preserve the *Chaubainhaa's* treasure; to which effect he
spent two whole days in conveighing it away, it being so great
that a thousand men were for that space altogether imployed
therein; at the end of these two days the King went very
early in the morning to an hill, called *Beidao*, distant from his
quarters some two or three flight-shoot, and then caused the
captains that were at the guard of the gates to leave them,
and retire away; whereupon the miserable city of *Martabano*
was delivered to the mercy of the souldiers, who at the
shooting off of a cannon, which was the signal thereof, entred
presently into it pell-mell, and so thronging together, that at
the entring into the gates, it is said, above three hundred men
were stifled; for as there was there an infinite company of
men of war of different nations, the most of them without
king, without law, and without the fear and knowledge of
God, they went all to the spoil with closed eyes, and therein
shewed themselves so cruel minded, that the thing they made
least reckoning of was to kill an hundred men for a crown;
and truly the disorder was such in the city, as the King
himself was fain to go thither six or seven times in person for
to appease it. The sack of this city endured three days and
an half, with so much avarice and cruelty of these barbarous
enemies, as it was wholly pillaged, without any thing left that

might give an eye cause to covet it. That done, the King
with a new ceremony of proclamations caused the *Chaubainhaa's* palaces, together with thirty or forty very fair rich
houses of his principal lords, and all the *Pagodes* and temples
of the city to be demolished; so that according to the opinion
of many, it was thought that the loss of those magnificent
edifices amounted to above 10 millions of gold : wherewith not
yet contented he commanded all the buildings of the city that
were still afoot, to be set on fire, which by the violence of the
winde, kindled in such manner, as in that onely night there
remained nothing unburnt, yea the very walls, towers, and
bulwarks were consumed even to the foundations. The
number of them that were killed in this sack was threescore
thousand persons ; nor was that of the prisoners much less.
There were an hundred and forty thousand houses, and
seventeen hundred temples burnt, wherein also were consumed
threescore thousand statues, or idols of divers metalls; during
this siege they of the city had eaten three thousand elephants.
There was found in this city six thousand pieces of artillery,
what of brass and iron, an hundred thousand quintals of
pepper, and as much of sanders, benjamin, lacre, lignum
aloes, camphire, silk, and many other kindes of rich merchandise, but above all an infinite number of commodities, which
were come thither from the *Indiaes* in above an hundred
vessels of *Cambaya, Achem, Melinda, Ceilam,* and of all the
Streight of *Mecqua,* of the *Lequios,* and of *China.* As for
gold, silver, precious stones, and jewels, that were found
there, one truly knows not what they were, for those things
are ordinarily concealed ; wherefore it shall suffice me to say,
that so much as the King of *Bramaa* had for certain of the
*Chaubainhaa's* treasure, amounted to an hundred millions of
gold, whereof, as I have said before, our King lost the moity,
as well for our sins, as through the malice and envy of wicked
dispositions. The next day after the city was pillaged, demolished, and burnt, there was seen in the morning upon the
hill where the King was, one and twenty pair of gallows,
twenty of the which were of equal height, and the other a
little lower erected on pillars of stone, and guarded by an
hundred *Bramaa* horsmen ; there were also round about the

place very large trenches, where a great many banners spotted
with drops of bloud were planted. As this novelty promised
somewhat which no man had heard of before, six of us
*Portugals* ran thither to learn what the matter might be; and
as we were going along we heard a great noise made by the
men of war from the camp, whereupon we saw come out of
the Kings quarter a number of horsemen, who with lances in
their hands prepared a great street, and cried out aloud; *Let
no man upon pain of death appear in arms, nor utter that with
his mouth which he thinks in his heart.* A pretty way off from
these horse was thē *Xemimbrum*, with an hundred armed
elephants, and a good many foot; after them went fifteen
hundred *Bramaas* on horsback, cast into four orders of files,
each of them six in a rank, whereof the *Talanagybras*, Viceroy of
*Tangu*, was commander: then marched the *Chauferoo Siammon*
with three thousand *Siammes*, armed with *Harquebuses* and
lances, all in one battalion: in the midst of these were an
hundred and twenty women tied and bound four and four
together, and accompanied with *Talagrepos*, men of great
austerity, and are such as the *Capuchins* amongst us, who
laboured all they might to comfort them in this last act of
life; behinde them were twelve ushers with maces, that went
before *Nhay Canatoo*, daughter to the King of *Pegu*, from
whom this *Bramaa* tyrant had usurped his kingdom, and wife
to the *Chaubainhaa*, with four children of hers, which were
carried by so many horsmen: all these sufferers were the
wives or daughters of the principal commanders that the
*Chaubainhaa* had with him in the city, upon whom in the
way of a strange revenge this *Bramaa* tyrant desired to wreak
his spight, and the hatred that he had always born unto
women. The most of these poor wretches were between
seventeen and five and twenty years of age, all of them very
white and fair, with bright auborn hair, but so weak in body,
that often-times they fell down in a swoon, out of which
certain women upon whom they leaned, endeavoured still to
bring them again, presenting them comfits, and other such
things fit for that purpose, but they would take none of them,
for that they were, as I have said, so feeble and benummed,
as they could scarce hear what the *Talegrepos* spake unto

them ; onely now and then lifted up their hands to heaven.
After this princess marched threescore *Grepos*, in two files,
praying with their looks fixed on the ground, and their eyes
watered with tears, saying ever and anon in a dolefull tone ;
*Thou which holdest Thy Being of none but Thy self, so justifie
our works, that they may be agreeable to Thy justice.*   Whereunto others answered weeping ; *Grant, Lord, that it may be so
that through our fault we lose not the rich gifts of Thy promises.*
After these *Grepos* followed a procession of three or four
hundred little children, quite naked from the girdle-sted
downwards, having in their hands great white wax lights,
and cords about their necks ; these, like the others, with a
sad and lamentable voice, which moved every one to compassion, uttered these words : *We most humbly beseech Thee,
O Lord, to give ear unto our cries and groans, and shew mercy
to these Thy captives, that with a full rejoycing they may have
a part of the graces and benefits of Thy rich treasures* ; and
much more they said to that purpose, in favour of these poor
sufferers : behinde this procession was another guard of foot-
men, all *Bramaas*, and armed with lances, arrows, and some
*Harquebuses.*   As for the rearward, it consisted of an hundred
elephants, like to them that marched first of all, so that the
number of the men of war that assisted at this execution, as well
for the guard, as for the pomp thereof, was ten thousand foot,
and two thousand horse, besides the two hundred elephants,
and a world of other people, both strangers and natives, that
came thither to behold the end of so mournfull and lamentable
an action.

---

## CHAPTER XLIII.

In what sort the sentence of death was executed on the person of the
Chaubainhaa King of Martaban, Nhay Canatoo his wife, and an
hundred and forty women ; with that which the King of Bramaa did
after his return to Pegu.

THESE poor sufferers having been led in the order before
mentioned clean through the camp, they came at last
to the place of execution, where the six ushers with a loud

voice made this proclamation : *Let all manner of people see and observe the bloudy justice, which is here to be done by the living God, Lord of all truth, and our King the Sovereign of our heads, Who of His absolute power doth command that these hundred and forty women be put to death, and thrown into the air, for that by their counsel and incitement their fathers and husbands stood out against us in this city, and at times killed twelve thousand* Bramaas *of the kingdom of* Tangu. Then at the ringing of a bell all the officers and ministers of justice, pell-mell together with the guards, made such a cry, as was most dreadfull to hear ; whereupon the cruel hangmen being ready to put the sentence of death in execution, those poor wretches embraced one another, and shedding abundance of tears they addressed themselves to *Nhay Canatoo*, who lay at that time almost dead in the lap of an old lady, and with their best complements one of them spake for all the rest unto her in this manner ; *Excellent lady, that art as a crown of roses upon our heads, now that we thy humble servants are entring into those mournful mansions where death doth reside, comfort us we beseech thee with thy dear sight, that so we may with less grief quit these bodies full of anguish, for to present ourselves before that Almighty just Judge, of whom we will for ever implore His justice for a perpetual vengeance of the wrong that is done us.* Then *Nhay Canatoo* beholding them with a countenance more dead then alive, answered them with a feeble voice, that could scarce be heard, *Go not away so soon, my sisters, but help me to sustain these little children.* That said, she leaned down again on the bosom of that lady, without speaking a word more ; whereupon the ministers of the arm of vengeance, so they term the hangmen, laid hold on those poor women, and hanged them up all by the feet, with their heads downwards, upon twenty gibbets, namely, seven on each one : now so painfull a death as this was, made them give strange and fearfull groans and sobs, untill at length the bloud stifled them all in less then an hour. In the mean time *Nhay Canatoo* was conducted by the four women, upon whom she leaned, directly to the gallows, whereon she and her four children were to be hanged, and there the *Rolim* of *Mounay*, who was held amongst them for a holy man, used some speeches unto her

for to encourage her the better to suffer death; whereupon
she desired them to give her a little water, which being
brought unto her, she filled her mouth with it, and so spurted
it upon her four children, whom she held in her arms; then
having kissed them many times, she said unto them weeping,
*O my children, my children, whom I have conceived anew within*
*the interior of my soul, how happy would I think my self if I*
*might redeem your lives with loss of mine own a thousand times*
*over, if it were possible ! for in regard of the fear and anguish*
*wherein I see you at this present, and wherein every one sees me*
*also, I should receive death with as good an heart from the hand*
*of this cruel enemy, as I willingly desire to see my self in the*
*presence of my Sovereign Lord of all things, within the repose*
*of His celestial habitation.*   Then turning her to the hangman,
who was going to binde her two little boys, *Good friend,* said
she, *be not I pray thee, so void of pity, as to make me see my*
*children die, for in so doing thou wouldst commit a great sin :*
*wherefore put me first to death, and refuse me not this boon*
*which I crave of thee for Gods sake.*   After she had thus
spoken she took her children again in her arms, and kissing
them over and over in giving them her last farewell, she
yielded up the ghost in the ladies lap upon whom she leaned,
not so much as once stirring ever after; which the hangman
perceiving, ran presently unto her and hanged her as he had
done the rest, together with her four little children, two on
each side of her, and she in the middle.   At this cruel and
pitiful spectacle there arose from amongst all this people so
great and hideous a cry, that the earth seemed to tremble
under the feet of them that stood upon it, and withall there
followed such a mutiny throughout the whole camp, as the
King was constrained to fortifie himself in his quarter with
6000 *Bramaa* horse, and 30000 foot, and yet for all that he
thought not himself secure enough from it, had not the night
come, which onely was able to calm the furious motions of
these men of war; for of seven hundred thousand which were
in the camp, six hundred thousand were by nation *Pegu's,*
whose king was the father of this queen, that was thus put
to death; but this Tyrant of *Bramaa* had so disarmed and
subjected them, as they durst not so much as quich upon any

occasion. Behold in what an infamous manner *Nhay Canatoo* finished her days, a princess every way accomplished, wife to the *Chaubainhaa* King of *Martabano*, and the daughter of the King of *Pegu*, Emperour of 9 kingdoms, whose yearly revenue amounted unto 3 millions of gold. As for the infortunate king her husband, he was the same night cast into the river with a great stone tied about his neck, together with 50 or 60 of his chiefest lords, who were either the fathers, husbands, or brothers of those hundred and forty ladies, that were most unjustly put to such an ignominious death, amongst the which there were 3, whom the King of *Bramaa* had demanded in marriage at such time as he was but a simple earl, but not one of their fathers would condescend unto it; whereby one may see how great the revolutions of time and fortune are.

After the Tyrant of *Bramaa* had caused this rigorous justice to be done, he stayed there 9 whole days, during the which many of the inhabitants of the city were also executed; at last he departed for to go to *Pegu*, leaving behinde him *Bainhaa Chaque*, lord steward of his house, to take order for all things that might conduce to the pacifying of that kingdom, and to provide for the repairing of what the fire had consumed; to which purpose he placed a good garison there, and carried with him the rest of his army; *Joano Cayeyro* followed him also with seven hundred *Portugals*, not above three or four remaining behinde in the ruines of *Martabano*, and those too not very considerable, except it were one, named *Goncalo Falcan*, a gentleman well born, and whom the *Gentiles* commonly called *Crisna Pacau*, that is to say, *Flower of Flowers*, a very honourable title amongst them, which the King of *Bramaa* had given him in recompence of his services: now forasmuch as at the departure from *Malaca*, *Pedro de Faria* had given me a letter directed unto him, whereby he desired him to assist me with his favour, in case I had need of it in the affair for which he sent me thither, as well for the service of the King, as for his own particular; as soon as I arrived at *Martabano*, where I found him resident, I delivered him this letter, and withall gave him an account of the occasion that brought me thither, which was to confirm the ancient League of Peace that the *Chaubainhaa* had made by his ambassadours with them of *Malaca*, at such time as *Pedro de Faria* was first governour of it, and whereof he could not chuse but have some knowledge; adding moreover, how to that effect I had brought the *Chaubainhaa* letters full of great protestations of amity, and a present of certain very rich pieces of *China*. Hereupon the *Goncalo Falcan* imagining that by means hereof he might insinuate himself much more into the good grace of the King of *Bramaa*, to whose side he turned at the siege of *Martabano*, quitting that of the *Chaubainhaa*, whom formerly he served, he went three days after the Kings departure to his said governour, and told him that I was come thither, as ambassadour from the captain of *Malaca* to treat with the *Chaubainhaa*, unto whom the captain sent an offer of great forces against the King of *Bramaa*; in so much that they of the country were upon the point of fortifying themselves in *Martabano*, and chasing away the *Bramaa's* out of the kingdom; whereunto he added so many other such like matters, that the Governour sent presently to apprehend me; and after he had put me into safe custody, he went directly to the junck, in which I came from *Malaca*, and seized upon all the goods that were in her, which were worth an hundred thousand ducates, committing the *Necoda*, captain and master of the junck, to prison, as also all the rest that were in her, to the number of an hundred threescore and four persons, wherein comprized forty rich merchants, *Malayes*, *Menancabo's*, *Mahumetans*, and *Gentiles*, natives of *Malaca*. All these were incontinently condemned to the confiscation of their goods, and to remain the Kings prisoners, as well as I, for being complices in the treason, which the captain of *Malaca* had plotted in secret with the *Chaubainhaa* against the King of *Bramaa*. Having thus caused them to be put into a deep dungeon, he made them to be so cruelly scourged, that within a moneth after their imprisonment, of an hundred sixty four of them, which they were, there died nineteen, either of a lethargy, or of hunger, or thirst. As for the rest, they were put into a miserable shallop without sails or oars, wherein they were exposed down the river; being delivered in this sort to the mercy of fortune, they were cast by the winde into a desert island,

*Pulho Canuida*, seated 20 leagues within the sea of this bar, where they furnished themselves with some sea-fish and such fruits as they found in the woods ; and in this necessity making a kinde of sail of the clothes they had, and with 2 oars, which it may be they met withall there, or made themselves, they took their course all along by the coast *Juncalan*, and from thence to another place, wherein they imployed the space of 2 moneths, arriving at length at the river of *Parles*, in the kingdom of *Queda*, where they all died of certain imposthumes, which rose in their throats, like unto carbuncles, two onely excepted, who came to *Malaca*, and recounted to *Pedro de Faria* the whole success of this sad voyage, and how that I was condemned to die, as indeed I expected every hour to be led to execution, when it pleased God to deliver me miraculously ; for as soon as the *Necoda*, and the merchants were banished in the manner that I have declared, I was committed to another prison farther off, where I remained six and thirty days laden with chains and irons in a most cruel and insupportable manner. During all that time the traitor *Goncalo* exhibited against me daily new and false allegations, wherein he charged me with a world of things which I never so much as thought of, and that to no other intent but to procure my death, that so he might rob me, as he had done all the rest that were in the junck. To which end, having questioned me 3 several times in judgment, I never answered any thing to his interrogatories that was to purpose, whereat he and other of my enemies were much enraged, saying, that I did it out of pride, and in contempt of justice ; so that for a punishment thereof they caused me to be openly whipped, and a great deal of lacre, which is like unto hard wax to be dropped scalding hot upon me, whereof the pain was such as it had almost killed me ; and indeed all that were by held me for a dead man. Now because for the most part I knew not what I spake, but talked like a desperate man, I happened 3 or 4 times to say, that for to rob me of my goods I had all these false accusations put upon me, but that Captain *Joano Cayeyro*, who was at *Pegu*, would ere it were long acquaint the King with this cruel usage of me, which was the cause of saving my life ; for even as this wicked Governour was going to have

the sentence executed, which was given against me, some of
his friends counselled him to forbear, saying, that if he put me
to death no doubt but that all the *Portugals*, which were at
*Pegu* would complain of him to the King, and tell him, that
for to rob me of an hundred thousand ducates, which I had
there in Commodities, appertaining to the captain of *Malaca*,
he had most unjustly taken away my life ; and that this being
so, the King would demand an account of him of all those
commodities, or of the money for them ; and that if he
rendered him even all that he had taken from me, yet would
not that content him, imagining still there was somewhat
more, whereby he would so put himself out of the good grace
of the King, as he would never recover it again, which would
be the cause of the utter overthrow both of himself and his
children, besides the dishonour that would redound to him
over and above. This dog the Governour *Bainhaa Chaque*,
fearing lest that should come to pass which they had said, desisted from his former obstinacy, and correcting the sentence he
had given, he ordained, that I should not die, but that my goods
should be confiscated, and my self arrested for the Kings
prisoner. As indeed, so soon as I was healed of the hurts
which the burning of the lacre, and the stripes of the whips
had made upon me, I was conducted in chains to *Pegu*, and
there as a prisoner was put into the hands of a *Bramaa*,
treasurer to the King, named *Diosoray*, who had also in his
custody 8 other *Portugals*, whose sins had procured them the
same misfortune which mine had caused unto me ; for it was
now full 6 moneths since these poor wretches had been in his
power, being taken in the ship of *Don Anrique Deca* of
*Cananor*, which by a tempest was cast on that coast. Now
seeing that hitherto I have discoursed of the success of my
voyage to *Martabano*, and of the benefit that redounded to me
by my going thither for the service of the King, which was no
other then to loss of my goods, and the imprisonment of my
person ; before I engage my self further in these relations, I
am resolved to entreat of the divers fortunes which I ran in
that kingdom for the space of 2 years and a half that I
travelled therein, being the time of my captivity, as also of the
several countries through which I was carried by my crosses

and mishaps; as holding it altogether necessary for the declaration of that which I am going on withal. I say then, that after this the King of *Bramaa* was departed from the city *Martabano,* as I have related before, he journeyed so long that at length he came to *Pegu,* where, before he dismissed his commanders, he caused a muster to be made of his army, and found that of seven hundred thousand men, which he had carried along with him to the besieging of the *Chaubainhaa,* there was fourscore and six thousand of them wanting. And for as much as he had about that time some inckling how the King of *Avaa* confederated with the *Savadis* and *Chaleus,* would give entry unto the *Sianmon* (whose country borders on the west and north-west side of the *Calaminhan,* Emperour of the indomitable forces of the elephants of the earth, as I will shew hereafter when I speak of him) to the end he might win from this *Bramaa* the chiefest strengths of his kingdoms, he like a good captain as he was, and very cunning in matter of war, before he passed on further, caused men to be levied, with whom, as also with all other necessary things, he furnished those principal fortresses from whence his greatest fear proceeded. Then having resolved to go and besiege the city of *Prom,* he retained the army which he had already a-foot, and made new and great preparations throughout the kingdom, using such diligence therein, and in six moneths time he had got together the number of nine hundred thousand men, whom he imbarqued in 12000 rowing vessels, whereof 2000 were *Seroos, Laulers, Caturos,* and *Foists.* Now all this great fleet set forth from *Pegu* the 9*th* of *March,* 1545, and going up the river of *Ansedaa,* it went to *Danapluu,* where it was furnished with all such provisions as were necessary From this place following on their way through a great river of fresh water, called *Picau Malacou,* which was above a league broad, at length upon the 13*th* of *April* they came within view of *Prom.* There, by some whom they took that night, they learned, that the King was dead, and how he had left for his successour to the kingdom a son of his of 13 years of age, whom the King his father before he died had married to his wives sister, the aunt of the said young prince, and daughter to the King of *Avaa.* The young King was no sooner advertised of the King of *Bramaa* his coming to besiege him in his city of *Prom*, but he sent presently away to the King his father in law for succour, which he instantly granted, and to that end speedily raised an army of 30000 *Mons, Tarées*, and *Chalems*, choice men and trained up in the wars, of whom he made a son of his, and brother to the Queen, General. In the mean time the *Bramaa*, having intelligence thereof, used all possible diligence for to besiege the city before so great a succour might arrive. To which purpose, having landed his army in a plain, called *Meigavotau*, some 2 leagues below the city, he continued there 5 days in making ready such preparations as were needfull. Having given order for all things, he caused his army to march one morning before day directly to the city, with the sound of drums, fifes, and other such instruments of war; where being arrived about noon without any opposition, he began presently to settle his camp; so that before it was night, the whole city was environed with trenches, and very great ditches, as also with six rows of cannons, and other pieces of ordnance.

---

## CHAPTER XLIV.

That which passed between the Queen of Prom, and the King of Bramaa, together with the first assault that was given to the city, and the success thereof.

THE King of *Bramaa* had been now five days before the city of *Prom*, when as the Queen that governed the State in the place of her husband, seeing her self thus besieged, sent to visit this her enemy with a rich jewel of precious stones, which was presented unto him by a *Talagrepo*, or religious man, of above an hundred years old, who was held amongst them for a saint, together with a letter, wherein was written [*an offer to pay homage if the city was spared*].

The *Bramaa* received this letter and ambassage with a great deal of authority, and entertained the religious man that delivered it unto him with much honour, as well in regard of

his age, as for that he was held as a saint amongst them ; with
all he granted him certain things which were at first demanded,
as a cessation of arms till such time as articles should be
agreed on ; as also a permission for the besieged to converse
with the besiegers, and other such things of little consequence.
In the mean time judging with himself that all those offers,
which this poor queen made him, and the humble submissions
of her letters, proceeded from weakness and fear, he would never
answer the ambassadour clearly, or to purpose. Contrarily
he caused all the places there abouts that were weak, and unarmed, to be secretly ransaked, and the poor inhabitants thereof to be unmercifully butchered by their barbarous enemies,
whose cruelty was so great, that in five dayes, according
to report, they killed fourteen thousand persons, the most part
whereof were women, children, and old men, that were not
able to bear arms. Hereupon the *Rolim*, who brought this
letter, relying no longer on the false promises of the Tyrant,
and discontented with the little respect he used towards him,
demanded leave of him to return to the city, which the *Bramaa*
gave him, together with this answer : that if the Queen would
deliver up her self, her treasure, her kingdom, and her vassals
to him, he would recompence her another way for the loss of
her State ; but withall that she was to return him a peremptory
answer to this propositions of his the very same day, which
was all the time he could give her, that so he might upon the
knowledge of her resolution determine upon what he had to do.
The *Rolim* went herewith back to the city, where he gave the
Queen an account of all things, saying, That this Tyrant was
a man without faith, and replete with damnable intentions ;
for proof whereof he represented unto her the siege of
*Martabano*, the usage of the *Chaubainhaa* after he had
rendred himself unto him upon his word, and how he had
put him, his wife, his children, and the chiefest nobility of his
kingdom, to a most shamefull death. These things considered
it was instantly concluded, as well by the Queen, as by all
those of her Councel, that she should defend the city, till such
time as succour came from her father, which would be within
15 days at the furthest. This resolution taken, she (being of
a great courage) without further delay took order for all things

that were thought necessary for the defence of the city,
animating to that end her people with great prudence, and a
man-like spirit, though she was but a woman.  Moreover, as
she liberally imparted to them of her treasure, so she promised
every one throughly to acknowledg their services with all
manner of recompences and honours, whereby they were
mightily encouraged to fight.  In the mean space the King
of *Bramaa*, seeing that the *Rolim* returned him no answer
within the time prefixt, began the next day to fortifie all
the quarters of his camp with double rows of cannon, for to
batter the city on every side ; and for assaulting of the walls
he caused a great number of ladders to be made, publishing
withall throughout his whole army, that all souldiers upon pain
of death should be ready within three days to go to the assault.
The time then being come, which was the 3rd of *May*, 1545,
about an hour before day the King went out of his quarter,
where he was at anchor upon the river with two thousand
vessels of choice men, and giving the signal to the commanders
which were on land, to prepare themselves, they altogether in
one body assailed the walls, with so great a cry, as if heaven
and earth would have come together, so that both sides falling
to encounter pell-mell with one another, there was such a
conflict betwixt them, as within a little while the air was seen
all on fire, and the earth all bloody ; whereunto being added
the clashing of weapons, and noise of guns, it was a spectacle
so dreadful, that we few *Portugals*, who beheld these things,
remained astonished, and almost besides our selves.  This
fight indured full five hours, at the end whereof the tyrant of
*Bramaa* seeing those within defend themselves so valiantly,
and the most part of his forces to grow faint, he went to land
with ten or eleven thousand of his best men, and with all
diligence re-inforcing the companies, that were fighting, the
bickering renewed in such sort, as one would have said it did
but then begin, so great was the fury of it.  The second trial
continued till night, yet would not the King desist from the
fight, what counsel soever was given him to retire ; but contrarily he swore not to give over the enterprise begun, and
that he would lie that night within the inclosure of the city
walls, or cut off the heads of all those commanders that were

not wounded at their coming off. In the mean time this obstinacy was very prejudicial to him, but continuing the assault till the moon was gone down, which was two hours past midnight, he was then forced to sound a retreat, after he had lost in this assault, as was the next day found upon a muster, fourscore thousand of his men, besides those which were hurt, which were thirty thousand at the least, whereof many died for want of dressing; whence issued such a plague in the camp, as well through the corruption of the air, as the water of the river, (that was all tainted with blood and dead bodies), that thereby about fourscore thousand more perished, amongst whom were five hundred *Portugals*, having no other buriall then the bodies of vultures, crows, and such like birds of prey, which devoured them all along the coast where they lay.

The King of *Bramaa*, having considered that this first assault had cost him so dear, would no more hazard his men in that manner, but he caused a great terrace to be made with bavins, and above ten thousand date-trees, which he commanded to be cut down, and on that he raised up a platform so high, as it over-topped the city two fathoms, and more, where he placed 80 pieces of ordnance, and with them continually battering the city for the space of nine dayes together, it was for the most part demolished, with the death of fourteen thousand persons, which quite abated the Queens courage, especially when she came to understand that she had but six thousand fighting men left, all the rest, which consisted of women, children, and old men, being unfit and unable to bear arms. The miserable besieged seeing themselves reduced to such extreamity, assembled together in councel, and there, by the advice of the chiefest of them, it was concluded, that all in general should anoint themselves with the oil of the lamps of the chapel of *Quiay Nivandel*, God of Battel of the field *Vitau*, and so offering themselves up in sacrifice to him, set upon the platform, with a determination either to dye, or to vanquish, in vowing themselves all for the defence of their young king, to whom they had so lately done homage, and sworn to be true and faithful subjects. This resolution taken, which the Queen and her nobility approved of for the best and most assured, in a time wherein all things were wanting to them for the longer

defending themselves, they promised to accomplish it in the
manner aforesaid by a solemn oath, which they all took.
Now there being no further question but to see how they
should carry themselves in this affair, they first of all made
an uncle of the Queens the captain of this resolute band, who
assembling these six thousand together, the same night, about
the first quarter of the watch, made a sally out of the two
gates that were neerest to the terrace and platform, and so
taking courage from their despair, and resolution to dye, they
fought so valiantly that in less then half an hour the whole
camp was put in disorder, the terrace gained, the fourscore
pieces of cannon taken, the King himself hurt, the pallisado
burnt, the trenches broken, and the *Xenimbrum*, General of
the army, slain, with above fifteen thousand men more,
amongst the which were five hundred *Turks*; there were
moreover forty elephants taken, besides those that were killed,
and eight hundred *Bramaas* made prisoners; so that these six
thousand resolute men did that which an hundred thousand,
though valiant enough, could hardly have effected. After this
they retreated an hour before day, and upon a review they
found, that of six thousand which they were, there was but
seven hundred slain. This bad success so grieved and incensed
the King of *Bramaa*, as attributing the cause thereof to the
negligence of some of his captains in the ill guarding of the
terrace, that the day following he caused two thousand *Pegu's*
to be beheaded, which had stood sentinel that night. This
adventure rendred things quiet for the space of twelve days,
during which the besieged stirred not; in the mean time one of
the four principal captains of the city, named *Xemim Meleytay*,
fearing that which all others in general misdoubted, namely,
that they could not escape from falling into the hands of so
cruel an enemy, treated secretly with the Tyrant, and upon
condition that he would continue him in his charge, nor
meddle with any of the houses of his friends, and make him
*Xemin* of *Ansedaa* in the kingdom of *Pegu*, with all the
revenue which the *Bainhaa* of *Malacou* had there, being thirty
thousand ducates a year, he would deliver him up the city by
giving him entrance into it through the gate which he commanded. The King of *Bramaa* accepted hereof, and for a gage

of performance on his part, he sent him a rich ring from off
his finger. This treason so concluded, was effected on the
23rd of *August*, in the year 1545. wherein this Tӯrant of
*Bramaa* carried himself with all the barbarousness and
cruelty that he used to practice in the like cases. And for
as much as I conceive that I should never have done, if I
should recount here at large how this affair past, I will say no
more, but that the gate was opened, the city delivered up, the
inhabitants all cut in pieces, without so much as sparing one ;
the king and queen made prisoners, their treasurers taken, the
buildings and temples demolished, and many other inhumani-
ties exercised with such outragiousness, the belief whereof is
beyond the imagination and thought of man; and truly I never
represent unto my self in what manner it was done, as having
seen it with mine own eyes, but that I remain as it were
astonished and besides my self at it. For as this tyrant was
touched to the quick with the affront he had lately received,
so he executed all the cruelties he could imagine against those
miserable inhabitants, for to be revenged of the ill success he
had had in the siege, which could not proceed from any other
but a base mind and vile extraction ; for it ordinarily falls out,
that barbarousness finds place in such kind of people, rather
then in generous and valiant hearts; whereunto may be added,
that he was a man without faith, and of an effeminate disposition, though he was nevertheless an enemy to women, albeit
there were in that kingdom, and in all the others whereof he
was lord, those that were very white and fair. After the
bloudy ruine of that wretched city, the Tyrant entred into it
in great pomp, and as it were in triumph, through a breach
that was made of purpose in the wall, and by his express
commandment. When he was arrived at the young kings
palace, he caused himself to be crowned King of *Prom*; and
during the ceremony of this coronation, he made that poor
prince, whom he had deprived of his kingdom, to continue
kneeling before him, with his hands held up, as if he adored
some god, and ever and anon they constrained him to stoop
down and kiss the Tyrants feet, who in the mean time made
shew as if he were not pleased therewith. This done, he went
into a balcone, which looked on a great market place, whither

he commanded all the dead children, that lay up and down the streets, to be brought; and then causing them to be hacked very small, he gave them, mingled with bran, rice, and herbs, to his elephants to eat. Afterward, with a strange kind of ceremony, at the sound of trumpets, drums, and other such like instruments, there was above an hundred horses led in, loaden with the quarters of men and women, which also he commanded to be cut small, and then cast into a great fire, kindled expresly for it. These things so done, the queen was brought before him, that was wife to the poor little king, who, as I said before, was but thirteen years of age, and she thirty and six, a woman very white, and well favoured, aunt to her own husband, sister to his mother, and daughter to the King of *Avaa*, which is the country from whence the rubies, saphirs, and emeralds do come to *Pegu*; and it was the same lady, whom the *Bramaa* had sent to demand in marriage of her father, as it was then spoken, but that he refused him, saying to his ambassador, for an answer, That the thoughts of his daughter soared a pitch higher then to be the wife of the *Xemim* of *Tanguu*, which was the family whence this Tyrant was issued ; but now that she was fallen into his hands as his slave, whether he used her so, either out of a revenge of that affront, or out of scorn and contempt, so it was that he made her to be publiquely stript stark naked, and to be torn and mangled with whipping, and then in that manner to be led up and down all the city, where amidst the cries and hooting of the people, he exposed her to other cruel torments, wherewith she was tortured till she gave up the ghost. When she was dead, he made her to be bound to the little king her husband, who was yet living ; and having commanded a great stone to be tyed about their necks, they were cast into the river, which was a kind of cruelty very dreadful to all that beheld it. To these barbarous parts he added many others so inhumane, as it is not likely that any other but he could imagine the like. And for a conclusion of his cruelties, the next day he caused all the gentlemen that were taken alive, being some three hundred, to be impaled, and so spitted like rosted pigs, to be also thrown into the river, whereby may be seen how great and unheard of the injustice of this Tyrant was, which he exercised on these miserable wretches.

## CHAPTER XLV.

The King of Bramaa his besieging of the Fortress of Meleytay, with his going from thence to Avaa ; and that which passed there.

FOURTEEN days were past since the doing of these things, during the which the Tyrant employed himself in fortifying the city with a great deal of diligence and care, when as his spies, whom he had sent out, brought him word, that from the city of *Avaa* a fleet of four hundred rowing vessels was come down the river of *Queitor*, wherein there were thirty thousand *Siamon* souldiers, besides the mariners, of which the King of *Avaa's* son, and brother to the poor queen, was general; for this prince having received advertisement of the taking of the city of *Prom*, and of the death of his sister and brother-in-law, went and lodged in the fortress of *Meleytay*, which was some twelve leagues up the river from *Prom*. This news much troubled the Tyrant, howbeit he resolved to go himself in person against his enemies before that other succours came to joyn with them, as indeed the report went, that fourscore thousand, all *Mons* by nation, and led by the King of *Avaa*, were on their way thither. With this resolution the Tyrant of *Bramaa* set forth towards *Meleytay* with an army of three hundred thousand men, namely, two hundred thousand by land alongst the rivers side, whereof the *Chaumigrem* his foster-brother was the commander in chief, and the other hundred thousand under his own conduct, being all choyce men, and imbarqued in two thousand *Seroes*. Being come within sight of *Meleytay*, the *Avaas* desiring to shew that the resolution wherewith they were come thither was of far more power with them, then any fear they could have, and that also their enemies might not receive any benefit by their fleet which lay on the river, and do them an affront beside by taking it, they set all their vessels on fire, and burnt them every one. Then, without any dread of that which the flesh doth naturally most fear, they got all into the field, and ranged themselves into four battalions, in three of which, whereof each one made ten thousand men, were the thirty thousand *Mons*; and in the other, that were somewhat bigger, were all the mariners of the four hundred vessels they had burnt. These same they placed in the vaunt-guard, with an intention that they should weary the enemies, with whom they made a cruel fight, which lasted about half an hour, wherein all these mariners were cut in pieces; presently after them the thirty thousand *Mons*, close compacted together in three battalions, presented themselves, and with wonderful violence set upon their enemies, between whom and them followed so extraordinary and cruel a battel, as not longer to insist upon it, nor to recount in particular how things past, which also I cannot well do, it shall suffice me to say, that of the thirty thousand *Mons*, eight hundred only escaped out of it; who being routed made their retreat into the fortress of *Meleytay*; but that which was most memorable herein was, that of the King of *Bramaas* two hundred thousand men, an hundred and fifteen thousand lay dead in the field, and all the rest for the most part were wounded. In the mean time the Tyrant, which came along on the river in the two thousand *Seroos*, arrived at the place of battel, where beholding the strange massacre which the *Mons* had made of his people, he became so enraged at it, that dis-imbarquing his forces, he instantly layd siege unto the fortress, with a purpose, as he said, to take all those eight hundred that were in it alive. This siege continued seven whole days together, during the which those without gave five assaults to it, and the besieged defended themselves always very valiantly; howbeit seeing that the last hour of their life was come, and that they could no longer hold that place for their king, as they had hoped they might, by reason of the fresh forces which the King of *Bramaa* had landed, like couragious men, as they were, they resolved to dye in the field, as their companions had done, and valiantly revenge their deaths with that of their enemies; whereunto they were the more willingly carryed, because they perceived well that if they continued still in the place, they should never make use of their valour, as they desired to do, for that the Tyrants ordnance would by little and little consume them. This resolution taken, they under the favour of a very dark and rainy night sallyed forth, and first of all fell upon the two first courts of guard that were on the lands side, cutting all in

pieces that they met withall. Then following their design
they passed on like desperate men; and whether they did it,
either to shew that they regarded not death which threatened
them, or for the desire they had to gain honor, so it was that
they behaved themselves so couragiously, and pressed the
Tyrant so neer, as they forced him to leap into the river, and
swim for his life, insomuch that all the camp was in disorder,
and broken through in I know not how many places, with the
death of above twelve thousand men; amongst whom were
fifteen hundred *Bramaas*, two thousand strangers of divers
nations, and all the rest *Pegu's*. This fight lasted not above
half an hour, in which time the eight hundred *Mons* were all
slain, there being not so much as one of them that would yield
upon any composition whatsoever. Hereupon the Tyrant of
*Bramaa* seeing the fight ended, and all things quiet, went and
reassembled his forces together, and so entered the fortress of
*Meleytay*, where he presently commanded the *Xemims* head to
be cut off, saying, that he was the sole cause of that disaster,
and that he who had been a traytor to his king could not be
faithful unto him : behold the recompence which this traytor
made him for delivering up the city of *Prom* unto him, howsoever it justly belonged unto him for a punishment of his
perfidiousness, that carried him to betray his king and his own
country into the power of his enemies. After this they fell to
dressing of the hurt men, which were in very great number.

We past all this night with much apprehension, always
keeping good watch; and the next morning as soon as it was
day, the first thing that we did was to rid away the dead
bodies, which were in so great number all over the camp, that
the ground was quite covered with them. After this we took
a view of those that were killed, as well on the one, as the
other party, and we found that on the *Bramaas* side there
were an hundred and fourscore thousand, and on the Prince
of *Avaas* forty and two thousand, wherein were comprized the
thirty thousand *Mons*. That done, after the Tyrant had fortified the city of *Prom*, as also the fort of *Meleytay*, and made
two other forts upon the bank of the river, in such places as
he judged to be most important for the safety of that kingdom,
he went up the river or *Queitor* in a thousand rowing *Seroos*,

wherein were imbarqued seventy thousand men. In this
voyage. his intention was to go in his own person, for to
observe the kingdom of *Avaa*, and to see the city himself,
the better to consider the strength of it, and thereby judge
what forces he should bring for to take it. So he proceeded
still on for the space of eight and twenty days, and during that
time passed by many goodly places, which within the kingdom
of *Chaleu* and *Jaeupalaon* were upon the bank of the river. At
length he arrived at the city of *Avaa*, the 13th of *October*, the
same year, 1545. Being come to the port, he remained there
thirteen days, and that while burned between two and three
thousand vessels that he found there. Moreover, he set fire
on many villages thereabout, which cost him not so little but
that he lost in all these degasts eight thousand of his men,
amongst the which were threescore and two *Portugals*. Now
whereas this city was very strong, as well in regard of the
scituation of it, as of the fortifications which were newly made
there, it had besides within it twenty thousand *Mons*, who (as
it was said) were come thither some five days before from
the mountains of *Pondaleu*, where the King of *Avaa*, by the
permission of the *Siamon*, emperour of that monarchy, was
levying above fourscore thousand men for to go and regain the
city of *Prom*: for as soon as that king had received certain
news of the death of his daughter and son-in-law, perceiving
that he was not strong enough of himself to revenge the
wrongs this Tyrant had done him, or to secure himself from
those which he feared to receive of him in time to come,
namely, the depriving him of his kingdom, as he was threatened, he went in person with his wife and children and cast
himself at the *Siamons* feet, and acquainting him with the
great affronts he had received, and what his desire was, he
made himself his tributary at threescore thousand bisses by
the year, which amount to an hundred thousand ducates of
our money, and a *gueta* of rubies, being a measure like to our
pint, therewith to make a jewel for his wife; of which tribute
it was said that he advanced the payment for ten years before-
hand, besides many other precious stones, and very rich plate,
which he presented him with, estimated in all at two millions;
in recompence whereof the *Siamon* obliged himself to take him

into his protection, yea and to march into the field for him as
often as need should require, and to restablish him within a
year in the kingdom of *Prom*, so as for that effect he granted
him those thirty thousand men of succour, which the *Bramaa*
defeated at *Meleytay*; as also the twenty thousand that were
then in the city, and the fourscore thousand which were to
come to him, over whom the said King of *Avaa* was to be the
general. The Tyrant having intelligence thereof, and apprehending that this, above all other things he could fear, might
be the cause of his ruine, he gave present order for the fortifying of *Prom* with much more care and diligence then formerly:
howbeit, before his departure from this river where he lay at
anchor, being about some league from the city of *Avaa*, he
sent his treasurer, named *Diocory* (with whom we eight
*Portugals*, as I have related before, remained prisoners)
embassador to the *Calaminhan*; a prince of mighty power,
who is seated in the midst of this region in a great and
spacious extent of country, and of whom I shall say something
when I come to speak of him. The subject of this embassage
was to make him his brother in arms by a league and contract
of new amity, offering for that effect to give him a certain
quantity of gold and precious stones; as also to render unto
him certain frontier lands of his kingdom, upon condition that
the spring following he should keep the *Siamon* in war for to
divert him from succouring the King of *Avaa*, and thereby
give him means the more easily to take his city from him,
without fear of that assistance which the King hoped should
serve for an obstacle to his design. This embassadour departed
then after he had imbarqued himself in a *Laulea*, that was
attended on by twelve *Seroos*, wherein there were three
hundred men of service, and his guard, besides the watermen
and mariners, whose number was little less. The presents
which he carried to the *Calaminhan* were very great, and
consisted in divers rich pieces, as well of gold as of precious
stones, but above all in the harness of an elephant, which
according to reports was worth above six hundred thousand
ducates; and it was thought that all the presents put together
amounted to a million of gold. At his departure, amongst
other favours which the king his master conferred on him, this

same was not the least for us, that he gave us eight unto him
for to be his perpetual slaves. Having clothed us then very
well, and furnished us abundantly with all things necessary,
he seemed to be exceedingly contented with having us along
with him in this voyage, and ever after he made more account
of us, then of all the rest that followed him.

---

## CHAPTER XLVI.

Our going with the King of Bramaa's ambassadour to the Calaminham,
with the course which we held until we arrived at the Temple or Pagode
of Timagoogoo.

IT seems fit unto me, and conformable to that which I am
relating, to leave for a while this Tyrant of *Bramaa* (to
whom I will return again when time shall serve) for to entreat here of the way we held for to go into *Timplan*, the
capital city of the Empire of the *Calaminham*, which signifies,
*Lord of the world*; for in their language *Cala* is Lord, and
*Minham* the world. This prince also entitles himself, *The
absolute Lord of the indomiptable force of the Elephants of the
Earth*. And indeed I do not think that in all the world there is
a greater lord than he, as I shall declare hereafter. This ambassadour then departing from *Avaa* in the moneth of *October*,
1545, took his course up the river of *Queitor*, steering west, south-
east, and in many places eastward, by reason of the winding of
the water ; and so in this diversity of rhombes we continued
our voyage seven days together, at the end whereof we arrived
at a channel, called *Guampanoo*, through which the *Rhobamo*,
who was our pilot, took his course, that he might decline the
*Siamons* country, being so commanded to do by the express
order of the King. A while after we came to a great town,
named *Gataldy*, where the ambassadour stayed three days to
make provision of certain things necessary for his voyage.
Having left this place we went on still, rowing up through
his channel eleven days longer, during which time we met not
with any place that was remarkable, only we saw some small

villages, the houses whereof were covered with thatch, and peopled with very poor folks, and yet for all that the fields are full of cattel, which seemed to have no master, for we killed twenty and thirty of them in a day in the sight of those of the country, no man so much as finding fault with it, but contrarily they brought them in courtesie to us, as if they were glad to see us kill them in that sort. At our going out of this channel of *Guampanoo*, we entred into a very great river, called *Angegumaa*, that was above three leagues broad, and in some places six and twenty fathom deep, with such impetuous currents as they drove us often-times from our course. This river we coasted above seven dayes together, and at length arrived at a pretty little walled town, named *Gumbim*, in the kingdom of *Jangromaa*, invironed on the lands side for five or six leagues space with forrests or *Binjamin*, as also with plains of lacre, wherewith they ordinarily traded to *Martabano*, and do also lade there many vessels with those commodities for to transport them into divers countries of the *Indiaes*, as to the Streight of *Mecqua*, to *Alcocer*, and *Judaa*. There is also in this town great store of musk, far better then that of *China*, which from thence is carried to *Martabano* and *Pegu*, where those of our nation buy of it, therewith to traffique at *Narsingua*, *Orixaa*, and *Masulopatan*. The women of this country are all very white and well-favoured; they apparel themselves with stuffs made of silk and cotton-wool, wear links of gold and silver about their legs, and rich carcanets about their necks. The ground there is of it self exceedingly fertile in wheat, rice, millets, sugar, wax, and cattel. This town, with ten leagues of circuit about it, yields every year to the King of *Jangomaa* threescore altars of gold, which are seven hundred thousand ducates of our money. From thence we coasted the river southward, for the space of above seven dayes, and arrived at a great town, named *Catammas*, which in our language signifies, *the Golden Crevice*, being the patrimony of *Raudiavaa Tinhau*, the *Calaminhams* second son. The *Naugator* of this town gave good entertainment to the ambassadour, and sent him many sorts of refreshment for his followers; withall he gave him to understand that the *Calaminham* was at the city of *Timplan*. We departed from this place on

a *Sunday* morning, and the day after about evening we came
to a fortress, called *Campalagor*, built in the midst of the
river in the form of an island upon a rock, and invironed with
good free-stone, having three bulwarks and two towers seven
stories high, wherein, they told the ambassadour, was one of
the four and twenty treasures, which the *Calaminham* had in
this kingdom, the most part whereof consisted in lingots of
silver, of the weight of six thousand *Caudins*, which are four
and twenty thousand quintals; and it was said, that all this
silver was buried in wells under ground.  After this we still
continued our course for the space of thirteen days, during
the which we saw on both sides of the river many very goodly
places, whereof the most were fair towns, and the rest stately
high trees, delicate gardens, and great plains full of corn, as
also much cattel, red deer, shamoises, and rhinocerots, under
the keeping of certain men on horsback, who looked to them
whilst they fed.  On the river there were a great number of
vessels, where in much abundance was all things to be sold
which the earth produceth, wherewith it hath pleased God to
enrich these countries more then any other in the world.
Now forasmuch as the ambassadour fell sick here of an impos-
tume in his stomack, he was counselled to proceed no further
till he was healed, so that he resolved to go with some of his
train for to be cured to a famous hospital, some twelve leagues
from thence, in a *Pagode*, named *Tinagoogoo*, which signifies
*the God of thousand Gods*, and so departing at the same instant
he arrived there on *Saturday* about night.

[*Here follows an account of the Temple of Tinagoogoo,
ommitted.*]

---

## CHAPTER XLVII.

The great and sumptuous procession made in this Pagode, together with
their sacrifices; and other particularities.

WHILEST this feast of these *Gentiles*, as also the fair,
which was kept all the time thereof, endured for the
space of fifteen days, with an infinite concourse of merchants

and pilgrims, that came flocking thither from all parts, as I
have declared before, there were many sacrifices made there
with different ceremonies, not a day passing without some
new thing or other. For amongst many of great charge, and
very worthy of observation, one of the chiefest was a *Jubile*,
after their manner, which was published the fifth day of the
moon, together with a procession, that was above three leagues
in length, as we could guess. It was the common opinion of
all, that in this procession there were forty thousand priests
of the four and twenty sects, which are in this empire; most
of them were of different dignities, and called *Grepos*, *Talagrepos*, *Roolims*, *Neepois*, *Bicos*, *Sacarens* and *Chanfarauhos*.
Now by the ornaments they wear, as also by the devices and
ensigns which they carry in their hands, they may be dis-
tinguished; and so every of them is respected according to
his dignity. Howbeit these went not on foot as the other
ordinary priests, for that they were on this day forbidden upon
pain of great sin to tread upon the ground, so that they caused
themselves to be born in *Pallaquins*, or arm-chairs, upon the
shoulders of other priests their inferiors, apparelled in green
sattin, with their stoles of carnation damask. In the midst of
the ranks of this procession were all the inventions of their
sacrifices to be seen, as also the rich custodes of their idols,
for the which each of them had a particular devotion. They
that carried them were clothed in yellow, having each of them
a big wax candle in his hand; and between every fifteen of
those custodes went a triumphant charet, all which charets
put together were in number an hundred twenty and six. All
these charets were four, and some five stories high, with as
many wheels on either side. In each of them there were at
the least two hundred persons, what with the priests and the
guards, and on the top of all an idol of silver, with a miter of
gold on its head, and all of them had rich chains of pearl and
precious stones about their necks; round about every charet
went little boys, carrying siver maces on their shoulders, and
behind them were a many of caskets full of exquisite perfumes,
as also divers persons with censers in their hands, who ever
and anon censed the idol to the tune of certain instruments of
musick, saying three times, with a lamentable voyce, *Lord*,

*asswage the pains of the dead, to the end they may praise Thee peaceably*; whereunto all the people answered with a strange noise, *Such may Thy pleasure be, and so may it come to pass every day wherein Thou shewest us the sun.* Each of these charets was drawn by above three thousand persons, who for that purpose made use of very long cords, covered with silk, and thereby gained to themselves plenary remission of their sins, without restitution to be made of any thing at all. Now that many might participate of this absolution by drawing the coard, they set their hands to it one after and close to another, continuing doing so to the very end, in such sort that the whole coard was covered with hands, and nothing else to be seen; but that they also which were without might gain this indulgence, they helped those that had their hands on the coard by putting theirs about their shoulders; then they that were behind them did the like, and so consequently all the rest. In this manner throughout the whole length of the coard there were six or seven ranks or files, and in each of them above five hundred persons. This procession was environed with a great number of horsemen, that carryed staves with pikes at both ends, who riding all about, went crying to the people, which were infinite in number, that they should make way, and not interrupt the priests in their prayers. Many times also they struck those so rudely whom they first met withal, as they beat down three or four together, or hurt them grievously, no man daring to find fault with, or so much as speak a word against it. In this order this marvelous procession passed through above an hundred streets, which to that end were all adorned with boughs of palms and myrtle, amongst the which were many standards and banners of silk planted. There were also many tables set up in divers places, where all that desired it for Gods sake were admitted to eat of free-cost; yea and in other parts they had clothes and money given them. There likewise enemies reconciled themselves one to another, and the rich men forgave them their debts which were not able to pay. In a word, so many good works were done there, more proper for Christians than for Gentiles, as I must needs conclude, that if they had been done with faith, and baptism, for the love of our Lord Jesus

Christ, and without any mixture of the things of this world, assuredly they would have been acceptable to him. But alas! the best was wanting to them, and that both for theirs and our sins. Whilest this procession, together with the chariots wherein the idols were, passed along in this manner, and that with a dreadful noise of drums, and other such instruments, behold where out of certain wooden sheds made expresly for the purpose, six, seven, eight, or ten men, all besmeared with odours, and wrapped up in silk, wearing gold bracelets about their wrists, start forth all at once, and room being instantly made them by the people, after they had saluted the idol which was on the top of the chariot, they went and laid themselves down athwart on the ground, so that the wheels coming to go over them crush'd them all to pieces, which the assistants beholding, cried out aloud together, *My soul be with thine.* Presently whereupon nine or ten of the priests descending from the chariot took up these blessed, or rather accursed, creatures, that sacrificed themselves in this sort, and putting the head, bowels, and all the other members so crushed in pieces into great bowls made for that purpose, they shewed them to the people from the highest part of the chariot where the idol stood, saying with a pitifull voice, *Miserable sinners, fall ye to praying, that God may make you worthy to be a saint, as this here is, who hath now offered himself up as a sweet smelling sacrifice.* Whereunto all the people, prostrated on the ground, answered with a fearfull noise, *We hope that the God of a thousand Gods will permit it to be so.* In this manner many other of these poor wretches sacrificed themselves, to the number, as we were told by certain merchants worthy of credit, of six hundred and more. After these followed other martyrs of the devil, whom they called *Xixaporaus*, which sacrificed themselves before the said chariots, by most merci-lesly slashing themselves with sharp rasors, that to behold them how they did it, one could not think but that they were altogether insensible; for they cut off great gobbets of their flesh, and holding them on high at the end of arrows, as if they would shoot them up to heaven, they said, *That they made a present thereof to God for the souls of their fathers, of their wives, of their children, or of such an one, for whose sake they did this wicked' work.* Now wheresoever this gobbet of flesh chanced to fall, there ran so much people to catch it up, as oftentimes many were stifled in the press, for they held it as a very great relick. In this sort these miserable wretches stood upon their feet, all bathed in their own bloud, without noses, without ears, and without any resemblance at all of a man, untill at length they fell down stark dead on the earth; then came the *Grepos* in all haste down from the top of the chariot, and cutting off their heads, shewed them to all the people, who kneeling on the ground, and lifting up their hands to heaven, cried out with a loud voice, *Let us, O Lord, live to that time, wherein for thy service we may do as this same here hath done.* There were others also whom the devil drew thither after another manner. Those same craving an alms, said, *Give me an alms for Gods sake, or if thou dost it not, I will kill my self.* So that if they were not presently contented they would instantly cut their own throats with rasors which they held in their hands, or stab themselves into the belly, and so drop down stark dead, whereupon the *Grepos* ran suddenly to them, and having cut off their heads, shewed them, as before, to the people, who reverenced them prostrated on the ground.

Of the 15 days that this feast was to last, 9 being past, all the people, which were there assembled, feigning that the gluttonous serpent of the house of smoke (who is their *Lucifer,* as I have said elsewhere) was come for to steal away the ashes of them that were dead in these several sacrifices, and so to keep their souls from going into heaven, there arose among them so great and dreadfull a noise, as words are not able to express it; for to the confused voices that were heard from every part, there was adjoyned such a ringing of bells and basins, beating of drums, and winding of horns, as it was not possible to hear one another; and all this was done to fright away the devil. Now this noise endured from one of the clock in the afternoon till the next morning; and it is not to be believed what a world of lights and torches were spent that night, besides the infinite number of fires that were kindled every where; the reason hereof was, as they said, *For that* Tinagoogoo, *the God of thousand Gods, was in quest of the glut-*

*tonous serpent, for to kill him with a sword which had been
given him from heaven.* After the night had been past thus
amidst this infernal noise and tumult, assoon as it was day,
the whole hill, whereon the temple was built, appeared full of
white banners, which the people beholding, they fell straight
to giving thanks unto God, and to that end they prostrated
themselves on the ground with great demonstrations of joy,
and then began to send presents one to another, for the good
news they received from the priests by the shew of those white
banners, an assured sign that the gluttonous serpent was
killed. So all the people, transported with incredible gladness,
fell to going up the hill, whereon the temple stood, by four and
twenty several accesses that there were unto it, for to give
thanks unto the idol, and chaunt his praises, for the victory he
had the night past obtained over the gluttonous serpent, and
cutting off his head. This throng of people continued three
days, and three nights; so during that time it was not possible
to break through the press on the way, but with much pain.
Now we *Portugals* having little to do, resolved to go thither
also to see those abuses, wherefore we went to ask leave of the
embassadour, but he denied us for the present, willing us to
stay till the next day, and that then we should wait on him
thither, for in his last sickness he had vowed to visit it; hereat
we were very glad, because we thought that by this means we
should the more easily see all that we desired. The morrow
after, which was the third day of this assembly, the greatest
croud being over, we went along with him to the Temple of
*Tinagoogoo*, and at length arrived, though with much ado, at
the hill whereon it was built. There we saw six very fair long
streets, all full of scales hanging on great rods of brass. In
these scales a number of people weighed themselves, as well
for the accomplishment of the vows they had made in their
adversities and sickness, as for the remission of all the sins
they had committed till that present; and the weight which
each of them laid in the other scale was answerable to the
quality of the fault they had done. So they that found themselves culpable of gluttony, and had not all that year used any
abstinence, weighed themselves with honey, sugar, eggs, and
butter, which were things not displeasing to the priests, from

23

whom they were to receive absolution. They that were addicted to sensuality weighed themselves with cotton-wool, feathers, cloth, apparel, wine, and sweet odours; because, say they, those things incite a man to that sin. They that were uncharitable to the poor weighed themselves with coin of copper, tin, and silver, or with pieces of gold. The slothfull with wood, rice, coals, pork, and fruit; and the envious, because they reap no benefit by their maligning the prosperity of others, expiated their sin by confessing it publickly, and suffering a dozen boxes on the ear to be given them in the memory and praise of the twelve moons of the year. As for the sin of pride, it was satisfied with dried fish, brooms, and cow-dung, as being the basest of things. And touching them that had spoken ill of their neighbours, without asking them forgiveness, they put for that a cow into the scale, or else a hog, a sheep, or a stag; so that infinite was the number of those which weighed themselves in the scales that were in those six streets, from whom the priests received so much alms, as there were great piles of all sorts of things made up all along. Now for the poor that had nothing to give for the remission of their sins, they offered their own hair, which was presently cut off by above an hundred priests, who for that effect sate in order one by another on low stools, with sizzars in their hands. There also we saw great heaps of that hair, whereof other *Grepos*, which were a thousand at least, and ranked also in order, made wreathes, tresses, rings, and bracelets, which one or another bought for to carry home to their houses, even as our pilgrims use to do, that come from *Santiago de Compostella*, or other such places. Our embassadour, being amazed at the sight of these things, inquired further of the priests concerning them, who besides other particulars told him, that all those alms, and other offerings which were given there during the fifteen days of this assembly, amounted to a great revenue and that even of the hair of the poor alone there were raised every year above an hundred thousand *Pardanis* of gold, which are fourscore and ten thousand ducates of our money; whereby one may judge what a world of wealth was made of all the rest. After that the embassadour had staid some time in the streets of the scales, he passed on through all the other

quarters, where were comedies, dancing, wrestling, and excellent consorts of all kinds of musick, till at length we arrived
at *Tinagoogoo*, but with much labour and pain, because the
throng was so great, as none could hardly break through it.
This temple had but one isle, that was very long and spacious,
and full of great wax lights, each of them having ten or eleven
wicks in it, set up all about in silver candlesticks; there was
also great store of perfumes of aloes and benjamin. As for the
image of *Tinagoogoo*, it was placed in the midst of the temple
upon a stately tribunal, in the form of an altar, environed
with a number of silver candlesticks, and a many of children,
attired in purple, which did nothing but cense it at the sound
of instruments of musick, whereon the priests played reasonable well. Before this idol danced, to the tune of the said
instrument, certain ladies, which were wonderfull fair, and
richly clad, to whom the people presented their alms and
offerings, which the priests received for them, and then laid
them before the tribunal of the idol with a great deal of ceremony and complement, ever and anon prostrating themselves
on the ground. The statue of this monster was seven and
twenty spans high, having the face of a giant, the hair of a
negro, wide distorted nostrils, mighty great lips, and a very
sowre and ill-favoured countenance. He had in his hand an
hatchet in the form of a cooper's addis, but with a far longer
handle. With this addis, as the priests made the people
believe, *this monster the night before killed the gluttonous
serpent of the house of smoke, for that he would have stoln away
the ashes of those that sacrificed themselves.* There also we
saw the serpent amidst the place before the tribunal in the
form of an adder, more horrible to behold then the wit of man
can imagine, and done so to the life, as all that looked on it
trembled for fear. It was laid all along, with the head cut off,
being eight fathom long, and the neck of it as thick as a
bushel, so lively represented, that though we knew it to be an
artificial thing, yet could we not chuse but be afraid of it.
In the mean time all the assistants ran thronging about it,
some pricking it with the points of their halberds, and some
with their daggers, every one with railing speeches, cursing
and calling it, *Proud, presumptuous, accursed, infernal monster,*

*pool of damnation, envious against God's goodness, hunger-starved dragon, in the midst of the night,* and many other names, which they delivered in such extraordinary terms, and so fitted to the effects of this serpent, as we could not but admire them. That done, they put into basins which stood at the foot of the idols tribunal a world of alms, of gold, silver, jewels, pieces of silk, fine callicoes, money, and a hundred other things in very great abundance. After we had seen all these things, we continued following the embassadour, who went to see the grots of the hermits or penitents, which were at the utmost end of the wood, all cut out of the hard rock, and in such order, as one would have thought that nature, rather then the hand of man, had laboured in it. There were an hundred forty and two of them, in some of the which remained divers men, whom they held for saints, and that did very great and austere penance. They in the first grots wore long robes like the *Bonzes* of *Japan,* and followed the law of an idol, that had sometimes been a man, called *Situmpor Michay,* who during his life enjoyned those of his sect to lead their lives in great austerity, assuring them that the onely and true way to gain heaven, was to subdue the flesh, and that the more they laboured to afflict themselves, the more liberally God would grant them all they could demand of him. They which accompanied us thither, told us, that they seldom eat any thing but herbs boiled, a few beans of *Aricot* rosted, and wilde fruit, which were provided for them by other priests, who as the purveyors of a cloister took care to furnish these penitents with such things as were conformable to the law whereof they made profession. After these we saw in a grot others of a sect of one of their saints, or rather of a devil, named *Angemacur*; these lived in deep holes, made in the midst of the rock, according to the rule of their wretched order, eating nothing but flies, ants, scorpions, and spiders, with the juice of a certain herb growing in abundance thereabouts, much like to sorrel. These spent their time in meditating day and night, with their eyes lifted up to heaven, and their hands closed one within another, for a testimony that they desired nothing of this world, and in that manner died like beasts; but they are accounted greater saints then all the rest, and as such, after they are dead, they burn them in fires, whereinto they cast great quantities of most precious perfumes. The funeral pomp being celebrated with great state, and very rich offerings, they have sumptuous temples erected unto them, thereby to draw the living to do as they had done, for to obtain this vain-glory, which is all the recompense that the world gives them for their excessive penance. We likewise saw others of a sect altogether diabolical, invented by a certain *Gileu Mitray*. These have sundry orders of penance, and are not much different in their opinions from the *Abissins* of *Ethiopia*. Now that their abstinence may be the more agreeable to their idol, some of them eat nothing but bitter fruits and herbs brought to them from the wood, by reason whereof they live but a short time, and have so bad a look and colour, as they fright those that behold them. I will pass by them of the sect of *Godomem*, who spend their whole life in crying day and night on those mountains, *Godomem, Godomem*, and desist not from it untill they fall down stark dead to the ground for want of breath. Neither will I speak of them which they call *Taxilacons*, who die more brutishly then the rest; for they shut themselves up in certain grots made of purpose for it, that are very little and close, stopped on all sides, and then burning green thistles and thorns in them, they choke themselves with the smoke thereof. Whereby one may see how by such rude and different ways of living these miserable creatures render themselves the devil's martyrs, who in reward thereof gives them everlasting hell-fire; and verily it is a pitifull thing to behold the great pains which these wretches take to lose themselves, and the little that we do to be saved.

---

## CHAPTER XLVIII.

What we saw in the continuing of our voyage, until we arrived at the city of Timplan.

AFTER we had seen all these things with wonder enough, we departed from this *Pagode* of *Tinagoogoo*, and continued on our way for thirteen days together, at the end whereof we arrived at two great towns, scituated on the bank of the river, just opposite the one against the other, about the distance of a stones cast, one of the which was called *Manavedea*, and the other *Singilapau*. In the midst of this same river, which was there somewhat narrow, there was an island by nature formed round, and in it a rock six and thirty fathom high, and a cross-bow shot broad ; upon this rock was a fort built, with nine bulwarks and five towers ; without the rampire of the wall it was invironed with two rows of great iron gates, and from the bulwarks to the other side of the river ran a huge chain of iron, to keep vessels from passing along, so that nothing could possibly enter there. At one of these two towns, which was called *Singilapau*, the ambassadour landed, where he was exceedingly well entertained by the *Xemimbrum*, or governour of it, who likewise furnished all his train with great store of refreshments. The next morning we left this place, accompanied with twenty *Laules*, wherein there were a thousand men and better, and about evening we arrived at the customhouses of the kingdom, which are two strong places, and from the one to the other run five mighty great chains of latten all athwart the whole breadth of the river, so that nothing can pass in and out without leave. Hither came a man in a swift *Seroo* to the ambassadour, and told him that he was to go ashore at *Campalagro*, which was one of the two castles on the southside, for to shew the letter which this king had sent by him to the *Calaminham*, to see if it were written in the form that was required in speaking to him, as was usually observed. The ambassadour presently obeyed, and being come to land he was lead into a great hall, where were three men set at a table, with a great many gentlemen, who gave him good entertainment, and demanded of him the occasion of his coming thither, as they that knew nothing of it. Whereunto the ambassadour answered ; *That he came thither from the King of* Bramaa, *Lord of* Tanguu, *and that he had a message to deliver unto the holy* Calaminham *concerning matters greatly importing his estate.* Then having made further answer to other questions, which were put to him in a way of ceremony by the three principal persons that were at the table, he showed them the letter, wherein they corrected some words, which were not of the style wherewith they were accustomed to speak to the *Cala-minham*; together with this letter the ambassadour shewed them the present which he had brought for him, whereat they very much wondred, especially when they saw the chair for an elephant of gold and precious stones, which in the judge-ment of divers lapidaries was worth above six hundred thou-sand ducates, besides the other rich pieces that he carried him also, as I have before related. After we had our dispatch from this first custom-house, we went to the other, where we found more venerable men then the former, who with another new ceremony looked likewise on the letter, and the present, and put to all the several parcels of it strings of wreathed carnation silk,* with three seals in lacre, which was as the conclusion of the receiving of the ambassy by the *Calaminham.* The same day there came a man from the next town of *Queitor,* sent by the governour of the kingdom to visit the ambassadour with a present of refreshments of flesh, fruit, and other such things after their manner. During nine days that the ambas-sadour stayed in this place he was abundantly furnished with all things necessary, both for his own person, and his train, and withal was entertained with sundry sports of hunting and fishing, as also with feasts, accompained with musick and comedies represented by very beautiful women, and richly attired. In the mean time we *Portugals* went, with the permission of the ambassadour, to see certain things which they of the country had much commended unto us, namely very antique buildings, rich and sumptuous temples, very fair gardens, houses and castles that were all along the side of this river, made after a strange fashion, well fortified, and of great charge, amongst the which there was an hospital for to lodge pilgrims in called *Manicafaran,* signifying in our tongue, *The Prison of the Gods,* which was above a league in breadth. Here we saw twelve streets, all vaulted over, and in every one of them two hundred and forty houses, namely, sixscore on each side, which made in all two thousand, eight hundred, and fourscore, all full of pilgrims, who the whole year through came thither in pilgrimage from divers countries; for, as they hold, this pilgrimage ought to be of far greater

---

* The first mention in history of red-tape?

merit then all others, because that these idols imprisoned by strangers have need of company. All these pilgrims, which, as they of the country say, are all the year long without discontinuing above six thousand, have meat given them the whole time of their abode there, at the charge, and out of the revenue of the house. They are served by four thousand priests of *Manicafaran*, who with many others reside within the same inclosure in sixscore religious houses, where there are also as many women that serve in like manner. The temple of this hospital was very great, with three isles after the fashion of ours, in the midst whereof was a remarkable chappel built round, and invironed with three very big ballisters of latten; within it there were fourscore idols of men and women, besides many other little gods, that lay prostrated on the ground; for the forescore great idols onely stood upright, and were all tied together with chains of iron. As for the little ones, they were, as I said, laid along on the pavement, as the children of these greater, and tied six to six by the middle with other sleighter chains. Moreover without the ballisters in two files there stood two hundred, forty and four, giants of brass, six and twenty spans high, with their halberds and clubs upon their shoulders, as if they had been set there for the guard of the captive gods. There was over-head upon iron rods, that traversed the isles of the temple, great store of lamps hanging, having seven or eight matches apiece in them, in the fashion of candlesticks, like to them of the *Indiaes*, all varnished without, as also the walls were, and every thing else that we saw there, in token of mourning, by reason of the captivity of these gods. Being amazed as well at that which I have recounted, as at many other things which I pass over in silence, and not able to comprehend what they meant by the imprisonment of these gods, we demanded the signification of it of the priests, whereunto one amongst them, that seemed of more authority then the rest, made us this answer. *Since I see that being strangers you desire to learn of me that which I know very well, and which you have never heard spoken, nor read of in your books, I will declare the matter unto you as it past, according as it is truly delivered by our histories. Know then, that it is now seven thousand, three hundred, and twenty moons, which make six hundred and ten years, after the supputation of other nations, since the time that an holy Cala-minham, named* Xixivarem Melentay, *commanding over the monarchy of the six and twenty kingdoms of this crown, waged wars with the* Siamon, *Emperour of the Mountains of the Earth insomuch that there assembled, what on the one part and the other, threescore and two kings, who putting themselves into field, fought so cruel and bloody a battel, as it endured from an hour before day till night, and there was slain on both sides sixteen* Laquesaas *of men, each of which makes an hundred thousand. At length the victory remaining to our* Calaminham, *without any more resting alive of his forces then two hundred and thirty thousand, he ruined in four moneths space all the enemies countries, with such a destruction of people, as (if credit may be given our histories, or to what any other besides have assured) there died fifty* Laquesaas *of persons. This battel was fought in the first of the said seven thousand, three hundred, and twenty moons, in the renowned field* Vitau, *where* Quiay Nivandel *appeared to the* Calaminham, *sitting in a chair of wood, who acquired unto himself in this place a greater and more famous title of honour, then all the other gods of the* Mons *and* Siammes; *in regard whereof so often as they that inhabit the earth desire to make oath of things which pass the belief of men, they use for the more authorizing thereof to swear by the holy* Quiay Nivandel, God of Battels of the field *Vitau. Now in a great city named* Sarocatam, *where five hundred thousand persons were slain, all these gods, which here you see before you, were made prisoners in despight of the kings that believed in them, and the priests that served them with the perfumes in their sacrifices. Thus by reason of so glorious a victory all those people become subject to us, and tributaries to the crown of the* Calaminham, *who at this day holds the scepter of this monarchy, whereunto he was not raised but with much labour, and the shedding of a world of blood, during the threescore and four rebellions made by the said people since that time until this present; who not able to endure the captivity of their gods, for that, to say the truth, is a mighty affront unto them, they do still in memory of so unhappy a success continue making great demon-strations of sorrow for it, renewing every year the vow they have made not to celebrate any feast, nor to rejoyce in any kind of sort whatsoever, until they have provided for the deliverance of these prisoners ; which also is the cause that no lamps are seen in their temples, and that they are resolved to light up none during the captivity of their idols.* Some of us seeming to doubt the verity hereof, because it seemed strange unto them, the *Grepo* swore that it was most true, and that also there had been killed at sundry times, about the deliverance of these Gods, whom there we saw captive, above three millions of men, besides those that fell in precedent battels ; whereby one may clearly see in what a strange manner the devil keeps these poor blinded wretches subjected unto him, and with how much abuse and extravagancy he precipitates them into hell. When we had well observed all the singularities of this temple, we went to see another, called *Urpanesendoo* ; to speak of which I desire to be excused, that I may not be forced to treat of infamous and abominable matters ; wherefore omitting the great abundance of riches, and other things which we saw there ; it shall suffice me to say, that this temple is served by none but women, who are all of them the daughters of princes, and of the principal lords of the kingdom, which dedicate them from their infancy to offer up their honour in sacrifice there. Now this filthy and sensual sacrifice is performed with so great charge, that many of them bestow above ten thousand ducats in it, besides the offerings which are made to this idol *Urpanesendoo*, to whom they sacrifice their honour. This idol is in a chappel that is round, and gilt all over ; it is made of silver, and set upon a tribunal in form of an altar, environed over-head with a great number of candlesticks, which are all of silver likewise, every light in them having six wicks. Round about this tribunal are many other idols gilded over, of very comely and well-favoured women, who with their knees on the ground, and hands lifted up, adore this idol. These same, as the priests told us, are the holy souls of certain young ladies, which finished their days there to the great honour of their parents, who made more esteem of that then of all the King could give them. They assured us, that the revenue belonging to the idol was three hundred thousand ducates by the year, besides the offerings and rich

ornaments of their abominable sacrifices, which was yet
worth more. In this diabolical temple were shut up within
many religious houses that we saw above five thousand women,
being all of them old, and for the most part exceeding rich ;
so that coming to die, they make a donation of all their
wealth to the *Pagode* ; wherefore it is no marvel, if it have
the revenue I spoke of. From this place we went to see the
companies of strangers, which came thither in pilgrimage in
the manner that I have declared. These companies were forty
and six in number, every one of an hundred, 200, 300, 400,
or 500 persons ; nay, some of them were more, and were all
lodged along by the river, as if it had been a camp. Amidst
these troops of strangers we met by chance with a *Portugal*
woman, whereat we wondred more then at all we had seen
before ; so that desiring to know of her the reason of so
strange an accident, she told us, with tears, who she was,
what occasion had brought her thither, and how she was at
that instant the wife of one of those pilgrims, to whom she
had been married three or four and twenty years ; whereunto
she further added, that not daring to go and live amongst
Christians, because of her sin, she continued still in her
wickedness, but that she hoped God would at length be pleased
to bring her into some country, where before she ended her
days, she might repent her of her life past ; and that although
we found her in the company of people devoted to the service
of the devil, yet she left not for all that to be still a true
Christian ; we remained much amazed at so strange a relation,
and not a little sorrowfull also to see and understand to what
a point of misfortune this poor woman was reduced, so that
we told her our opinion, and what we thought was fit for her
to do ; whereupon she concluded to go along with us to
*Timplam*, and so to *Pegu*, and from thence to set sail for
*Coromandel*, there to finish her days in the island of *St. Tomé*.
Having vowed unto us to do thus we quitted her, not doubting
that she would lose so good an opportunity to retire her self
out of the errours wherein she was, and to restore her self to
an estate wherein she might be saved, since it had pleased
God to permit her to meet with us in a country so far distant
from that which she could hope for. Howbeit she performed

nothing, for we could never see nor hear of her afterwards, which made us to believe, that either something had befallen her that kept her from coming to us ; or that through the obstinacy of her sins, she deserved not to make her profit of the grace which our Lord had offered to her out of His infinite goodness and mercy.

---

## CHAPTER XLIX.

The magnificent reception of the King of Bramaa his Ambassadour, at the city of Timplam.

NINE days after the King of *Bramaa* his ambassadour had reposed himself there by way of ceremony, according to the fashion of the country, for the more honour of his ambassage, one of the governours of the city, called *Campanogrem*, came to fetch him, accompanied with fourscore *Seroos* and *Laulees*, very well equipped, and full of lusty able men. Throughout this fleet they played on so many barbarous and ill accorded instruments, as bells, 'cymbals, drums, and sea-cornets, that the din thereof coming to joyn with the noise which the rowers made, terrified all those that heard it ; and indeed one would have thought it at first to be some inchantment, or to say better, a musick of hell, if there be any there. Amidst this stir we drew near to the city, where we arrived about noon.  Being come to the first key, that was named *Campalarraia*, we saw a great many men, both horse and foot, all richly accoutred, as also a number of fighting elephants, very well furnished, having their chairs and fore-head pieces garnished with silver, and their warlike *Panores* fastened to their teeth, which rendered them very terrible.  The ambassadour was no sooner come on shore, but the *Campanogrem* took him by the hand, and falling on his knees presented him to another great man that attended for him at the key in great pomp.  This same was called *Patedacan*, one of the chiefest of the kingdom, as we were told.  After he had with a new complement of courtesie received the ambassadour, he offered him an elephant furnished with a chair and harness of gold ;

but whatsoever the *Mandarin* could do to make the ambassadour accept of it, he could by no means draw him thereunto;
whereupon he caused another almost as well furnished to be
brought, and gave it to him.    As for us nine *Portugals*, and
fifty or threescore *Bramaas*, they provided horses, on which
we mounted.    In this manner we departed from that place,
having his chariots before us full of men, that amidst the
acclamations of the people played upon divers kindes of
instruments; namely, on silver cymbals, bells, and drums.
Thus we were conducted through many long streets, whereof
nine were environed with ballisters of lattin, and at the
entrance into them, there were arches very richly wrought, as
also many chapiters of pillars gilt, and great bells, which like
unto clocks, struck the hours, nay, the quarters of the hour of
the day, whereby the people were ordinarily directed.    After
that with much ado, by reason of the great press of people
that was in the streets, we were come to the outward court of
the *Calaminhan's* palace, which was as long, or little less, as
a faulcons shot, and broad proportionably thereunto, we saw
in it above six thousand horses, all trapped with silver and
silk, and those that were mounted on them were armed with
corslets of lattin and copper, head-pieces of silver, carrying
ensigns in their hands of divers colours, and targets at their
saddle-bows.    The commander of these troops was the *Quietor*
of Justice, who is as the superintendent over all the other civil
and criminal ministers, which is a jurisdiction separate by it
self, from whence there is no appeal.    The ambassadour being
come near unto him, who was also advanced to receive him,
and the two governours, they all prostrated themselves on the
ground three times, which is amongst them a new kinde of
complement, whereupon the *Quietor* spake not a word to the
ambassadour, but onely laid his hand on his head, and then
gave him a rich scymitar that he wore by his side, which the
ambassadour accepted of very thankfully, and kissed it thrice.
That done the *Quietor* set the ambassadour on his right hand,
and leaving the two *Mandarins* a little behinde, they passed
along through two rows of elephants, which made a kinde of
a street of the length of the outward court, they being fifteen
hundred in number, all furnished with castles, and rich chairs

of divers inventions, as also with a great many of silk banners, and gorgeous coverings; round about were a great company of halberdiers, and many other shews of greatness and majesty, which made us believe that this prince was one of the mightiest in the country. When we were come to a great gate, that stood between two high towers, two hundred men which guarded it no sooner saw the *Quietor*, but they all fell down on their knees. Through this gate, we entered into another very long outward court, where the Kings second guard was, composed of a thousand men, who were all in gilt arms, their swords by their sides, and on their heads helmets wrought with gold and silver, wherein stuck gallant plumes of several colours. After we had past through the middle of all this guard we arrived at a great hall, where there was a *Mandarin*, uncle to the king, called the *Monvagaruu*, a man of above seventy years of age, accompanied with a great number of nobility, as also with many captains and officers of the kingdom. About him were twelve little boys richly clad, with great chains of gold three or four times double about their necks, and each of them a silver mace upon his shoulder. Assoon as the ambassadour was come near him, he touched him on the head with a *Ventiloe* that he held in his hand, and beholding him, *May thy entrance*, said he, *into this palace of the Lord of the World be as agreeable to his eyes, as the rain is to our field of rice, for so shall he grant thee all that thy King demands of him.* From thence we went up an high pair of stairs, and entered into a very long room, wherein there were many great lords, who seeing the *Monvagaruu* stood up on their feet, as acknowledging him for their superior. Out of this room we entered into another, where there were 4 altars, very well accommodated with idols of silver; upon one of these altars we saw the statue of a woman as big as a giant, being eighteen spans high, and with her arms all abroad looking up to heaven. This idol was of silver, and her hair of gold, which was very long, and spread over her shoulders. There also we saw a great throne, encompassed round about with thirty giants of brass, who had gilded clubs upon their shoulders, and faces as deformed as those they paint for the devil. From this room we passed into a manner of a gallery,

adorned from the top to the bottom with a number of little
tables of ebony, inlayed with ivory, and full of mens heads,
under every one of the which the name of him to whom it
belonged was written in letters of gold. At the end of this
gallery there were a dozen of iron rods gilt, whereon hung a
great many silver candlesticks of great value, and a number
of perfuming pans, from whence breathed forth a most excellent odour of *amber*, and *calambuco*, or *lignum aloes*, but
such as we have none in *Christendom*. There on an altar
environed all about with three rows of ballisters of silver, we
saw thirteen kings visages of the same metall, with golden
mitres upon their heads, and under each of them a dead mans
head, and below many candlesticks of silver, with great white
wax lights in them, which were snuffed ever and anon by little
boys, who accorded their voices to those of the *Grepos* that
sung in form of a letany, answering one another. The *Grepos*
told us that those thirteen dead mens heads which were under
the visages were the skulls of thirteen *Calaminhans*, which in
times past gained this empire from certain strangers, called
*Roparons*, who by arms had usurped the same upon them of
the country. As for the other dead mens heads which we saw
there, they were the skulls of such commanders as by their
heroic deeds had honourably ended their days in helping to
recover this empire, in regard whereof it was most reasonable,
that though death had deprived them of the recompence which
they had merited by their action, yet their memory should not
be abolished out of the world. When we were gone out of the
gallery, we proceeded on upon a great bridge, that was in the
form of a street, railed on either sides with ballisters of
lattin, and beautified with a many of arches curiously
wrought, upon which were scutcheons of arms, charged with
several devices of gold, and the crest over them were silver
globes, five spans in circumference, all very stately and majestical to behold. At the end of this bridge was another building, the doors whereof we found shut, whereupon we knocked
4 times, they within not deigning to answer us, which is a
ceremony observed by them in such occasions. At the length
after we had rung a bell 4 times more, as it were in haste, out
comes a woman of about 50 years of age, accompanied with 6

little girls, richly attired, and scymitars upon their shoulders garnished with flowers wrought in gold. This ancient woman having demanded of the *Monvagaruu* why he had rung the bell, and what he would have, he answered her with a great deal of respect, *That he had there an ambassadour from the King of* Bramaa, *the Lord of* Tanguu, *who was come thither to treat at the feet of the* Calaminhan *about certain matters much importing his service*. By reason of the great authority which this woman was in she seemed little to regard this answer, whereat we wondred much, because he that spake to her was one of the chiefest lords of the kingdom, and uncle to the *Calaminhan*, as it was said. Nevertheless one of the 6 girls that accompanied her, spake thus in her behalf to the *Monvagaruu*, *My Lord, may it please your greatness, to have a little patience till we may know whether the time be fit for the kissing of the foot of the throne of this Lord of the World, and advertising him of the coming of this stranger, and so according to the grace which our Lord will shew him therein, his heart may rejoyce, and we with him*. That said, the door was shut again for the space of three or four *Credo's*, and then the six girls came and opened it, but the ancient woman that at first came along with them we saw no more; howbeit instead of her there came a boy of about nine years of age, richly apparelled, and having on his head an *Hurfangua* of gold, which is a kinde of mitre -(but that it is somewhat more closed all about, and without any overture) he had also a mace of gold, much like a sceptre, which he carried upon his shoulder; this same, without making much reckoning of the *Monvagaruu*, or of any of the other lords there present, took the embassadour by the hand, and said unto him, *The news of thy arrival is come unto the feet of* Binaigaa *the* Calaminhan, *and sceptre of the kings that govern the earth, and is so agreeable to his ears, that with a smiling look he now sends for thee to give thee audience concerning that which is desired of him by the King, whom he newly receives into the number of his brethren, with the love of the son of his entrals, that so he may remain powerfull and victorious over his enemies*. Thereupon he caused him, together with the Kings uncle, and the other governours that accompanied him, to come in, leaving all the rest without; the embassadour then

seeing none of his train follow him, looked three or four times
back, seeming by his countenance to be somewhat discontented, which the *Monvagaruu* perceiving, spake to the *Quietor*,
who was a little behinde, that he should cause the strangers to
be let in, and none else; the doors being then opened again,
we *Portugals* began to go in with the *Bramaas*; but such a
number of others came thrusting in amongst us, as the
gentlemen ushers who were above twenty, had much ado to
keep the doors, striking many with battoons which they had
in their hands, and (of those) some that were persons of
quality, and yet could they not therewith, neither with their
cries, nor menaces, stop them all from entering. Thus being
come in, we past along through the midst of a great garden,
made with such art, and where appeared so many goodly
things, so divers, and so pleasing to the eye, as words are not
able to express them. For there were there many alleys
environed with ballisters of silver, and many arbors of extraordinary scent, which we were told had so much sympathy
with the moons of the year, that in all seasons whatsoever
they bare flowers and fruits; withall there was such abundance
and variety of roses and other flowers, as almost passeth
belief. In the midst of this garden we saw a great many
young women, very fair, and well clad, whereof some past
away their time in dancing, and others in playing on sundry
sorts of instruments much after our manner, which they performed with so much harmony, as we were not a little delighted
therewith: some also bestowed themselves in making of
curious needle-works and gold-strings, some in other things,
whilest their companions gathered fruit to eat; and all this
was done so quietly, and with such order and good behaviour,
as made us admire it. At our going out of this garden, where
the *Monvagaruu* would needs have the embassadour to stay a
while, that he might there observe something worthy to entertain his king with at his return to *Pegu*, we went into a very
great antichamber, where many commanders and lords were
sitting, as also some great princes, who received the embassadour with new ceremonies, and complements, and yet not one
of them stirred from his place. Through this antichamber
we came to a door, where there were six gentlemen ushers

24

with silver maces, by which we entered into another room
very richly furnished : in this was the *Calaminhan* seated on
a most majestical throne, encompassed with three rows of
ballisters of silver. At the foot of the degrees of his throne
sate twelve women that were exceeding beautifull, and most
richly apparelled, playing on divers sorts of instruments,
whereunto they accorded their voices. On the top of the
throne, and not far from his person, were twelve young damsels
about nine or ten years old, all of them on their knees round
about him, and carrying maces of gold in the fashion of
sceptres; amongst them there was also another that stood on
her feet and fanned him. Below, all along the whole length
of the room, were a great many of old men, wearing mitres
of gold on their heads, and long robes of sattin and damask,
curiously embroidered, every one having silver maces on their
shoulders, and ranked in order on either side against the walls.
Over all the rest of the room were sitting, upon rich *Persian*
carpets, about two hundred young ladies, as we could guess,
that were wonderfull fair, and exceeding well-favoured. Thus
did this room, both for the marvellous structure of it, and for
the excellent order that was observed therein, represent so
great and extraordinary a majesty, as we heard the embassadour say afterwards, talking of it, that if God would grant
him the grace to return to *Pegu*, he would never speak of it
to the King, as well for fear of grieving him, as of being
taken for a man that reports things which seem altogether
incredible.

Assoon as the embassadour was entered into the room
where the *Calaminhan* was, accompanied with the four princes
that conducted him, he prostrated himself five times on the
ground, without so much as daring to behold the *Calaminhan*,
in sign of the great respect he carried towards him, which the
*Monvagaruu* perceiving, willed him to advance forward; so
that being arrived near to the first degree of his throne, with
his face still bending downward, he said to the *Calaminhan*,
with so loud a voice as every one might hear him; *The clouds
of the air, which recreate the fruits whereof we eat, have published over the whole monarchy of the world the great majesty of
thy power, which hath caused my King, desiring to be honoured*

*with thy amity, as with a rich pearl, to send me for that purpose,
and to tell thee from him, that thou shalt much oblige him, if
thou pleasest to accept of him for thy brother, with the honourable obedience which he will always render to thee, as to him
that is the elder, as thou art. And for that end it is, that he
sends thee this letter, which is the jewel of all his treasure that
he prizes most, and wherein his eyes take more pleasure, for the
honour and contentment they receive by it, then being lord of the
kings of* Avaa, *and of all the precious stones of the mountain of*
Falent, *of* Jatir, *and* Pontau. Hereunto the *Calaminhan* made
him this answer following, and that with a grave and severe
countenance; *For my part, I accept of this new amity, thereby
to give full satisfaction to thy king, as to a son newly born of my
intrals.* Then began the women to play on instruments of
musick, and six of them danced with little children for the
space of three or four *Credo's.* After that, other six little girls
danced with six of the oldest men that were in the room,
which seemed to us a very pretty fantasticalness. This dance
ended, there was a very fine comedy represented by twelve
ladies, exceeding beautifull, and gorgeously attired, wherein
appeared on the stage a great sea-monster, holding in his
mouth the daughter of a king, whom the fish swallowed up
before them all, which the twelve ladies seeing went in all
haste weeping to an hermitage that was at the foot of a
mountain, from whence they returned with an hermit, who
made earnest supplications to *Quiay Patureu,* God of the Sea,
that he would bring this monster to the shore, so as they
might come to bury the damsel according to her quality. The
hermit was answered by *Quiay Patureu,* that the twelve ladies
should change their lamentations and complaints into so many
consorts of musick, that were agreeable to his ears, and he
would then command the sea to cast the fish upon the strand
to be done withall as they thought good; whereupon comes on
the stage six little boys with wings and crowns of gold upon
their heads, in the same manner as we use to paint angels, and
naked all over, who falling on their knees before the ladies,
presented them with three harps and three viols, saying, that
*Quiay Patureu* sent them these instruments from the heaven
of the moon, therewith to cast the monster of the sea into a

sleep, that so they might have their desire on him; whereupon
the twelve ladies took them out of the hands of the little boys,
and began to play upon them, tuning them unto their voices
with so lamentable and sad a tone, and such abundance of
tears, that it drew some from the eyes of divers lords that
were in the room.   Having continued their musick about half
a quarter of an hour, they saw the monster coming out of the
sea, and by little and little as it were astonished, making to
the shore where these fair musicians were; all which was
performed so properly, and to the life, that the assistants could
hardly imagine it to be a fable, and a matter devised for pleasure, but a very truth, besides the scene was set forth with a
world of state and riches.   Then one of the twelve ladies
drawing out a poniard, all set with precious stones, which she
wore by her side, ripped up the fish, and out of the belly of it
drew the *Infanta* alive, which presently went and danced to
the tune of their instruments, and so went and kissed the
*Calaminhan's* hand, who received her very graciously, and
made her sit down by him.   It was said that this young lady
was his niece, the daughter of a brother of his; as for the
other twelve, they were all the daughters of princes, and of
the greatest lords of the country, whose fathers and brothers
were there present.   There were also three or four comedies
more like this, acted by other young ladies of great quality,
and set forth with so much pomp and magnificence, as more
could not be desired.   About evening the *Calaminhan* retired
into another room, accompanied with women onely; for all
the rest they went along with the *Monvagaruu*, who took the
embassadour by the hand, and led him back to the outermost
room of all, where with many complements, after their manner,
he took his leave of him, and so committed him to the *Queitor*,
who straightway carried him to his house, where he lodged all
the while that he was there, being two and thirty days, during
which time he was feasted by the principal lords of the court,
in a splendid and sumptuous manner, and continually entertained with several sports of fishing, hunting, hawking, and
other such like recreations.

[*Here follows a discourse on the Christian religion between a
priest and the Portuguese, omitted.*]

## CHAPTER L.

An ample relation of the empire of the Calaminham, and of the kingdoms of Pegu, and Bramaa, with the continuance of our voyage, and what we saw among the same.

A MONETH after our arrival at this city of *Timplan,* where the court then was, the ambassador demanded an answer to his ambassie, and it was immediately granted him by the *Calaminham,* with whom he spake himself, and being graciously entertained by him, he referred him for his dispatch to the *Monvagaruu,* that was, as I have heretofore delivered, the chief man in governing the kingdom, who gave him an answer on the behalf of the *Calaminham,* as also a present.in exchange of that which the King of *Bramaa* had sent him, withal he wrote him a letter [*entering into the proposed alliance with him*]. The ambassador having received this letter, departed from the court the 3rd of November, 1546, accompanied with certain lords, who by the express commandment of the *Calaminham* went along with him to *Bidor,* where they took their leave of him, after they had made him a great feast, and presented him with divers gifts. But before I entreat of the way which we held from this place till we came to *Pegu,* where the King of *Bramaa* was, I think it convenient and necessary to make a relation here of certain things which we saw in this country, wherein I will acquit my self as succinctly as I can, as I have done in all other matters whereof I have spoken heretofore ; for if I should discourse in particular of all that I have seen, and of that which hath past as well in this empire, as in other kingdoms, where I have been during my painful voyages, I had then need to make another volume far bigger then this same, and be indued with a wit much above that I have : howbeit that I may not wholly conceal things so remarkable, I am contented to say so much thereof as my gross stile will permit me to deliver. The kingdom of *Pegu* hath in circuit an hundred and forty leagues, is scituate on the south side in sixteen degrees, and in the heart of the country towards the rhomb of the east it hath an hundred and forty leagues, being invironed all above with a high ground, named

*Pangavirau*, where the nation of the *Bramaas* doth inhabit, whose country is fourscore leagues broad, and two hundred long. This monarchy was in times past one sole kingdom, which now it is not, but is divided into thirteen estates of sovereigns, who made themselves masters of it by poysoning their king in a banquet which they made him in the city of *Chaleu*, as their histories relate: of these thirteen estates, there are eleven that are commanded by other nations, who by a tract of another great country are joyned to all the bounds of the *Bramaas*, where two great emperors abide, of which the one is called the *Siamon*, and the other the *Calaminham*, who is the same I purpose onely to treat of. According to report, the empire of the prince is above three hundred leagues breadth, and as much in length, and it is said that anciently it contained seven and twenty kingdoms, the inhabitants whereof spake all one language: within this empire we saw many goodly cities, exceedingly well peopled, and abounding with all provisions necessary for mans life, as flesh, fresh water, fish, corn, pulse, rice, pastures, vines, and fruits; the chief of all these cities is *Timplan*, where this emperor, the *Calaminham*, with his court commonly resides: it is seated along by a great river, named *Pituy*, and invironed all about with two broad walls of earth, made up with strong stone on either side, having very broad ditches, and at each gate a castle with high towers. Certain merchants affirmed unto us, that this city had within it some four hundred thousand fires; and albeit the houses are for the most part not above two stories high, yet in recompence thereof they are built very stately, and with great charge, especially those of the nobility, and of the merchants, not speaking of the great lords, which are separated by great inclosures, where are spacious outward courts, and at the entring into them arches after the manner of *China*, as also gardens, and walks planted with trees, and great ponds, all very handsomely accommodated to the plea-sures and delights of this life, whereunto these people are very much inclined. We were also certified, that both within the inclosure of the city, and a league about it, there were six and twenty hundred *Pagodes*, some of which, wherein we had been, were very sumptuous and rich; indeed (for the rest) the most

of them were but petty houses in the fashion of hermitages.
These people follow four and twenty sects, all different one
from another, amongst the which there is so great a confusion
of errors, and diabolical precepts, principally in that which
concerns their bloody sacrifices, as I abhor to speak of them;
but the idol which is most in vogue amongst them, and most
frequented, is that whereof I have already made mention,
called *Quiay Frigau*, that is to say, *The God of the Moats of
the Sun*; for it is in this false god that the *Calaminham*
believes, and does adore him, and so do all the chiefest lords
of the kingdom, wherefore the *Grepos, Menigrepos,* and *Talagrepos* of this false god, are honored far more then all others,
and held in the reputation of holy personages; their superiours,
who by an eminent title are called *Cabizondos,* never know
women, as they say; but to content their bructish and sensual
appetites they want not diabolical inventions, which are more
worthy of tears then recital. During the ordinary fairs of this
city, called by them *Chanduhos,* we saw all things there that
nature hath created, as iron, steel, lead, tin, copper, lattin,
salt-peter, brimstone, oyl, vermillion, honey, wax, sugar, lacre,
benjamin, divers sorts of stuffes and garments of silk, pepper,
ginger, cinamon, linnen cloth, cotton wool, alum, borax, corna-
lines, cristal, camphire, musk, ivory, cassia, rhubarbe, turbith,
scamony, azure, woad, incense, cochenel, saffron, myrrhe, rich
porcelain, gold, silver, rubies, diamonds, emeraulds, saphirs,
and generally all other kind of things that can be named, and
that in so great abundance, as it is not possible for me to speak
that which I have seen, and be believed; women there are
ordinarily very white and fair, but that which most commends
them is, that they are of a good nature, chast, charitable, and
much inclined to compassion. The priests of all these four
and twenty sects, whereof there are a very great number
in this empire, are cloathed in yellow, like the *Roolims* of *Pegu*;
they have no money either of gold or silver, but all their commerce is made with the weight of *cates, cacis, maazes,* and
*conderins.* The court of the *Calaminham* is very rich, the
nobility exceeding gallant, and the revenue of the lords and
princes very great, the king is seated and respected in a marvellous manner; he hath in his court many commanders that

are strangers, unto whom he giveth great pensions, to serve him for the safety of his person ; our ambassador was assured, that in the city of *Timplan*, where most commonly the court is, there are above threescore thousand horse, and 10000 elephants.  The gentlemen of the country live very hand-somely, and are served in vessels of silver, and sometimes of gold, but as for the common people they use porcelain and lattin ; in summer they are apparelled in sattin, damask, and wrought taffeties, which come from *Persia*, and in winter in gowns furred with marterns ; there is no going to law amongst them, nor does any man enter into bond there ; but if there be any difference among the common people, certain magistrates, like to our aldermen of wards, do decide it ; and if contention happens to arise between persons of an higher quality, then they submit to the judgement of certain religious men, who are expresly deputed for that purpose, and from them matters pass on in manner of appeal to the Queitor of Justice, which is as the superintendent thereof, from whose sentence there is no appeal, how great and important soever the business be.   The monarchy of these seven and twenty kingdoms hath seven hundred provinces, that is six and twenty in every kingdom ; and in the capital town of each of those provinces doth a governor preside, all of them being of like and equal power. Now on every new moon, each captain is bound to muster the souldiers that are under his charge, which ordinarily are two thousand foot, five hundred horse, and fourscore fighting elephants, one of the which is called by the name of the capital town of the same province ; so that if one should make a just computation of all those men of war that are in those seven hundred companies of those provinces, they would appear to be seventeen hundred and fifty thousand, whereof there are three hundred and fifty thousand horse, and five and fifty thousand elephants; for in regard of the great number that there are of those beasts in that country, this emperor stiles himself, in his titles, Lord of the indomitable force of Elephants.  The revenue which the monarch draws from his royal prerogatives, by them called, *the price of the Scepter*, as also from his mines, amounts to twenty millions of gold, without comprising therein the presents which are given him

by the princes, lords and captains, and a great quantity of
money that is distributed amongst the men of war, according
to every one's merit, which are not of that account. In all this
country, pearl, amber, and salt, are very much esteemed of,
because they are things that come from the sea, which is far
distant from the city of *Timplan*; but of all other commodities
they have infinite store. The country of it self is very healthy,
the air very good, and likewise the waters. When they sneeze
they use to say, *the God of truth is three and one*, whereby one
may judge that these people have had some knowledge of the
Christian religion.

Being departed from the town of *Bidor*, we held on our
course down the great river of *Pituy*, and the same day at
night we went and lodged at a certain *Abby* of the land of
*Quiay Jarem*, the god of married folks; this abby is seated on
the bank of the river in a plain, where are a great many of
trees planted, and very rich buildings, here the ambassador
was well entertained by the *Cabizondo* and the *Talagrepos*;
then continuing our voyage seven days longer, we arrived at a
town named *Pavel*, where we staid three days, to furnish our
vessels with some provisions which we needed; in this place
the ambassador bought divers knacks of *China*, and other
commodities that were sold there at a very cheap rate, as
musk, fine porcelains, wrought silks, ermins, and many other
sorts of furs, which are much used in that country, because it
is extreme cold there; these wares were brought thither by
great troops of elephants and rhinocero's from a certain far
distant province, as the merchants told us, called *Friouca-
raniaa*, beyond the which, they said, was a kind of people
called *Calogens*, and *Funcaos*, tawny men, and great archers,
having their feet like unto oxen, but hands like unto other
men, save that they are exceeding hairy, they are naturally
inclined to cruelty, and have below at the end of the backbone
a lump of flesh as big as ones two fists, their dwelling is in
mountains that are very high and rough on some parts, where
there are mighty deep pits, or caves, from whence are heard
in winter nights most dreadful cries, and doleful lamentations.
We were told likewise, that not far from these people there
were others, called *Calouhos*, *Timpates*, and *Bugems*, and a

good way beyond them some, named *Oquens* and *Magores*, who feed on wild beasts which they catch in hunting, and eat raw, as also on all kind of contagious creatures, as lizards, serpents, and adders; they hunt those wild beasts mounted on certain animals, as big as horses, which have three horns in the midst of their foreheads, with thick short legs, and on the middle of their backs a row of prickles, wherewith they prick when they are angry, and all the rest of the body is like a great lizard; besides they have on their necks, instead of hair, other prickles far longer and bigger then those on their backs, and on the joynts of their shoulders short wings like to the fins of fishes, wherewith they fly, as it were, leaping the length of five or six and twenty paces at a jump. These creatures are called *Banazes*, upon which these savages ride into the country of their enemies, with whom they hold continual war, and whereof some pay them tribute in salt, which is the thing they make most account of, in regard of the need they have of it, for that they are very far distant from the sea. We spake also with other men called *Bumioens*, who live on high mountains, where there are mines of alum and lacre, and great store of wood; of this nation, we saw a troop conducting of above two thousand oxen, on ¦whom they had put pack saddles, and so made them to carry their merchandise; these men were very tall, and had eyes and beards like the *Chineses*. We saw others likewise, that had reasonable long beards, their faces full of freckles, and their ears and nostrils pierced, and in the holes thereof small threds of gold made into clasps, these were called *Ginaphogaas*, and the province whereof they were natives *Surobosay*, which within the mountains of the *Lauhos* are bounded with the lake of *Chiammay*, and are cloathed with hairy skins, going bare-foot and bare-headed, certain merchants told us that these had great riches, and that all their traffique was in silver, whereof they had great store. We spake also with another sort of men, called *Tuparoens*, who are tawny, great eaters, and much addicted to the pleasures of the flesh; these gave us better entertainment then all the rest, and oftentimes feasted us. Now because in a certain banquet, where we nine *Portugals* were with the ambassador, one of us, named *Francisco Temuda*, challenged them to drink, they taking it for a great affront, caused the feast to continue the longer for the recovery of their honour; but the *Portugal* set on them so lustily, twenty that they were, as he laid them all along drunk on the ground, himself remaining still sober; when they were out of their drink, the *Sapiton*, that was their captain, and in whose house the feast had been made, called his company together, which were above three hundred, and, whether the *Portugal* would or no, made him to mount upon an *Elephant*, and so lead him through all the town, accompanied with a great multitude of people that followed him at the sound of trumpets, drums, and other such instruments; the captain himself, as also the ambassador, and the rest of us, together with all the *Bramaas*, marching on foot after him, with boughs in our hands, and two men before him on horseback, that rode crying, *O all ye people, praise with gladness the beams which proceed from the midst of the sun, who is the god that makes our rice to grow, for that you have lived to see a man so holy, that knowing how to drink better then all the men of the world, hath laid on the ground twenty of the principal drinkers of our troop, to the end his renown may be dayly more and more augmented.* Whereunto all the crowd of people that accompanied him, answered with such cries and acclamations, as the very noise thereof frighted all that heard it. In this equipage they lead the *Portugal* to the ambassadors house, where they set him down with a great deal of respect and many complements; then on their knees they rendred him to the ambassador, desiring him to have a care of him as of an holy man, or the son of some great king, for, said they, it cannot be otherwise, seeing God hath bestowed so great a gift on him, as to know how to drink so well. Whereupon having made a gathering for him, they got together above two hundred lingots of silver, which they gave him; and until the time that we departed he was continually visited by the inhabitants, whereof many presented him with rich pieces of silk, and other gifts, as if they had made an offering to some saint upon a solemn day of his invocation. After these we saw other men that were very white, named *Pavilens*, great archers, and good horsemen, apparrelled in cassocks of silk like those of *Japon*, and that carried their meat to their mouths with little sticks, after the manner of the *Chineses*; these same told us that their country was called *Binagorem*, and that it was distant from thence about two hundred leagues up the river; their merchandize was store of gold in powder, like to that of *Meuancabo*, of the island of *Sumatra*, as also lacre, aloes, musk, tin, copper, silk, and wax, which they exchanged for pepper, ginger, salt, wine, and rice : the wives of these men which we saw there are very white, of better conversation then all the rest of those countrys, well natured, and exceeding charitable; demanding of them what was their law, and what was the divinity that they adored, they answered us, *That their gods were the sun, the heaven, and the stars, for that from them they received by an holy communication all the good that they enjoyed upon earth; and furthermore, that the soul of man was but a breath which ended in the death of the body, and that afterwards tumbling up and down in the air she mingled her self with the clouds, until such time as coming to be dissolved into water, she died again upon the earth, as the body had done before.* I omit an infinite many of such extravagances which were told us, and that gave us good cause to wonder at the blindness and confusion of these wretches, and doth also oblige us to render thanks continually unto God for delivering us from these errors, and this false belief. Now from the diversity of these unknown nations, which we saw in these parts, it is easie to infer, that in this monarchy of the world there are many countries yet undivided, and unknown to us.

---

## CHAPTER LI.

### Our arrival at Pegu.

CONTINUING our course from this town of *Pavel*, we came the next day to a village, called *Luncor*, invironed about the space of three leagues, with a great number of trees of *Benjamin*, which from this place is transported into the kingdoms of *Pegu*, and *Siam*. From thence we sailed for nine days together down that great river, all alongst the which we saw many goodly towns; and then we arrived at another river, called *Ventrau*, through the which we continued our voyage to *Penauchin*, the first borrough of the kingdome of *Jangumaa*, where the ambassador registred his vessels, and all that were within them, because such was the custom of the country. Being departed from thence, we went and lay that night at the *Rauditens*, which are two strong places belonging to the Prince of *Pancanor*. Five days after we came to a great town, called *Magdaleu*, which is the country from whence lacre is brought to *Martabano*; the prince thereof, during the time that we stayed there, shewed the ambassador a general muster of all the men of war that he had levied against the King of the *Lauhos*, with whom he was at difference, because he had repudiated a daughter of his, which he had married three years before, intending to espouse a gentlewoman by whom he had had a son that he had legitimated, and made choice of for heir of his kingdom, thereby frustrating his nephew (by his daughter) of his right. Passing on then through the streight of *Madur*, wherein we sailed five days, we arrived at a village called *Mouchell*, the first place of the kingdom of *Pegu*; there one *Chalagonim*, a famous Pyrat, that went up and down robbing in this place with thirty *Seroos*, well equipped, and full of warlike men, assailed us one night, and fighting with us till it was almost day, he handled us in such sort, as it was the great grace of God that we escaped out of his hands; nevertheless it was not without the loss of five of the twelve vessels that we had, together with an hundred and fourscore of our men, whereof two were *Portugals*. The ambassador himself had a cut on one of his arms, and two wounds besides with arrow shot, which had almost cost him his life; all of us likewise were cruelly hurt; and the present which the *Calaminham* sent to the King of *Bramaa*, being worth above an hundred thousand ducates, was taken by the pyrat, together with a great deal of rich merchandize that was in the five vessels, whereof he had made himself master. In this sad equipage we arrived three days after at the city of *Martabano*, from whence the ambassador wrote the King a letter, wherein he rendred him an account of all that had hapned to him in his voyage, as also in his disaster. Whereupon the King sent presently away a Fleet of sixscore *Seroos*, with a number of choice men, amongst which were an hundred *Portugals* in quest of this pyrat. This fleet having by good fortune discovered him, found that he had put on shore his thirty *Seroos*, wherewith he had assailed us, and was with all his forces retired into a fortress, which was full of divers prizes that he had taken in several parts thereabout; our men immediately attacqued the place, and carried it easily at the very first assault, only with the loss of some few *Bramaas* and one *Portugal*, howbeit many were hurt with arrows, but they recovered in a short time without the maiming of any one. As soon as the fortress was gained, all that were found within it were put to the sword, not sparing the life of any, but that of the pyrat, and sixscore others of his company, which were led alive to the King of *Bramaa*, who caused them to be cast to his elephants, that instantly dismembred them. In the mean time the taking of this fortress was so advantagious to the *Portugals* that were sent thither, as they returned from thence all very rich; and it was thought that five or six of them got each of them the value of five and twenty, or thirty thousand ducates apiece, and that he which had least had the worth of two or three thousand for his share. After that the ambassador was cured at *Martabano* of the hurts which he had received in the fight, he went directly to the city of *Pegu*, where, as I have declared, the King of *Bramaas* court was at that time; who being advertised of his arrival, and of the letter which he brought him from the *Calaminham*, (whereby he accepted of his amity, and allied himself with him) he sent the *Chaumigrem*, his foster-brother, and brother-in-law, to receive him; to which end he set forth, accompanied with all the grandees of the kingdom, and four battalions of strangers, amongst the which were a thousand *Portugals* commanded by *Antonio Ferreira*, born in *Braguenca*, a man of great understanding, and to whom this king gave twelve thousand ducates a year pension, besides the presents which he bestowed on him in particular, that came to little less. Hereupon the King of *Bramaa* seeing that by this new league God had contented his desire, he resolved to shew himself thankful for so great a favour, wherefore he caused great feasts to be made amongst these people, and a number of sacrifices to be offered in the temples, where there was no spare of perfumes, and wherein it was thought there were killed above a thousand stags, cows, and hogs, which were bestowed for an alms among the poor, besides many other works of charity, as the cloathing of five thousand poor folks, and imploying great sums of money in the releasing of a thousand prisoners which were detained for debt. After that these feasts had continued seven whole days together, with a most ardent zeal, and at the incredible charge of the King, lords, and people, news came to the city of the death of the *Aixquendoo, Roolim* of *Mounay*, who was as it were their sovereign bishop, which caused all rejoicings to cease in an instant, and every one to fall into mourning, with great expressions of sorrow.

[*Here follows a description of the funeral ceremonies and an account of the installation of the new Roolim, omitted.*]

---

## CHAPTER LII.

### That which the King of Bramaa did after his arrival at the city of Pegu, together with his besieging of Savady.

TWO and twenty dayes after the King of *Bramaa* arrived at the city of *Pegu*, he perceived by the letter which his ambassadour brought him from the *Calaminham*, that he had concluded the league with him against the *Siamon*; yet in regard the season was not fit for him, either to commence that war, or to assail the kingdom of *Avaa*, as he desired, he resolved to send his foster-brother, unto whom, as I have already declared, he had given the title of lawfull brother, to the siege of *Savady*, which was some hundred and thirty leagues from thence to the north-east. Having assembled an army then of an hundred and fifty thousand men, amongst whom were thirty thousand strangers of divers nations, and

five thousand fighting elephants, besides three thousand others
that carried the baggage, and the victualls; the *Chaumigrem*
departed from *Pegu* with a fleet of thirteen hundred rowing
vessells, the 15th of the moneth of *March*. Fourteen dayes
after he arrived in the sight of *Savady*; and having cast
anchor neer to a great plain, called *Gumpalaor*, he arrived
there six dayes in attending the five thousand elephants which
were to come to him by land, which were no sooner arrived,
but he began to besiege the town; so that having begirt it
round, he assaulted it three times in the open day, and retreated still with very great loss, as well in regard of the
notable resistance which they within made against him, as
of the extream trouble his people were at in planting their
ladders against the walls, by reason of their bad scituation,
which was all of slate; whereupon consulting with his commanders about what he should do, they were all of opinion to
have it battered with the canon on the weakest side, untill
that by the overthrow of some part of the wall, a breach
might be made, whereby they might enter with more ease and
less danger. This resolution was as soon executed as taken,
so that the ingineers fell to making of two manner of bull-
works on the outside upon a great platform, composed of great
beams and bavins, which in five dayes they raised up to such
an height, as it surpassed the wall two fathom at the least.
This done, they planted on each bulwark twenty great pieces
of ordnance wherewith they began to batter the town so
valiantly, that in a little time they beat down a pane of the
wall; and besides those pieces of battery, there were above
three hundred falcons that shot incessantly, with an intention
only to kill those that were in the streets, as indeed they made
a great havoc, which was the cause that seeing themselves so
ill entreated, and their people slain in that manner, they resolved, like valiant men as they were, to sell their lives as
dearly as they could; so that one morning having sallied
forth by the same breach of the wall which the cannon had
made, they gave so valiantly upon those of the camp, that in
less then an hour they almost routed the *Bramaas* whole
army. Now because it began to be day, the *Savadis* thought
it fit to re-enter into the town, leaving eight thousand of their

enemies dead on the place. After this they repaired the breach in a very little time by the means of a rampire of earth, which they made up with bavins and other materialls, that was strong enough to resist the cannon. Hereupon the *Chaumigrem* seeing the bad success he had had, resolved to make war, both upon the places neer about, as also upon the frontiers that were furthest off from the town; for which purpose he sent *Diosanay*, high treasurer of the kingdom, whose slaves we *Portugals* were, colonel of five thousand men, to spoil a certain borrough, called *Valeutay*, which furnished the besieged town with provisions; but this voyage was so infortunate unto him, that before his arrivall at the designed place, his forces were by two thousand *Savadis*, whom he incountred by the way, all cut in pieces in less then half an hour, not one escaping with life that fell into their enemies hands. Nevertheless, it pleased our Lord that amidst this defeat we saved our selves by the favour of the night, and without knowing whither we went, we took the way of a very craggy mountain, where we marched in exceeding great pain three dayes and an half, at the end whereof we entred into certain Moorish plains, where we could meet with no path or way, nor having other company then tygers, serpents, and other savage beasts, which put us into a mighty fear. But as our God, whom incessantly we invoked with tears in our eyes, is the true guide of travellers, He out of His infinite mercy permitted, that at length we perceived one evening a certain fire towards the east, so that continuing our course towards that place where we saw this light, we found our selves the next morning neer to a great lake, where there were some cottages, which in all likelihood were inhabited by very poor people; howbeit not daring to discover our selves as yet, we hid us all that day in certain hanging precipices that were very boggy, and full of horsleaches, which made us all gore blood. As soon as it was night we fell to marching again untill the next morning, when as we arrived neer to a great river, all alongst the which we continued going for five dayes together. At last with much pain we got to another lake, that was far greater then the former, upon the bank whereof was a little temple in the form of an hermitage, and

25

there we found an old hermite, who gave us the best entertainment that possibly he could.  This old man permitted us to
repose our selves two dayes with him, during which time we
demanded many things of him that made for our purpose;
whereunto he alwayes answered according to the truth, and
told us, that we were still within the territories of the King
of *Savady*, that this lake was called *Oreguantor*, that is to
say, *the opening of the night* ; and the hermitage, *the God of
succour*.  Whereupon being desirous to know of him the
signification of this abuse, he laid his hand on an horse of
brasse, that stood for the idol upon the altar, and said that
he often read in a book, which entreated of the foundation of
the kingdom, that some two hundred, thirty, and seven years
before, this lake being a great town, called *Ocumhaleu*, a king
that was named *Avaa* had taken it in war, that in acknowledgement of this victory, his priests, by whom he was wholly
governed, counselled him to sacrifice unto *Quiay Guator*,
the god of war, all the young male children which had
been made captives; and in case he did not so, they would
when they became men regain the kingdom from him.  The
King apprehending the event of this threatning, caused all
these children, being fourscore and five thousand in number,
to be brought all into one place, and so upon a day that was
kept very solemn amongst them, he made them to be put
most inhumanely to the edge of the sword, with an intent to
have them burned the next morning in sacrifice ; but the
night following there came a great earthquake, and such
lightning and fire from heaven upon the town, as within less
then half an hour it was quite demolished, and all that was
in it reduced to nothing ; so that by this just judgement of
God, the King, together with all his, were stricken dead, not
so much as one escaping ; and besides them thirty thousand
priests in like manner, who ever since during all the new
moons are heard to cry and roar so dreadfully, that all the
inhabitants thereabouts were ready to go besides themselves
with fear ; by reason whereof the country was utterly depopulated, no other habitation remaining therein, save only fourscore and five hermitages, which were erected in memory of
the fourscore and five thousand children, whom the King had
caused to be butchered through the evill counsell of his priests.

## CHAPTER LIII.

A continuation of the success which we had in this voyage, with my departure from Goa to Zunda, and what passed during my abode there.

WE past two dayes in this hermitage, where, as I declared before, we were very well entertained by the hermite; the third day after betimes in the morning we took our leave of him, and departed from thence not a little afflicted with that which we had heard, and so all the same day and the night following we continued on our way along by the river; the next morning we arrived at a place where were a great many of sugar canes, of which we took some, for that we had nothing else to nourish us withall. In this manner we marched still along by this river, which we kept for a guide of our voyage, because we judged that how long soever it were, yet would it at last ingulfe it self in the sea, where we hoped that our Lord would raise us up some remedy for our miseries. The day ensuing we arrived at a village called *Pommiseray*, where we hid our selves in a very thick wood from being descried by passengers, and two hours within night we continued our design in following the current of the river, being resolved to take our death in good part, if it should please God to send it us, for to put an end to so many sufferings as we had undergone day and night; and without lying, the apprehension and visions of this last end troubled us more then death it self, wherewith we imagined our selves to be already ensnared. At the end of seventeen dayes, that this painfull and sad voyage had lasted, God shewed us so much grace, that during the obscurity of a very rainy night we discovered a certain light little more then a faulcon shot before us; the fear we were in at the first that we were neer some town, made us to stand still for a good space, without knowing what to resolve upon, untill we observed that this light seemed to move, whereby we conjectured that it was some vessel which went from one port to another; as indeed half an hour after we perceived one, wherein there were nine persons, who approaching to the bank of the river, neer to the place where we were, landed all in a creek that was there in the form of an haven, and presently making a fire, they began to prepare their supper, which was no sooner ready, but they fell to eating with great demonstrations of mirth, wherein they bestowed a pretty good time. At length when they were well replenished with meat and drink, it happened that all nine of them, amongst whom there were three women, fell fast asleep; whereupon seeing that we could not find a more favourable occasion to make our benefit of this adventure, we went all eight of us very softly into the barque, that stuck half in the ouze, and was tyed fast to a great stake, which pushing forth with our shoulders we set aflote; and then imbarquing our selves in it with all speed, we began to row down the river with as little noyse as possibly we could make. Now in regard the current of the water and the wind were both very favourable unto us, we found our selves the next morning above ten leagues from the place whence we parted, namely, neer to a *Pagode*, called *Quiay Hinarel*, that is to say, *the God of Rice*, where we met but only with one man and seven and thirty women, the most of them old, and religionaries of this temple, who received us with a great deal of charity, although in my opinion they did it rather out of fear of us, then any will that they had to do us good. Having questioned them about many things which served for our purpose, they could give us no pertinent answer thereunto, alledging still, that they were but poor women, who upon a solemn vow had renounced all things in the world, and confined themselves into this inclosure, where they bestowed all their time in continuall prayer to *Quiay Ponuedea*, which moves the clouds of heaven, that he would be pleased to give them rain, whereby their grounds might be made fruitfull to produce them abundance of rice. In this place we spent all the day in caulking our barque, and furnishing our selves at these religious womens cost, with rice, sugar, *French* beans, onyons, and some smoak-dried flesh, wherewith they were sufficiently provided. Being parted from hence about an hour within night, we continued our course with our oars and sails for seven whole dayes together, without so much as once daring to touch the land, so much were we in fear of some disaster that might easily arrive to us from those places which we saw all alongst the river. But as it is impossible to avoid that here below which is determined there above, just at the instant as we were continuing on our course, all confused as we were, and in a perpetuall alarm, by reason of the danger that was alwayes present before our eyes, as well for that which we saw, as for that we were in doubt of, our ill hap would have it, that an hour before day, as we past thorough the mouth of a channell, three *Paraos* of pyrats assaulted us with such violence, and with so many different sorts of darts, which they showred upon us, that within less then two *Credoes*, they had killed three of our companions; as for us five that remained, we cast our selves into the sea, all bloudy as we were with the wounds which we had received, whereof two others died a little after. When as we were got ashore we hid our selves in the woods, where we past all that day in lamenting our present mishap after so many fortunes as we had run thorough before time. Thus wounded as we were, parting from thence in more hope of death then life, we proceeded on our way by land, with so much pain and irreso-lution concerning what we were to do, as we fell many times a weeping, without being able to comfort one another, in regard of the small likelihood there was of saving our lives by any humane means. As we were reduced to this deplor-able estate, with two of our companions ready to die, it pleased our Lord (whose succour doth ordinarily supply our defects) that in a place where we found our selves upon the bank of the water, there chanced to pass by a vessel, wherein there was a Christian woman, named *Violenta*, who was married to a *Pagan*, to whom this vessel appertained, which he had laden with cotton wooll to sell off at *Cosmin*; this woman no sooner perceived us, but moved with pity at the sight of us, *Jesus*, cried she, *these are Christians which I behold!* that said, she caused the vessel wherein she was to come to the shore, and leaping on land, together with her husband, they fell both of them to imbracing us with tears in their eys, and then made us to be imbarqued with them; presently whereupon this vertuous dame took a care to have our wounds drest, and provided us of cloaths the best that

she could, rendring us many other good offices of a true and
charitable Christian. Then setting aside all fear, we parted
from this place with all speed, and five dayes after thorough
Gods grace we arrived safely at the town of *Cosmin*, which is
a part of the sea in the kingdom of *Pegu*, where in the house
of this good Christian woman we were so well looked unto,
that in a short time we found our selves thoroughly cured of
all our hurts. Now whereas there is never any want in the
grace which God doth to his creatures, it pleased Him that at
that very time we met in this port with a ship, whereof *Luis
de Montorrayo* was master, who was upon the poynt of setting
sail for *Bengala*; so that after we had taken our leave of our
hostess, to whom we rendred many thanks for all the benefits
which we had received of her, we imbarqued our selves with
the said *Luis de Montorrayo*, who likewise entreated us exceeding well, and furnished us abundantly with all that was
necessary for us. At our arrivall at the port of *Chatigan* in
the kingdom of *Bengala*, where there was at that time many
*Portugals*, I instantly imbarqued my self in the foist of a
certain merchant, called *Fernando Caldeyra* who was bound
for *Goa*, where it pleased God I arrived in good health. There
I found *Pedro de Faria*, who had been Captain of *Malaca*, and
by whom I had been sent as ambassador to the *Chaiubanhaa*
of *Martabano*, as I have declared heretofore. To him I rendred an exact account of all that had past, for which he
shewed himself very sorrowful, and accommodated me with
divers things, whereunto his conscience and generosity obliged
him, in regard of the goods which I had lost for his occasion.
A little after, that I might not lose the opportunity of the
season, I imbarqued my self with an intention to go to the
southward, and once more to try my fortune in the kingdoms
of *China* and *Japan*, to see if in those countries where I had
so many times lost my coat, I could not find a better then
that I had on.

Being imbarqued at *Goa* in a junck that belonged to *Pedro
de Faria*, which was bound in way of trade for *Zunda*, I
arrived at *Malaca* the same day that *Ruy vas Pereyra*, termed
*Marramaque* died, who was then captain of the fortress there.
Being departed from that place to go to *Zunda*, at the end of

seventeen days I arrived at *Banta*, where the *Portugals* are
accustomed to traffique.  And because there was at that time
great scarcity of pepper over all the country, and that we
came thither of purpose for it, we were constrained to pass
the winter there, with a resolution to go for *China* the year
following.  We had been almost two moneths in this port,
where we exercised our commerce very peaceably, when as
from the King of *Demaa*, Emperor of all the islands of *Jaoa*,
*Angenia*, *Bala*, *Madura*, and of the rest of the islands of that
*Archipelago*, there landed in this country a widow woman,
named *Nhay Pombaya*, about the age of threescore years, who
came as ambassador to *Tagaril*, King of *Zunda*, that was also
his vassal as well as all the rest of that monarchy, for to tell
him that he was within the term of six weeks to be in person
at the town of *Japara*, where he was then making preparation
to invade the kingdom of *Passaruan*.  When this woman
arrived in this port, the King went in person to the vessel
where she was, from whence he carried her to his palace with
great pomp, and put her into the company of his wife for her
better entertainment, whilest he himself retired to another
lodging farther off to do her the more honor.  Now that one
may know the reason wherefore this ambassage was executed
rather by a woman then a man, you must note, that it hath
always been the custom of the Kings of this kingdom to treat
of the most important matters of their state by mediation of
women, especially when it concerns peace, which they observe
not only in particular messages that are sent by the lords to
their vassals, (such as this was) but also in matter of publique
and general affairs, which is performed by ambassage from one
king to another ; and all the reason they give for it, is ; *That
God hath given more gentleness and inclination to courtesie, yea
and more authority to women then to men, who are severe, as
they say, and by consequent less agreeable to those unto whom
they are sent.*  Now it is their opinion, that every one of those
women which the kings are accustomed to send about affairs
of importance, ought to have certain qualities for well executing of an ambassage, and worthily discharging the commission
which is granted to them : for first of all, they say, *That she
must not be a maid, for fear she chance to lose her honor in*

*going out of her house, because that even as with her beauty she
contents every one, so by the same reason she may be a motive
of discord and unquietnes in matters where unity is required,
rather then an access to concord, and the peace which is pretended unto.* To this they add, *that she must be married, or at
leastwise a widow after a lawful marriage ; that if she have had
children, she must have a certificate how she hath given them all
suck with her own breasts, alledging thereupon, that she who
hath born children, and doth not nourish them if she can, is
rather a carnal, voluptuous, corrupted, and dishonest woman,
then a true mother.* And this custom is observed so exactly
over all this country, principally amongst persons of quality,
that if a mother hath a child which she cannot give suck unto
for some valuable consideration, she must make an attestation
thereof, as of a thing very serious, and much importing her
honor. That if being young too she happens to lose her
husband, and becomes a widdow, she must for the better
testifying of her vertue enter into religion, to the end she may
thereby shew, that she did not formerly marry for the pleasure
which she expected from her marriage, but to have children,
according to the pure and honest intention, wherewith God
joyned together the first married couple in the terrestial
paradise. Furthermore, that there might be nothing to be
found fault with in the purity of their marriage, and that it
might be altogether comformable to the law of God, they say,
that after a woman is with child, she ought no longer to have
the company of her husband, because the same could not then
be but dishonest and sensual. To these conditions they add
many others which I will pass over in silence, for that I think
it unreasonable to use prolixity in matters that I hold worthy
of excuse, if I do not relate them at length. In the mean
time after that *Nhay Pombaya* had delivered her embassage to
the King of *Zunda*, as I have declared before, and treated
with him about the occasion which brought her thither, she
presently departed from this town of *Banta* ; whereupon the
King having speedily prepared all things in readiness, he set
sail with a fleet of thirty *Calaluzes*, and ten *Juripangoes*, well
furnished with ammunition and victual, in which forty vessels
there were 7000 fighting men, besides the mariners and rowers.

Amongst this number were forty *Portugals*, of six and forty that we were in all, in regard whereof they did us many particular favors in the business of our merchandize, and publikely confessed, that they were much obliged to us for following them as we did, so that we should have had little reason to have excused our selves from accompanying them in this war.

## CHAPTER LIV.

### The expedition of the Pangueyran, Emperor of Jaoa, and King of Demaa, against the King of Passeruan, and all that which passed in this war.

THE King of *Zunda* being departed from the port of *Banta* the 5th day of *January*, in the year 1546, arrived on the 19th of the same at the town of *Japara*, where the King of *Demaa*, Emperor of this island of *Jaoa*, was then making his preparatives, having an army on foot of eight hundred thousand men. This prince being advertised of the King of *Zunda's* coming, who was his brother-in-law and vassal, he sent the King of *Panaruca*, Admiral of the fleet, to receive him, who brought along with him an hundred and threescore *Calaluzes*, and ninety *Lanchares*, full of *Luffons* from the Isle of *Borneo* : with all this company he arrived where the King of *Zunda* was, who entertained him very courteously, and with a great deal of honor. Fourteen days after our coming to this town of *Japara*, the King of *Demaa* went and imbarqued himself for the kingdom of *Passaruan* in a fleet of two thousand and seven hundred sails, amongst the which were a thousand high built juncks, and all the rest were vessels with oars. The 11th of *February* he arrived at the river of *Hicandurea*, which is at the entrance of the bar ; and because the King of *Panaruca*, Admiral of the fleet, perceived that the great vessels could not pass unto the port, which was two leagues off, by reason of certain shelves of sand that were in divers parts of the river, he caused all those that were in them to be disimbarqued, and the other vessels with oars to go and anchor in the road before the town, with an intention to burn the ships that were in the port, which indeed was accordingly executed. In this army was the Emperor *Pangueyran* in person, accompanied with all the grandees of the kingdom ; the King of *Zunda*, his brother in law who was General of the army, went by land with a great part of the forces, and being all arrived at the place where they meant to pitch their camp, they took care in the first place for the fortifying thereof, and for placing the canon in the most commodious places to batter the town, in which labour they bestowed the most part of the day. As for the night ensuing it was spent in rejoycings, and keeping good watch until such time as it was day, when as each captain applied himself to that whereunto his duty obliged him, all in general imploying themselves according to the ingineers directions, so that by the second day the whole town was invironed with high *Pallisadoes*, and their platforms fortified with great beams, whereupon they planted divers great pieces of ordnance, amongst the which were eagles and lions of metal, that the *Achems* and *Turks* had cast, by the invention of a certain *Renegado*, born in the kingdom of *Algarues*, appertaining to the crown of *Portugal* ; and by reason this wicked wretch had changed his belief, he called himself *Coia Geinal* : for as for the name which he had before when he was a Christian, I am contented to pass it over in silence for the honor of his family, being indeed of no mean extraction. In the mean time the besieged having taken notice how ill-advised they had been in suffering the enemies to labor two whole days together peaceably in fortifying of their camp, without any impeach-ment of theirs ; and taking the same for a great affront, they desired their King to permit them to fall upon them the night following, alledging how it was probable that men wearied with labor, could not make any great use of their arms, nor be able to resist this first impetuosity. The King, who at that time commanded the kingdom of *Passaruan*, was yong, and indued with many excellent qualities which made him to be exceedingly beloved of all his subjects ; for as it was reported of him, he was very liberal, no maner of tyrant, exceedingly affable to the common people, a friend to the poor, and so charitable towards widows, that if they acquainted him with their necessities, he relieved them instantly, and did them more good then they asked of him. Besides these perfections that were so recommendable, he possessed some others so comfortable to mens desires, as there was not any one that would not have exposed his life a thousand times for his service if need had been. Furthermore he had none but choice men with him, even the flower of all his kingdom, besides many strangers, upon whom he conferred much wealth, honor, and many graces, which he accompanied with good words, that being indeed the means whereby the minds both of great and small are so strongly gained, that they make them lions of sheep, whereas carrying ones self other ways, of generous lions, they are made fearful hares. This king then examining the request which his people made unto him, and referring himself to the advice of the antientest and most prudent councellors of his state which were with him, there was a great contention about the success that the affairs might have ; but in the end, by the counsel of all in general, it was concluded, *That in case fortune should be altogether adverse unto them in this sally which they meant to make against their enemies, yet would it be a much less evil, and less considerable affront, then to see the King so besieged by vile people, who against all reason would reduce them by force to quit their belief, wherein they had been bred by their fathers, to imbrace another new one by the suscitation of the* Farazes, *who place their salvation in not eating of swines flesh, and marrying of seven wives, whereby the best advised may easily judge, that God was so much their enemy, as he would not assist them in any thing, seeing that with so great offence. they would under pretext of religion, and with reasons so full of contradiction, compel their king to become a Mahometan, and render himself tributary to them.* To these reasons they added many others which the King, and they that were with him, found to be so good, as they all with one common consent agreed thereunto, which is an evident mark, that it is a thing no less natural for a good subject to expose his life for his king, then for a vertuous wife to conserve her chastity for the husband which God hath given her : this being so, said they, a matter of so great importance was no longer to be deferred, but we all in general, and each one in particular, are by this sally to make demonstration of the extreme affection which we bear to our good king, who we are assured will never be unmindful of them that shall fight best for his defence, which is all the inheritance we desire to leave to our children.  Whereupon it was resolved that the night following they should make a sally upon their enemies.

Whereas the joy, which this designed sally brought to all the inhabitants of the town, was general, they never stayed till they were called, but two hours after midnight, and before the time which the King had appointed, they assembled all in a great place, which was not far from the royal palace, and where they of the country had accustomed to keep their fairs, and to solemnize their most remarkable feasts on those principal days which were destined to the invocation of their *Pagodes*.  The King in the mean time, wonderfully content to see such heat of courage in them, of seventy thousand inhabitants which were in the town, drew out twelve thousand only for this enterprise, and divided them into four companies, each of them containing three thousand, whereof an unkle of the Kings was General, a man whom experience had rendred very knowing in such undertakings, and that marched in the head of the first company.  Of the second was captain another of the principal *Mandarins*; of the third a stranger, a *Champaa* by nation, and born in the island of *Borneo*; and of the fourth one called *Panbacaluio*; all of them good commanders, very valiant, and exceeding expert in matters of war.  When they were all ready, the King made them a speech, whereby he succinctly represented unto them the confidence which he had in them touching this enterprise. After which, the better to encourage them, and assure them of his love, he took a cup of gold and drunk to them all, causing the chiefest of them to pledge him, and craving pardon of the rest, for that the time would not permit them to do the like.  This gracious carriage of his so encouraged the souldiers, that without further delay the most part of them went and anointed themselves with *Minhamundi*, which is a certain confection of an odoriferous oyl, wherewith these people are accustomed to frote themselves with, when they have taken a full resolution to die, and these same are ordinarily called *Amacos*. The hour being come wherein this sally was to be made, four of twelve gates that were in the town were opened, thorow each of the which sallied forth one of the four captains with his company, having first sent out for spies into the camp six *Orobalons*, of the most valiant that were about the King, whom he had honored with new titles, and with such special favors as use to give courage to them that want it, and to encrease it in them that are endued with some resolution. The four captains marched a little after the six spies, and went and joyned all together in a certain place, where they were to fight with the enemies : whereupon falling into the midst of them with a marvellous impetuosity, they fought so valiantly, that in less then an hours time, which the fight endured, the twelve thousand *Passaruans* left about thirty thousand enemies upon the place, besides those that were wounded, which were in a far greater number, and whereof many died afterwards. Furthermore they took prisoner three kings, and eight *Pates*, which are as the dukes amongst us ; the King of *Zunda* too, with whom we forty *Portugals* were, could not so save himself, but that he was hurt with a lance in three places, a number being killed in defending him. Thus was the camp put in so great disorder, as it was almost destroyed, the *Pangueyran* himself being wounded with a dart, and constrained to leap into the water, where little lacked but that he had been drowned. Whereby one may see what the force of a number of resolute and fearless men is against such as are surprised when least they think of it ; for before that the enemies could know what they did, or the commanders could put their souldiers into order, they were twice routed. The next morning, as soon as the day gave them leave to know the truth of the business, the *Passeruans* retired into the town, where they found that they had not lost above nine hundred of their men, nor more then two or three thousand hurt.

It is scarcely to be believed how much the King of *Demaa* was grieved with the disaster of the former day, as well for the affront which he received from those within by the loss of his people, as for the bad success of the beginning of this

siege, whereof he seemed in some sort to impute the fault
unto our King of *Zunda*, saying, that this fortune had hapned
by the bad directions he had given to the sentinels.  Now
after he had commanded that the wounded should be drest,
and the dead buried, he called to councel all the kings,
princes, and captains of the forces that he had, both by
land and water, unto whom he said, *That he had made a
solemn vow, and oath upon the Mazapho of* Mahomet, *which
is their Alcoran, or the book of their law, never to raise the
siege from before this town, until he had utterly destroyed
it, or lost his own state therein.*  Whereunto he added, *That
he protested he would put to death whomsoever should oppose
this resolution of his, what reason soever he could alledge
thereupon*; which begot so great a terror in the minds of all
that heard him, as there was not one that durst contradict
his will, but contrarily they infinitely approved and commended it.  He used then all kind of diligence for the new
fortifying of the camp with good ditches, strong pallisadoes,
and divers bulworks made of stone and timber, garnished
on the inside with their platforms, where he caused a great
many of cannons to be planted, so that by this means the
camp was stronger then the town it self, in regard whereof
the besieged did often times jeer the sentinels without,
telling them, *That it must needs be concluded they were
notorious cowards, since instead of besieging their enemies
like valiant men, they besieged themselves like feeble women,
wherefore they bid them return home to their houses,
where it was fitter for them to fall to spinning, then to
make war.*  These were the jeers which they ordinarily
put upon the besiegers, who were greatly offended with them.
This town had been almost three moneths besieged, and yet
had the enemies advanced but little ; for during all that time,
wherein there had been five batteries and three assaults given
to it, with above a thousand ladders planted against the
walls, the besieged defended themselves still like valiant and
couragious men, fortifying themselves with counter-mires which
they opposed to the breaches, which they made with pieces of
timber taken from the houses ; so that all the power of the
*Pangueyran*, which (as I have declared) was about eight

hundred thousand men, whereof the number was much
diminished, was not able ·to give him entrance into it.
Hereupon the principal ingineer of the camp, who was a
renegado of *Maillorque*, seeing that this affair had not a
success answerable to what he had promised the King, he
resolved to take another far different course. To that effect,
with a great amass of earth and bavins he framed a kind of a
platform, which he fortified with six rows of beames, and
wrought so, that in nine days he raised it a fathom higher
then the wall; that done, he planted forty great pieces of
cannon upon it, together with a number of bases and faulconets, wherewith he fell to battering the town in such sort,
as the besieged were therewith mightily damnified, so that the
King perceiving that this invention of the enemy was the only
thing in the world that could most incommodate him in the
town, he resolved by the means of ten thousand volunteers,
who had offered themselves unto him for that purpose, and to
whom for a mark of honor he gave the title of *Tygers of the
World*, to attacque this fort, and they that were upon it; this
matter was no sooner resolved upon, but was presently put in
execution, and for the better incouragement of them, the King
himself would be their captain, albeit this whole enterprise
was governed by the four *Panaricons*, which had formerly
commanded in the first sally. Having put themselves into
the field then with the rising of the sun, they fought so
valiantly without any fear at all of the dreadful ordnance,
which were planted on the platform, as in less then two
*Credoes* they got to the top of it, and there setting on the
enemies, who were thirty thousand in number, they defeated
them all in a very short time. The *Pangueyran* of *Pate* seeing
his forces thus routed, ran thither in person with twenty
thousand choice souldiers, intending to beat the *Passeruans*
from the place which they had ·gained; but they·defended it
so couragiously, as it is not possible to express it in words.
This bloody battel having indured till evening, the *Passeruan*,
who had lost the most part of his men, made his retreat into
the town by the gate that was next to the platform, whereunto
having first set fire in six or seven places, it took hold of some
barrels of powder, whereof there was great store there,

which inflamed it so terribly in several parts, as it was not possible to approach unto it by the space of a flight shoot; this accident was very favorable to the besieged, because the enemies were thereby kept from joyning together, and so the town was for this time preserved from the great danger where-withal it was threatned; howbeit the *Passeruans* scap't not so scot-free, but that of the ten thousand volunteers imployed in this service, six thousand remained dead on the top of the platform. True it is, that in the *Pangueyran* part there was above forty thousand killed, amongst the which were three thousand strangers of divers nations, the most part *Achems*, *Turks*, and *Malabares*, as also twelve *Pates*, or dukes, five kings, with many other commanders, and men of quality.

---

## CHAPTER LV.

### The death of the King of Demaa by a very strange accident, and that which ensued thereupon.

TO come again now to our history, you are to understand, that the *Pangueyran* of *Pata*, King of *Demaa*, being certified by some of the enemies whom his men had taken prisoners, of the piteous estate whereunto the besieged were reduced, the most part of them dead, their ammunition failing, and their king dangerously hurt; all these things together carried him more ardently than ever to the assault, which he had purposed with himself to give to the besieged town. He resolved then to scale it in plain day, and to assault it with more violence then before, so that instantly great preparations were made over all the camp, where divers serjeants at arms, on horseback, and carrying maces on their shoulders, went proclaiming aloud, after the men of war had been made to assemble together with the sound of trumpets, *The* Pangueyran *of* Para *by the power of him who hath created all things, Lord of the Lands which inviron the Seas, being willing to discover unto all in general the secret of his soul, doth let you know, that nine days hence he will have you be in a readiness, to the end that*

*with the courages of tygers, and redoubled forces, you assist him*
*in the assault which he intends to give unto the town, for a*
*recompence whereof he liberally promiseth to do great favors, as*
*well in money, as in honorable and remarkable titles, to those*
*five souldiers which first of all shall plant colours on the enemies*
*walls, or that shall perform actions which shall be agreeable to*
*him. Whereas, contrarily, they which do not carry themselves*
*valiantly in this enterprise, conformably to his pleasure, shall be*
*executed by the way of justice, without any regard had to their*
*condition.* This ordinance of the kings, full of menaces, being
published over every part of the camp, put them into such an
alarm, as the commanders began incontinently to make themselves ready, and to provide all things necessary for this
assault, without scarce taking any rest either day or night,
making withal so great a noise, by intermingling their hues
and cries with the sounds of drums, and other instruments of
war, as it could not be heard without much terror. In the
mean time, whereas of the nine days, destined for the purpose
aforesaid, seven were already past, so as there rested no more
but two, at the end whereof an assault was to be given to the
town, one morning as the *Pangueyran* sate in councel, to resolve
of the affairs of this siege with the principal lords of his army,
as also of the means, of the time, and places, whereby they
were to assault the town, and of other necessary things, it was
said, that from the diversity of opinions, which the one and
the other had, there arose so great a contention amongst
them, as the king was constrained to take every ones advice
in writing. During this time, whereas he had always neer
about him a young page, who carried *Bethel*, an herb whose
leaves are like unto plaintain, which these Pagans are
accustomed to chaw, because it makes them have a sweet
breath, and also purges the humours of the stomack; he asked
this page then for some of it, who at first seemed not to hear
him, being much about twelve or thirteen years old, for I hold
it fit to make mention of his age, in regard of that I am to say
of him hereafter. Now to return to the *Pangueyran,* as he
was continuing his discourse with his councel of war, thorow
much speaking, and somewhat in choler, his mouth became
dry, so that he asked the page again for some *Bethel,* which

he ordinarily carried in a little box of gold, but he heard him
no more this second time then he had done the first; insomuch
as the King having asked him for some the third time, one of
the lords that was neer to the page pulled him by the sleeve,
and bid him *give the King some Bethel,* which immediately he
did, and falling on his knees he presented him with the box
which he had in his hands ; the King then took two or three
leaves of it, as he used to do, and without being otherwise angry,
giving him a light touch with his hand on the head, *art thou
deaf,* said he unto him, *that thou couldst not hear me?* and
thereupon re-entred into discourse with them of his councel.
Now because these *Jacas* are the most punctillious and
perfidious nation of the world, and that withal they of this
country hold it for the greatest affront that can be done them,
when one gives them a touch on the head, this young page
imagining that the King had touched him so out of a mark of
so great a contempt, as he should thereby be made infamous
for ever, though indeed none of the company took notice of
it, he went aside weeping and sobbing by himself, and in the
end resolved to revenge the injury which the King had done
him, so that drawing out a little knife which he wore at his
girdle, he stabbed the King with it into the midst of the left
pap, and so because the blow was mortal, the King fell
instantly down on the ground, not able to say any more then
these two or three words, *I am dead*: wherewith all those of
the council were so frighted, as it is not possible to express
it.   After that this commotion was a little calmed, they fell
first unto looking to the King, to see if some remedy might not
be applied to his wound; but because he was hurt just in the
heart there was no hope of recovery, so that he died within a
very short time after.   Presently they seized on the page,
whom they put to torture, by reason of some suspitions which
they had upon this accident, but he never confessed any thing,
and said nought else, save, *That he had done it of his own free
will, and to be revenged of the blow which the King had given
him on his head by way of contempt, as if he had struck some
dog that was barking up and down the streets in the night,
without considering that he was the son of the* Pate Pondan,
*Lord of* Surebayaa.   The page then was impaled alive, with

a good big stake, which came out at the nape of his neck. As much was done to his father, to three of his brothers, and to threescore and twelve of his kinsmen, so that his whole race was exterminated, upon which so cruel and rigorous an execution, many great troubles ensued afterwards in all the country of *Jaca*, and in all the islands of *Bale*, *Tymor*, and *Madura*, which are very great, and whereof the governours are sovereigns by their laws, and from all antiquity. After the end of this execution, question was made what should be done with the Kings body, whereupon there were many different opinions amongst them; for some said that to bury him in that place was as much as to leave him in the power of the *Passeruans*; and others, that if he were transported to *Demaa*, where his tomb was, it was not possible but that it would be corrupted before it arrived there; whereunto was added, that if they interred him so putrified and corrupted, his soul could not be received into *Paradise*, according to the law of the country, which is that of *Mahomet*, wherein he died. After many contestations thereupon, in the end they followed the counsel which one of our *Portugals* gave them, that was so profitable to him afterwards, as it was worth him above ten thousand ducates, wherewith the lords rewarded him as it were in vye of one other for a recompence of the good service which he did then to the deceased. This counsel was, that they should put the body into a coffin full of lime and camphire, and so bury it in a junck also full of earth; so that albeit the thing was not so marvellous of it self, yet left it not to be very profitable to the *Portugals*, because they all found it very good, and well invented, as indeed the success of it was such, as by means thereof the Kings body was carried to *Demaa*, without any kind of corruption or ill savour.

As soon as the Kings body was put into the junck appointed for it, the King of *Zunda*, General of the army, caused the great ordinance and the ammunition to be imbarqued, and with the least noyse that might be committed to safe custody the most precious things the King had, together with all the treasures of the tents. But whatsoever care and silence was used therein, the enemy could not be kept from having some inkling of it, and from understanding how things went in the

camp, so that instantly the King marched out of the town in
person, with onely three thousand souldiers of the past
confederacy, who by a solemn vow caused themselves to be
anointed with the oyl which they call *Minhamudi*, as men
resolved, and that had vowed themselves to death. Thus
fully determined as they were, they went and fell upon the
enemies, whom finding busie in trussing up their baggage, they
entreated so ill, as in less than half an hours space, for no
longer lasted the heat of the fight, they cut twelve thousand
of them in pieces. Withal they took two kings, and five *pates*,
or *dukes*, prisoners, together with above three hundred *Turks*,
*Abyssines*, and *Achems*, yea and their *Cacismoubana*, the sovereign dignity amongst the *Mahometans*, by whose counsel the
*Pangueyran* was come thither. There were also four hundred
ships burnt, wherein were the hurt men, so that by this means
all the camp was neer lost. After this the King retreated into
the town with his men, whereof he lost but four hundred.
In the mean time the King of *Zunda* having caused the
remainder of the army to be re-imbarqued with all speed
the same day, being the 9th of *March*, they set sail
directly for the city of *Demaa*, bringing along with them the
body of the *Pangueyran*, which upon the arrival thereof was
received by the people with great cries, and strange demonstrations of an universal mourning. The day after a review
was taken of all the men of war, for to know how many were
dead, and there was found missing an hundred and thirty
thousand; whereas the *Passeruans*, according to report, had
lost but five and twenty thousand; but be it as it will, and let
fortune make the best market that she can of these things, yet
they never arrive, but the field is dyed with the bloud of van-
quishers, and by a stronger reason with that of the vanquished,
to whom these events do always cost far dearer, then to the
others. The same day there was question of creating a new
*Pangueyran*, who, as I have said heretofore, the Emperour
over all the *Pates* and kings of that great *Archipelago*, which
the *Chineses*, *Tartar*, *Japon*, and *Lequio*, historians are wont
to call *Raterra Vendau*, that is to say, *the Eye-lid of the World*,
as one may see in the card, if the elevation of the heights
prove true. Now because that after the death of the *Panguey-*

*ran*, there was not a lawfull successor to be found that might inherit this crown, it was resolved that one should be made by election; for which effect by the common consent of all, eight men were chosen, as heads of all the people, to create a *Pangueyran*. These same assembled then together in a house, and after order had been taken for the pacifying of all things in the city, they continued seven whole days together without being able to come to any agreement about the election; for whereas there were eight pretendents of the principal lords of the kingdom, there were found amongst these electors many different opinions, which proceeded from this, that the most part, or all of them, were neerly allied to the eight, or to their kinsmen, so that each one laboured to make him *Pangueyran* which was most to his minde. Whereupon the inhabitants of the city, and the souldiers of the army, making use of this delay to their advantage, as men who imagined that this affair would never be terminated, and that there would be no chastisement for them, they began shamelessly to break out into all kinde of actions full of insolency and malice. And forasmuch as there was a great number of merchant ships in the port, they got aboard them, and fell pell-mell to rifling both of strangers and those of the country, with so much licentiousness, as it was said, that in four days they took an hundred junks, wherein they killed about six thousand men; whereof notice being given to the King of *Panaruca*, Prince of *Balambuam*, and Admiral of the Sea of this Empire, he ran thither with all speed, and of the number of those which were convicted of manifest robbery, he caused fourscore to be hanged all along the shore, to the terrour of those that should behold them. After this action, *Quiay Ansedeaa*, *Pate*, or Duke of *Cherbom*, who was Governour of the town, and greatly in authority, taking this which the King of *Panaruca* had done for a manifest contempt, because he had, said he, little respected the charge of governour, was so mightily offended at it, as having instantly got together about six or seven thousand men, he went and fell upon this kings palace, with an intent to seize upon his person; but the *Panaruca* resisted him with his followers, and as it was said, he endeavoured with many complements to justifie himself to him all that ever

he could ; whereunto *Quiay Ansedeaa* was so far from having
any regard, as contrarily entring by force into his house he
slew thirty or forty of his men ; in the mean time so many
people ran to this mutiny as it was a dreadful thing to behold.
For whereas these two heads were great lords, one Admiral of
the fleet, the other Governour of the town, and both of them
allied to the principal families of the country, the devil sowed
so great a division amongst them, as if night had not separated
the fight, it is credible that not one of them had escaped ;
nevertheless the difference went yet much farther, and ended
not so, for the men of war, who were at that time above six
hundred thousand in number, coming to consider the great
affront which *Quiay Ansedeaa*, Governour of the town, had
done to their admiral, they to be revenged thereof went all
ashore the same night, the *Panaruca* not being of power
enough to keep them from it, notwithstanding he laboured all
that he could to do it.   Thus all of them animated and transported with wrath ; and a desire of revenge, went and set
upon *Quiay Ansedeaa's* house, where they slew him, and ten
thousand men ; wherewith not contented, they assaulted
the town in ten or eleven places, and fell to killing and
plundering all that · ever they met with, so that they
carried themselves therein with so much violence, as in three
days alone, which was as long as the siege of this town
lasted, nothing remained that was not an insupportable object
to the sight.   There was withall so great a confusion of howl-
ing, weeping, and heavy lamentation, as all that heard it could
think no other but that the earth was going to turn topsy-
turvy.   In a word, and not to lose time in aggravating this
with superfluous speeches, the town was all on fire, which
burnt to the very foundations, so that according to report there
were above an hundred thousand houses consumed, above three
hundred thousand persons cut in pieces, and almost as many
made prisoners, which were led away slaves, and sold in divers
countries.   Besides, there was an infinite of riches stollen,
whereof the value, as it was said, onely in silver and gold,
amounted even to forty millions, and all put together, to an
hundred millions of gold.   As for the number of prisoners,
and of such as were slain, it was near five hundred thousand

persons; and all these things arrived by the evil counsel of a young king, bred up amongst young people like himself, who did every thing at his own pleasure, without any body contradicting him.

———

## CHAPTER LVI.

That which befell us, untill our departure towards the port of Zunda, from whence we set sail for China, and what afterwards happened unto us.

THREE days after so cruel and horrible a mutiny, whenas all things were peaceable, the principal heads of this commotion fearing assoon as a *Pangueyran* should be elected, that they should be punished according to the enormity of their crime, they all of them set sail without longer attending the danger which threatened them. They departed away then in the same vessels wherein they came, the King of *Panaruca*, their admiral, being not possibly able to stay them, but contrarily was twice in jeopardy of losing himself in endeavouring to do it with those few men that were of his party. Thus in the space of two days onely, the two thousand sails that were in the port went away, leaving the town still burning, which was the cause that those few lords, which remained, being joyned together, resolved to pass unto the town of *Iapara*, some five leagues from thence towards the coast of the *Mediterranean* Sea. This resolution being taken, they put it presently in execution, to the end that with the more tranquillity (for the popular commotion was not yet well appeased) they might make election of the *Pangueyran*, which properly signifies *Emperour*. As indeed they created one, called *Pate Sudayo*, Prince of *Surubayaa*, who had been none of those eight pretendents of whom we have spoken; but this election they made, because it seemed to them necessary for the common good, and the quiet of the country. All the inhabitants too were exceedingly satisfied with it, and they immediately sent the *Panaruca* for him to a place some dozen leagues from thence, called *Pisammenes*, where he at that time lived. Nine days after he was sent for he failed not to come, accompanied with above two hundred thousand men, imbarqued in fifteen hundred *Calaluzes* and *Juripangos*  He was received by all the people with great demonstration of joy, and a little after he was crowned with the accustomed ceremonies, as *Pangueyran* of all the countries of *Jaoa, Bala,* and *Madura,* which is a monarchy that is very populous, and exceeding rich and mighty.   That done, he returned to the town of *Demaa,* with an intent to have it rebuilt anew, and to restore it to its former estate.   At his arrival in that place, the first thing he did was to give order for the punishing of those which were found attainted and convicted of the sacking of the town, who proved not to be above five thousand, though the number of them was far greater, for all the rest were fled away, some here, some there.   These wretches suffered onely two kindes of death, some were impaled alive, and the rest were burned in the very same ships wherein they were apprehended ; and of four days, wherein this justice was executed, there past not one without the putting to death of a great number, which so mightily terrified us *Portugals* that were there present, as seeing the commotion very great still over the whole country, and no likelihood that things would of a long time be peaceable, we humbly desired the King of *Zunda* to give us leave to go to our ship which lay in the port of *Banta,* in regard to the season for the voyage to *China* was already come.   This King having easily granted our request, with an exemption of the customs of our merchandise, presented every of us besides with an hundred ducates ; and to each of the heirs of fourteen of ours, which were slain in the war, he gave three hundred, which we accepted of as a very honourable reward, and worthy of a most liberal, and good natured prince.   Thus went we presently away very well satisfied of him to the Port of *Banta,* and there we remained twelve whole days together, during the which we made an end of preparing our selves for our voyage. After this, we set sail for *China* in the company of other four ships, who were bound for the same place, and we took along with us the same *Joano Rodriguez,* whom we encountred at *Passeruan,* as I have before declared, that had made himself a Brachman of a *Pagode,* called *Quiay Nacorel* ; and as for him he had named himself *Gauxitau Facalem,* which is as much to

say as, *the Council of the Saint.* The same *Joano Rodriguez*
no sooner arrived at *China,* but he imbarqued himself for
*Malaca,* where (through the grace of God) he was reconciled
anew to the Catholick faith; and after he had continued a
year there, he died with great demonstrations of a good and
true Christian, whereby it seems we may believe that our
Lord received him to mercy, since after so many years
profession of an infidel, He reserved him to come and die in
His service, for which be He praised for evermore. Our five
ships then, with which we parted from *Zunda,* being arrived at
*Chincheo,* where the *Portugals* at that time traded, we abode
three moneths and an half there with travel and danger enough
of our persons; for we were in a country, where nothing but
revolts and mutinies were spoken of. Withall, there were
great armies afoot all along the coast, by reason of many
robberies which the pirats of *Japon* had committed thereabout;
so that in this disorder there was no means to exercise any
commerce, for the merchants durst not leave their houses to
go to sea. By reason of all this we were constrained to pass
unto the port of *Chabaquea,* where we found at anchor sixscore
juncks, who having set upon us, took three of our five vessels,
wherein four hundred Christians were killed, of which fourscore
and two were *Portugals.* As for the other two vessels, in one
of the which I was, they escaped as it were by miracle. But
because we could not make to land, by reason of the easterly
windes which were contrary to us all that same moneth, we
were constrained (though to our great grief) to regain the coast
of *Jaoa.* At length after we had continued our course by the
space of two and twenty days with a great deal of travel and
danger, we discovered an island called *Pullo Condor,* distant
eight degrees, and one third of heighth from the bar of the
kingdom of *Camboya.* Whereupon as we were even ready to
reach it, so furious a storm came from the south-coast, as we
were all in jeopardy to be cast away. Nevertheless driving
along we got to the Isle of *Lingua,* where a tempest surprised
us at west and south-west, with so impetuous a winde, as
struling against the billow, it kept us from making use of our
sails; so that being in fear of rocks and shelves of sand, which
were in the prow-side, we steered the other way, untill that

after some time the fore-keel of our poup opened within nine hand-bredths of the water, which was the cause, seeing our selves so near unto death, that we were enforced to cut down our two masts, and to cast all our merchandises into the sea, whereby our ship was somewhat eased. This done, whereas we had left our ship the rest of the day, and a good part of the night, to the mercy of the sea, it pleased our Lord out of an effect of His divine justice, that without knowing how, or without seeing any thing, our ship ran her self against a rock, with the death of seventy and two persons. This miserable success so deprived us of all our understandings and forces, that not so much as one of us ever thought of any way saving himself, as the *Chineses*, whom we had for mariners in our junck had done, for they had so bestirred themselves all the night long, that before it was day they had made a raft of such planks and beams as came to their hands, tying them together in such sort with the cordage of their sails, that forty persons might abide upon it with ease. Now whereas we were in an imminent danger, and in a time wherein (as they say) the father does nothing for his son, nor the son for the father, no man took care but for himself alone, whereof we had a fair example in our *Chinese* mariners, whom we accounted but as our slaves; for *Martin Estevez*, the captain and master of the junck, having intreated his own servants who were upon the raft, to receive him amongst them, they answered him, that they could not do it at any hand, which coming to the ears of one of ours called *Ruy de Moura*, whereas he could not endure that those perfidious villains should use us with so much discourtesie and ingratitude, he got him up on his feet from a place where he lay hurt, and made unto us a short speech, whereby he represented unto us, *That we were to remember how odious a thing cowardice was*; and withall, *how absolutely it imported us to seize upon this raft for the saving of our lives.* To these words he added many other such like, which so encouraged us, that with one accord, and with one and the same resolution, whereunto the present necessity obliged us, being but eight and twenty *Portugals*, we set upon the forty *Chineses* which were upon the raft. We opposed our swords then to their iron hatchets, and fought so lustily with them, as we

killed them all in the space of two or three *Credo's*. It is
true indeed, that of us eight and twenty *Portugals*, sixteen
were slain, and twelve escaped, but so wounded that four of
them died the next day. This was an accident, whereof no
doubt the like hath seldom been heard of, or seen, whereby
one may clearly perceive how great the misery of humane life
is, for it was not twelve hours before, when as we all embraced
each other in the ship, and behaved our selves like right
brethren, intending to die for one another ; and so soon after
our sins carried us to such great extremity, as hardly sus-
taining our selves upon four scurvy planks, tied together
with two ropes, we killed one another with as much bar-
barism, as if we had been mortal enemies, or something
worse. It is true, that the excuse which may be alledged
thereupon is, that necessity, which hath no law, compelled us
thereunto.

When as we were masters of this raft, which had cost us
and the *Chineses* so much bloud, we set upon it eight and
thirty persons of us that we were, of which there were twelve
*Portugals*, some of their children, our servants, and the
remainder of those that were hurt, whereof the most part
died afterwards. Now forasmuch as we were so great a
number upon a very little raft, where we floated at the
mercy of the waves of the sea, the water came up to our
middles, and in this fashion we escaped from that dangerous
and infortunate rock, on Saturday, being *Christmas* day, 1547,
with one onely piece of an old counter-point, which served us
for a sail, having neither neelle nor compass to guide us.
True it is, that we supplied this defect with the great hope
which we had in our Lord, whom we invoked incessantly with
groans and sighs, that were accompanied with abundance of
tears. In this pitifull equipage we navigated four whole days
without eating anything, so that upon the fifth day necessity
constrained us to feed on a *Caphar* which died amongst us,
with whose body we sustained our selves five days longer,
which made up the nineth of our voyage ; so that during
other four, wherein we continued in this case, we had nothing
else to eat but the foam and slime of the sea ; for we resolved
to die with hunger rather then feed on any of those four

*Portugals* which lay dead by us. After we had wandered thus at the mercy of the sea, it pleased our Lord out of His infinite goodness to let us discover land on the twelfth day, which was so agreeable a sight to us, as the joy of it proved mortal to some of ours; for of fifteen of us that were still alive, four died suddenly, whereof three were *Portugals*; so that of eight and thirty persons which had been imbarqued on the raft, there was but eleven that escaped, namely, seven *Portugals*, and four of our boys. In the end, having got to land, we found our selves in a shallow rode, fashioned much like to an haven, where we began to render infinite thanks to God for having thus delivered us from the perils of the sea, promising our selves also, that through His infinite mercy He would draw us out of those of the land. Having then made provision of certain shell-fish, as oisters, and sea-crabs, to nourish our selves withall, because we had observed how all this country was very desert, and full of elephants and tigres, we got up into certain trees, to the end we might avoid the fury of these beasts, and some others which we saw there; then when we thought that we might proceed on our way with less danger, we gathered us together, and went on through a wood, (where to secure our lives) we had recourse to loud cries, and hollowings. In the mean time, as it is the property of the divine mercy never to forsake the poor sufferers that are upon the earth, it permitted us to see coming along in a chaunel of fresh water, that ran ingulphing it self into the sea, a little barque, laden with timber and other wood, wherein were nine *Negroes*, *Jaoas*, and *Papuas*. As soon as these men saw us, imagining that we were some devils, as they confessed to us afterwards, they leapt into the water, and quite left the vessel, not so much as one of them abiding in her. But when they perceived what we were, they abandoned the fear they were in before, and coming unto us they questioned us about many particulars, whereunto we answered according to the truth, and withall, desired them, for Gods sake, to lead us whithersoever they would, and there to sell us as slaves to some that would carry us to *Malaca*; adding that we were merchants, and that in acknowledgment of so good an office, they should get a great deal of money for us, or as much in commodities

as they would require. Now whereas these *Jaoas* are naturally inclined to avarice, when they heard us talk of their
interest, they began to be more tractable, and gave us better
words, with hope of doing that which we desired of them;
but these courtesies lasted no longer but till such time as they
could get again into their barque, which they had quitted; for
as soon as they saw themselves aboard her, they put off from
the land, and making as though they would part without
taking us in, they told us, that to be assured of what we had
said to them, they would have us before they proceeded any
further, to yield up our arms to them, whereas otherwise they
would never take us in, no not though they saw us eaten up
with lions. Seeing our selves thus constrained by necessity,
and by a certain despair of finding any other remedy to our
present extremity, we were enforced to do all that these men
required of us, so that having brought their barque a little
nearer, they bid us swim to them, because they had never a
boat to fetch us from the shore, which we presently resolved
to do. Whereupon two boys and one *Portugal* leapt into the
sea to take hold on a rope, which they had thrown out to us
from off the poup of the barque; but before they could reach
it, they were devoured by 3 great lizards, nothing of the bodies
of these three appearing to us, but onely the bloud, wherewith
the sea was all dyed. Whilest this passed so, we the other 8 that
remained on the shore were so seized with fear and terrour,
as we were not our selves a long time after, wherewith those
dogs which were in the barque were not a whit moved; but
contrarily, clapping their hands together in the sign of joy,
they said in the way of jearing, *O how happy are these three,
for that they have ended their days without pain!* Then when
as they saw that we were half sunk up into the ouze, without
so much strength as to get our selves out of it, 5 of them leaped
a shore, and tying us by the middle, drew us into their barque,
with a thousand injuries and affronts. After this setting sail
they carried us to a village called *Cherbam*, which was some
dozen leagues from thence, where they sold all eight of us,
namely, six *Portugals*, one *Chinese* boy, and a *Caphar*, for the
sum of 13 *pardains*, which are in value 300 *reals* of our money.
He that bought us was a Pagan merchant of the Isle of *Zele-*

*bres*, in whose power we continued for six or eight and twenty days, and without lying, we had no lack with him, either of clothes or meat. The same merchant sold us afterwards for twelve pistols to the King of *Calapa*, who used so great a magnificence towards us, as he sent us freely to the port of *Zunda*, where there were three *Portugal* vessels, where *Jeronimo Gomez Surmento* was general, who gave us a very good reception, and furnished us abundantly with all that was necessary for us, untill such time as he put to sea from the port, to set sail to *China*.

---

## CHAPTER LVII.

My passing from Zunda to Siam, where in the company of the Portugals
I went to the war of Chiammay; and that which the King of Siam
did, untill he returned into his kingdom, where his queen poisoned
him.

AFTER we had been very near a moneth in this port of *Zunda*, where a good number of *Portugals* were assembled together, so soon as the season to go to *China* was come, the three vessels set sail for *Chincheo*, no more *Portugals* remaining ashore, but onely two, who went to *Siam* in a junck of *Patana* with their merchandise. I bethought me then to lay hold on this occasion, and put my self into their company, because they offered to bear my charges in this voyage, yea and to lend me some money for to try fortune once more, and see whether by the force of importuning her, she would not use me better then formerly she had done. Being departed then from this place, in six and twenty days we arrrived at the city of *Odiaa*, the capital of this empire of *Sarnau*, which they of this country ordinarily call *Siaam*, where we were wonderfully well received and intreated by the *Portugals*, which we found there. Now having been a moneth and better in this city, attending the season for the voyage to *China*, that so I might pass to *Japan* in the company of six or seven *Portugals*, who had imbarqued themselves for that purpose, I made account to imploy in commodities some

hundred ducates, which those 2, with whom I came from
*Zunda,* had lent me. In the mean time very certain news
came to the King of *Siam,* who was at that time with all his
court at the said city of *Odiaa,* that the King of *Chiammay,*
allied with the *Timocouhos, Laaos,* and *Gucos,* people which on
the north-east hold the most part of that country above
*Capimper* and *Passiloco,* and are all sovereigns, exceeding rich
and mighty in estates, had laid siege to the town of *Quiteruan,*
with the death of above thirty thousand men, and of *Oyaa
Capimper,* Governour and Lieutenant General of all that
frontire. The King remained so much appalled with this
news, that without further temporising, he passed over the
very same day to the other side of the river, and never
standing to lodge in houses, he went and encamped under
tents in the open field, thereby to draw others to do the like
in imitation of him. Withall he caused proclamation to be
made over all the city, *That all such as were neither old nor
lame, and so could not be dispensed with for going to this war,
should be ready to march within 12 days at the uttermost, upon
pain of being burned alive, with perpetual infamy for themselves,
and their descendants, and confiscation of their estates to the
Crown:* to which he added many other such great and
dreadfull penalties, as the onely recital of them struck terrour,
not onely into them of the country, but into the very strangers,
whom the King would not exempt from this war, of what
nation soever they were, for if they would not serve, they
were very expresly enjoyned to depart out of his kingdom
within three days. In the mean time so rigorous an edict
terrified every one in such sort, as they knew not what counsel
to take, or what resolution to follow. As for us *Portugals,* in
regard that more respect had always been carried in that
country to them, then to all other nations, this King sent to
desire them that they would accompany him in this voyage,
wherein they should do him a pleasure, because he would trust
them onely with the guard of his person, as judging them
more proper for it then any other that he could make choice
of; and to oblige them the more thereunto, the message was
accompanied with many fair promises, and very great hopes
of pensions, graces, benefits, favours, and honours, but above

all, with a permission which should be granted them to
build churches in his kingdom, which so obliged us, that of
an hundred and thirty *Portugals* which we were, there were
sixscore of us that agreed together to go to this war. The
twelve days limited being past, the King put himself into the
field with an army of four hundred thousand men, whereof
seventy thousand were strangers of divers nations. They
imbarqued all in three hundred *Seroos*, *Lauleas*, and *Iangas*,
so that on the nineth day of this voyage the King arrived at a
frontier town, named *Suropisem*, some 12 or 13 leagues from
*Quitiruan*, which the enemies had besieged. There he abode
above seven days to attend four thousand elephants which
came to him by land. During that time, he was certified that
the town was greatly prest, both on the rivers side, which the
enemies had seized upon with two thousand vessels, as also
towards the land, where there were so many men, as the
number of them was not truly known, but as it was adjudged
by conjecture, they might be some three hundred thousand,
whereof forty thousand were horse, but no elephants at all.
This news made the King hasten the more, so that instantly
he made a review of his forces, and found that he had five
hundred thousand men ; for since his coming forth many had
joyned with him by the way, as also four thousand elephants,
and two hundred carts with field-pieces. With this army he
parted from *Suropisem*, and drew towards *Quitiruan*, marching
not above four or five leagues a day. At the end of the third,
then he arrived at a valley called *Siputay*, a league and a half
from the place where the enemies lay. Then all these men of
war, with the elephants, being set in battel-aray by the three
masters of the camp, whereof two were *Turks* by nation, and
the third a *Portugal*, named *Domingos de Soixas*, they proceeded
on in their way towards *Quitiruan*, where they arrived before
the sun appeared. Now whereas the enemies were already prepared, in regard they had been advertised by their spies of the
King of *Siam's* forces, and of the design which he had, they
attended him resolutely in the plain field, relying much on their
forty thousand horse. Assoon as they discovered him, they
presently advanced, and with their vant-guard, which were the
said forty thousand horse, they so charged the King of *Siam's*

rereward, composed of threescore thousand foot, that they
routed them in less than a quarter of an hour, with the loss
of three princes that were slain upon the place. The King of
*Siam* seeing his men thus routed, resolved not to follow the
order which he had formerly appointed, but to fall on with
the whole body of his army, and the four thousand elephants
joyned together. With these forces he gave upon the battalion
of the enemies with so much impetuosity, as at his first shock
they were wholly discomfited, from whence ensued the death
of an infinite company of men; for whereas their principal
strength consisted in their horse, as soon as the elephants,
sustained by the harquebuses and the field-pieces, fell upon
them, they were defeated in less than half an hour, so that
after the routing of these same, all the rest began instantly to
retreat. In the mean time the King of *Siam*, following the
honour of the victory, pursued them to the rivers side, which
the enemies perceiving, they formed a new squadron of those
that remained of them, wherein there were above an hundred
thousand men, as well sound as hurt, and so past all the
same day there, joyned together in one entire body of an
army, the King not daring to fight with them, by reason he
saw them fortified with two thousand ships, wherein there
were great numbers of men. Nevertheless, as soon as it was
dark night the enemies began to march away with all speed
all along the river, wherewith the King was nothing displeased,
because the most part of his souldiers being hurt, they were
necessarily to be drest, as indeed that was presently executed,
and the most part of the day and the night following imployed
therein.

After the King of *Siam* had obtained so happy a victory,
the first thing that he did was to provide with all diligence for
the fortifications of the town, and whatsoever else he thought
to be necessary for the security thereof. After that he commanded a general muster to be made of all his men of war,
that he might know how many he had lost in the battel;
whereupon he found that some fifty thousand were wanting,
all men of little reckoning, whom the rigour of the King's
edict had compelled to serve in the war, ill provided, and
without defensive arms. As for the enemies, it was known

the next day that an hundred and thirty thousand of them had been slain. As soon as the hurt men were recovered, the King, having put into the principal places of his frontier such guards as seemed requisite to him, was counselled by his lords to make war upon the kingdom of *Guibem*, which was not above fifteen leagues thence on the north side, to be revenged on the Queen of *Guibem*, for having given free passage through her dominions to those of *Chiammay*, in regard whereof he attributed to her the loss of *Oyaa Capimper*, and the thirty thousand men that had been killed with him. The King approving of this advice, parted from this town with an army of four hundred thousand men, and went and fell upon one of this queen's town, called *Fumbacor*, which was easily taken, and all the inhabitants put to the sword, not one excepted. This done, he continued his voyage till he came to *Guitor*, the capital town of the kingdom of *Guibem*, where the Queen then was, who being a widow governed the State under the title of *Regent*, during the minority of her son, that was about the age of nine years. At his arrival he laid siege to the town, and forasmuch as the Queen found not her self strong enough to resist the King of *Siam's* power, she fell to accord with him to pay him an annual tribute of five thousand *Turmes* of silver, which are threescore thousand ducates of our money, whereof she paid him five years advance in hand. Besides that, the young prince her son did him homage as his vassal, and the King led him away with him to *Siam*. Hereupon he raised his siege from before the town, and passed on towards the north-east to the town of *Taysiran*, where he had news that the King of *Chiammay* was fallen off from league aforesaid. In the mean time, whereas he had been six days march in the enemies territories, he sacked as many places as he met withall, not permitting the life of any male whatsoever to be saved. So proceeding onward, he arrived at the lake of *Singipamor*, which ordinarily is called *Chiammay*, where he staid six and twenty days, during the which he took twelve goodly places, environed with ditches and bulwarks after our fashion, all of brick and mortar, without any stone or lime in them, because in the country it is not the custome to build so; but they had no other artillery then some faulconets, and certain muskets of brass.⊗ Now forasmuch as winter began to approach, and that it was very rainy weather, the King too feeling himself not very well, he retired back again to the town of *Quitiruan*, where he tarried three and twenty days and better, in which space he made an end of fortifying it with walls, and many broad and deep ditches, so that having put this town into an estate of being able to defend it self against any attempt, he imbarqued his army in the three thousand vessels which brought him thither, and so returned towards *Siam*. Nine days after he arrived at *Odiaa*, the chief city of his whole kingdom, where for the most part he kept his Court. At his arrival the inhabitants gave him a stately reception, wherein they bestowed a world of money upon divers inventions, which were made against his entry. Now whereas during the six moneths of the King's absence, the Queen his wife had committed adultery with a purveyor of her house, named *Uquum-cheniraa*, and that at the Kings return she found her self gone four moneths with childe by him, the fear she was in lest it should be discovered made her, for the saving of her self from the danger that threatned her, resolve to poison the King her husband, as indeed, without further delaying her pernicious intention, she gave him in a mess of milk, which wrought that effect, as he died of it within five days after; during which time he took order by his testament for the most important affairs of his kingdom, and discharged himself of the obligation wherein he stood ingaged to the strangers which had served him in this war of *Chiammay*. In this testament, when as he came to make mention of us *Portugals*, he would needs have this clause added thereunto, *It is my intent that the six-score* Portugals, *which have always so faithfully watched upon the guard of my person, shall receive for a recompence of their good services, half a years tribute which the Queen of* Guibem *gives me; and that in my custom-houses their merchandise shall pay no custom for the space of three years. Moreover my intent is, that their priests may throughout all the towns of my kingdom publish the law whereof they make profession, namely, of a God made man for the salvation of mankinde, as they have many times assured me.* To these things he added many others such like, which well deserve to be reported here, though I

pass them over in silence, because I hope to make a more
ample mention of them hereafter. Furthermore, he desired
all the grandees of his Court which were present with him,
that they would give him the consolation before he died, to
make his eldest son be declared king, which was incontinently
executed. For which effect, after that all the *Oyaas*, *Conchalis*, and *Monteos*, which are sovereign dignities over all the
rest of the kingdom, had taken the oath of allegiance to this
young prince, they shewed him out at a window to all the
people, who were in a great place below, and they set upon
his head a rich crown of gold in the form of a mitre, and put
a sword into his right hand, and a pair of balances in his left,
a custom which they always observe in such a like ceremony.
Then *Oya Passilico*, who was the highest in dignity in the
kingdom, falling on his knees before the new king, said unto
him with tears in his eyes, and so loud that every one might
hear him, *Blessed childe, that in so tender an age doth hold
from the good influence of thy star the happiness to be chosen by
heaven there above for Governor of this Empire of* Sornau; *see
how God puts it into thy hand by me who am thy vassal, to the
end thou maist take thy first oath, whereby thou dost protest to
hold it with obedience to His divine will, as also to observe justice
equally to all the people, without having any regard to persons,
whether it be in chastising or recompensing the great or small,
the mighty or the humble, that so in time to come thou maist not
be reproached for not having accomplished that which thou hast
sworn in this solemn action. For if it shall happen, that humane
considerations shall make thee swerve from that which for thy
justification thou art obliged to do before so just a Lord, thou
shalt be greatly punished for it in the profound pit of the house
of smoke, the burning lake of insupportable stench, where the
wicked and damned howl continually with a sadness of obscure
night in their entrails. And to the end thou maist oblige thy self
to the charge which thou takest upon thee, say now* Xamxaimpom, *which is as much as to say, amongst us, Amen.* The
*Passilico* having finished his speech, the young prince said
weeping *Xamxaimpom;* which so mightily moved all the
assembly of the people, as there was nothing heard for a good
while together, but sighing and wailing. At length, after that

this noise was appeased, the *Passilico* proceeding on with his discourse in looking on the young king. *This sword,* said he unto him, *which thou holdest naked in thy hand, is given thee as a scepter of sovereign power upon earth for the subduing of the rebellious, which is also to say that thou art truly obliged to be the support of the feeble and poor, to the end that they which grow lofty with their power, may not overthrow them with the puffe of their pride, which the Lord doth as much abhor, as he doth the mouth of him that blasphemeth against a little infant which hath never sinned. And that thou mayest in all things satisfie the fair enamelling of the stars of heaven, which is the perfect, just, and good God, whose power is admirable over all things of the world, say once again* Xamxaimpom; whereunto the Prince answered twice weeping, *Maxinau, Maxinau,* that is to say, *I promise so to do.* After this, the *Passilico* having instructed him in divers other such like things, the young prince answered seven times *Xamxaimpom,* and so the cere-mony of his coronation was finished, only there came first a *Talagrepo,* of a sovereign dignity above all the other priests, named *Quiay Ponuedea,* who it was said was above an hundred years old. This same prostrating himself at the feet of the prince, gave him an oath upon a golden bason full of rice; and that done, they put an end to it, after they had created him thus anew; for time would not permit them to hold him there longer, in regard the king his father was at the point of death; besides there was so universall a mourning amongst the people, that in every place there was nothing heard but lamentations and wailing.

------

## CHAPTER LVIII.

The lamentable death of the King of Siam, with certain illustrious and memorable things done by him during his life; and many other accidents that arrived in this kingdom.

WHEN as the day and the night following had been spent in the manner that I have related, the next morning about eight of the clock the infortunate king yielded up the

406 THE TRAVELS, VOYAGES, AND ADVENTURES

ghost in the presence of the most part of the lords of his kingdom, for the which all the people made so great demonstrations
of mourning, as every where there was nothing but wailing
and weeping.  Now forasmuch as this prince had lived in the
reputation of being charitable to the poor, liberall in his benefits and recompences, pitifull and gentle towards every one,
and above all incorrupt in doing of justice, and chastising the
wicked ; his subjects spake so amply thereof in their lamentations, as if all that they said of it was true ; we are to believe
that there was never a better king then he, either amongst
these Pagans, or in all the countries of the world.

[*Here follows an account of the memorable things done by the
late king, omitted.*]

   It is not to be believed with what infinite sorrow, both all
the great lords, and generally all the subjects of this kingdom,
bewailed the death of their good king ; but at length an
assembly was made of all the priests of this city, who as it
was said, were twenty thousand in number ; by whose direction the principall persons of the kingdom concluded upon the
funerall pomp, and ceremonies which were to be used thereabout, according to the custom of the country : whereupon a
mighty great pile was forthwith erected, made of sandal, aloes,
calembaa, and benjamin ; on the which the body of the
deceased king being laid, fire was put to it, with a strange
ceremony : during all the time that the body was a burning,
the people did nothing but wail and lament beyond all expression ; but in the end, it being consumed to ashes, they put
them into a silver shrine, which they imbarqued in a *Laulea*
very richly equipped, that was accompanied with forty *Seroos*
full of *Talagrepos*, which are the highest dignity of their
Gentile priests, and a great number of other vessells, wherein
there was a world of people : after them followed an hundred
small barques laden with divers figures of idols, under the
forms of adders, lizards, tygers, lions, toads, serpents, bats,
geese, bucks, dogs, elephants, cats, vultures, kites, crows, and
other such like creatures, whose figures were so well represented to the life, as they seemed to be living.  In another

very great ship was the king of all these idols, which they called, *The gluttonous Serpent of the profound pit of the house of smoak.* This idol had the figure of a monstrous adder, was as big about as an hogshead, and writhed into nine circles; so that when it was extended, it was above an hundred spans long; it had the neck standing upright, and out of the eyes, throat, and breast, issued flames of artificiall fire, which rendred this monster so dreadfull and furious, as all that beheld it trembled for fear. Now upon a theatre three fathom high, and richly gilt, was a very beautiful little boy, about four or five years old, covered all over with pearls, and chains, and bracelets of precious stones, having wings, and a bush of hair of fine gold, much after the manner as we use to paint angels. This child had a rich curtelas in his hand; by which invention these Pagans would give to understand, *That it was an angel of heaven sent from God to imprison all those many devils, to the end they should not steal away the kings soul, before it should arrive at the place of rest, which was prepared for it there above in glory, for a recompence of the good works which he had done below in the world.* In this order all these vessells got to land at a *Pagode,* called *Quiay Poutor,* where after that the silver shrine, in which the Kings ashes were, was placed, and the little boy taken from thence, fire was put to all that infinite number of idolls, just in the manner as they stood in the barques; and this was accompanied with so horrible a din of cries, great ordnance, harquebuses, drums, bells, cornets, and other different kinds of noyse, as it was impossible to hear it without trembling. This ceremony lasted not above an hour; for whereas all these figures were made of combustible stuffe, and the vessels filled with pitch and rozen, so dreadfull a flame ensued presently thereupon, as one might well have said that it was a very pourtraiture of hell; so that in an instant the vessells, and all that were in them were seen to be reduced to nothing. When as this, and many other very lively inventions, which had cost a great deal of money, were finished, all the inhabitants, which were come thronging thither, and whereof the number seemed to be infinite, retired back to their houses, where they remained with their doors and windows shut, not one appearing in the streets for the space of ten dayes, during

which time all places were unfrequented, and none were seen
stirring but some poor people, who in the night went up and
down begging with strange lamentations. At the end of the
ten dayes wherein they had shut themselves up so, they opened
their doors and windows, and their *Pagodes*, or temples, were
adorned with many ensigns of rejoycing, together with a world
of hangings, standards, and banners of silk. Hereupon there
went through all the streets certain men on horseback,
apparelled in white damask, who at the sound of very har-
monious instruments, cryed aloud with tears in their eyes, *Ye
sad inhabitants of this Kingdom of* Siam, *hearken, hearken to
that which is made known to you from God, and with humble
and pure hearts praise ye all His holy name; for the effects of
His Divine justice are great; withall laying aside your mourning, come forth of your abodes wherein you are shut up, and
sing the praises of the goodness of your God; since He hath been
pleased to give you a new King, who fears Him, and is a friend
of the poor.* This proclamation being made, all the assistants,
with their faces prostrated on the ground, and their hands
lifted up, as people that rendred thanks to God, answered
aloud weeping: *We make the angells of heaven our attorneys,
to the end they may continually praise the Lord for us.* After
this, all the inhabitants of the city coming out of their houses,
and thinking of nothing but dancing and rejoycing, went to the
Temple of *Quiay Fanarel*, that is to say, *the god of the joyfull*,
where they offered sweet perfumes, and the poorest sort, fruits,
pullen, and rice, for the entertainment of the priests. The
same day the new king shewed himself over all the city with
a great deal of pomp and majesty, in regard whereof the people
made great demonstrations of joy and gladness. And forasmuch as the King was but nine years old, it was ordained by
the four and twenty *Bracalons* of the Government, that the
Queen his mother should be the Protectress or Regent of him,
and that she should bear rule over all the officers of the crown.
Things past thus for the space of four moneths and an half,
during the which there was no manner of disorder, but all was
peaceable in the kingdom; howbeit, at the end of that time,
the Queen coming to be delivered of a son which she had had
by her Purveyor, being displeased with the bad report that

went of her, she resolved with her self to satisfie her desire, which was to marry with the father of this new son, for that she was desperately in love with him : and further, she wickedly enterprised to make away the new king, her lawfull child, to the end that by this means the crown might pass to the bastard by right of inheritance. Now to execute this horrible design of hers, she made shew that the excess of her affection to the young king her son kept her always in fear, lest some attempt should be made upon his life ; so that one day having caused all the Councell of the State to be assembled, she represented unto them, that having but this only pearl enchaced in her heart, she desired to keep it from being plucked from thence by some disaster ; for which effect she thought it requisite, as well to secure her from her apprehensions, as to prevent the great mischiefs which carelessness is wont to bring in such like cases, that there should be a guard set about the palace, and the person of the King. This affair was immediately debated in the Councell, and accorded to the Queen, in regard the matter seemed good of it self. The Queen seeing then that her design had succeeded so well, took instantly for the guard of the palace, and the person of her son, such as she judged were proper for the executing of her damnable enterprise, and in whom she most confided. She ordained a guard then of two thousand foot, and five hundred horse, besides the ordinary guard of her house, which were six hundred *Cauchins* and *Lequios*, and thereof she made captain one called *Tileuhacus*, the cozen of the same Purveyor, by whom she had had a child, to the end that by this mans favour she might dispose of things as she pleased, and the more easily bring to pass her pernicious design. Whereupon relying on the great forces which she had already on her party, she began to revenge her self upon some of the great ones of the kingdom, because she knew they despised her, and held her not in that esteem she desired. The two first whom she caused to be laid hands on were two deputies of the Government, making use of this pretext, that they held secret intelligence with the King of *Chiammay*, and were to give him an entry into the kingdom thorough their lands ; so that under colour of justice she caused them to be both executed, and confiscated their

estates, whereof she gave the one to her favourite, and the
other to a brother-in-law of his, who (it was said) had been a
smith.   But in regard this execution had been done precipi-
tously, and without any proof, the greatest part of the lords of
the kingdom murmured against the Queen for it, representing
unto her the merit of them whom she had put to death, the
services they had rendred to the Crown, the quality of the
persons, and the nobility and antiquity of their extractions, as
being of the blood royall, and lineally descended from the
kings of *Siam*; howbeit, she made no reckoning thereof, but
contrarily a little after making shew as if she had not been
well, she in a full Councill renounced her regency, and conferred it on *Uquumcheniraa*, her favourite, to the end that by
this means bearing rule over all others, he might dispose of
the affairs of the kingdom at his pleasure, and give the most
important charges thereof to such as would be of his party,
which he thought to be the most assured way for him to usurp
this crown, and make himself absolute lord of the Empire of
*Sornau*, whereof the revenue was twelve millions of gold,
besides other comings in, which amounted to as much more.
With all these inventions this Queen used so great diligence
for the contenting of the desire which she had to raise her
favourite to the royalty, to marry her self to him, and to make
the illegitimate son, which she had had by him, successor of
the crown, as within the space of eight moneths, fortune
favouring her designes, and hoping more fully to execute her
wicked plot, she caused most of the great men of the kingdom
to be put to death, and confiscated all their lands, goods and
treasures, which she distributed amongst such of her creatures
as she daily drew to her party.   Now forasmuch as the young
king her son served for the principall obstacle to her intentions, this young prince could not escape her abominable fury,
for she her self poysoned him even as she had poysoned the
king his father.   That done, she married with *Uquumcheniraa*,
who had been one of the purveyors of her house, and caused
him to be crowned King in the city of *Odiaa*, the 11th of
*November*, 1545.   But whereas heaven never leaves wicked
actions unpunished, the year after, 1546, and on the 15th of
*January*, they were both of them slain by *Oyaa Passilico*, and

the King of *Cambaya*, at a certain banquet which these princes made in a temple, that was called *Quiay Figrau*, that is to say, *the God of the Atoms of the Sun*, whose solemnity was that day celebrated : so that, as well by the death of these two persons, as of all the rest of their party, whom these princes also killed with them, all things became very peaceable, without any further prejudice to the people of the kingdom ; only it is true, that it was despoyled of the most part of the nobility, which formerly it had, by the wicked inventions, and pernicious practices, whereof I have spoken before.

---

## CHAPTER LIX.

The King of Bramaa's enterprize upon the Kingdom of Siam : and that which past untill his arrivall at the city of Odia ; with his besieging of it, and all that ensued thereupon.

THE Empire of *Siam* remaining without a lawfull successor, those two great lords of the kingdom, namely, *Oyaa Passilico*, and the King of *Cambaya*, together with four or five more of the trustiest that were left, and which had been confederate with them, thought fit to chuse for king a certain religious man, named *Pretiem*, in regard he was the naturall brother of the deceased prince, husband to that wicked queen of whom I have spoken ; whereupon this religious man, who was *Talagrepo* of a *Pagode*, called *Quiay Mitran*, from whence he had not budged for the space of thirty years, was the day after drawn forth of it by *Oyaa Passilico*, who brought him on the 17th of *January* into the city of *Odiaa*, where on the 19th he was crowned King with a new kind of ceremony, and a world of magnificence, which (to avoid prolixity) I will not make mention of here, having formerly treated of such like things. Withall passing by all that further arrived in this Kingdom of *Siam*, I will content my self with reporting such things as I imagine will be most agreeable to the curious. It happened then that the King of *Bramaa*, who at that time reigned tyrannically in *Pegu*, being advertised of the deplorable estate whereinto the Empire of *Sornau* was reduced, and of

the death of the greatest lords of the country, as also that the
new king of this monarchy was a religious man, who had no
knowledge either of arms or war, and withall of a cowardly
disposition, a tyrant, and ill beloved of his subjects, he fell to
consult thereupon with his lords in the town of *Anapleu*,
where at that time he kept his court. Desiring their advice
then upon so important an enterprise, they all of them told
him, that by no means he should desist from it, in regard this
kingdom was one of the best of the world, as well in riches,
as in abundance of all things; thereunto they added, that the
season which was then so favourable for him, promised it to
him at so good a rate, as it was likely it would not cost him
above the revenue of one only year, what expence soever he
should make of his treasure; besides, if he chanced to get it,
he should remain monarch of all the emperours of the world,
and therewithall he should be honoured with the sovereign
title of *Lord of the white Elephant*; by which means the
seventeen Kings of *Capimper*, who made profession of his law,
must of necessity render him obedience. They told him moreover, that having made so great a conquest, he might, thorough
the same territories, and with the succour of the princes his
allies, pass into *China*, where was the great city of *Pequin*, the
incomparable pearl of all the world; and against which the
great *Cham* of *Tartaria*, the *Siamon*, and the *Calaminham*, had
brought such prodigious armies into the field. The King of
*Bramaa*, having heard all these reasons, and many others
which his great lords alledged unto him, wherein his interest
was especially concerned, which alwayes works powerfully on
every man, was perswaded by them, and resolved to undertake
this enterprise. For this effect he went directly to *Martabano*,
where in less then two moneths and an half, he raised an
army of eight hundred thousand men, wherein there were an
hundred thousand strangers; and amongst them a thousand
*Portugals*, which were commanded by *Diego Suarez d'
Albergaria*, called *Galego* by way of nick-name. This *Diego
Suarez* departed out of the kingdom of *Portugal* in the year
1538, and went into the *Indias* with the fleet of the Vice-roy,
*Don Garcia de Noronha*, in a junck, whereof *Joano de
Sepulveda*, of the town of *Euora*, was captain; but in the

time of which I speak, namely, in the year 1548, he had of the King of *Bramaa* two hundred thousand ducats a year, with the title of his brother, and governour of the kingdom of *Pegu.* The King departed then from the town of *Martabano* the Sunday after Easter, being the 7th of *April* 1548. His army, as I have already said, was eight hundred thousand men, whereof only forty thousand were horse, and all the rest foot, threescore thousand of them being harquebuziers; there were moreover five thousand warlike elephants, with whom they fight in those countries, and also a world of baggage, together with a thousand pieces of cannon, which were drawn by a thousand couples of buffles and rhinocerots; withall, there was a like number of yokes of oxen for the carriage of the victualls. Having taken the field then with these forces, he caused his army to march still on, untill at length he entred into the territories of the King of *Siam*, where after five days he came to a fortress called *Tapurau*, containing some two thousand fires, commanded by a certain *Mogor*, a valiant man, and well verst in matters of war. The King of *Bramaa* having invested it, gave three assaults to it in the open day, and laboured to scale it with a world of ladders which he had caused to be brought thither for that purpose; but not being able to carry it, in regard of the great resistance of them within, he retreated for that time. But having by the counsel of *Diego Suarez*, who was generall of the camp, and by whom he was wholly governed, caused forty great pieces of ordnance, whereof the most of them shot bullets of iron, to be planted against it, he fell to battering it with so much fury, as having made a breach in the wall twelve fathom wide, he assaulted it with ten thousand strangers, *Turks*, *Abyssins*, *Moors*, *Malauares*, *Achems*, *Jaaos*, and *Malayos*; whereupon ensued so terrible a conflict between the one and the other, that in less than half an hour, the besieged, which were six thousand *Siamites*, were all cut in pieces, for not so much as one of them would render himself. As for the King of *Bramaa*, he lost above three thousand of his men, whereat he was so inraged, as that to be revenged for this loss he caused all the women to be put to the sword, which no doubt was a strange kind of cruelty: after this execution, he drew

directly towards the town of *Sacotay*, which was nine leagues
beyond, desiring to make himself master of that, as well as
of the other. He arrived in the sight of this town on
Saturday about sun-set, and incamped all along the river of
*Lebrau*, which is one of the three that issue out of the lake
of *Chiammay*, whereof I have formerly made mention, with
a design to march thorough it directly to *Odiaa*, the capital
city of the empire of *Sornau*; for he had already been
advertised that the King was there in person, and that he
was making preparation to fight with him in the field; he no
sooner received this advice, but his lords counselled him to
make no tarrying in any place, as well that he might not lose
time, as that he might keep himself from insensibly consuming
his forces, in lying before places which he pretended to take,
that were so well fortified as they would cost him dear if he
amused himself about them; so that at his arrivall at *Odiaa*
he would find the most part of his men wanting, and his
victualls quite spent. The King having approved of this
advice caused his army to march away the next day thorough
woods that were cut down by threescore thousand pioners,
whom he had sent before to plane the passages and wayes:
which with much ado they performed. When he was come
to a place, called *Tilau*, which is besides *Juncalau*, on the
south-east coast, neer to the kingdom of *Quedea*, an hundred
and forty leagues from *Malaca*, he took guides that were very
well acquainted with the way, by whose means in nine days
journey he arrived in the sight of *Odiaa*, where he pitched
his camp, which he invironed with trenches and strong
pallisadoes.

During the first five days that the King of *Bramaa* had been
before the city of *Odiaa*, he had bestowed labour and pains
enough, as well in making of trenches and pallisadoes, as in
providing all things necessary for this siege; in all which time
the besieged never offered to stir, whereof *Diego Suarez*, the
marshall of the camp being aware, as also of the little
reckoning which the *Siamites* made of so great a power as
was there assembled, and not knowing whereunto he should
attribute the cause of it, he resolved to execute the design
for which he came; to which effect, of the most part of the

men which he had under his command, he made two separated
squadrons, in each of which there were six battalions of six
thousand a piece. After this manner he marched in battell
array, at the sound of many instruments, towards the two
poynts which the city made on the south side, because the
entrance there seemed more facile to him then any other
where. So upon the 19th day of *June*, in the year 1548, an
hour before day, all these men of war, having set up above a
thousand ladders against the walls, endeavoured to mount up
on them; but the besieged opposed them so valiantly, that in
less than half an hour there remained dead on the place above
ten thousand on either part. In the mean time the King, who
incouraged his souldiers, seeing the ill success of this fight,
commanded these to retreat, and then made the wall to be
assaulted afresh, making use for that effect of five thousand
elephants of war which he had brought thither, and divided
into twenty troops, of two hundred and fifty apiece, upon
whom there were twenty thousand *Moens* and *Chaleus*, choice
men, and that had double pay. The wall then was assaulted
by these forces with so terrible an impetuosity, as I want
words to express it. For whereas all the elephants carried
wooden castles on their backs, from whence they shot with
muskets, brass culverins, and a great number of harquebuses a crock, each of them ten or twelve spans long, these
guns made such an havock of the besieged, that in less then
a quarter of an hour the most of them were beaten down;
the elephants withall setting their trunks to the target fences,
which served as battlements, and wherewith they within
defended themselves, tore them down in such sort, as not one
of them remained entire; so that by this means the wall was
abandoned of all defence, no man daring to shew himself
above. In this sort was the entry into the city very easy to
the assailants, who being invited by so good success to make
their profit of so favourable an occasion, set up their ladders
again which they had quitted, and mounting up by them to
the top of the wall, with a world of cries and acclamations,
they planted thereon, in sign of victory, a number of banners
and ensigns. Now because the *Turks* desired to have therein
a better share then the rest, they besought the King to do

them so much favour as to give them the vantguard, which
the King easily granted them, and that by the counsell of
*Diego Suarez*, who desired nothing more then to see their
number lessened, always gave them the most dangerous
imployments.   They in the mean time extraordinarily contented, and proud to see themselves preferred before so many
other nations as were in the camp, resolved to come off with
honour from this service which they had undertaken.   For
which purpose having formed a squadron of twelve hundred
men, wherein some *Abyssins* and *Janizaries* were comprised,
they mounted with great cries by those ladders up to the top
of the wall, which, as I have declared was at that time in the
power of the King of *Bramaa's* people.   These *Turks* then,
whither more rash, or more infortunate then the rest, sliding
down by a pane of the wall, descended through a bulwark
into a place which was below, with an intent to open a gate,
and give an entrance unto the King, to the end they might
rightly boast, that they all alone had delivered to him the
capital city of the kingdom of *Siam*, and so might gain the
recompence which they might well expect for so brave an
action; for the King had before promised to give unto whomsoever should deliver up the city unto him, a thousand bisses
of gold, which in value are five hundred thousand ducates of
our money.   These *Turks* being gotten down, as I have said,
laboured to break open a gate with two rams which they had
brought with them for that purpose; but as they were
occupied about it, upon a confidence that they alone should
gain the thousand bisses of gold, which the King had promised
to whomsoever should open him the gates, they saw themselves suddenly charged by three thousand *Jaos*, all resolute
souldiers, who fell upon them with such fury, as in little more
then a quarter of an hour there was not so much as one *Turk*
left alive in the place, wherewith not contented, they mounted
up immediately to the top of the wall with a wonderfull
courage, and so flesht as they were, and covered over with the
bloud of the *Turks*, whom they had newly cut in pieces, they
set upon the *Bramaa's* men which they found there, and
fought with them so valiantly, that they durst not make head
against them, so that most of them were there slain, and the

NATIVES OF PEGU AND THE MOLUCCAS.

rest tumbled down over the wall. The King of *Bramaa* redoubling his courage more then before, would not for all that give over this assault, but contrarily resolved to undertake it anew : so as imagining that those elephants alone would be able to give him an entry into the city, he caused them once again to approach unto the wall. At the noise hereof, *Oyaa Passilico*, captain general of the city, ran in all haste to this part of the wall, accompanied with fifteen thousand men, whereof the most part were *Luzons*, *Borneos*, and *Champaa's* with some *Menancabo's* among, and caused the gate to be presently opened, through which the *Bramaa* pretended to enter, and then sent him word, that whereas he was given to understand how his Highness had promised to give a thousand bisses of gold to whomsoever should open him the gates, that so he might thereby enter into the city, he had now performed it, so that he might enter if he would, provided that like a great king as he was, he would make good his word, and send him the thousand bisses of gold, which he stayed there to receive. The King of *Bramaa* having received this jear, would not vouchsafe to give an answer, thereby to shew his contempt of *Oyaa Passilico* ; but instantly he commanded the city to be assaulted, which was presently executed with a great deal of fury ; for the fight began so terrible, as it was a dreadfull thing to behold, the rather for that the violence of it lasted above three whole hours, during the which time the gate was twice forced open, and twice the assailants got an entrance into the city, which the King of *Siam* no sooner perceived, and that all was in danger to be lost, but he ran speedily to oppose them with his followers, which were about thirty thousand in number, and the best souldiers that were in all the city : whereupon the conflict grew much hotter then before, and continued half an hour and better, during the which I do not know what past, nor can say any other thing, save that we saw streams of bloud running every where, and the air all of a light fire ; there was also on either part such a tumult and noise, as one would have said the earth had been tottering ; for it was a most dreadfull thing to hear the discord and jarring of those barbarous instruments, as bells, drums, and trumpets, intermingled with the noise of the great ordnance and smaller shot, and the dreadfull yelling of six thousand elephants, whence ensued so great a terrour, that it took from them that heard it both courage and sense ; withall, that place at the city gate, whereof the *Bramaa* had been master, was all covered over with bodies drowned in bloud, a spectacle so horrible, that the very sight of it put us almost besides our selves. *Diego Suarez* then, seeing their forces quite repulsed out of the city, the most part of the elephants hurt, and the rest so scared with the noise of the great ordnance, as it was impossible to make them return unto the wall ; as also that the best of those that had fought at the gate were slain, and that the sun was almost down, came to the King, and counselled him to sound a retreat, whereunto the King yielded, though much against his will, because he observed, that both he and the most part of the *Portugals* were wounded, but it was with a purpose to return to the same enterprise again the next morning.

The King being retired to his quarter, found himself wounded with the shot of an arrow which he received in that days conflict, and which he felt not untill then, by reason of the heat of the fight. This accident hindred the executing of the resolution he had taken to give another assault to the city the next day ; for he was constrained to keep his bed twelve days together ; but at seventeen days end, when he was fully cured of his hurt he undertook again the prosecution of his design, and to effect that which he had so resolved upon, namely, not to raise the siege from before the city untill he had made himself master of it, though it cost him both his life and his whole state. He gave then a second assault unto the city, which proved like unto the former, for he lost a world of men in it, so that he was forced to retreat ; but his wilfulness was such, as nothing daunted with the great slaughter of his men, he gave five assaults more to it in the open day, wherein he made use of many warlike strata- gems, which a *Greek* enginier daily invented for him ; but whatsoever he could do, he was always fain to retire with loss, whereat he was greatly troubled. In the mean time, whereas the siege of this city had already endured four moneths and an half, he commanded a general muster of his souldiers to be

made, and he found that an hundred and forty thousand of
them were wanting. Whereupon seeing to what estate he
was reduced, for the putting of an end to the business, he
resolved to assault the city again with another new invention,
and this assault was the eighth he had already given to it,
during the siege, which he enterprised by the council of war,
and that under the favour of the night; for they alledged unto
him, that darkness would make the assault less dangerous,
and the scaling of the walls more facile. This resolution
taken, he instantly commanded all preparations necessary for
this design to be made, so that in seventeen days they built
up six and twenty castles of strong pieces of timber, whereof
each one was set upon six and twenty wheels of iron, which
facilitated the motion of so great a frame. Every castle was
fifty foot broad, threescore and five long, and five and twenty
high, and all of them were re-inforced with double beams,
covered over with sheets of lead. Moreover each of them
was full of wood, and had fastened to them before great iron
chains, and that were very long in regard of the fire. Things
thus prepared, on *Friday* about midnight, being very dark and
rainy, the King of *Bramaa* caused three times one after
another all the great ordnance of the camp to be discharged,
which, as I remember, I have already said, consisted of an
hundred and threescore great pieces, whereof the most part
shot iron bullets, besides a many of falconets, bases, and
muskets, to the number of fifteen hundred; so that from all
these guns shot off together three times one after another,
proceeded so horrible and dreadfull a noise, as I cannot think
that any where but in hell the like could be; for on whatsoever the imagination can be fixt, it cannot meet with any
thing that may be rightly compared thereunto. At this time,
it was not onely the great pieces of ordnance, whereof I have
spoken before, and the small ones too, which were shot off,
but the like was done by all the guns which were both within
the city, and without the camp, of what bigness soever they
were, being at least an hundred thousand in all; for whereas
there were, as I have already said, threescore thousand
harquebusiers in the King of *Bramaa's* army, there were thirty
thousand also in the city, besides seven or eight thousand

falconets and bases; so that to hear all these shot off continually for the space of three hours together, and intermingled with thunder, lightning, and the tempest of the night, was, to say the truth, a thing which was never seen, read of, or imagined, and such indeed as put every one almost besides himself; for some fell flat on the ground, some crept behind walls, and others got into walls.  During the great violence of this horrible and furious tempest, they set fire on the six and twenty castles which they had before brought close to the walls, so that by the force of the winde, which was at that time very great, and by the means of barrels of pitch that had been put into them, they fell a flaming in such a strange manner, as there was anew to be seen so dreadful a picture of hell (for it is the onely name that can be given it, because there is nothing upon earth that may rightly be resembled unto it) that if even those which were without trembled at it, I leave you to think with how much more reason were they to fear it whom necessity constrained to abide the violence of it. Hereupon began a most bloody conflict on either part, they without falling to scale the walls, and the besieged; who took no less care for all things then they, valiantly to defend themselves, so that no advantage was to be found on either side, but rather both of them were in a condition to be utterly destroyed; for whereas the one and other reinforced themselves continually with fresh supplies, and that the King of *Bramaas* obstinacy was such, as he went himself in person amongst his souldiers, incouraging them with his speeches, and the great promises that he made them, the fight proceeded so far, and increased so mightily, as being unable to deliver the least part of that which passed therein, I leave it to the understanding of every one to imagine what it might be.  Four hours after midnight, the six and twenty castles being quite burned to the ground, with so terrible a blaze, as no man durst come within a stones cast of it, the King of *Bramaa* caused a retreat to be sounded, at the request of the captains of the strangers; for there were so many hurt men amongst them, as all the day, and most part of the night following, was employed in dressing of them.

## CHAPTER LX.

The King of Bramaa's raising his siege from before the City of Odiaa.

THE King of *Bramaa*, seeing that neither the great ordnance wherewith he had battered the city, nor the assaults which he had given unto it, nor his inventions of castles, accompanied with so many artifices of fire, whereon he had so much relied, had served him to any purpose for the execution of that which he had so mightily desired, and being resolved not to desist from the enterprise which he had begun, he called a councel of war, wherein all the princes, dukes, lords, and commanders that were in the army were present. Having then propounded his desire and intention unto them, he required them to give him their advice there-upon; immediately the affair being put into deliberation, and thorowly debated on either part, they concluded in the end, that the King was by no means to raise this siege, in regard this enterprise was the most glorious, and most profitable of all that ever might be offered unto him; they represented more-over unto him the world of treasure that he had imployed therein, and that if he continued battering the city without desisting from his assaults, at length the enemy would be spent, because it was apparent (as they were informed) that they were no longer able to withstand the least attempt that should be made against them. The King being exceedingly contented, for that their opinions proved to be conformable to his desire, testified the great satisfaction that he received thereby, so that he gave them many recompences in money, and vowed to them, that if they could take the city, he would confer upon them the greatest commands of the kingdom, with very honorable titles and revenues. This resolution being taken there was no further question but of considering in what manner the business should be carried; whereupon by the counsel of *Diego Suarez*, and of the ingineers it was con-cluded, that with bavins and green turf a kind of platform should be erected higher then the walls, and that thereon should be mounted good store of great ordnance, wherewith the principal fortifications of the city should be battered, since that in them alone consisted all the enemies defence. Order then was presently given for all that was judged necessary thereunto, and the threescore thousand pioneers which were in the camp were imployed about it, who in twelve days brought the fort or platform into the estate which the King desired. There were already planted on it then forty pieces of cannon for the battering of the city the day ensuing, when as a post arrived with letters to the King, whereby he was advertised, *That the* Xemindoo *being risen up in the Kingdom of* Pegu, *had cut fifteen thousand* Bramaas *there in pieces, and had withal seized on the principal places of the country*. At these news the King was so troubled, that without further delay he raised the siege, and imbarqued himself on a river, called *Pacarau*, where he stayed but that night, and the day following, which he imployed in retiring his great ordnance and ammunition. Then having set fire on all the pallisadoes, and lodgings of the camp, he parted away on Tuesday, the 15th of *October*, 1548, for to go to the town of *Martabano*. Having used all possible speed in his voyage; at seventeen days end he came thither, and there was amply informed by the *Chalagonim*, his captain of all the *Xemindoos* proceedings, in making himself King, and seizing on his treasure; by killing fifteen thousand *Bramaas*, and that in divers places he had lodged five hundred thousand men, with an intention to stop his passage into the kingdom. This news very much perplexed the King of *Bramaa*, so that he fell to thinking with himself what course he should take for the remedying of so great a mischief as he was threatned with. In the end he resolved to tarry a while at *Martabano*, to attend some of his forces that were still behind, and then to go and fight a battel with his enemy; but it was his ill luck, that in the space of fourteen days onely which he abode there, of four hundred thousand men which he had, fifty thousand quitted him. For whereas they were all *Pegues*, and consequently desirous to shake off the *Bramaas* yoke, they thought it best to side with the new King the *Xemindoo*, who was a *Pegu* as well as they; and they were the rather induced thereunto, by understanding, that this prince was of an eminent condition, liberal, and so affable to every one, that he thereby won most men to be of his party. In the mean time the King of

*Bramaa,* fearing lest the defection of his souldiers should daily more and more increase, was advised by his counsel to stay no longer there, in regard the longer he should tarry, the more his forces would diminish, for that a great part of his army was *Pegues,* which were not likely to be very faithful unto him. This counsel was approved of by the King, who presently marched away towards *Pegu,* neer unto which he was no sooner arrived, but he was certified that the *Xemindoo,* being advertised of his coming, was attending ready to receive him. So these two kings being in view of one another, incamped in a great plain, some two leagues from the city of *Pegu,* the *Xemindoo* with six hundred thousand men, and the *Bramaa* with three hundred and fifty thousand. The next day these two armies being put into battel array, came to joyn together on Friday, the 16th of *November,* the same year, 1548. It was about six of the clock in the morning when first they began their incounter, which was performed with so much violence, as a general defeat ensued thereupon, yet fought they with an invincible courage on either part; but the *Xemindoo* had the worse, for in less than three hours his whole army was routed, with the slaughter of three hundred thousand of his men, so that in this extremity he was forced to save himself onely with six horse in a fortress, called *Battelor,* where he stayed but one hour, during the which, he furnished himself with a little vessel, wherein he fled the night ensuing up the river to *Cedaa.* Let us leave him now flying, until we shall come to him again when as time shall serve, and return to the King of *Bramaa,* who exceedingly contented with the victory which he had gotten, marched the next morning against the city of *Pegu;* where as soon as he arrived, the inhabitants rendred themselves unto him, on condition to have their lives and goods saved. Whereupon he took order for the dressing of them that were hurt; as for those that he lost in this battel, they were found to be threescore thousand in number, amongst the which were two hundred and fourscore *Portugals,* all the rest of them being grievously wounded.

[*Here follows a description of the Kingdom of Siam,* omitted.]

## CHAPTER LXI.

A continuation of that which hapned in the Kingdom of Pegu, as well
during the life, as after the death of the King of Bramaa.

TO return now unto the history which hitherto I have
left, you must know that after the King of *Bramaa*
had obtained that memorable victory neer to *Pegu*, as I
have declared heretofore, by means whereof he remained
peaceable possessor of the whole kingdom, the first thing
he imployed himself in was to punish the offendors, which
had formerly rebelled ; for which effect he cut off the heads
of a great many of the nobility, and commanders, all whose
estates were confiscated to the crown, which (according
to report) amounted unto ten millions of gold, besides plate
and jewels, whereby that common proverb, which was common
in the mouths of all, was verified, namely, *That one mans
offence cost many men very dear*.   Whilest the King continued
more and more in his cruelties, and injustice, which he executed against divers persons during the space of two moneths
and a half, certain news came to him, that the city of *Martabano*
was revolted, with the death of two thousand *Bramaas*, and
that the *Chalogomin*, governour of the same city, had declared
himself for the *Xemindoo*.  But that the cause of this revolt may
be the better understood by such as are curious, I will (before
I proceed any further) succinctly relate, how this *Xemindoo*
had been of a religious order in *Pegu*, a man of noble extraction, and (as some affirmed) neer of kin to the precedent king,
whom this *Bramaa* had put to death twelve years before, as I
have already declared.  This *Xemindoo* had formerly to name
*Xoripam Xay*, a man of about forty-five years of age, of a
great understanding, and held by every one for a saint: he
was withal very well versed in the laws of their sects and false
religion, and had many excellent parts, which rendered him so
agreeable unto all that heard him preach, as he was no sooner
in the pulpit, but all the assistants prostrated themselves on
the ground, saying at every word that he uttered, *Assuredly
God speaks in thee*.  This *Xemindoo*, seeing himself then in
such great credit with the people, spurred on by the generosity

of his nature, and the occasion which was then so favourable
unto him, resolved to try his fortune, and see to what degree
it might arrive. To this end, at such a time as the King of
*Bramaa* was fallen upon the kingdom of *Siam*, and had laid
siege to the city of *Odiaa*, the *Xemindoo* preaching in the
temple of *Conquiay* at *Pegu*, which is as it were the cathedral
of all the rest, where there was a very great assembly of people,
he discoursed at large of the loss of this kingdom, of the
death of their lawful king, as also of the great extortions,
cruel punishments, and many other mischiefs which the
*Bramaas* had done to their nation ; with so many insolences,
and with so many offences against God, as even the very
houses which have been founded by the charity of good people,
to serve for temples wherein the divine word might be
preached, were all desolated and demolished; or if any were
found still standing, they were made use of, either for stables,
lay stalls, or other such places accustomed to lay filth or dung
in. These, and many other such like things, which the
*Xemindoo* delivered, accompanied with many sighs and tears,
made so great an impression in the minds of the people, as
from thenceforward they acknowledged him for their lawful
king, and swore allegeance unto him ; so that instead of calling
him, as they did before, *Xoripam Xay*, they named him
*Xemindoo*, as a sovereign title which they gave him above all
others. Seeing himself raised then to the dignity of king, the
first thing during the heat and fury of this people, was to go
to the King of *Bramaas* palace, where having found five
thousand *Bramaas*, he cut them all in pieces, not sparing the
life of one of them ; the like did he afterwards to all the rest
of them that were abiding in the most important places of the
state, and withal he seized on the King's treasure, which was
not small. In this manner he slew all the *Bramaas* that were
in the kingdom, which were fifteen thousand, besides the
women of that nation of what age soever, and seized on the
places where they resided, which were instantly demolished;
so that in the space of three and twenty days onely he became
absolute possessor of the kingdom, and prepared a great army
to fight with the King of *Bramaa*, if he should chance to return
upon the bruit of this rebellion, as indeed he fought with him to

his great damage, being defeated by him, as I have heretofore
declared. And thus having methinks said enough for the intelligence of that which I am to recount, I will come again to
my first discourse. This King of *Bramaa* being advertised of the
revolt of the town of *Martabano*, and of the death of those two
thousand *Bramaa's*, gave order immediately to all the lords
of the kingdom for their repair unto him with as many men
as they could levy, and that within the term of fifteen days at
the furthest, in regard the present necessity would not endure
a longer delay., This done, he parted the day following with a
small train from the city of *Pegu*, to give example to others to
do the like, and went and lodged at a town called *Mouchan*,
with an intention to tarry there those fifteen days he had
limited the lords to come unto him. Now when as six or
seven of them were already past, he was advertised that *Xemin
de Satan*, governour of a town so named, had secretly sent a
great sum of gold to the *Xemindoo*, and withall had done him
homage for the same town where he commanded. This news
somewhat troubled the King of *Bramaa*, who devising with
himself of the means which he might use to meet with the
mischief that threatned him, he sent for *Xemin de Satan*,
who was then in the said town of his government, with a
purpose to cut off his head ; but he, betaking himself to his
bed, and making shew of being sick, answered, that he would
wait upon the King assoon as he was able to rise. Now in
regard he found himself to be guilty, and misdoubting the
cause wherefore he was sent for, he communicated this affair
to a dozen of his kinsmen who were there present with him,
who all of them concluded together, how since there was no
better way to save himself then in killing the King, that
without further delay it was to be put in execution ; so that
all of them offering secretly to assist him in this enterprise,
they speedily assembled all their confidents, without declaring
unto them at first the occasion wherefore they did it ; and
withall, drawing others unto them with many fair promises,
they made up, all being joyned together, a company of six
hundred men. Whereupon being informed that the King was
lodged in a certain *Pagode*, they fell upon it with great
violence ; and fortune was so favourable unto them, that

finding him almost alone in his chamber, they slew him
without incurring any danger. That done, they retired into
an outward court, where the Kings guard having had some
notice of this treason, set upon them, and the conflict was so
hot between them, that in half an hours space, or thereabout,
eight hundred men lay dead in the place, whereof the most
part were *Bramaa's*. After this *Xemin de Satan* making away
with four hundred of his followers, went to a place of large
extent, called *Poutel*, whither all those of the country round
about resorted unto him, who being advertised of the death of
the King of *Bramaa*, whom they mortally hated, made up a
body of five thousand men, and went to seek out the three
thousand *Bramaa's* which the King had brought thither with
him. And forasmuch as these same were dispersed in several
places, they were all of them easily slain, not scarce so much
as one escaping. With them also were slain fourscore of three
hundred *Portugals* that *Diego Suarez* had with him, who, together with all the rest which remained with their lives saved,
rendered themselves upon composition, and were received to
mercy, upon condition that for the future they should faithfully
serve *Xemin de Satan*, as their proper king, which they easily
promised to do. Nine days after this mutiny, the rebell seeing
himself favoured by fortune, and such a multitude of people at
his devotion, which were come to him out of this province, to
the number of thirty thousand men, caused himself to be
declared the King of *Pegu*, promising great recompences to
such as should follow and accompany him, untill he had
wholly gotten the kingdom, and driven the *Bramaa's* out of
the country. With this design he retired to a fortress called
*Tagalaa*, and resolved to fortifie himself there out of the fear
he was in of the forces which were to come to the succour of
the deceased king, thinking to finde him alive, having been
advertised that many were already set forth from the city of
*Pegu* for that purpose. Now of those *Bramaa's* which *Xemin
de Satan* had slain, one by chance escaped, and cast himself
all wounded as he was into the river, and swimming over,
never left travelling all that night, and the day following, for
fear of the *Pegu's*, untill he arrived at a place, called *Coutasa-
rem*, where he encountred with the *Chaumigrem*, the deceased

Kings foster-brother, who was encamped there with an army
of an hundred and fourscore thousand men, whereof there
were but onely thirty thousand *Bramaa's*, all the rest *Pegu's*;
finding him then upon the point of parting from thence, in
regard of the heat that would be within two hours after, he
acquainted him with the death of the King, and all that had
past besides.  Now though the news greatly troubled the
*Chaumigrem*, yet he dissembled it for the present with so
much courage and prudence, as not one of his followers
perceived any alteration in him.  But contrarily, putting on
a rich habit of carnation sattin, embroidered with gold, and
a chain of precious stones about his neck, he caused all the
lords and commanders of his army to assemble before him,
and then speaking to them with the semblance of a joyfull
man, *Gentlemen*, said he, *this fellow which you saw come to me
but now in such haste, hath brought me this letter, which I have
here in my hand, from the King, my Lord and yours; and
although by the contents thereof he seeemeth to blame us for our
carelesness in lingring thus, yet I hope ere long to render him
such an account of it, as his Highness shall give us all thanks
for the service we have done him.  By this letter too he certifies
me, that he hath very certain intelligence, how the* Xemindoo
*hath raised an army, with an intent to fall upon the towns of*
Cosmin *and* Dalaa, *and to gain all along the rivers of* Digon
*and* Meidoo, *the whole province of* Danapluu *even to* Ansedaa;
*wherefore he hath expresly enjoyned me, that as soon as possibly
I may, I put into those places (as the most important) such
forces as shall be able to resist the enemy; and that I take
heed nothing be lost through my negligence, because in that
case he will admit of no excuse.  This being so, it seems to me
very important and necessary for his service, that you my Lord*
Xemimbrum *go instantly without all delay, and put your self
with your forces into the town of* Dalaa; *and your brother-in-
law* Bainhaa Quem *into that of* Digon, *with his fifteen thousand
men; as for Colonel* Gipray *and* Monpocasser, *they shall go
with their thirteen thousand souldiers into* Ansedaa, *and*
Danapluu, *and* Ciguamcan, *with twenty thousand men shall
march along to* Xaraa, *and so to* Malacou; *moreover* Quiay
Brazagaran, *with his brethren and kinsmen, shall go for General*

*of the Frontier, with an army of fifty thousand men, to the end that assisted with these forces he may in person give order wheresoever need shall be. Behold, what the King hath written to me, whereof I pray you let us make an agreement, and all sign it together, for it is no reason that my head should answer for your want of care, and imprudence.* His commanders presently obeyed him, and without longer tarrying there, each of them went straight to the place whither his commission directed him. The *Chaumigrem,* by the means of this so cunning and well dissembled a sleight, rid himself in less then three hours of all the hundred and fifty thousand *Pegu's,* who he knew, if once they came to hear of the Kings death, would fall upon the thirty thousand *Bramaa's* that he had there with him, and not leave one of them alive. This done, assoon as it was night, turning back to the city, which was not above a league from thence, he seized with all speed on the deceased Kings treasure, which amounted, according to report, unto above thirty millions of gold, besides jewels that were not to be estimated; and withall, he saved all the *Bramaa's* wives and children, and took as many arms and as much ammunition as he could carry away. After this, he set fire on all that was in the magazines, caused all the lesser ordnance to be rived asunder, and the greater, which he could not use so, to be cloyed. Furthermore, he made seven thousand elephants that were in the country to be killed, reserving onely two thousand for the carriage of his treasure, ammunition, and baggage. As for all the rest, it was consumed with fire, so that neither in the palace, where were chambers all sieled with gold, nor in the magazines and arsenals, nor on the river where were two thousand rowing vessels, remained ought that was not reduced to ashes. After this execution, he departed in all haste, an hour before day, and drew directly towards *Tanguu,* which was his own country, from whence he came some fourteen years before to the conquest of the kingdom of *Pegu,* which in the heart of the country was distant from thence about an hundred and threescore leagues. Now whereas fear commonly adds wings to the feet, it made him march with such speed, as he and his arrived in fifteen days at the place whither they were

a going. In the mean time, whereas the *Chaumigrem* had
cunningly sent away the hundred and fifty thousand *Pegu's,*
as I have declared already, it happened that two days after
they understood how the King of *Bramaa* was dead.   Now in
regard they were mortal enemies of that nation, sixscore
thousand of them in one great body turned back in haste for
to go in quest of the thirty thousand *Bramaa's ;* but when
they arrived at the city, they found that they were gone from
thence three days before; this making them to follow in
pursuit of them with all the speed that possibly they could,
they came to a place, called *Guinacoutel,* some forty leagues
from the city whence they came; there they were informed,
that it was five days since they passed by; so that despairing
of being able to execute the design which they had, of cutting
them in pieces, they returned back to the place from whence
they were parted, where they consulted amongst themselves
about that which they were to do, and resolved in the end,
since they had no lawfull King, and that the land was quite
freed of the *Bramaa's,* to go to *Xemin de Satan,* as incontinently they did, who received them, not onely with a great
deal of joy and good entertainment, but promised them mighty
matters, and much honour, by raising them to the principal
commands of the kingdom, assoon as time should serve, and
that he was more peaceably setled.   Thereupon he went
directly to the city of *Pegu,* where he was received with the
magnificence of a king, and for such crowned in the temple
of *Comquiay,* which is the chiefest of all the rest.

## CHAPTER LXII.

That which arrived at the time of Xenim de Satan, and an abominable case
that befell to Diego Suarez ; together with the Xemindoo's Expedition
against Xenim de Satan ; and that which ensued thereupon.

THREE moneths and nine days had this tyrant *Xenim de
Satan* already peaceably possessed the city and kingdom
of *Pegu,* when as without fearing any thing, or being contra-
dicted by none, he fell to distributing the treasure and revenues

of the crown to whomsoever he pleased; whereupon great
scandals ensued, which were the cause of divers quarrels and
divisions amongst many of the lords, who for this cause, and
the injustice which this tyrant did them, retired into several
forreign countries and kingdoms. Some also went and sided
with the *Xemindoo*, who began at that time to be in reputation
again. For after he had fled from the battel onely with six
horse, as I have declared heretofore, he got into the kingdom
of *Ansedaa*, where as well by the efficacy of his sermons, as
by the authority of his person, he won so many to his devotion, as assisted by the favour and forces of those lords as
adhered to him, he made up an army of threescore thousand
men, with which he marched to *Meidoo*, where he was very
well received by those of the country. Now setting aside
what he did in those parts, during the space of four moneths
that he abode there, I will in the mean time pass to a strange
accident which in a few days fell out in this city, that one
may know what end the good fortune of the great *Diego
Suarez* had, who had been Governour of this kingdom of
*Pegu*; and the recompence which the world is accustomed
to make at last unto all such as serve and trust in it, under
the semblance of a good countenance which she shews them
at first. The matter past in this sort. There was in this city
of *Pegu* a merchant, called *Manbagoaa*, a rich man, and that
of good reputation in the country. This same resolved to
marry a daughter of his to a young man, the son of a worship-
full and very rich merchant also, named *Manicaniandarim*,
about that time that *Diego Suarez* was in the greatest height
of his fortune, and termed the Kings brother, and in dignity
above all the princes and lords of the kingdom. So the fathers
of this young couple being agreed on this marriage, and of
the dowry that was to be given, which by report was three
hundred thousand ducates; when as the day was come
wherein the nuptials were celebrated with a great deal of
state and magnificence, and honoured with the presence of
most of the gentlemen of chiefest quality in the city, it
happened that *Diego Suarez*, being come a little before sun-
set from the royal palace, with a great train both of horse
and foot, as his manner was to be always well accompanied,

passed by *Mambagoaa's* door, where hearing the musick and rejoicing that was in the house, asked what the matter was, whereunto answer being made him, that *Mambagoa* had married his daughter, and that the wedding was kept there, he presently caused the elephant on which he was mounted to stay, and sent one to tell the father of the bride, that he congratulated with him for this marriage, and wished a long and happy life to the new married couple; to these words he added many others by way of complement, yea and made him many offers if he would make use of him; wherewith the old father of the bride finding himself so exceedingly honoured, as not knowing how to acknowledge it, in regard the person who did him so much honour was no less than the King himself in greatness and dignity, the desire which he had to satisfie this obligation in part, if he could not wholly do it, made him go and take his daughter by the hand, accompanied with many ladies of quality, and so leading her to the street door, where *Diego Suarez* was, he prostrated himself on the ground with a great deal of respect, and with many complements, after his manner, thanked him · for the favour and honour that he had done him. Thereupon the new married bride, having taken from off her finger a rich ring, presented it on her knees by her fathers express commandment, to *Diego Suarez*; but he that naturally was sensual and lascivious, instead of using civility, whereunto the laws of generosity and friendship obliged him, having taken the ring which the maid presented unto him, he reached out his hand, and plucked her to him by force, saying, *God forbid that so fair a maid as you should fall into any other hands but mine*; whereupon the poor old man seeing *Diego Suarez* hale his daughter so rudely, lifting up both his hands to heaven, with his knees on the ground, and tears in his eyes, *My lord*, said he unto him, *I humbly beseech thee for the love and respect of the great God, whom thou adorest, and which was conceived without any spot of sin in the Virgin's womb, as I confess and believe, according to that which I have heard thereof, that thou wilt not forcibly take away my daughter; for if thou dost so, I shall assuredly die with grief and displeasure at it; but if thou desire of me that I should give thee her dowry, together with all that is in*

*my house, and that I deliver up my self unto thee for a slave,*
*I will instantly do it, provided thou wilt permit that her*
*husband may possess her, for I have no other good in the world*
*but she, nor will I have any other as long as I live.* Whereupon offering to lay hold on his daughter, *Diego Suarez,*
making no answer to him, turned himself about to the
captain of his guard, who was a *Turk* by nation, and said
unto him, *Kill this dog.* The *Turk* presently drew out his
scymitar to kill the poor old man, but he suddenly fled away,
leaving his daughter with all her hair about her ears in *Diego*
*Suarez* his hands. In the mean time the bridegroom came
running to this tumult, with his cheeks all bedewed with
tears; but he was scarcely arrived there, when as these
barbarians slew him, and his father too, with six or seven
other of his kinsmen. Whilest this past so, the women made
such fearfull cries in the house as terrified all those that heard
them, so that even the earth and the air seemed to tremble at
it, or to say better, they demanded vengeance of God for the
little respect which was had to His divine justice, and for so
great a violence as this was; and truly, if I do not more
amply report the particularities of so black and so abominable
an action, I desire to be excused, in regard I pass them by
for the honour of the *Portugal* nation. Wherefore it shall
suffice me to say, that this poor maid seeing her self upon
the point to be forced, strangled her self with a string that
she wore about her middle for a girdle; which she chose
rather to do, then suffer this sensual and brutish man to
carry her away with him by force; but he was therewith so
displeased, as he was heard to say, that he repented him
more for that he had not enjoyed her, then for using her in
that sort as he did. Now from the day of this abhorred act,
till four years after, the good old man, the father of the
bride, was never seen to go out of his house; but at length
to give a greater demonstration of his sorrow, and to shew
his extreme resentment of the matter, he covered himself
with an old tattered mat, and in that sad equipage went up
and down, begging an alms of his very slaves, never eating
any thing, but lying all along naked, and his face fixed on the
ground. Thus continued he in so sad a manner of life, untill

in the end he saw that the season invited him to have recourse
unto justice, which he demanded in this sort; perceiving that
in the kingdom there was another king, other governours, and
other jurisdiction, alterations which time ordinarily produceth
in every country, and in all kinde of affairs, he went out of his
house in the wretched fashion he had so long used, having a
big cord about his neck, and a white beard, reaching almost
down to his girdle, and got him into the midst of a great place,
where stood a temple called *Quiay Fantareu*, that is to say,
*the God of the afflicted*; there he took the idol from off the
altar, and holding it in his arms, he returned out of the temple,
to the said great place, where having cried out aloud three
times to draw the people together, as accordingly they came
flocking in unto him, he said with tears in his eyes; *O ye*
*people, ye people! who with a clean and peaceable heart make*
*profession of the truth of this god of the afflicted, which you see*
*here in my arms, come forth like lightning in a dark and rainy*
*night, and joyn with me in crying so loud, that our cries may*
*pierce the heavens, to the end the pitifull ear of the Lord may be*
*drawn to hear our heavy lamentations, and by them he may know*
*the reason we have to demand justice against this accursed*
*stranger, as the most wicked man that ever was born in the*
*world; for this abominable wretch hath not been contented with*
*spoiling us of our goods, but hath also dishonoured our families;*
*wherefore whosoever shall not with me accompany the god which*
*I hold in my hands, and water with my tears, in detesting so*
*horrible a crime, let the gluttonous serpent of the profound pit*
*of smoke abridge his days miserably, and tear his body in pieces*
*at midnight.* This old mans words so mightily terrified the
assistants, and made so deep an impression in their minds,
that in a short time fifty thousand persons assembled in that
place, with so much fury and desire of revenge, as was wonderfull to behold. Thus the number of the people still more
and more increasing, they ran thronging strait to the Kings
palace, with so horrible a noise, as struck terrour unto all that
heard them. In this disorder, being arrived at the outward
court of the palace, they cried out six or seven times with a
dreadfull tone; *Oh King come out of the place where thou art*
*shut up, to hearken to the voice of thy god, who demands justice*

*of thee by the mouth of thy poor people.* At these cries the
King put forth his head out of the window, and affrighted with
so strange an accident, would needs know of them what
they would have? whereunto they all answered unanimously
with such loud cries, as seemed to pierce the heavens, *Justice,
justice, against a wicked infidel, who to spoil us of our goods hath
killed our fathers, our children, our brothers, and our kinsmen.*
The King having thereupon inquired of them who it was: *It is,*
answered they, *an accursed thief, participating with the works
of the serpent, who in the Fields of Delight abused the first man
that God created. Is it possible,* said he unto them, *that there
should be any such thing as you tell me ?* Whereunto they all
replied, *This same is the most accursed man that ever was born
on the earth, and is so out of his wicked nature and inclination,
wherefore we all of us beseech thee in the name of this God of
the afflicted, that his veins may be as much emptied of his bloud,
as hell is filled with his wicked works.* At these words the King
turning towards them that were about him, *What do you think
hereof,* said he unto them? *What am I to do ? and how am I
to carry my self in so strange and extraordinary a matter ?* To
which they all answered, *My lord, if thou wilt not hearken to
that which this God of the afflicted comes to demand of thee, it
is to be feared that he will take care no longer to aid thee, and
will refuse to support thee in thy dignity.* Then the King turning himself again to the multitude that were below in the court,
bade them *go to the place where the great market was kept, and
he would give order that the man whom they required should be
delivered unto them to be disposed of at their pleasure.* Whereupon
having sent to the *Chirca* of Justice, who is as the sovereign
superintendent thereof above all others, he commanded him to
go and apprehend *Diego Suarez,* and deliver him bound hand
and foot to the people, that they might do justice upon him,
for he feared if he did otherwise, that God would execute it
upon him.

The *Chirca* of Justice went immediately to *Diego Suarez* his
house, and told him that the King had sent for him; he in the
mean time was so troubled to see the *Chirca* come for him, that
he remained a pretty while not able to answer him, as a man
that was almost besides himself, and had lost his understand-

ing; but at length being somewhat come to himself again; *He carnestly desired him to dispense with him at this time for going with him, in regard of a great pain that he had in his head, and that in acknowledgment of so good an office, he would give him forty bisses of gold.* Whereunto the *Chirca* replied, *The offer which thou makest me is too little for me to take upon me that great pain which thou sayest thou hast in thine head, wherefore thou must go along with me, either by fair means or by force, since thou obligest me to tell thee the truth.* Diego Suarez then, seeing that there was no means to excuse him, would have taken along with him six or seven of his servants, and the *Chirca* not permitting it; *I must,* said he unto him, *fulfill the Kings command, which is, that thou shalt come alone, and not with six or seven men, for the time is now past wherein thou wert wont to go so well accompanied, as I have oftentimes seen thee do; all thy support is gone by the death of the tyrant of* Bramaa, *who was the quill wherewith thou blowedst up thy self to unsupportable pride, as is apparent by the wicked actions which thou hast committed, which at this present accuse thee before the justice of God.* This said, he took him by the hand, and led him along with him, environed with a guard of three hundred men, whereat we remained very much dismayed. Thus marching from one street to another, he arrived in the end at the *Bazor*, which was a publick place where all kinde of wares was sold; but as he was going thither, he met by chance with *Balthazar Suarez* his son, who came from a merchants house, whither his father had sent him that morning to receive some money that was owing to him. The son, seeing his father in this plight, alighted presently from his horse, and casting himself at his feet; *What means this, my lord,* said he unto him with tears in his eyes, *and whence comes it that you are led along in this sort?* *Ask it of my sins,* answered *Diego Suarez, and they will tell thee, for I protest unto thee, my son, that in the case I am in, all things seem dreams unto me.* Thereupon embracing one another, and mingling their tears together, they continued so, untill such time as the *Chirca* commanded *Balthazar Suarez* to get him gone, which he would not do, being loth to part from his father; but the ministers of justice haled him away by force, and pushed him so rudely, as he fell and broke his head, yea and withall they gave him many blows besides, whereat his father fell into a swoun. Being come again to himself, he craved a little water, which he had no sooner taken, but lifting up his hands to heaven, he said with tears in his eyes, *Si iniquitates observaberis, Domine, Domine quis sustinebit ? But, O Lord,* added he, *out of the great confidence I have in the infinite price of Thy precious bloud, which Thou hast shed for me upon the cross, I may say with more assurance, Misericordias Domini in æternum cantabo.* Thus altogether desolated as he was in this last affliction, when he was come in sight of the place whither the King had commanded him to be conducted, it is said, that perceiving so many people, he remained so exceedingly dismayed, that turning himself to a *Portugal,* who was permitted to accompany him, *Jesus,* said he unto him, *have all these accused me to the King ?* Whereunto the *Chirca* made him this answer, *It is no longer time for thee to think of this, for thou hast wit enough to know, that the people are of so unruly a humour, that they always follow evil whereunto they are naturally inclined.* It is not that, replied *Diego Suarez* with tears in his eyes, *for I know that if there be any unruliness in them, it proceeds from my sins. Thou seest thereby,* said the *Chirca, that this is the ordinary recompence which the world is accustomed to give to them, who during this life have lost the memory of the divine justice, as thou hast done, and God give thee the grace that in this little time thou hast to live thou mayest repent thee of the faults thou hast committed, which possibly may avail thee more then all the gold that thou leavest behinde thee, for an inheritance to him, who peradventure is the cause of thy death.* Here *Diego Suarez* falling down on his knees, and lifting up his eyes to heaven, *O Lord Jesus Christ,* cried he, *my true Redeemer, I beseech Thee by the pains which Thou hast suffered upon the cross, to permit that the accusation of these hundred thousand hunger-starred dogs against me, may serve to satisfie the chastisement of Thy divine justice in my behalf, to the end that the inestimable price which Thou hast imployed for the salvation of my soul, without any merit of mine, may not be unprofitable unto me.* This said, he ascended the stairs which led to the market-place, and the *Portugal* that assisted him told me, how at every step he

kissed the ground, and called upon the Name of Jesus; at
length when he was come to the top, the *Manbagoao*, who held
the idol in his arms, animating the people with great cries, said
unto them, *Whosoever shall not for the honour of this god of
the afflicted, whom I have here in my arms, stone this accursed
serpent, let him for ever be miserable, and let the brains of his
children be consumed in the midst of the night, to the end that
by the punishment of so great a sin, the righteous judgement of
the Lord above may be justified in them.* He had no sooner
made an end of speaking thus, but there fell so great a shower
of stones on *Diego Suarez*, as in less then a quarter of an hour
he was buried under them, and they that flung them at him
did it so indiscreetly, as the most part of them hurt one another
therewith. An hour after they drew forth the poor *Diego
Suarez* from under the stones, and with another new tumult of
cries and voices they tore him in pieces, with so much fury and
hatred of the whole people in general, as there was not he
which did not believe that he did a charitable and holy work
in giving a reward to the most mutinous amongst those which
dragged his members and entrails up and down the streets.
This execution done, the King willing to confiscate his goods,
sent men to his house for that purpose, where the disorder was
so great, in regard of the extreme avarice which these hungry
dogs had, they left not a tile unmoved; and because they found
not so much as they expected, they put all his slaves and
servants to torture, with such an excess of cruelty, as eight
and thirty of them remained dead in the place, amongst them
were seventeen *Portugals*, who bore the pain of a thing whereof they were not guilty. In all this spoil there were no more
then six hundred bisses of gold found, which are in value three
hundred thousand ducates, besides some pieces of rich hous-
hold-stuff, but no precious stones, nor jewels at all, which
perswaded men that *Diego Suarez* had buried all the rest;
howsoever it could never be found out, notwithstanding all the
search that was made for it, and yet it was verified by the
judgement of some who had seen him in his prosperity, that
he had in means above three millions of gold, according to the
supputation of the country. Behold what was the end of the
great *Diego Suarez*, whom fortune had so favoured in this

kingdom of *Pegu*, as she had raised him up to the deg.ee of the King's brother, the highest and most absolute title of all others, and given him withall two hundred thousand ducates yearly rent, with the charge of general of eight hundred thousand men, and sovereign over all the other govexnours and vice-roys of fourteen kingdoms, which the King of *Bramaa* had at that time in his possession. But it is the ordinary course of the goods of this world, especially of such as are ill gotten, always to serve for a way to disgraces and misfortunes.

I return now to the *Xemindoo*, of whom I have not spoken a long time. Whereas that tyrant and avaricious King *Xemin de Satan* gave daily new increases to the cruelties and tyrannies which he exercised against all sorts of persons, never ceasing killing and robbing (indifferently) those, who were thought to have money; nor sparing any thing that he could lay his hands on, his rapines proceeded so far, as it was that in the space of seven moneths onely, wherein he was peaceable possessour of this kingdom of *Pegu*, he put to death six thousand very rich merchants, besides many ancient lords of the country, who by way of right of inheritance held their estates from the crown. These extortions rendered him so odious, as the most part of those that were with him abandoned him to side with the *Xemindoo*, who had for him at that time the towns of *Digon*, *Meidoo*, *Dalaa*, and *Coulam*, even to the confines of *Xaraa*, from whence he parted in haste to go and besiege this tyrant with an army of two hundred thousand men, and five thousand elephants. When he was arrived at the city of *Pegu*, where *Xemin de Satan* then kept his court, he invested it round about with palisadoes and very strong trenches, yea, and gave some assaults to it, but he could not enter it so easily as he believed, in regard of the great resistance he found from them within; wherefore, judging it requisite for him to alter his minde, being prudent as he was, he came very subtilly to a truce of twenty days with the tyrant upon certain conditions, whereof the principal was, that if within the term of those twenty days he gave him a thousand bisses of gold, which are in value five hundred thousand ducates, he would desist from the pretention and right which he had to this kingdom; and all this he did (as I have already said) cunningly, hoping by this means to bring him to his bowe with less peril. So the time of the truce beginning to run on, all things remained peaceable on either side, and the besiegers fell to communicate with the besieged. During this pacification every morning two hours before it was day, they of the *Xemindoo's* camp played after their manner upon divers sorts of instruments very melodiously, at the sound whereof all they of the city ran to the walls to see what the matter was. Whereupon those instruments ceasing to play, a proclamation was made by a priest, accounted by every man a holy personage, who said these words with a very sad voice, *O ye people, ye people ! unto whom Nature hath given ears to hear, hearken to the voice of the holy captain* Xemindoo, *of whom God will make use for the restoring you to your liberty and former quiet ; in order whereunto he admonisheth you from* Quiay Nivandel, *the God of battels and of the field* Vitau, *that none of you be so hardy as to lift up your hand against him, nor against this holy assembly which he hath made, out of a holy zeal towards these people of* Pegu, *as brother, that he is, to the least of all the poor. Otherwise whosoever shall come against the army of the servants of God, or shall have the will to do them any harm, let him be accursed for it, and as deformed and vile as the children of the night, who foaming with poyson make horrible cries, and be delivered into the burning jaws of the dragon of discord, whom the true Lord of all the Gods hath cursed for ever ; whereas contrarily, to those that shall be so happy as to obey this proclamation, as his holy brethren and allies, shall be granted in this life a perpetual peace, accompanied with a great deal of wealth and riches ; and after their death their souls shall be no less pure and agreeable to God, then those of the saints which go dancing amidst the beams of the sun in the celestial repose of the Lord Almighty.* This publication made, the musick began to play again with a great noise as before, which made such an impression in the hearts of them that heard it, as in seven nights that it continued above threescore thousand persons went and rendered themselves to the *Xemindoo* ; for most of them which heard those words gave as much credit thereunto, as if an angel from heaven had spoken them. In the mean time the besieged tyrant, seeing that these secret proclamations of the enemy were so prejudicial unto him, as they could not chuse but turn to his utter ruine, brake the truce at twelve days end, and deliberated with his council what he should do, who advised him by no means to suffer himself to remain any longer besieged, for fear lest the inhabitants should mutiny, and fall from him to the enemy; and that the best and surest way was, to fight with the *Xemindoo* in the open field, before he grew to any further strength. This resolution being approved of by *Xenim de Satan*, he prepared himself for the execution of it; to which effect he, two days after, before it was day, sallied out at five gates of the city, with fourscore thousand men, which then he had, and charged the enemies with strange fury. They then, in the mean time, who always stood upon their guard, received them with a great deal of courage; whereupon ensued so cruel a conflict between them, that in less then half an hour, for so long lasted the heat of the fight, there fell on both sides about forty thousand men; but at the end of that time the new King *Xenim* was born from his elephant by an harquebuse shot, discharged at him by a *Portugal*, named *Goncalo Neto*, which caused all the rest to render themselves, and the city likewise, upon condition that the inhabitants should have their goods and lives saved. By this means the *Xemindoo* entred peaceably into it, and the very same day, which was a *Saturday*, the 23*rd* of *February*, 1551, he caused himself to be crowned King of *Pegu* in the greatest temple of the city. As for *Goncalo Neto*, he gave him in recompence for killing the tyrant twenty bisses of gold, which are ten thousand ducates; and to the other *Portugals*, being eighty in number, he gave five thousand ducates, besides the honours and priviledges which they had in the country; he also exempted them for three years from paying any custome for their merchandise, which was afterwards very exactly observed.

## CHAPTER LXIII.

That which the Xemindoo did, after he was crowned King of Pegu, with
the Chaumigrems; the King of Bramaa's foster-brothers coming against
him, with an army; and divers other memorable things.

THE *Xemindoo* seeing himself crowned King of *Pegu*, and
peaceable lord of all the kingdom, began to have thoughts
far different from those which *Xemin de Satan* had had, being
raised to the same dignity of King; for the first and principal
thing wherein he imployed himself with all his endeavour, was
to maintain his kingdom in peace, and to cause justice to
flourish; as, indeed, he established it with so much integrity,
as no man how great soever he was, durst wrong a lesser then
himself: withall in that which concerned the government of
his kingdom, he proceeded with so much virtue and equity, as
it filled the strangers that were there with admiration, so that
one could not without marvel consider the peace, the quiet,
and union of the wills of the people; during the happy and
peaceable estate of this kingdom, which continued the space of
a year, and better; at the end whereof the *Chaumigrem*, foster-
brother to the same King of *Bramaa*, whom *Xemin de Satan*
had slain, as I have before declared, having received advertisement, that by reason of the rebellions and wars, which
since his departure from thence had happened in the kingdom
of *Pegu* the principal men of state there, had lost their lives;
and the *Xemindoo* who then reigned was unprovided of all
things necessary for his defence; he resolved once again to
adventure upon the same enterprise which had formerly been
undertaken by his late king. With this design, he entertained into his pay a mighty army of strangers, unto whom
he gave a tineal of gold by the moneth, which is five ducates
of our money; when as he had prepared all things in a readiness, he departed from *Tanguu*, the place of his birth. On
the 9th day of *March*, 1552, with an army of three hundred
thousand men, whereof onely fifty thousand were *Bramaa's*,
and all the rest *Mons, Chaleus, Calaminhans, Sauanis, Pam-
crus*, and *Auaas*. In the mean time the *Xemindoo*, the new
King of *Pegu*, having certain intelligence of these great forces,

which were coming to fall upon him, made preparation to go
and meet them, with a design to give them battel; for which
effect he assembled in the same city where he was, a huge
army of nine hundred thousand men, which were all *Pegu's* by
nation, and consequently of a weak constitution, and less warlike then all the others, whereof I have spoken; and on
*Tuesday* the 4th of *April*, about noon, having received advice
that the enemies army was encamped all along the river of
*Meleytay*, some twelve leagues from thence, he used such
expedition, as the same day, and the next night, all his
souldiers were put into battel-aray, for whereas they had
prepared every thing long before, and had also been trained
by their captains, there needed no great ado to bring them
into order. The day ensuing, all these men of war began
about nine of the clock in the morning, to march at the sound
of an infinite number of warlike instruments, and went and
lodged that night some two leagues from thence near to the
river *Potareu*. The next day, an hour before sun-set the
*Bramaa Chaumigrem* appeared with so great a body of men,
as it took up the extent of a league and an half of ground;
his army being composed of seventy thousand horse, of two
hundred and thirty thousand foot, and six thousand fighting
elephants, besides as many more which carried baggage and
victuals; and in regard it was almost night, he thought fit to
lodge himself all along by the mountain, that he might be in
the greater safety. Thus the night past with a good guard,
and a strange noise that was made on either part. The day
following, which was a *Saturday*, the 7th of *April*, in the
year 1553, about five of the clock in the morning, these two
armies began to move, but with different intentions; for the
design of the *Bramaa* was to pass the ford, and recover an
advantageous piece of ground, which lay near to another
river; and the *Xemindoo* had a desire to keep him from it,
and to stop his passage; upon this contention, some skirmishes ensued, which continued most part of the day, and
wherein above five hundred men on the one side and the other
were slain, howbeit the advantage remained with the *Chaumigrem*, because he gained the place whereunto he pretented,
and passed all the night there in banquetting, and making

great bonfires for this good successe. The next day, betimes
in the morning, the *Xemindoo*, King of *Pegu*, presented the
battail to his enemies, who did not refuse it; so that they
encountred one another with all the fury that a cruel hatred
is accustomed to kindle in such like cases; the two vantgards
then, who were the best souldiers amongst them, fell so lustily
unto it, that in lesse then half an hour, all the field was covered
with dead bodies, and the *Pegues* began to lack courage.
Whereupon the *Xemindoo*, seeing his men give ground, came
to succour them with a body of three thousand elephants,
wherewith he set upon the seventy thousand horse so
couragiously, and to the purpose, as the *Bramaa's* lost all
that they had gained; which perceived by the *Chaumigrem*,
who was better experienced in matters of warre, knowing full
well what he was to do, to recover all again, made shew of
retyring, as if he had been vanquished; the *Xemindoo* thereupon, who understood not this stratagem, and that thought
of nothing but the victory, pursued his enemy about a quarter
of a league : but incontinently the *Bramaa* facing about with
all his forces, fell upon his enemy with such violence and
horrible cryes, as not only men, but even the very earth, and
all the other elements seemed to tremble at it.   By this means
the conflict renewed in such sort, as in a little time the ayre
was seen all on fire, and the ground watered all over with
bloud; for the *Pegu* lords and commanders, beholding their
King so farre ingaged in the battle, and likely to lose the day,
ran instantly to his succor; the like did the *Panonsaray*, the
*Bramaa's* brother, on his side, with fourty thousand men, and
two thousand elephants; so that there ensued betwixt them
so bloudy and dreadfull a fight, as words are not able to
expresse the truth of it; wherefore I shall say no more, but
that half an hour, or there about, before sun-set, the army
of nine hundred thousand *Pegues* was utterly discomfited;
and (as it was said) four hundred thousand of them were
left dead on the place, and all the rest, or the most part of
them, grievously wounded; which the *Xemindoo* seeing, fled
out of the field, and so escaped.   Thus did the victory remain
unto the *Chaumigrem*, who thereupon caused himself to be
crowned King of *Pegu*, with the same royal ensignes, magni-

ficence, and triumph, as the other King of *Bramaa*, whom *Xemin de Satan* slew, had formerly been. And in regard it was already night, they bestowed the time in no other thing, but in dressing the hurt men, and keeping good watch in the camp.

The next day, as soon as it was light, all the victorious souldiers, as well wounded as unwounded, ran to the spoil of the dead bodies; wherewith divers amongst them were mightily enriched; for they found there great store of gold and jewels, by reason the custome of those Gentiles is, (as I think, I have heretofore delivered) to carry all their wealth about them to the war. The souldiers being well satisfied in this particular, the new king of this miserable kingdome parted forthwith from the place were he had gotten the victory, and marched towards the citie of *Pegu*, distant some three leagues from thence. Now forasmuch as he would not that day enter into it, for certain considerations which I will relate hereafter, he set himself down in the view of it, about half a league off, in a plain, called *Sunday Patir:* and after he had thus encamped his army, he gave order for the guard of the four and twenty gates thereof, by placing at each of them a *Bramaa* commander with five thousand horse. In this manner he remained there five dayes, without being able to resolve to enter into the citie, out of the fear he was in, lest the strangers should require of him the pillage of it, as indeed, he was obliged to grant it to them by the promise which he had made them for it at *Tanguu.* Now the custom of men of war, who live but upon their pay, being to have regard to nothing but their interests, these six nations seeing the King thus defer his entry into the citie, which they could not brook, began to mutinie, and this by the instigation of a *Portugal*, named *Christonano Surnento*, a man of a turbulent spirit, but otherwise a good and valiant commander; and this mutinie proceeded so far, as the King of *Bramaa* for his own safty was constrained to retire into a *Pagode*, where he fortified himself with his *Bramaa's*, untill that the next morning about nine of the clock he came to a truce with them, and causing them to assemble together, from the top of a wall he spake to them in this sort, *My worthy friends, and valiant commanders, I have caused you to come to this holy resting-place of the dead, to the end that with a solemn oath I may discover unto you my intentions ; whereof, with my knees on the ground, and my eyes lift up unto heaven, I take to witness* Quiay Nivandel, *the God of battel of the field* Vitau, *beseeching him to be judg of this between you and me, and to strike me dumb, if I do not tell you the truth. I very well remember the promise I made you at* Tanguu, *which was, to give you the pillage of this tumultuous citie ; as well because I believed your valour would be as it were the minister of my revenge, as in some sort to satisfie your avarice, whereunto I know you are naturally very much inclined. Now having given you this promise for a gage of my faith, I acknowledg that I am altogether obliged not to break my word with you. But when, on the other side, I come to consider the great inconveniences which may accrue to me thereby, and the strict account which I shall one day render for it before the equitable and rigorous justice of the Lord above, I must confesse unto you, that I am very much affraid of charging my self with so heavie a burthen : wherefore reason advises me to render my self faulty towards men, rather than to fall into the displeasure of God. Besides, it is not reasonable that the innocent should pay for the guilty, and of whom I am sufficiently satisfied with the death which they have received in this last battel by your hands. Behold, how I earnestly intreat you, as children that you are of my bowels, that having regard to my good intention, you will not kindle this fire wherein my soul will be burnt, since you see well enough how reasonable that is which I desire of you, and how unjust it would be for you to refuse it me. Nevertheless, to the end you may not remain altogether without recompense, I do here promise you to contribute thereunto all that shall seem reasonable to you, and so supply this default in part with my own goods, with my person, with my kingdom, and with my state.* Hereupon the commanders of those six nations hearing the King's justification, and the promise which he made them, yeelded to agree unto whatsoever he would do : howbeit, they prayed him above all things to have regard unto souldiers pretensions, who were not at any hand to be discontented, but greatly to be made account of. Whereunto the King

replyed, *That they had reason, and that in all things he would
endeavour to conform himself to whatsoever they should judg
reasonable.* In the mean time, to avoid disputes which might
ensue hereupon, it was concluded, that they should referr
themselves to arbitrators : for which effect the mutiners were
to name three on their side, and the King three others on his,
which made six in all, whereof three were to be religious men
and the rest strangers, that so the judgment might be given
with lesse suspicion. This resolution being taken between
them, they agreed together, that the three religious men
should be the *Menigrepos* of a *Pagode*, that was named *Quiay
Hifaron*, that is to say, the God of Povertie ; and that for the
other three strangers, the King and the mutiners should cast
lots, to see who should chuse one or two of them on his side.
The election being fallen to the King, he made a choice of two
*Portugals*, of an hundred and forty that were then in the
citie ; whereof the one was *Gonsalo Pacheco*, the King our
masters factor for lacre, a worthie man, and of a good conscience ; and the other a worshipful merchant, named *Nuno
Fernandez Teixeyra*, whom the King held in good esteem, as
having known him in the life time of the deceased king. By
the same means the commanders of the mutiners elected
another stranger, whose name I do not know. Things thus
concluded, the judges destined for the resolution of this affair
were sent for, because the King was not willing to stirre out
of the place where he was, untill the matter was determined ;
to the end he might dismisse them all peaceably before he
entred into the citie, for fear lest if they entred with him, they
should not keep their word. For this purpose then the King
about midnight sent a *Bramaa* on horseback to the *Portugals*
quarter, who were in no lesse fear then the *Pegues* of being
plundered and killed. After that the *Bramaa* was come into
the citie, and that he had asked aloud (for so they use to do
when they come from the King) where the captain of the
*Portugals* was, he was presently conducted to his lodging,
where being arrived, *It is a thing* (said he to the captain) *as
proper to the nature of that Lord above, who hath created the
firmament and the whole heavens, to make good men for the
conversion of the wicked, as it is ordinary with the pernicious*

*dragon to nourish in his bosome spirits of commotion and tumult,
to bring disorder unto the peace which conserves us in the holy
law of the Lord. I mean hereby* (continued he) *that amongst
all those of your nation there is one wicked man found, vomiting
out of his infernal stomack flames of discord and sedition, by
means whereof he hath caused the three strange nations of the*
Chalons, Meleytes, *and* Savadis *to mutinie in the King my
masters army, whereupon hath ensued so great a mischief, that
besides almost the utter ruine of the camp, three thousand*
Bramaa's *have been slain, and the King himself hath been in
such danger, as he was fain to retire into a fort, where he hath
remained three dayes, and still is there, not daring to come out,
because he cannot put any trust in those strangers. Howbeit,
for a remedy of so great unquietnesse, it hath pleased God, who
is the true Father of concord, to inspire the King's heart with
patience to endure this injurie, being prudent as he is, to the end
he may by that means pacifie the tumult and rebellion of these
three turbulent nations, who inhabit the most desart parts of the
mountains of* Mons, *and are the most accursed of God amongst
all people. Now, to make an entry into this peace and union, a
treaty hath been had between the King and the commanders of
the mutiners, whereby it hath been concluded on either part,
with an oath, That to exempt this city from the plundering
which had been promised to the souldiers, the King shall give
them out of his own estate, as much as six men, deputed for
that purpose, shall award; of which number there are already
four; so that to make up the whole six, there wants none but
thee, whom the King hath chosen for him; and another Portugal,
whose name is written in this paper, whereby thou shalt be
ascertained of that which I have said unto thee.* Thereupon he
delivered a letter unto him from the King of *Bramaa*; which
*Gonsalo Pacheco* received upon his knees, and laid upon his
head, with exterior complements so full of civilitie and courtesie, as the *Bramaa* remained very much contented and
satisfied therewith, and said unto him, *Surely, the King my
master must needs have a great knowledge of thee, in that he
hath chosen thee for a judge of his honour and estate.* Hereupon *Gonsalo Pacheco* read the letter aloud before all the
*Portugals*, who heard it standing, with their hats in their

hands. The contents of it were to this effect, *Captain* Gonsalo Pacheco, *my dear friend, and that appears before my eyes
like a precious pearl, as being no less vertuous in the tranquillitie
of thy life, then the holiest Menigrepos which live in the desarts;
I, the ancient* Chaumigrem, *and now King of fourteen states,
which God hath now put into my hands by the death of the holy
King my master, do send thee a smile of my mouth, to the end
thou mayest be as agreeable to me, as those whom I cause to sit
at my table, in a day of joy and feasting. Know then, that I
have thought good to take thee for a judge of the affair that is in
question, and therefore have sent for thee, together with my good
friend,* Nuno Fernandez Teixyra, *to come presently unto me, for
to give an end to this business, which I wholly commit unto your
trust. And for so much as concerns the security of your persons,
in regard of the fear you may be in of the late mutiny, I do
engage my word, and swear to you by the faith which a king
ought to have, whom God himself hath anointed, that I will take
you, and all those of your nation, with all others that beleeve in
your God, into my protection.* After that this letter was read,
to the great astonishment of all us that heard it, we could
beleeve no other, but that by divine permission it came from
heaven for the assurance of our lives, whereof we stood in very
great doubt until then, *Gonsalo Pacheco* and *Nuno Fernandez*,
with ten other *Portugals*, which were chosen for that purpose, instantly prepared a present of divers rich pieces to carry
to the King, unto whom they went that very same night an
hour before day, in the company of the *Bramaa* who brought
the letter, in regard, the haste the King was in would brook
no delay.

*Gonsalo Pacheco, Nuno Fernandez,* and the other *Portugals*,
arrived at the camp an hour before sun-rising, and the King
sent to receive them one of the chiefest *Bramaa* commanders
that he had, and in whom he very much confided, who was
accompanied with above an hundred horse, and six serjeants
at armes that carried maces. This same received the *Portugals*, and lead them to the King, who did much honour unto
*Gonsalo Pacheco,* and *Nuno Fernandez*; and after he had talked
with them of divers matters, he put them in mind of the
importance of the businesse for which he had sent for them,

30

and willed them by any means, to leane rather to the commanders then to him, assuring them that he should be very well contented therewith, and said many things to them to that purpose. Then he caused them to be conducted by the same *Bramaa* lord to the tent, where the other four arbitrators were with the high treasurer, and two registers; when as they had commanded silence to all that were without, they fell to debating of the businesse for which they were assembled together; whereupon there were many opinions, which took up the most part of the day, but at last all six came to conclude; that albeit on the one side the King, by the promise which he had made at *Tanguu* to the forreigne souldiers, for to give them the spoil or pillage of the places which he should take by force, was exceedingly obliged to the performance thereof, yet seeing that on the other side this promise was of great and notable prejudice to the innocent, because it could not be put in execution without greatly offending God; these things considered, they ordained by their award; *That the King, in regard of the promise which he had made them, should pay unto them a thousand bisses of gold out of his own treasure; and that upon the souldiers receiving thereof they should passe over to the other side of the river, and retire directly into their countries; but that they should first be also paid all that was due to them before this mutiny began, and that they should be furnished with victuals sufficient for twenty daies.* This award being published was received with much content to either party; so that the King commanded it to be instantly and punctually executed; and for a greater testimony of his liberality, after he had payed them all this sum of mony, he bestowed upon the commanders and officers of each company many bountifull rewards, wherewith they were all of them very well pleased, and satisfied. In this sort were these three mutinous nations discharged; for the King would by no means trust, or make use of them any longer. Howbeit, he would not suffer these strangers to go all away together, but caused them to be divided into troups, each of them consisting of a thousand men, to the end that by this means they should give the lesse suspicion in their return, and should be lesse able to plunder the open towns, by which they were to passe; and

thus the next day they departed    As for *Gonsalo Pacheco*,
and *Nuno Fernandez Teixyra*, the King gave them ten bisses
of gold, for being his arbitrators in this affair, whereunto he
added a passport written with his own hand, whereby the
*Portugals* were permitted to retire freely into the *Indies*,
without paying any custome or duty for their merchandize,
whereof we made more account then of all the mony could
have been given us ; because that, for three years before, the
precedent kings had retayned us in this country, with exceeding much vexation and tyranny, whereby we were oftentimes
in great danger of our lives, by reason of the successe of that
which I have spoken heretofore.  This done, there were proclamations made by men on horseback, to give notice that the
day following, the King would enter into the city in a peaceable
manner, threatning all such as should do the contrary, with a
cruell death.  Accordingly, the next morning at nine of the
clock the King parted from the *Pagode*, whither he had retired
himself ; and about an hour after arrived at the city, whereinto
entring by the chiefest gate, he was received by an assembly
(in form of a *procession*) of six thousand priests of all the
twelve sects which are in this kingdome ; by one of whom,
called *Capizundo*, an oration was made unto him, whereof the
preface was thus, *Blessed and praised be that Lord, who ought
truly to be acknowledged of all men for such, in regard of the
holy works which He hath made with His Divine hands, testified
to us by the light of the day, the shining of the night, and all
the other magnificences of His mercy which He hath produced in
us ; praised be He, I say, for that by the effects of His infinite
power, which are agreeable unto Him, He hath been pleased to
establish thee on the earth above all the kings that govern it ;
and seeing we hold thee for His favorite, we humbly beseech
thee our lord, that thou wilt never more remember the faults and
offences which we have committed against thee, to the end that
these thy afflicted people may be comforted with the promise
thereof, which they hope thy Majesty will make them at this
present.*  This same request was likewise made unto him by
the six thousand *Grepos*, all prostrated on the ground, and
with their hands lifted up to heaven, who with a dreadfull
tumult of voices said unto him ; *Grant, our Lord and King,*

*peace and pardon for that is past to all the people of this thy
kingdom of Pegu, to the end they may not be troubled with the
fear of their offences, which they confesse publikely before thee.*
The King answered them that he was contented so to do, and
swore to them by the head of *Quiay Nivandel*, the God of Battle
of the field *Vitau*, for the confirmation thereof.  Upon this
promise all the people prostrated themselves with their faces
on the ground, and said unto him; *God make thee to prosper
for infinite years in the victory over thy enemies, that thou
mayest trample their heads under thy feet.*  Hereupon for a
token of great gladness, they fel to playing on divers instruments after their manner, though very barbarously, and
untunably; and the *Grepo Capizondo* set on his head a rich
crown of gold and precious stones of the fashion of a mitre,
wherewith the King made his entry into the city, with a great
deal of state and triumph, causing to march before him all the
spoile of the elephants and chariots, as also the statue of the
*Xemindoo*, whom he had vanquished, bound with a great iron
chain, and forty colours trayled on the ground; as for him, he
was seated on a very mighty elephant, harnessed with gold,
and invironed with forty serjeants at armes bearing maces:
there marched likewise all the great lords and commanders on
foot, with their scymitars covered with plates of gold, which
they carried on their shouldiers, and three thousand fighting
elephants, with their castles of divers inventions, besides a
world of other people, as well foot as horse, which followed
him without number.

------

## CHAPTER LXIV.

The finding of the Xemindoo, and bringing of him to the King; with the
manner of his execution and death; and other particularities concerning
the same.

AFTER that the King of *Bramaa* had continued peaceably
in this citie of *Pegu* for the space of six and twenty daies,
the first thing he did was to make himself master of the principal places of this kingdome, which not knowing the defeat of
the *Xemindoo*, held still for him.  To this purpose, having

given commission to some commanders for it, he wrote to the inhabitants of those places divers courteous letters, wherein he called them his dear children, and gave them an abolition of all that was past. He also promised them, by a solemn oath, to maintain them in peace for the time to come, and alwayes to minister justice to them, without any imposts or other oppression; but that he would (contrarily) do them new favours, as to the very *Bramaas* which served him in the warres. To these words he added many others, very well accommodated to the time and his desire; for the better crediting whereof, they that were already reduced under his obedience wrote their letters also unto them, wherein they made an ample relation of the franchises and immunities which the King had granted to them. All this, accompanied with the fame which ran thereof in all parts, wrought so great an effect, as all those places rendred unto him, and put themselves under his obedience: so that, in imitation of them all, the other cities, towns, states and provinces that were in the kingdom, did the like. For my part, I hold, that this kingdome whereof the King of *Bramaa* made at this time a new conquest, is the best, the most abundant, and richest in gold, in silver, and precious stones, that may be found in any part of the world. Things being thus accomplished, to the great advantage of the *Bramaa*, he dispatches divers horsemen with all speed into all parts, to go in quest of the *Xemindoo*; who (as I have already declared) had escaped from the past battel, and was so unhappy, that he was discovered in a place named *Faulau*, a league from the town of *Potem*, which separates the kingdom from *Aracam*: presently whereupon, he was lead with great joy, by a man of base condition, to this King of *Bramaa*, who in recompence thereof gave him thirty thousand ducates of yearly rent. Being brought before him, bound as he was with an iron collar, and manacles, he said unto him, in way of derision, *Thou art welcome (King of* Pegu) *and maist well kisse the ground which thou seest; for I assure thee, I have set my foot on it; whereby thou mayest perceive how much I am thy friend, since I do thee an honour which thou couldst never imagine.* To these words the *Xemindoo* made no answer; so that the King falling to jeer this miserable man anew, who lay

before him with his face on the ground, said unto him, *What
means this ? Art thou amazed to see me, or to see thy self in so
great honour ? Or what is the matter, that thou dost not answer
to that which I demand of thee ?* After this affront, the
*Xemindoo*, whether it were that he was troubled with his
misfortunes, or ashamed of his dishonour, answered him in
this sort ; *If the clouds of heaven, the sun, the moon, and the
other creatures, which cannot expresse in words that which God
hath created for the service of man, and for the beautifying of
the firmament, which hides from us the rich treasures of His
power, could naturally with the horrible voice of their dreadful
thunder explain to them which now look upon me, the estate
whereunto I see my self reduced before thee, and the extreme
affliction which my soul doth suffer, they would answer for me,
and declare the cause I have to be mute in the condition wherein
my sins have set me : and whereas thou canst not be judg of that
which I say, being the party that accusest me, and the minister
of the execution of thy designe, I hold my self for excused, if I do
not make thee an answer, as I would do before that blessed Lord,
who, how faulty soever I could be, would have pitie on me, moved
with the least tear that I should shed.* This said, he fell down
with his face on the ground, and twice together asked for a
little water : whereupon the King of *Bramaa*, the more to
afflict him, commanded that the *Xemindoo* should receive this
water from the hand of a daughter of his, (held by him as a
slave) whom he exceedingly loved, and had at that time of his
defeat promised to the Prince of *Nautir*, son to the King of
*Avaa*. The princesse no sooner saw her father lying in that
manner on the ground, but she cast her self at his feet, and
straitly embracing him, after she had kissed him thrice, she
said to him with her eyes all bathed in tears, *O my father, my
lord, and my king, I intreat you for the extreme affection which
I have alwayes born you, and for that also which you have at
all times shewed to me, that you will be pleased to lead me with
you, thus imbracing you as I do, to the end that in this sad
passage you may have one to comfort you with a cup of water,
now that for my sins the world refuses you that respect which is
due unto you.* It is said, that the father would fain have
answered to these words, yet could not possibly do it, so

much was he oppressed with grief and anguish of mind, to
see this daughter whom he so dearly loved, in such a taking;
but fell as it were in a swoun, and so continued a good
while; wherewith some lords that were there present were so
moved, as the tears came into their eyes; which observed by
the King of *Bramaa*, and that they were *Pegues*, who had formerly been the *Xemindoo's* subjects, fearing lest they should
betray him in time to come, he caused their heads to be
presently strucken off, saying with a disdainfull and fierce
countenance, *Seeing you have so great pitie of the* Xemindoo
*your King, get you before and prepare a lodging for him, and
there he will pay you for this affection which you testifie to have
for him.* After this, his wrath redoubled in such sort, as
instantly he caused this very daughter to be killed in her
fathers arms; which truly was more then a brutish and
savage cruelty, in seeking to hinder the affections which
nature hath imprinted in us. Then no longer enduring the
sight of the *Xemindoo*, he commanded him to be taken from
thence, and to be carried to a close prison, where he passed
all the night following under a sure guard.

The next morning, proclamation was made over all the city,
for the people to be present at the death of the unhappy
*Xemindoo*. Now, the chiefest reason why the *Bramaa* did
this, was, that the inhabitants seeing him dead, might for ever
lose all hope of having him for their king, as all generally
desired; for whereas he was their countryman, and the *Bramaa*
a stranger, they were in extreame fear, lest the *Bramaa* should
become in time like unto him whom *Xemin de Satan* slew,
and that had been during his reign a mortal enemy to the
*Pegues*; entreating them with such extraordinary cruelty, as
there scarcely passed a day, wherein he did not execute
hundreds of them; and all for matters of small importance,
and which deserved no punishment, had they been proceeded
against by the waies of true justice. About ten of the clock,
the unfortunate *Xemindoo* was drawn out of the dungeon where
he was, in the manner ensuing. Before him marched through
the streets, by which he was to passe, forty men on horseback
with lances in their hands, to prepare and clear the waies;
there were as many behind as before him, which carried naked

swords, crying aloud to the people, whereof the number was
infinite, to make room: after them followed about fifteen
hundred harquebusiers with their matches lighted; next to
these last, which they of the country use to call, the *avant
coureurs* of the Kings wrath, went an hundred and threescore
elephants armed with their castles, and covered with silk
tapestry, marching by five and five in a rank; after them rode
in the same order, by five in a rank, fifteen men on horseback, which carried black ensignes all bloudy, crying aloud, as
it were by way of proclamation; *Let those miserable wretches,
which are the slaves of hunger, and are continually persecuted
by the disgrace of fortune, hearken to the cry of the arm of
wrath, executed on them that have offended their king, to the
end that the astonishment of the pain, which is ordained them
for it, may be deeply imprinted in their memory.* Behind these
same were other fifteen, clothed with a kind of bloudy
garment, which rendred them dreadful and of a bad aspect;
who at the sound of five bells, which they rung in haste, said
with so lamentable a voice, as they that heard them were
moved to weep: *This rigorous justice is done by the living God,
the Lord of all truth, of whose holy body the hairs of our heads
are the feet. It is he that will have the* Xemindoo *put to death,
for usurping the estates of the great King of Bramaa, Lord of
Tanguu.* These proclamations were answered by a troupe of
people, which marched thronging before with such loud cryes,
as would have made one tremble to hear them, saying these
words; *Let him die without having pity on him, that hath
committed such an offence.* These were followed by a company
of five hundred *Bramaa* horse, and after them came another of
foot, whereof some held naked swords and bucklers in their
hands, and the rest were armed with corselets, and coats of
maile. In the midst of these came the poor patient, mounted
on a lean ill-favoured jade, and the hangman on the crupper
behind him, holding him up under both the armes. This
miserable prince was so poorly clad, that his naked skinne was
every where seen; withall, in an exceeding derision of his
person, they had set upon his head a crowne of straw, like
unto an urinall case; which crowne was garnished with
muscle-shells, fastned together with blew thred; and round

about his iron collar were a number of onions tyed. Howbeit, though he was reduced to so deplorable an estate, and that his face was scarce like to that of a living man, yet left he not (for all that) from having something of I know not what in his eyes, which manifested the condition of a king. There was besides observed in him a majestical sweetnesse, which drew tears from all that beheld him. About this guard which accompanied him there was another of above a thousand horsemen, intermingled with many armed elephants. Passing thus thorow the twelve principal streets of the city, where there was a world of people, he arrived at last at a certain street called *Cabam Bainhaa,* out of which he went but two and twenty days before, to go and fight with the *Bramaa,* in such pomp and greatness, as by the report of them that saw it, and of which number I was one, it was (without doubt) one of the most marvellous sights that ever hath been seen in the world ; whereof notwithstanding I will make no mention here, either in regard I cannot promise to recount rightly how all past, or for that I fear some will receive these truths for lies ; neverthelesse mine eyes having been the witnesses of these two successes, if I do not speak of the greatnesse of the first, I will at leastwise declare the miseries of the second, to the end by these two so different accidents, happening in so short a time, one may learn what little assurance is to be put in the prosperities of the earth, and in all the goods which are given to us by inconstant and deceitful fortune. When as the poor patient had past that street of *Cabam Bainhaa,* he arrived at a place where *Gonsalo Pacheco* our captain was, with above an hundred Portugals in his company ; amongst the which there was one of a very base birth, and of a mind yet more vile, who having been robbed of his goods some years before, as he said, at such time as the patient reigned, and complained to him of those who had done it, he would not vouchsafe to give him audience ; so that thinking to be revenged on him for it now, with extravagant and unseemly speech ; as soon as this poor prince came where *Gonsalo Pacheco* was, with all the other Portugals, the witlesse fellow said aloud to him, that all might hear him, *O Robber* Xemindoo, *remember how when I complained to thee of those that had robbed me of my goods, thou wouldest not do me justice* ; *but I hope that now thou shalt satisfie what thy works deserve* : *for I will at supper eat a piece of that flesh of thine, whereunto I will invite two dogs that I have at home.*  The sad patient having heard the words of this hair-brained fellow, lifted up his eyes to heaven, and after he had continued a while pensive, turning himself with a severe countenance towards him that uttered them, *Friend,* said he unto him, *I pray thee, by the great goodness of that God in whom thou believest, to pardon me that for which thou accusest me, and to remember that it is not the part of a Christian, in this painful estate wherein I see my self at this present, to put me in mind of that which I have done heretofore* ; *for besides that, thou canst not thereby recover the loss which thou sayest thou hast sustained, it will but serve to afflict and trouble me the more.*  *Pacheco* having heard what this fellow said, commanded him to hold his peace, which immediately he did ; whereupon the *Xemindoo* with a grave countenance made shew that this action pleased him ; so that seeming to be more quiet, it made him to acknowledge that with his mouth which he could not otherwise requite, *I must confess,* said he unto him, *that I could wish, if God would permit it, I might have one hour longer of life to profess the excellency of the faith wherein you Portugals live* ; *for, as I have heretofore heard it said, your God alone is true, and all other gods are lyers.*  The hangman had no sooner heard these words, but he gave him so great a buffet on the face, that his nose ran out with bloud, so that the poor patient stooping with his hands downward, *Brother* (said he unto him) *suffer me to save this bloud, to the end thou maist not want some to fry my flesh with all.*  So passing on in the same order as before, he finally arrived at the place where he was to be executed, with so little life as he scarcely thought of any thing. When he was mounted on a great scaffold, which had been expresly erected for him, the Chirca of Justice fell to reading of his sentence from an high seate, where he was placed ; the contents whereof were in few words these : *The living God of our heads, Lord of the crown of the Kings of* Avaa, *commands, that the perfidious* Xemindoo *be executed as the perturbator of the people of the earth, and the mortal enemy of the* Bramaa *Nation.*  This said, he made a sign with his hand, and instantly the hangman cut off his head at one blow, shewing it to all the people, which were there without number, and divided his body into eight quarters, setting his bowels and other interior parts which were put together, in a place by themselves ; then covering all with a yellow cloth, which is a mark of mourning amongst them, they were left there till the going down of the sun, at which time they were burnt in the manner ensuing.

[*Mendez Pinto embarks for Malacca, and thence for Japan, with a strange accident that occurs at the Port of Fucheo, omitted.*]

---

## CHAPTER LXV.

Our passing from the town of Fucheo, to the port of Hiamangoo ; and that which befell us there ; together with my departure from Malaca and arrival at Goa.

AFTER that this revolt had taken an end by the death of so many men on the one and the other side, we few *Portugals* that remained, as soon as time would permit us, got to the port of the town, where seeing the country desolated, the merchants fled away, and the King resolved to leave the town, we lost all hope of selling our commodities, yea and of being safe in this harbour, which made us set sail, and go ninety leagues further to another port, called *Hiamangoo*, which is in the bay of *Canguexumaa* ; there we sojourned two months and an half, not able to sell anything at all, because the country was so full of *Chinese* commodities, as they fell above half in half in the price : for there was not a port or road in all this island of *Japan*, where there were not thirty or forty *junks* at anchor, and in some places above an hundred ; so that in the very same year, at least two thousand merchants ships came from *China* to *Japan*. Now most of this merchandise consisted in silk, which was sold at so cheap a rate, that the piece of silk which at that time was worth an hundred taies in *China*, was sold in *Japan* for eight and twenty, or thirty at the most, and that too with much adoe ; besides, the prices of all other commodities were so low, as holding our selves utterly undone, we knew not what resolution or counsell to take. But whereas the Lord doth dispose of things according to his good pleasure, by waies which surpasse our understanding; he permitted, for reasons only known to himself, that on the new moon in December, being the fifth day of the month, there arose so furious a tempest of wind and rain, as all those vessels, saving a few, perished in it : so that the losse caused by this storm amounted unto a thousand, nine hundred, and seventy two *junks* ; amongst the which were six and twenty *Portugals* ships, wherein five hundred and two of our nation were drowned ; besides, a thousand Christians of other countries, and eight hundred thousand ducates worth of goods cast away. Of *Chinese* vessels, according to report, there were a thousand, nine hundred, thirty and six, lost, together with above two millions of gold, and an hundred and threescore thousand persons.   Now from so miserable a ship-wrack not above ten or eleven ships escaped, of which number was that wherein I was imbarqued, and that almost by miracle ; by reason whereof these same sold their commodities at what price they would.   As for us, after we had uttered all ours, and prepared our selves for our departure, we put to sea on a twelfth day in the morning ; and although we were well enough contented in regard of the profit we had made, yet were we not a little sad, to see things fall out so to the cost of so many lives and riches, both of those of our nation, and of strangers.   But when we had weighed anchor, and hoisted our sailes for the prosecution of our course, the ties of our main sail brake ; by which means, the sail-yard falling down upon the prow of the ship, brake all to pieces ; so that we were constrained, by this accident, to recover the port again, and to send a shallop on shore to seek for a sail-yard, and shipwrights to fit it for us.   To this effect, we sent a present to the captain of the place, that he might suddenly give us necessary succor, as accordingly he did ; so that the very same day, the ship was put into her former estate, and better then before.   Neverthelesse, as we were weighing anchor again, the cable of our anchor broke ; and because we had but one more in the ship, we were forced to endeavour all that we might for the recovery

thereof, by reason of the great need we stood in of it"; now, to
do this, we sent to land for such as could dive, who in consideration of ten ducates that we gave them, fell to diving into
the sea, where they found our anchor in six and twenty fathome
depth ; so that by the means of the cordage which we fastned
unto it, we hoisted it up, though with a great deal of labour,
wherein we all of us bestowed our selves, and spent the most
part of the night. As soon as it was day, we set saile, and
parting from this river of *Hiamangoo*, it pleased God, that in
fourteen daies, with a good wind, we arrived at *Chincho*, which
is one of the most renowned and richest ports of the kingdome
of *China* ; there we were advertised, that at the entrance of
this river, there lay at that time a famous pirate, called *Cheo-
pocheca*, with a mighty fleet, which put us into such a fear,
that in all haste we got away to *Lamau*, where we made some
provision of victuals, which lasted us untill our arrivall at
*Malaca*.

[*Here follows the narration of Mendez Pinto's adventures
until his arrival at the port of Zequa with a letter from the
King of Japan,* omitted.]

------

## CHAPTER LXVI.

What past after our departure from Zequa, till my arrival in the Indiaes,
and from thence into the Kingdom of Portugal.

FROM this port of *Zequa* we continued our course with
northerly winds, which were favourable unto us in this
season; and on the 4th of December we arrived at the port of
*Lampacau*, where we met with six *Portugal* ships, whereof
was general a certain merchant, called *Francisco Martinez*, the
creature of *Francisco Barreto*, at that time Governour of the
State of the *Indiaes* in the place of *Don Pedro Mascarenhas*.
And because that then the season for navigation into *India*
was almost past, our Captain *Don Francisco Mascarenhas*
stayed no longer there than was necessary for providing of
victual. We departed then from this port of *Lampacau* a

little before *Christmass*, and arrived at *Goa* the 17th of February. The first thing I did there was to go to *Francisca Barreto*, unto whom I gave an account of the letter which I brought from the King of *Japan*: but he having referred it to the day following, I failed not to deliver it to him the next morning, together with the arms, the scymitars, and the other presents which that pagan king had sent. Whereupon, after he had seen all at leasure, addressing himself unto me, *I assure you*, said he unto me, *that I prize these arms which you have brought me, as much as the Government of* India: *for I hope that by the means of this present, and this letter from the King of* Japan, *I shall render my self agreeable to the King our Sovereign Lord, that I shall be delivered from the fortune of* Lisbon, *where almost all us that govern this state, do go and land for our sins.* Then, in acknowledgment of this voyage, and the great expence I had been at, he made me many large offers, which I would by no means accept of at that time. Nevertheless I was well contented to justifie before him by attestations, and acts past expresly for it, how many times I had been made a slave for the service of the king our master; and how many times also I had been robbed of my merchandize: for I imagined that this would suffice to keep me, at my return into my country, from being refused that which I believed was due to me for my services: as indeed, the Viceroy past me an act of all these things, adding thereunto the certificates which I presented unto him: withal, he gave me a letter, addrest to the king, wherein he made so honorable a mention of me and my services, that relying on these hopes, grounded as they were on such apparant reasons as I had on my side, I imbarqued my self for to return into the kingdom of *Portugal*; so contented with the papers which I carried along with me, that I counted them the best part of my estate; at leastwise, I believed so, because I was perswaded that I should no sooner ask a recompence for so many services, but it would be presently granted me. Upon this hope being put to sea, it pleased our Lord, that I arrived safely at the city of *Lisbon*, the 22nd of September, 1558, at such time as the kingdom was governed by Madam *Katherina*, our queen of happy memory. Having delivered her the letter then from

the Vice-roy of the *Indiaes*, I told her by word of mouth all
that I thought was important for the good of my business:
whereupon she referred me to the minister of her state, who
had the charge of dealing in her affairs. At first he gave me
very good words, but far better hopes, as indeed I held them
for most assured, hearing what he said unto me. But in
stead of letting me see the effect thereof, he kept me these
miserable papers of mine four years and an half; at the end
of which, all the fruit I reaped thereby was no other, then the
labour and pains which to no purpose I had imployed in these
vain sollicitations, and which had been more grievous unto
me, then all the troubles I had suffered during my voyages.
Wherefore seeing of what little profit all my past services were
unto me, notwithstanding all the suit I could make, I resolved
to retire my self, and remain within the terms of my misery,
which I had brought along with me, and gotten by the means
of many misfortunes, which was all that was resting to me of
the time and wealth which I had bestowed in the service of
this kingdom, leaving the judgement of this process to the
Divine Justice. I put this design of mine then in execution,
not a little grieved that I had not done it sooner, because I
might thereby peradventure have saved a good piece of money.
For a conclusion, behold what the services have been which I
have done for the space of one and twenty years, during which
time, I was thirteen times a slave, and sold sixteen times, by
reason of the unlucky events of so long and painful a voyage,
whereof I have made mention amply enough in this book.
But although this be so, yet do I not leave to believe, that the
cause why I remained without the recompence whereunto I
pretented for so many services and travels, rather proceeded
from the Divine providence, which permitted it to be so for
my sins, then from the negligence and fault of him whom the
duty of his charge seemed to oblige to do me right. For it
being true, that in all the kings of this kingdom, who are the
lively source from whence all recompence do flow, though
many times they ran through pipes more affectionate then
reasonable, there is always found an holy and acknowledging
zeal, accompanied with a very ample and great desire, not
onely to recompence those which serve them, but also to con-

fer great estates on them which render them no service at all; whereby it is evident, that if I, and others, have not been satisfied, the same happens by the only fault of the pipes, and not of the source; or rather, it is a work of the Divine Justice, which cannot fail, and which disposeth of all things for the best, and as is most necessary for us; in regard whereof, I render infinite thanks to the King of Heaven, whose pleasure it hath been, that His Divine will should be this way accomplished, and do not complain of the kings of the earth, since my sins have me unworthy of meriting more.

FINIS.

UNWIN BROTHERS, THE GRESHAM PRESS, WOKING AND LONDON.

Made in the USA
Monee, IL
11 March 2022